INTRODUCTION TO
COMPUTING & PROGRAMMING
IN PYTHON®

INTRODUCTION TO COMPUTING & PROGRAMMING IN PYTHON®

A MULTIMEDIA APPROACH

Mark Guzdial and Barbara Ericson

College of Computing/GVU
Georgia Institute of Technology

Second Edition

Prentice Hall

Upper Saddle River   Boston   Columbus   San Francisco   New York
Indianapolis   London   Toronto   Sydney   Singapore   Tokyo   Montreal
Dubai   Madrid   Hong Kong   Mexico City   Munich   Paris   Amsterdam   Cape Town

Vice President and Editorial Director, ECS: *Marcia J. Horton*
Editor in Chief, CS: *Michael Hirsch*
Executive Editor: *Tracy Dunkelberger*
Assistant Editor: *Melinda Haggerty*
Editorial Assistant: *Allison Michael*
Director of Team-Based Project Management: *Vince O'Brien*
Senior Managing Editor: *Scott Disanno*
Production Liaison: *Irwin Zucker*
Production Editor: *Pavithra Jayapaul, TexTech International*
Senior Operations Specialist: *Alan Fischer*
Operation Specialist: *Lisa McDowell*
Marketing Manager: *Erin Davis*
Marketing Assistant: *Mark Patterson*
Art Director: *Kenny Beck*
Cover Designer: *Kristine Carney*
Cover Image: *Ian McKinnell/Taxi/Getty Images*
Art Editor: *Greg Dulles*
Media Editor: *Daniel Sandin*
Composition/Full-Service Project Management: *TexTech International*

Library of Congress Cataloging-in-Publication Data

Guzdial, Mark.
    Introduction to computing and programming in Python : a multimedia approach / Mark Guzdial and Barbara Ericson. — 2nd ed.
        p. cm.
    Includes bibliographical references and index.
    ISBN 0-13-606023-4 (alk. paper)
    1. Python (Computer program language) 2. Multimedia systems. I. Ericson, Barbara. II. Title.
    QA76.73.P98G99 2009
    006.7′6–dc22   2009016329

Prentice Hall
is an imprint of

www.pearsonhighered.com

10 9 8 7 6 5 4 3 2 1
ISBN-13:978-0-13-606023-9
ISBN-10:   0-13-606023-4

Dedicated to our children,
Matthew, Katherine, and Jennifer.

Contents

1 INTRODUCTION   1

Bibliography   391

Index   395

Preface to the Second Edition

We appreciate the interest in the first edition of the book, which has allowed us to prepare this second edition. We are grateful for the comments from our anonymous reviewers that guided our revision.

The major differences between the first edition and second edition are:

1. We increased our coverage of the Python language, including more of the standard libraries, global scope, and additional control structures.

2. There is an increased emphasis on abstraction and on creating reusable code.

3. The movie chapter includes instructions on how to create standard AVI and Quick-Time movies for sharing with others.

4. We increased the number of exercises at the end of each chapter significantly.

5. All indices start with zero instead of one. By starting with zero as the first index instead of one, we are more compatible with standard Python.

6. We removed the chapter on creating a user interface in Swing and the one on JavaScript.

7. We rewrote the chapter on design and debugging to include design and testing examples, with an emphasis on maintenance.

8. We split the chapter on creating and modifying text into two chapters. We added an example of steganography.

9. We split the language paradigms chapter (styles of programming) into two chapters to provide more content on functional (such as non-mutable functions) and object-oriented programming (including introducing objects through use of Logo-like turtles).

10. We have added in coverage of concepts that many teachers want to touch on in their introductory course, such as binary representations of negative numbers.

11. Overall, we have made the English clearer and removed some unnecessary detail. (We hope.)

12. There is no longer a CD in the back of the book. The latest versions of all software and materials can be found at http://mediacomputation.org.

The second edition adds a co-author who brings great experience to the project.

MARK GUZDIAL AND BARBARA ERICSON
Georgia Institute of Technology

Preface to the First Edition

Research in computing education makes it clear that one doesn't just "learn to program." One learns to program *something* [5, 22], and the motivation to do that something can make the difference between learning and not learning to program [8]. The challenge for any teacher is to pick a *something* that is a powerful enough motivator.

People want to communicate. We are social creatures and the desire to communicate is one of our primal motivations. Increasingly, the computer is used as a tool for communication even more than a tool for calculation. Virtually all published text, images, sounds, music, and movies today are prepared using computing technology.

This book is about teaching people to program in order to communicate with digital media. The book focuses on how to manipulate images, sounds, text, and movies as professionals might, but with programs written by students. We know that most people will use professional-grade applications to perform these type of manipulations. But, knowing *how* to write your own programs means that you *can* do more than what your current application allows you to do. Your power of expression is not limited by your application software.

It may also be true that knowing how the algorithms in a media applications work allows you to use them better or to move from one application to the next more easily. If your focus in an application is on what menu item does what, every application is different. But if your focus is on moving or coloring the pixels in the way you want, then maybe it's easier to get past the menu items and focus on what you want to say.

This book is not just about programming in media. Media-manipulation programs can be hard to write or may behave in unexpected ways. Natural questions arise, like "Why is the same image filter faster in Photoshop?" and "That was hard to debug—Are there ways of writing programs that are *easier* to debug?" Answering questions like these is what computer scientists do. There are several chapters at the end of the book that are about *computing*, not just programming. The final chapters go beyond media manipulation to more general topics.

The computer is the most amazingly creative device that humans have ever conceived. It is completely made up of mind-stuff. The notion "Don't just dream it, be it" is really possible on a computer. If you can imagine it, you can make it "real" on the computer. Playing with programming can be and *should* be enormous fun.

TO TEACHERS

The curricular content of this book meets the requirements of the "imperative-first" approach described in the ACM/IEEE *Computing Curriculum 2001* standards document [4]. The book starts with a focus on fundamental programming constructs: assignments, sequential operations, iteration, conditionals, and defining functions. Abstractions (e.g., algorithmic complexity, program efficiency, computer organization, hierarchical decomposition, recursion, and object-oriented programming) are emphasized later, after the students have a context for understanding them.

This unusual ordering is based on the findings of research in the learning sciences. Memory is associative. We remember new things based on what we associate them with. People can learn concepts and skills on the premise that they will be useful some day but the concepts and skills will be related only to the premises. The result has been described as "brittle knowledge" [9]—the kind of knowledge that gets you through the exam but is promptly forgotten because it doesn't relate to anything but being in that class.

Concepts and skills are best remembered if they can be related to many different ideas or to ideas that come up in one's everyday life. If we want students to gain *transferable* knowledge (knowledge that can be applied in new situations), we have to help them to relate new knowledge to more general problems, so that the memories get indexed in ways that associate with those kinds of problems [26]. In this book, we teach with concrete experiences that students can explore and relate to (e.g., conditionals for removing red-eye in pictures) and later lay abstractions on top of them (e.g., achieving the same goal using recursion or functional filters and maps).

We know that starting from the abstractions doesn't really work for computing students. Ann Fleury has shown that students in introductory computing courses just don't buy what we tell them about encapsulation and reuse (e.g., [13]). Students prefer simpler code that they can trace easily and they actually think that such code is *better*. It takes time and experience for students to realize that there is value in well-designed systems. Without experience, it's very difficult for students to learn the abstractions.

The **media computation** approach used in this book starts from what many people use computers for: image manipulation, exploring digital music, viewing and creating Web pages, and making videos. We then explain programming and computing in terms of these activities. We want students to visit Amazon (for example) and think, "Here's a catalog Web site—and I know that these are implemented with a database and a set of programs that format the database entries as Web pages." We want students to use Adobe Photoshop and GIMP and think about how their image filters are actually manipulating red, green, and blue components of pixels. Starting from a relevant context makes transfer of knowledge and skills more likely. It also make the examples more interesting and motivating, which helps with keeping students in the class.

The media computation approach spends about two-thirds of the time on giving students experiences with a variety of media in contexts that they find motivating. After that two-thirds, though, they naturally start to ask questions about *computing*. "Why is it that Photoshop is faster than my program?" and "Movie code is slow—How slow do programs get?" are typical. At that point, we introduce the abstractions and the valuable insights from computer science that answer *their* questions. That's what the last part of this book is about.

A different body of research in computing education explores why withdrawal or failure rates in introductory computing are so high. One common theme is that computing courses seem "irrelevant" and unnecessarily focus on "tedious details" such as efficiency [31, 1]. A communications context is perceived as relevant by students (as they tell us in surveys and interviews [15, 27]). The relevant context is part of the explanation for the success we have had with retention in the Georgia Tech course for which this book was written.

The late entrance of abstraction isn't the only unusual ordering in this approach. We start using arrays and matrices in Chapter 3, in our first significant programs. Typically, introductory computing courses push arrays off until later, because they are obviously more complicated than variables with simple values. A relevant and concrete context is very powerful [22]. We find that students have no problem manipulating matrices of pixels in a picture.

The rate of students withdrawing from introductory computing courses or receiving a D or F grade (commonly called the *WDF rate*) is reported in the 30–50% range or even higher. A recent international survey of failure rates in introductory computing courses reported that the average failure rate among 54 U.S. institutions was 33% and among 17 international institutions was 17% [6]. At Georgia Tech, from 2000 to 2002, we had an average WDF rate of 28% in the introductory course required for all majors. We used the first edition of this text in our course *Introduction to Media Computation*. Our first pilot offering of the course had 121 students, no computing or engineering majors, and two-thirds of the students were female. Our WDF rate was 11.5%.

Over the next two years (Spring 2003 to Fall 2005), the average WDF rate at Georgia Tech (across multiple instructors, and literally thousands of students) was 15% [21]. Actually, the 28% prior WDF rate and 15% current WDF rate are incomparable, since all majors took the first course and only liberal arts, architecture, and management majors take the new course. Individual majors have much more dramatic changes. Management majors, for example, had a 51.5% WDF rate from 1999–2003 with the earlier course, and had a 11.2% failure rate in the first two years of the new course [21]. Since the first edition of this book was published, several other schools have adopted and adapted this approach, and evaluated their result. All of them have reported similar, dramatic improvements in success rates [37, 36].

Ways to Use This Book

This book represents what we teach at Georgia Tech in pretty much the same order. Individual teachers may skip some sections (e.g., the section on additive synthesis, MIDI, and MP3), but all of the content here has been tested with our students.

However, this material has been used in many other ways.

- A short introduction to computing could be taught with just Chapters 2 (introduction to programming) and 3 (introduction to image processing), perhaps with some material from Chapters 4 and 5. We have taught even single-day workshops on media computation using just this material.
- Chapters 6 through 8 basically replicate the computer science concepts from Chapters 3 through 5 but in the context of sounds rather than images. We find the replication useful—some students seem to relate better to the concepts of iteration and conditionals when working with one medium than with the other. Further, it gives us the opportunity to point out that the same **algorithm** can have

similar effects in different media (e.g., scaling a picture up or down and shifting a sound higher or lower in pitch are the same algorithm). But it could certainly be skipped to save time.

- Chapter 12 (on movies) introduces no new programming or computing concepts. While motivational, movie processing could be skipped to save time.

- We recommend getting to at least some of the chapters in the last unit, in order to lead students into thinking about computing and programming in a more abstract manner, but clearly not *all* of the chapters have to be covered.

Python and Jython

The programming language used in this book is Python. Python has been described as "executable pseudo-code." We have found that both computer science majors and non-majors can learn Python. Since Python is actually used for communications tasks (e.g., Web site development), it's a relevant language for an introductory computing course. For example, job advertisements posted to the Python Web site (`http://www.python.org`) show that companies like Google and Industrial Light & Magic hire Python programmers.

The specific dialect of Python used in this book is *Jython* (`http://www.jython.org`). Jython *is* Python. The differences between Python (normally implemented in C) and Jython (which is implemented in Java) are akin to the differences between any two language implementations (e.g., Microsoft vs. GNU C++ implementations)—the basic language is *exactly* the same, with some library and details differences that most students will never notice.

TYPOGRAPHICAL NOTATIONS

Examples of Python code look like this: x = x + 1. Longer examples look like this:

```
def helloWorld():
    print "Hello, world!"
```

When showing something that the user types in with Python's response, it will have a similar font and style, but the user's typing will appear after a Python prompt (»>):

```
>>> print 3 + 4
7
```

User interface components of JES (Jython Environment for Students) will be specified using a small-caps font, like SAVE menu item and the LOAD button.

There are several special kinds of sidebars that you'll find in the book.

Computer Science Idea: An Example Idea
Key computer science concepts appear like this.

Common Bug: An Example Common Bug

Common things that can cause your program to fail appear like this.

Debugging Tip: An Example Debugging Tip

If there's a good way to keep a bug from creeping into your programs in the first place, it's highlighted here.

Making It Work Tip: An Example How to Make It Work

Best practices or techniques that really help are highlighted like this.

ACKNOWLEDGMENTS

Our sincere thanks go out to the following:

- Jason Ergle, Claire Bailey, David Raines, and Joshua Sklare, who made the initial version of JES with surprising quality in an amazingly short amount of time. Over the years, Adam Wilson, Larry Olson, Yu Cheung (Toby) Ho, Eric Mickley, Keith McDermott, Ellie Harmon, Timmy Douglas, Alex Rudnick, Brian O'Neill, and William Fredrick (Buck) Scharfnorth III have made JES into the useful and still understandable tool that it is today.

- Adam Wilson built the MediaTools that are so useful for exploring sounds and images and processing video.

- Andrea Forte, Mark Richman, Matt Wallace, Alisa Bandlow, Derek Chambless, Larry Olson, and David Rennie helped build course materials. Derek, Mark, and Matt created many example programs.

- There were several people who really made the effort come together at Georgia Tech. Bob McMath, Vice-Provost at Georgia Tech, and Jim Foley, Associate Dean for Education in the College of Computing, invested in this effort early on. Kurt Eiselt worked hard to make this effort real, convincing others to take it seriously. Janet Kolodner and Aaron Bobick were excited and encouraging about the idea of media computation for students new to computer science. Jeff Pierce reviewed and advised us on the design of the media functions used in the book. Aaron Lanterman gave me lots of advice on how to convey the digital material content accurately. Joan Morton, Chrissy Hendricks, David White, and all the staff of the GVU Center made sure that we had what we needed and that the details were handled to make this effort come together. Amy Bruckman and Eugene Guzdial bought Mark time to get the final version completed.

- We are grateful to Colin Potts and Monica Sweat who have taught this class at Georgia Tech and given us many insights about the course.

- Charles Fowler was the first person outside of Georgia Tech willing to take the gamble and trial the course in his own institution (Gainesville College), for which we're very grateful.

- The pilot course offered in Spring 2003 at Georgia Tech was very important in helping us improve the course. Andrea Forte, Rachel Fithian, and Lauren Rich did the assessment of the pilot offering of the course, which was incredibly valuable in helping us understand what worked and what didn't. The first teaching assistants (Jim Gruen, Angela Liang, Larry Olson, Matt Wallace, Adam Wilson, and Jose Zagal) did a lot to help create this approach. Blair MacIntyre, Colin Potts, and Monica Sweat helped make the materials easier for others to adopt. Jochen Rick made the CoWeb/Swiki a great place for CS1315 students to hang out.

- Many students pointed out errors and made suggestions to improve the book. Thanks to Catherine Billiris, Jennifer Blake, Karin Bowman, Maryam Doroudi, Suzannah Gill, Baillie Homire, Jonathan Laing, Mireille Murad, Michael Shaw, Summar Shoaib, and especially Jonathan Longhitano, who has a real flair for copyediting.

- Thanks to former *Media Computation* students Constantino Kombosch, Joseph Clark, and Shannon Joiner for permission to use their snapshots from class in examples.

- The research work that led to this text was supported by grants from the National Science Foundation—from the Division of Undergraduate Education, CCLI program, and from the CISE Educational Innovations program. Thank you for the support.

- Thanks to computing students Anthony Thomas, Celines Rivera, and Carolina Gomez for allowing us to use their pictures.

- Finally but most important, thanks to our children Matthew, Katherine, and Jennifer Guzdial, who allowed themselves to be photographed and recorded for Mommy and Daddy's media project and who were supportive and excited about the class.

MARK GUZDIAL AND BARBARA ERICSON
Georgia Institute of Technology

About the Authors

Mark Guzdial is a professor in the School of Interactive Computing in the College of Computing at Georgia Institute of Technology. He is one of the founders of the ACM's International Computing Education Research workshop series. Dr. Guzdial's research focuses on learning sciences and technology, specifically, computing education research. His first books were on the programming language Squeak and its use in education. He was the original developer of "Swiki" (Squeak Wiki), the first wiki developed explicitly for use in schools. Mark has published several books on the use of media as a context for learning computing, which have influenced undergraduate computing curricular around the world. He serves on the ACM Education Board as vice-chair and is on the editorial boards of the "Journal of the Learning Sciences" and "Communications of the ACM."

Barbara Ericson is a research scientist and the Director of Computing Outreach for the College of Computing at Georgia Tech. She has been working on improving introductory computing education since 2004.

She is currently the teacher education representative on the Computer Science Teachers Association board, the co-chair of the K-12 Alliance for the National Center for Women in Information Technology, and is on the Development Committee for the Advanced Placement Computer Science exams. She enjoys the diversity of the types of problems she has worked on over the years in computing including computer graphics, artificial intelligence, medicine, and object-oriented programming.

PART 1

INTRODUCTION

1

Introduction to Computer Science and Media Computation

Chapter Learning Objectives

- To explain what computer science is about and what computer scientists are concerned with.
- To explain why we digitize media.
- To explain why it's valuable to study computing.
- To explain the concept of an **encoding**.
- To explain the basic components of a computer.

1.1 WHAT IS COMPUTER SCIENCE ABOUT?

Computer science is the study of **process**: how we or computers do things, how we specify what we do, and how we specify what the stuff is that we're processing. That's a pretty dry definition. Let's try a metaphorical one.

Computer Science Idea: Computer Science Is the Study of Recipes

They're a special kind of recipe—one that can be executed by a computational device, but this point is only of importance to computer scientists. The important point overall is that a computer science recipe defines *exactly* what has to be done. ■

If you're a biologist who wants to describe how migration works or how DNA replicates, then being able to write a recipe that specifies *exactly* what happens, in terms that can be completely defined and understood, is *very* useful. The same is true if you're a chemist who wants to explain how equilibrium is reached in a reaction. A factory manager can define a machine-and-belt layout and even test how it works—before physically moving heavy things into position—using computer **programs**. A recipe that can run on a computer is called a *program*. Being able to exactly define tasks and/or simulate events is a major reason why computers have radically changed so much of how science is done and understood.

It may sound funny to call *programs* a recipe, but the analogy goes a long way. Much of what computer scientists study can be defined in terms of recipes.

- Some computer scientists study how recipes are written: Are there better or worse ways of doing something? If you've ever had to separate egg whites from yolks, you realize that knowing the right way to do it makes a world of difference. Computer science theoreticians worry about the fastest and shortest recipes, and the ones that take up the least amount of space (you can think about it as counter space—the analogy works). *How* a recipe works, completely apart from how it's written, is called the study of **algorithms**. Software engineers worry about how large groups can put together recipes that still work. (The recipes for some programs, like the one that keeps track of Visa/MasterCard records, have literally millions of steps!) The term **software** means a collection of computer programs (recipes) that accomplish a task.

- Other computer scientists study the units used in recipes. Does it matter whether a recipe uses metric or English measurements? The recipe may work in either case, but if you don't know what a pound or a cup is, the recipe is a lot less understandable to you. There are also units that make sense for some tasks and not others, but if you can fit the units to the tasks, you can explain yourself more easily and get things done faster—and avoid errors. Ever wonder why ships at sea measure their speed in *knots*? Why not use something like meters per second? Sometimes, in certain special situations—on a ship at sea, for instance—the more common terms aren't appropriate or don't work as well. The study of computer science units is referred to as **data structures**. Computer scientists who study ways of keeping track of lots of data in lots of different kinds of units are studying **databases**.

- Can recipes be written for anything? Are there some recipes that *can't* be written? Computer scientists know that there are recipes that can't be written. For example, you can't write a recipe that can absolutely tell whether some other recipe will actually work. How about *intelligence*? Can we write a recipe such that a computer following it would actually be *thinking* (and how would you tell if you got it right)? Computer scientists in **theory**, **intelligent systems**, **artificial intelligence**, and **systems** worry about things like this.

- There are even computer scientists who worry about whether people like what the recipes produce, like restaurant critics for a newspaper. Some of these are **human–computer interface** specialists who worry about whether people like how the recipes work ("recipes" that produce an *interface* that people use, like windows, buttons, scrollbars, and other elements of what we think about as a running program).

- Just as some chefs specialize in certain kinds of recipes, like crepes or barbecue, computer scientists also specialize in certain kinds of recipes. Computer scientists who work in *graphics* are mostly concerned with recipes that produce pictures, animations, and even movies. Computer scientists who work in *computer music* are mostly concerned with recipes that produce sounds (often melodic ones, but not always).

- Still other computer scientists study the *emergent properties* of recipes. Think about the World Wide Web. It's really a collection of *millions* of recipes (programs) talking to one another. Why would one section of the Web get slower at some point? It's a phenomenon that emerges from these millions of programs, certainly not something that was planned. That's something that **networking** computer scientists study. What's really amazing is that these emergent properties (that things just start to happen when you have many, many recipes interacting at once) can also be used to explain noncomputational things. For example, how ants forage for food or how termites make mounds can also be described as something that just happens when you have lots of little programs doing something simple and interacting.

The recipe metaphor also works on another level. Everyone knows that some things in a recipe can be changed without changing the result dramatically. You can always increase all the units by a multiplier (say, double) to make more. You can always add more garlic or oregano to the spaghetti sauce. But there are some things that you cannot change in a recipe. If the recipe calls for baking powder, you may not substitute baking soda. If you're supposed to boil the dumplings and then sauté them, the reverse order will probably not work well (Figure 1.1).

CHICKEN CACCIATORE

3 whole, boned chicken breasts
1 medium onion, chopped
1 tbsp chopped garlic
2 tbsp and later ¼ c olive oil
1 ½ c flour
¼ c Lawry's seasoning salt
1 bell pepper, chopped (optional)
    any color

1(28 oz) can chopped tomatoes
1(15 oz) can tomato sauce
1(6.5 oz) can mushrooms
1(6 oz) can tomato paste
½ of (26 oz) jar of spaghetti
    sauce*
3 tbsp Italian seasoning
1 tsp garlic powder (optional)

Cut up the chicken into pieces about 1 inch square. Saute the onion and garlic until the onion is translucent. Mix the flour and Lawry's salt. You want about 1:4–1:5 ratio of seasoning salt to flour and enough of the whole mixture to coat the chicken. Put the cut up chicken and seasoned flour in a bag, and shake to coat. Add the coated chicken to the onion and garlic. Stir frequently until browned. You'll need to add oil to keep from sticking and burning; I sometimes add up to ¼ cup of olive oil. Add the tomatoes, sauce, mushrooms, and paste. (And the optional peppers, too.) Stir well. Add the Italian seasoning. I like garlic, so I usually add the garlic powder, too. Stir well. Because of all the flour, the sauce can get too thick. I usually cut it with the spaghetti sauce, up to ½ jar. Simmer 20–30 minutes.

FIGURE 1.1
A cooking recipe—you can always double the ingredients, but throwing in an extra cup of flour won't cut it, and don't try to brown the chicken *after* adding the tomato sauce!

The same holds for software recipes. There are usually things you can easily change: the actual names of things (though you should change names consistently), some of the **constants** (numbers that appear as plain old numbers, not as variables), and maybe even some of the data **ranges** (sections of the data) being manipulated. But the order of the commands to the computer, however, almost always has to stay exactly as stated. As we go on, you'll learn what can be safely changed, and what can't.

1.2   PROGRAMMING LANGUAGES

Computer scientists write a recipe in a **programming language** (Figure 1.2). Different programming languages are used for different purposes. Some of them are wildly popular, like Java and C++. Others are more obscure, like Squeak and T. Others are designed to make computer science ideas very easy to learn, like Scheme or Python, but the fact that they're easy to learn doesn't always make them very popular or the best choice for experts building larger or more complicated recipes. It's a hard balance in teaching computer science to pick a language that is easy to learn *and* is popular and useful enough that students are motivated to learn it.

Why don't computer scientists just use natural human languages, like English or Spanish? The problem is that natural languages evolved the way they did to enhance

Python/Jython

```
def hello():
  print "Hello World"
```

Java

```
class HelloWorld {
  static public void main( String args[] ) {
    System.out.println( "Hello World!" );
  }
}
```

C++

```
#include <iostream.h>

main() {
    cout << "Hello World!" << endl;
    return 0;
}
```

Scheme

```
(define helloworld
    (lambda ()
            (display "Hello World")
            (newline)))
```

FIGURE 1.2
Comparing programming languages: a common simple programming task is to print the words "Hello, World!" to the screen.

communications between very smart beings—humans. As we'll explain more in the next section, computers are exceptionally dumb. They need a level of specificity that natural language isn't good at. Further, what we say to one another in natural communication is not exactly what you're saying in a computational recipe. When was the last time you told someone how a video game like *Doom* or *Quake* or *Super Mario Brothers* worked in such minute detail that they could actually replicate the game (say, on paper)? English isn't good for that kind of task.

There are so many different kinds of programming languages because there are so many different kinds of recipes to write. Programs written in the programming language *C* tend to be very fast and efficient, but they also tend to be hard to read, hard to write, and require units that are more about computers than about bird migrations, or DNA, or whatever else you want to write your recipe about. The programming language *Lisp* (and related languages like Scheme, T, and Common Lisp) is very flexible and is well suited to exploring how to write recipes that have never been written before, but Lisp *looks* so strange compared to languages like C that many people avoid it, and there are (as a natural consequence) few who know it. If you want to hire a hundred programmers to work on your project, it will be easier to find a hundred programmers who know a popular language than a less popular one—but that doesn't mean that the popular language is the best one for your task!

The programming language that we're using in this book is **Python** (visit `http://www.python.org` for more information on it). Python is a fairly popular programming language, used very often for Web and media programming. The Web search engine *Google* uses Python. The media company *Industrial Light & Magic* also uses Python. A list of companies using Python is available at `http://wiki.python.org/moin/OrganizationsUsingPython`. Python is easy to learn, easy to read, very flexible, but not very efficient. The same algorithm coded in C and in Python will probably be faster in C.

The version of Python used in this book is called **Jython** (`http://www.jython.org`). Python is normally implemented in the programming language C. Jython is Python implemented in *Java*—this means that Jython is actually a program written in Java. Jython lets us do multimedia that will work across multiple computer platforms. Jython is a real programming language that can be used for serious work. You can download a version of Jython for your computer from the Jython Web site that will work for all kinds of purposes. We will be using Jython in this book through a special programming *environment* called **JES** (*Jython Environment for Students*) that has been developed to make it easier to program in Jython. But anything you can do in JES, you can also do in normal Jython—and most programs that you write in Jython will also work in Python.

Here is an explanation of some of the important terms that we'll be using in this book:

- A **program** is a description in a programming language of a process that achieves some result that is useful to someone. A program can be small (like one that implements a calculator) or huge (like one your bank uses to track all of its accounts).
- An **algorithm** (in contrast) is a description of a process apart from any programming language. The same algorithm may be implemented in many different

languages in many different ways in many different programs—but they would all be the same **process** if we're talking about the same algorithm.

The term **recipe**, as used in this book, describes programs or portions of programs that do something. We're going to use the term recipe to emphasize the *pieces of a program that achieve a useful* **media-related** *task*.

1.3   WHAT COMPUTERS UNDERSTAND

Computational recipes are written to run on computers. What does a computer know how to do? What can we tell the computer to do in the recipe? The answer is "Very, very little." Computers are exceedingly stupid. They really only know about numbers.

Actually, even to say that computers *know* numbers is not really correct. Computers use **encodings** of numbers. Computers are electronic devices that react to voltages on wires. Each wire is called a **bit**. If a wire has a voltage on it, we say that it encodes a 1. If it has no voltage on it, we say that it encodes a 0. We group these wires (bits) into sets. A set of 8 bits is called a **byte**. So, from a set of eight wires (a byte), we have a pattern of eight 0's and 1's, e.g., 01001010. Using the **binary** number system, we can interpret this byte as a **number** (Figure 1.3). That's where we come up with the claim that a computer knows about numbers.[1]

A computer has a **memory** filled with bytes. Everything that a computer is working with at a given instant is stored in its memory. This means that everything a computer is working with is *encoded* in its bytes: JPEG pictures, Excel spreadsheets, Word documents, annoying Web pop-up ads, and the latest spam e-mail.

A computer can do lots of things with numbers. It can add them, subtract them, multiply them, divide them, sort them, collect them, duplicate them, filter them (e.g., "Make a copy of these numbers, but only the even ones."), and compare them and do things based on the comparison. For example, a computer can be told in a recipe,

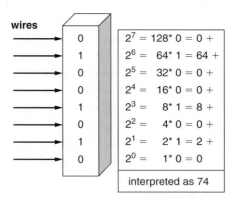

FIGURE 1.3
Eight wires with a pattern of voltages is a byte, which is interpreted as a pattern of eight 0's and 1's, which in turn is interpreted as a decimal number.

[1]We'll talk more about this level of the computer in the chapter on *speed*.

"Compare these two numbers. If the first one is less than the second one, jump to step 5 in this recipe. Otherwise, continue on to the next step."

So far, it looks like the computer is a kind of fancy calculator, and that's certainly why it was invented. One of the first uses of a computer was to calculate projectile trajectories during World War II ("If the wind is coming from the SE at 15 MPH, and you want to hit a target 0.5 miles away at an angle of 30 degrees East of North, then incline your launcher to . . .") Modern computers can do billions of calculations per second. But what makes the computer useful for general recipes is the concept of *encodings*.

> **Computer Science Idea: Computers Can Layer Encodings**
>
> Computers can layer encodings to virtually any level of complexity. Numbers can be interpreted as characters, which can be interpreted in sets as Web pages, which can be interpreted to appear as multiple fonts and styles. But at the bottom-most level, the computer *only* "knows" voltages, which we interpret as numbers.

If one of these bytes is interpreted as the number 65, it could simply be the number 65. Or it could be the letter *A* using a standard encoding of numbers to letters called the *American Standard Code for Information Interchange* (**ASCII**). If the 65 appears in a collection of other numbers that we're interpreting as text, and it's in a file that ends in ".html" it might be part of something that looks like this `<a href=`..., which a Web browser will interpret as the definition of a link. Down at the level of the computer, that *A* is just a pattern of voltages. Many layers of recipes up, at the level of a Web browser, it defines something that you can click on to get more information.

If the computer understands only numbers (and that's a stretch already), how does it manipulate these encodings? Sure, it knows how to compare numbers, but how does that extend to being able to alphabetize a class list? Typically, each layer of encoding is implemented as a piece or layer in software. There's software that understands how to manipulate characters. The character software knows how to do things like compare names because it has encoded that *a* comes before *b* and so on, and that the numeric comparison of the order of numbers in the encoding of the letters leads to alphabetical comparisons. The character software is used by other software that manipulates text in files. That's the layer that something like Microsoft Word or Notepad or TextEdit would use. Still another piece of software knows how to interpret *HTML* (the language of the Web), and another layer of the same software knows how to take HTML and display the right text, fonts, styles, and colors.

We can similarly create layers of encodings in the computer for our specific tasks. We can teach a computer that cells contain mitochondria and DNA, and that DNA has four kinds of nucleotides, and that factories have these kinds of presses and these kinds of stamps. Creating layers of encoding and interpretation so that the computer is working with the right units (recall back to our recipe analogy) for a given problem is the task of **data representation** or defining the right **data structures**.

If this sounds like a lot of software, it is. When software is layered this way, it slows the computer down a bit. But the powerful thing about computers is that they're *amazingly* fast—and getting faster all the time!

Computer Science Idea: Moore's Law

Gordon Moore, one of the founders of Intel (maker of computer processing chips for computers running Windows operating systems), claimed that the number of transistors (a key component of computers) would double at the same price every 18 months, effectively meaning that the same amount of money would buy twice as much computing power every 18 months. This means that computers keep getting smaller, faster, and cheaper. This law has held true for decades.

■

Computers today can execute literally *billions* of recipe steps per second. They can hold in memory literally encyclopedias of data! They never get tired or bored. Search a million customers for an individual card holder? No problem! Find the right set of numbers to get the best value out of an equation? Piece of cake!

Process millions of picture elements or sound fragments or movie frames? That's **media computation**. In this book you will write recipes that manipulate images, sounds, text, and even other recipes. This is possible because everything in the computer is represented digitally, even recipes. By the end of the book, you will have written recipes to implement digital video special effects that create Web pages in the same way that Amazon and eBay do, and that filter images like PhotoShop.

1.4   MEDIA COMPUTATION: WHY DIGITIZE MEDIA?

Let's consider an encoding that would be appropriate for pictures. Imagine that pictures are made up of little dots. That's not hard to imagine: look really closely at your monitor or at a TV screen and you will see that your images are *already* made up of little dots. Each of these dots is a distinct color. Physics tells us that colors can be described as the sum of *red*, *green*, and *blue*. Add the red and green to get yellow. Mix all three together to get white. Turn them all off and you get a black dot.

What if we encoded each dot in a picture as a collection of three bytes, one each for the amount of red, green, and blue at that dot on the screen? And we collect a bunch of these three-byte sets to determine all the dots of a given picture? That's a pretty reasonable way of representing pictures, and it's essentially how we're going to do it in Chapter 3.

Manipulating these dots (each referred to as a **pixel** or *picture element*) can take a lot of processing. There are thousands or even millions of them in a picture that you might want to work with on your computer or on the Web. But the computer doesn't get bored, and it's very fast.

The encoding that we will be using for sound involves 44,100 two-byte sets (called a sample) for each *second* of time. A three-minute song requires 158,760,000 bytes (twice that for stereo). Doing any processing on this takes a *lot* of operations. But at a billion operations per second, you can do lots of operations to every one of those bytes in just a few moments.

Creating encodings of this kind for media requires a change to the media. Look at the real world: it isn't made up of lots of little dots that you can see. Listen to a sound: Do you hear thousands of little bits of sound per second? The fact that you *can't* hear little bits of sound per second is what makes it possible to create these encodings. Our eyes and ears are limited: we can only perceive so much, and only things that are just so small. If you break up an image into small enough dots, your eyes can't tell that it's not a continuous flow of color. If you break up a sound into small enough pieces, your ears can't tell that the sound isn't a continuous flow of auditory energy.

The process of encoding media into little bits is called **digitization**, sometimes referred to as "*going digital*." *Digital* means (according to the *American Heritage Dictionary*) "Of, relating to, or resembling a digit, especially a finger." Making things digital is about turning things from continuous and uncountable to something that we can count, as if with our fingers.

Digital media, done well, feel the same to our limited human sensory apparatus as the original. Phonograph recordings (ever seen one?) capture sound continuously as an **analog** signal. Photographs capture light as a continuous flow. Some people say that they can hear a difference between phonograph recordings and CD recordings, but to our ears and most measurements, a CD (which *is* digitized sound) sounds just the same, or maybe clearer. Digital cameras at high enough resolutions produce photograph-quality pictures.

Why would you want to digitize media? Because then the media will be easier to manipulate, to replicate exactly, to compress, and to transmit. For example, it's hard to manipulate images that are in photographs, but it's very easy when the same images are digitized. This book is about using the increasingly digital world of media and manipulating it—and learning computation in the process.

Moore's Law has made media computation feasible as an introductory topic. Media computation relies on the computer doing lots and lots of operations on lots and lots of bytes. Modern computers can do this easily. Even with slow (but easy to understand) languages, even with inefficient (but easy to read and write) recipes, we can learn about computation by manipulating media.

When we manipulate media, we need to be respectful of the author's digital rights. Modifying images and sounds for educational purposes is allowed under fair use laws. However, sharing or publishing manipulated images or sounds could infringe on the owner's copyright.

1.5   COMPUTER SCIENCE FOR EVERYONE

Why should you learn about computer science by writing programs that manipulate media? Why should anyone who doesn't want to be a computer scientist learn about computer science? Why should you be interested in learning about computation by manipulating media?

Most professionals today manipulate media: papers, videos, tape recordings, photographs, drawings. Increasingly, this manipulation is done with a computer. Media are very often in a digitized form today.

We use software to manipulate these media. We use Adobe Photoshop for manipulating our images, and Audacity to manipulate our sounds, and perhaps Microsoft

PowerPoint for assembling our media into slideshows. We use Microsoft Word for manipulating our text, and Netscape Navigator or Microsoft Internet Explorer for browsing media on the Internet.

So why should anyone who does *not* want to be a computer scientist study computer science? Why should you learn to program? Isn't it enough to learn to *use* all this great software? The following sections provide answers to these questions.

1.5.1   It's About Communication

Digital media are manipulated with software. *If you can only manipulate media with software that **someone else** made for you, you are limiting your ability to communicate.* What if you want to say something that can't be said in software from Adobe, Microsoft, Apple, and the rest? Or what if you want to say something in a way they don't support? If you know how to program, even if it would take you *longer* to do it yourself, you have the freedom to manipulate the media your way.

What about learning these tools in the first place? In all our years working with computers, we have seen many types of software come and go as *the* package for drawing, painting, word processing, video editing, and so on. You can't learn just a single tool and expect to be able to use it for your entire career. If you know *how* the tools work, you have a core understanding that can transfer from tool to tool. You can think about your media work in terms of the *algorithms*, not the *tools*.

Finally, if you're going to prepare media for the Web, for marketing, for print, for broadcast, or for any use whatsoever, it's worthwhile for you to have a sense of what's possible and what can be done with media. It's even more important as a consumer of media that you know how the media can be manipulated, to know what's true and what could be just a trick. If you know the basics of media computation, you have an understanding that goes beyond what any individual tool provides.

1.5.2   It's About Process

In 1961, Alan Perlis gave a talk at MIT in which he argued that computer science, and programming explicitly, should be part of a liberal education [17]. Perlis is an important figure in the field of computer science. The highest award in computer science is the ACM Turing Award. Perlis was the first recipient of that award. He's an important figure in software engineering and he started several of the first computer science departments in the United States.

Perlis's argument can be made in comparison with calculus. Calculus is generally considered part of a liberal education: not *everyone* takes calculus, but if you want to be well educated, you will typically take at least a term of calculus. Calculus is the study of *rates*, which is important in many fields. Computer science, as stated earlier in this chapter, is the study of **process**. Process is important to nearly every field, from business to science to medicine to law. Knowing process formally is important for everyone. Using a computer to automate processes has changed every profession.

More recently, Jeannette Wing has argued that everyone should learn **computational thinking** [34]. She views the types of skills taught in computing as critical skills for all students. This is what Alan Perlis predicted: that automating computation would change the way we learn about our world.

PROBLEMS

1.1 *Every* profession uses computers today. Use a Web browser and a search engine like Google to find sites that relate your field of study with computer science or computing or computation. For example, search for "biology computer science" or "management computing."

1.2 Find an ASCII table on the Web: a table listing every character and its corresponding numeric representation. Write down the sequence of numbers whose ASCII values make up your name.

1.3 Find a Unicode table on the Web. What's the difference between ASCII and Unicode?

1.4 Consider the representation for pictures described in Section 1.4, where each dot (pixel) in the picture is represented by three bytes, for the red, green, and blue components of the color at that dot. How many bytes does it take to represent a 640 by 480 picture, a common picture size on the Web? How many bytes does it take to represent a 1024 by 768 picture, a common screen size? (What do you think is meant now by a "three megapixel" camera?)

1.5 One bit can represent 0 or 1. With two bits you have four possible combinations 00, 01, 10, and 11. How many different combinations can you make with four bits or eight bits (one byte)? Each combination can be used to represent a binary number. How many numbers can you represent with 2 bytes (16 bits)? How many numbers can you represent with four bytes?

*1.6 How can you represent a *floating-point number* in terms of bytes? Do a search on the Web for "floating point" and see what you find.

1.7 Look up Alan Kay and the *Dynabook* on the Web. What does he have to do with media computation?

1.8 Look up Grace Hopper on the Web? How did she contribute to programming languages?

1.9 Look up Philip Emeagwali on the Web? What computing prize did he win?

1.10 Look up Alan Turing on the Web. What does he have to do with our notion of what a computer can do and how encodings work?

1.11 Look up the Harvard computers on the Web. What did they contribute to astronomy?

1.12 Look up Adele Goldberg on the Web. How did she contribute to programming languages?

1.13 Look up Kurt Gödel on the Web. What amazing things did he do with encodings?

1.14 Look up Ada Lovelace on the Web. What amazing things did she do before the first mechanical computer was built?

1.15 Look up Claude Shannon on the Web. What did he do for his master's thesis?

1.16   Look up Richard Tapia on the Web. What has he done to encourage diversity in computing?

1.17   Look up Frances Allen on the Web. What computing prize did she win?

1.18   Look up Mary Lou Jepsen on the Web. What new technology is she working on?

1.19   Look up Ashley Qualls on the Web. What did she create that is worth a million dollars?

1.20   Look up Marissa Mayer on the Web. What does she do?

TO DIG DEEPER

James Gleick's book *Chaos* describes more on emergent properties—how small changes can lead to dramatic effects, and the unintended impacts of designs because of difficult-to-foresee interactions.

Mitchel Resnick's book *Turtles, Termites, and Traffic Jams: Explorations in Massively Parallel Microworlds* [33] describes how ants, termites, and even traffic jams and slime molds can be described pretty accurately with hundreds or thousands of very small processes (programs) running and interacting all at once.

Exploring The Digital Domain [3] is a wonderful introductory book on computation with lots of good information about digital media.

Introduction to Programming

Chapter Learning Objectives

The media learning goals for this chapter are:

- To make and show pictures.
- To make and play sounds.

The computer science goals for this chapter are:

- To use JES to enter and execute programs.
- To create and use variables to store values and objects, such as pictures and sounds.
- To create functions.
- To recognize different types (encodings) of data, such as integers, floating-point numbers, and media objects.
- To sequence operations in a function.

2.1 PROGRAMMING IS ABOUT NAMING

> **Computer Science Idea: Much of Programming Is About Naming**
>
> A computer can associate names, or *symbols*, with just about anything: with a specific byte; with a collection of bytes making up a numeric variable or a bunch of letters; with a media element like a file, sound, or picture; or even with more abstract concepts, like a named recipe (a *program*) or a named encoding (a *type*). A computer scientist sees a choice of names as being high-quality in the same way that a philosopher or mathematician might: the naming scheme (the names and what they name) should be elegant, parsimonious, and usable. Naming is a form of abstraction. The name is used to refer to the thing you are naming.

Obviously, the computer itself doesn't *care* about names. Names are for humans. If the computer were just a calculator, then remembering words and their association with values would be just a waste of the computer's memory. But for humans, this is *very* powerful. It allows us to work with the computer in a natural way, even a way that extends how we think about recipes (processes) altogether.

A **programming language** is really a set of names that a computer has encodings for, such that the names make the computer do expected actions and interpret our data in expected ways. Some of the programming languages' names allow us to define *new* names that in turn allow us to create our own layers of encoding. Assigning a variable to a value is one way of defining a name for the computer. Defining a function is giving a name to a recipe.

A **program** is made from a set of names and their values, where some of these names have values of instructions to the computer ("*code*"). Our instructions will be in the Python programming language. Combining these two definitions means that the Python programming language gives us a set of useful names that have a meaning to the computer, and that our programs are then a selection of Python's useful names, plus names that we define, that together let us tell the computer what we want it to do.

> **Computer Science Idea: Programs Are for People, Not Computers**
> Remember that names are only meaningful for people, not for computers. Computers just take instructions. A good program is meaningful (understandable and useful) for humans.

There are good names and bad names. This has nothing to do with curse words or with TLAs (three-letter acronyms). A good set of encodings and names allows us to describe recipes in a way that's natural, without having to say too much. The variety of different programming languages can be thought of as a collection of sets of namings and encodings. Some are better for some tasks than others. Some languages require you to write more to describe the same recipe than others—but sometimes that "more" leads to a much more (humanly) readable recipe that helps others to understand what you're saying.

Philosophers and mathematicians look for very similar senses of quality. They try to describe the world in a few words, seeking an elegant selection of words that cover many situations but remain understandable to their fellow philosophers and mathematicians. That's exactly what computer scientists do.

How the units and values (**data**) of a recipe can be interpreted is often also named. Remember how we said in Section 1.3 that everything is in bytes, but bytes can be interpreted as numbers? In some programming languages, you can say explicitly that some value is a *byte*, and later tell the language to treat it as a number, an *integer* (or sometimes *int*). Similarly, you can tell the computer that this particular series of bytes is a collection of numbers (an **array of integers**), a collection of characters (a **string**), or even a more complex encoding of a single floating-point number (a **float**—any number with a decimal point in it).

In Python, we will explicitly tell the computer how to interpret our values, but we will very rarely tell it that certain names are only associated with certain encodings. Languages such as Java and C++ are *strongly typed*: in these languages names are strongly associated with certain types or encodings. They require you to say that this name will only be associated with integers and that one will only be a floating-point number. Python still has *types* (encodings that you can reference by name), but they're not as explicit. Python also has **reserved words**. Reserved words are words that you can't use to name things since they already have meaning in the language.

2.1.1   Files and Their Names

A programming language isn't the only place where computers associate names and values. Your computer's **operating system** takes care of the files on your disk and associates names with them. Operating systems you may be familiar with or use include Windows 95, Windows 98 (Windows ME, NT, XP. . .), Vista MacOS, and Linux. A **file** is a collection of values (bytes) on your **hard disk** (the part of your computer that stores things after the power is turned off). If you know the name of a file and tell it to the operating system, you will be given the values associated with the name.

You may be thinking, "I've been using the computer for years, and I've *never* given a filename to the operating system." Maybe you didn't realize that you were doing it, but when you pick a file from a file-choosing dialog in Photoshop, or double-click a file in a *directory* window (or Explorer or Finder), you are asking some software somewhere to give the name you're picking or double-clicking to the operating system, and get the values back. When you write your own recipes, though, you'll be explicitly getting filenames and asking for their values.

Files are *very* important for media computation. Disks can store acres and acres of information on them. Remember our discussion of Moore's Law? Disk capacity per dollar is increasing *faster* than computer speed per dollar! Computer disks today can store whole movies, hours (days?) of sounds, and the equivalent of hundreds of film rolls of pictures.

These media are not small. Even in a *compressed* form, screen-size pictures can be over a million bytes large, and songs can be 3 million bytes or more. You need to keep them someplace where they'll last past the computer being turned off and where there's lots of space.

In contrast, your computer's **memory** is impermanent (it disappears when the power does) and relatively small. Computer memory is getting larger all the time, but it's still just a fraction of the amount of space on your disk. When you're working with media, you will load the media from the disk into memory, but you wouldn't want it to stay in memory after you're done. It's too big.

Think about your computer's memory as a dorm room. You can get to things easily in a dorm room—they're right at hand, easy to reach, and easy to use. But you wouldn't want to put everything you own (or everything you hope to own) in that one dorm room. All your belongings? Your skis? Your car? Your boat? That's silly. Instead, you store large things in places designed to store large things. You know how to get them when you need them (and maybe take them back to your dorm room if you need to or can).

When you bring things into memory, you will name the value so that you can retrieve it and use it later. In that sense, programming is something like *algebra*. To write equations and functions that were generalizable (i.e., that worked for any number or value), you wrote them with *variables*, like $PV = nRT$ or $e = Mc^2$ or $f(x) = sin(x)$. Those P's, V's, R's, T's, e's, M's, c's, and x's were names for values. When you evaluated $f(30)$, you knew that the x was the name for 30 when computing f. We'll be naming media (as values) in the same way when using them in programming.

2.2 PROGRAMMING IN PYTHON

The programming language that we're going to be using in this book is called **Python**. It's a language invented by Guido van Rossum. He named his language for the famous British comedy troupe *Monty Python*. Python has been used for years by people without formal computer science training—it's aimed at being easy to use. The particular form of Python that we're going to be using is **Jython** because it lends itself to cross-platform multimedia.

You'll actually be programming using a tool called **JES** (**Jython Environment for Students**). JES is a simple **editor** (tool for entering program text) and interaction tool so that you can try things out in JES and create new recipes within it. The media names (functions, variables, encodings) that we'll be talking about in this book were developed to work from within JES (i.e., they're not part of a normal Jython distribution, though the basic language we'll be using is normal Python).

You can read the instructions on installing JES at `http://mediacomputation.org`. The process there will lead you to install Java, Jython, and JES, and give you a nice icon to double-click on to start JES. JES is available for Windows, Macintosh, and Linux.

> **Debugging Tip: Getting Java, If You Have To**
>
> For most people, dragging the JES folder onto their hard disk is all they need to do to get started. However, if you have Java installed, and it's an older version that can't run JES, you might have trouble getting JES started. If you do have problems, get a new version of Java from the Sun site at `http://www.java.sun.com`. ∎

2.3 PROGRAMMING IN JES

How you start JES depends on your platform. In Windows and Macintosh, you'll have a JES icon that you'll simply double-click. In Linux, you'll probably `cd` into your Jython directory and type a command like `./JES.sh`. See the instructions at the Web site for what will work for your computer.

> **Common Bug: JES Can Be Slow To Start**
>
> JES can take a while to load. Don't worry—you may see the splash screen for a long time, but if you see the splash screen, it will load. It will often start faster after the first use. ∎

Common Bug: Making JES Run Faster

As we'll talk more about later, when you're running JES, you're actually running Java. Java needs memory. If you find that JES runs slowly, give it more memory. You can do this by quitting out of other applications you're running. Your e-mail program, your instant messenger, and your digital music player all take up memory—sometimes lots of it! Quit out of those and JES will run faster.

Once you start JES, it will look something like Figure 2.1. There are two main areas in JES (the bar between them moves so that you can differentially resize the two areas).

- The top part is the **Program Area**. This is where you write *your* recipes: the programs that you're creating and their names. This area is simply a text editor—think of it as Microsoft Word for your programs. The computer doesn't actually try to interpret the names that you type up in the program area until you press the LOAD PROGRAM button, and you can't press LOAD PROGRAM until you've saved your program (by using the SAVE menu item which is under the FILE menu).

  Don't worry if you hit LOAD PROGRAM before you remember to save. JES won't load the program until it's saved, so it will give you a chance to save the program then.

- The bottom part is the **Command Area**. This is where you literally *command* the computer to do something. You type your commands at the >>> prompt, and when you hit the RETURN (Apple) or ENTER (Windows) key, the computer will interpret

FIGURE 2.1
JES with areas labelled.

your words (i.e., apply the meanings and encodings of the Python programming language) and do what you have told it to do. This interpretation will include whatever you typed and loaded from the program area as well.

- The area on the right is the **Help Area**. You can select something and then click the Explain button for help on that item.

Other features of JES are visible in Figure 2.1, but we won't be doing much with them yet. The watcher button opens up the **watcher** (**a debugger**), a window with tools for watching how the computer executes your program. The STOP button allows you to stop a running program (e.g., if you think it's been running too long, or if you realize that it's not doing what you wanted it to do).

Making It Work Tip: Get To Know Your Help!

An *important* feature to start exploring is the HELP menu. There is a lot of great help for programming and for using JES available under this menu. Start exploring it now so that you have a sense of what's there when you start writing your own programs. ∎

2.4   MEDIA COMPUTATION IN JES

We're going to start out by simply typing commands in the Command Area—not defining new names yet, but simply using the names that the computer already knows from within JES.

The name print is an important one to know. It's always used with something following it. The meaning for print is "Display a readable representation of whatever follows." Whatever follows can be a name that the computer knows, or an *expression* (literally, in the algebraic sense). Try typing print 34 + 56 by clicking in the command area, typing the command, and hitting ENTER—like this:

```
>>> print 34 + 56
90
```

34 + 56 is a numeric expression that Python understands. Obviously, it's composed of two numbers and an operation (in our sense, a *name*) that Python knows how to do, + meaning "add." Python understands other kinds of expressions, not all of them numeric.

```
>>> print 34.1/46.5
0.7333333333333334
>>> print 22 * 33
726
>>> print 14 - 15
-1
>>> print "Hello"
Hello
>>> print "Hello" + "Mark"
HelloMark
```

Python understands quite a few standard math operations. It also knows how to recognize different kinds or **types** of numbers: integer and floating point. A floating-point number has a decimal point in it. An integer number does not have a decimal point in it. Python also knows how to recognize *strings* (sequences of characters) that are started and ended with " (quote) marks. It even knows what it means to "add" two strings together: it simply puts one right after the other.

Common Bug: Python's Types Can Produce Odd Results

Python takes types seriously. If it sees you using integers, it thinks you want an integer result from your expressions. If it sees you use floating-point numbers, it thinks you want a floating-point result. Sounds reasonable, no? But how about:

```
>>> print 1.0/2.0
0.5
>>> print 1/2
0
```

1/2 is 0? Well, sure! 1 and 2 are integers. There is no integer equal to 1/2, so the answer must be 0! Adding ".0" to an integer convinces Python that we're talking about floating-point numbers, so the result is in floating-point form.

Python also understands about **functions**. Remember functions from algebra? They're a "box" into which you put one value, and out comes another. One of the functions that Python knows takes a character as the *input* value (the value that goes into the box) and returns or outputs (the value that comes out of the box) the number that is the ASCII mapping for that character. The name of this function is ord (for *ordinal*), and you can use print to display the value that the function ord returns:

```
>>> print ord("A")
65
```

Another function that's built into Python is named abs—it's the absolute value function. It returns the absolute value of the input value.

```
>>> print abs(1)
1
>>> print abs(-1)
1
```

Debugging Tip: Common Typos

If you type something that Python can't understand at all, you'll get a syntax error.

```
>>> pint "Hello"
Your code contains at least one syntax
error, meaning it is not legal Jython.
```

If you try to access a word that Python doesn't know, Python will say that it doesn't know that name.

```
>>> print a
A local or global name could not be found. You need to define
the function or variable before you try to use it in any way.
```

A *local name* is a name defined inside a function, and a *global name* is a name available to all functions (such as pickAFile). ∎

Another function that JES knows is one that allows you to pick a file from your disk. You may notice that we have switched from saying "Python knows" to "JES knows". print is something that all Python implementations know. pickAFile is something that we built for JES. In general, you can ignore the difference, but if you try to use another kind of Python, it will be important to know what is common and what is not. It takes no input, as ord did, but it does return a string which is the name of the file on your disk. The name of the function is pickAFile. Python is very picky about capitalization—neither pickafile nor Pickafile will work! Try it like this: print pickAFile(). When you do, you will get something that looks like Figure 2.2.

You're probably already familiar with how to use a file picker or file dialog:

- Double-click on folders/directories to open them.
- Click to select and then click OPEN, or double-click, to select a file.

Once you select a file, what gets returned is the *full filename* as a string (a sequence of characters). (If you click CANCEL, pickAFile returns the *empty string*—a string of characters, with no characters in it, e.g., "".) Try it: do print pickAFile() and OPEN a file.

FIGURE 2.2
The file picker.

```
>>> print pickAFile()
C:\ip-book\mediasources\beach.jpg
```

What you get when you finally select a file will depend on your operating system. On Windows, your filename will probably start with C: and will have backslashes in it (e.g., \). On Linux or MacOS, it will probably look /Users/guzdial/ip-book/ mediasources/beach.jpg. There are really two parts to this filename:

- The character between words (e.g., the / between "Users" and "guzdial") is called the **path delimiter** or **path separator**. Everything from the beginning of the filename to the last path delimiter is called the *path* to the file. That describes exactly *where* on the hard disk (in which **directory**) a file exists.

- The last part of the file (e.g., "beach.jpg") is called the **base filename**. When you look at the file in the Finder/Explorer/Directory window (depending on your operating system), that's the part you see. The last three characters (after the period) are called the **file extension**. They identify the encoding of the file.

Files that have an extension of ".jpg" are **JPEG** files. They contain pictures. (To be more literal, they contain data that can be *interpreted* to be a *representation* of a picture—but it's close enough to say "they contain pictures.") JPEG is a standard *encoding* (representation) for any kind of image. The other media files that we'll be using frequently are ".wav" files (Figure 2.3). The ".wav" extension means that these are **WAV** files. They contain sounds. WAV is a standard encoding for sounds. There are many other kinds of extensions for files, and there are even many other kinds of media extensions. For example, there are also GIF (".gif") files for images and AIFF

FIGURE 2.3
File picker with media types identified.

("`.aif`" or "`.aiff`") files for sounds. We'll stick to JPEG and WAV in this text, just to avoid too much complexity.

2.4.1 Showing a Picture

So now we know how to get a complete filename: path and base name. This *doesn't* mean that we have the file itself loaded into memory. To get the file into memory, we have to tell JES how to interpret it. *We* know that JPEG files are pictures, but we have to tell JES explicitly to read the file and make a picture from it. There is a function for that, too, named `makePicture`.

`makePicture` *does* require a **parameter**—some input to the function. Just like `ord`, the input is specified inside parentheses. It takes a filename. Lucky us—we know how to get one of those.

```
>>> print makePicture(pickAFile())
Picture, filename C:\ip-book\mediasources\barbara.jpg
    height 294 width 222
```

The result from `print` suggests that we did in fact make a picture, from a given filename and a given height and width. Success! Oh, you wanted to actually *see* the picture? We'll need another function! (Did we mention somewhere that computers are stupid?) The function to show the picture is named `show`. `show` *also* takes a parameter—a `Picture`.

But, we have a problem. We didn't name the picture that we just created and so we don't have any way to refer to it again. We can't just say show the picture that we created a second ago, but didn't name. Computers don't remember things unless we name them. Creating a name for a value is also called *declaring a variable*.

Let's start over and this time let's first name the file that we pick. We will also name the picture that we create. Then we can show the named picture as shown in Figure 2.4.

You can pick and name a file using `file = pickAFile()`. This means create a name `file` and set it to refer to the value returned from the function `pickAFile()`. We have seen that the function `pickAFile()` returns the name of the file (including the path). We can name and create a picture using `pict = makePicture(file)`. This passes the filename into the function `makePicture` and then returns the created picture. The name `pict` refers to that created picture. We can then show the created picture by passing the name `pict` to the function `show`.

Another way to do all of this is to do it all at once because the output from one function can be used as the input for another function: `show(makePicture(pickAFile()))`. That's what we see in Figure 2.5. This will start by allowing you to pick a file and then pass the name of that file to the `makePicture` function and pass the resulting picture to the `show` function. But again, we didn't name the picture so we can't refer to it again.

Try it both ways yourself. Congratulations! You've just worked your first media computation!

If you try `print show(pict)`, you'll notice that the output from `show` is `None`. Functions in Python don't *have* to return a value, unlike real mathematical functions. If a function *does* something (like opening up a picture in a window), it can be useful without also needing to return a value. Computer scientists use the term **side-effect** for when

FIGURE 2.4
Picking, making, and showing a picture, and naming the pieces.

FIGURE 2.5
Picking, making, and showing a picture, using each function as input to the next.

a function does computation other than through its input-to-return value computation. Displaying windows and making sounds is a type of side-effect computation.

2.4.2 Playing a Sound

We can replicate this entire process with sounds.

- We still use pickAFile to find the file we want and get its filename. This time we pick a file that ends with .wav.
- We now use makeSound to make a sound. makeSound, as you might imagine, takes a filename as input.
- We will use play to play the sound. play takes a sound as input but returns None.

Here are the same steps we saw previously with pictures:

```
>>> file = pickAFile()
>>> print file
C:\ip-book\mediasources\hello.wav
>>> sound = makeSound(file)
>>> print sound

Sound of length 54757
>>> print play(sound)
None
```

(We'll explain what the length of the sound means in the next chapter.) Please try this on your own, using JPEG files and WAV files that are on your own computer, that you make yourself, or that are available at http://www.mediacomputation.org. (We will talk more about where to get the media and how to create it in future chapters.)

2.4.3 Naming Values

As we saw in the last section, we name data using =. We can check our namings using print, just as we have been doing.

```
>>> myVariable=12
>>> print myVariable
12
>>> anotherVariable=34.5
>>> print anotherVariable
34.5
>>> myName="Mark"
>>> print myName
Mark
```

Don't read = as "equals." That's what it means in mathematics, but that's not at all what we're doing here. Read = as "becomes a name for." myVariable=12 thus means "myVariable becomes a name for 12." The reverse (putting the *expression* on the left and the name on the right) thus makes no sense: 12=myVariable would then mean "12 becomes a name for myVariable."

```
>>> x = 2 * 8
>>> print x
16
>>> 2 * 8 = x
Your code contains at least one syntax error, meaning
it is not legal Jython.
```

We can use names more than once.

```
>>> print myVariable
12
>>> myVariable="Hello"
>>> print myVariable
Hello
```

The *binding* (or association) between the name and the data only exists until (a) the name gets assigned to something else or (b) you quit JES. The relationship between names and data (or even names and functions) only exists during a session of JES.

Remember that data have encodings or types. How data act in expressions depends in part on their types. Note how the *integer* 12 and the *string* "12" act differently for multiplication below. Both are doing something reasonable for their type, but they are very different actions.

```
>>> myVariable=12
>>> print myVariable*4
48
>>> myOtherVariable="12"
>>> print myOtherVariable*4
12121212
```

We can assign names to the *results* of functions. If we name the result from pickAFile, we will get the same result each time we print the name. We don't rerun pickAFile. Naming code in order to re-execute it is what we're doing when we define functions, which comes up in just a few pages.

```
>>> file = pickAFile()
>>> print file
C:\ip-book\mediasources\640x480.jpg
>>> print file
C:\ip-book\mediasources\640x480.jpg
```

In the following example, we assign names to the filename and the picture.

```
>>> myFilename = pickAFile()
>>> print myFilename
C:\ip-book\mediasources\barbara.jpg
>>> myPicture = makePicture(myFilename)
>>> print myPicture
Picture, filename barbara.jpg
height 294 width 222
```

Note that the algebraic notions of *substitution* and *evaluation* work here as well. myPicture = makePicture(myFilename) causes the exact same picture to be created as if we had executed makePicture(pickAFile()),[1] because we set myFilename to be equal to the result of pickAFile(). The values are substituted for the names when the expression is evaluated. makePicture(myFilename) is an expression that

---

[1]Assuming, of course, that you picked the same file.

is expanded, at evaluation time, into makePicture("C:/ip-book/mediasources/ barbara.jpg") because "C:/ip-book/mediasources/barbara.jpg" is the name of the file that was picked when pickAFile() was evaluated and the returned value was named myfilename.

We can also replace the function *invocations* (or *calls*) with the *value* returned. pickAFile() returns a *string*—a bunch of characters enclosed inside quotes. We can make the last example work like this, too.

```
>>> myFilename = "C:/ip-book/mediasources/barbara.jpg"
>>> print myFilename
C:/ip-book/mediasources/barbara.jpg
>>> myPicture = makePicture(myFilename)
>>> print myPicture
Picture, filename C:/ip-book/mediasources/barbara.jpg
height 294 width 222
```

Or even substitute for the name.

```
>>> myPicture = makePicture("C:/ip-book/mediasources/
    barbara.jpg")
>>> print myPicture
Picture, filename C:/ip-book/mediasources/barbara.jpg
height 294 width 222
```

Computer Science Idea: We Can Substitute Names, Values, and Functions
We can substitute a value, a name assigned to that value, and the function returning the same value *interchangeably*. The computer cares about the value, not whether it comes from a string, a name, or a function call. The key is that the computer is *evaluating* the value, the name, and the function. As long as these *expressions* evaluate to the same thing, they can be used interchangeably.

We actually don't need to use print every time we ask the computer to do something. If we want to call a function that doesn't return anything (and so is pretty useless to print), we can just call the function by typing its name and its input (if any) and hitting return.

```
>>> show(myPicture)
```

We tend to call these statements to the computer that are telling it to do things *commands*. print mypicture is a command. So is myfilename = pickAFile(), and show(mypicture). These are more than expressions: they're telling the computer to *do* something.

2.5   MAKING A PROGRAM

We have now used names to stand for values. The values are substituted for the names when the expression is evaluated. We can do the same for programs. We can name a series of commands and then just use the name whenever we want the commands to be executed. In Python, the name we define will be a *function*. A *program* in Python, then, is a collection of one or more functions that perform a useful task. We're going to use the term *recipe* to describe programs (or portions of programs) that perform a useful media operation, even if whatever is covered by the term is not enough to make a useful program in itself.

Remember when we said earlier that just about anything can be named in computers? We've seen naming values. Now we'll see naming recipes.

Making It Work Tip: Try *Every* Recipe!

To really understand what's going on, type in, load, and execute *every* recipe in the book. *EVERY* one. None of them are long, and the practice will go a long way to convince you that the programs work, to develop your programming skill, and to help you understand *why* they work.

∎

The name that Python understands as *defining* the name of new recipes is def. def isn't a function—it's a command like print. def is used to *define* new functions. There are certain things that have to come after the word def, though. The structure of what goes on the line with the def command is referred to as the **syntax** of the command—the words and characters that have to be there for Python to understand what's going on and the order of those things.

def needs three things to follow it on the same line:

- The name of the recipe you're defining, like showMyPicture.
- Whatever *inputs* this recipe will take. The recipe can be a function that takes inputs, like abs or makePicture. The inputs are named and placed between parentheses separated by commas. If your recipe takes no inputs, you simply enter () to indicate no inputs.
- The line ends with a colon, :.

What comes after this are the commands to be executed, one after the other, whenever the recipe is told to execute. We create a collection of commands by defining a **block**. The block of commands that follow a def command (or *statement*) are the ones associated with the name of the function.

Most real programs that do useful things, especially those that create user interfaces, require the definition of more than one function. Imagine that you have several def commands in the program area. How do you think Python will figure out that one function has ended and a new one has begun? (Especially because it *is* possible to define functions *inside of* other functions.) Python needs some way of figuring out where the *function body* ends—which statements are part of this function and which are part of the next.

The answer is **indentation**. All the statements that are part of the definition are slightly indented after the def statement. We recommend using exactly two spaces—it's enough to see, it's easy to remember, and it's simple. (In JES, you could also use one *tab*—a single press of the tab key.) You enter the function in the program area like this (where ⊔ indicates a single space, a single press of the spacebar):

```
def hello():
⊔⊔print "Hello"
```

We can now define our first recipe. You type this into the program area of JES. When you're done, save the file: Use the extension ".py" to indicate a Python file. (We saved ours as `pickAndShow.py`.)

Program 1: Pick and Show a Picture

```
def pickAndShow():
  myFile = pickAFile()
  myPict = makePicture(myFile)
  show(myPict)
```

You'll notice a thin blue box around the body of the function while you're typing. The blue box indicates the blocks in your program (Figure 2.6). All the commands in the same block as the statement containing the cursor (the vertical bar where you're typing) are enclosed in the same blue box. You know that you have the indentation right when all the commands you *expect* to be in the block *are* in the box.

Once you've typed in your recipe and saved it, you can load it. Click the LOAD PROGRAM button.

Debugging Tip: Don't Forget To Load!

The most common mistake with JES is typing in the function, saving it, and then trying the function in the command area before you load it. You have to click the LOAD PROGRAM button to make it available in the command area.

Now you can execute your recipe. Click in the command area. Since you aren't taking any input and aren't returning any value (i.e., this isn't a strict mathematical function), simply type the name of your recipe as a command:

FIGURE 2.6
Visualizing the blocks in JES.

```
>>> pickAndShow()
>>>
```

We can similarly define our second recipe to pick and play a sound.

Program 2: Pick and Play a Sound

```
def pickAndPlay():
  myFile = pickAFile()
  mySound = makeSound(myFile)
  play(mySound)
```

Making It Work Tip: Name the Names You Like

In the last section, we used the names myFilename and myPicture. In this recipe, we used myFile and myPict. Does it matter? It doesn't matter to the computer at all. We could call all our pictures myGlyph or even myThing. The computer doesn't care what names you use—they're entirely for your benefit. Pick names that are (a) meaningful to you (so that you can read and understand your program), (b) meaningful to others (so that anyone you show your program to can understand it), and (c) easy to type. Names with 25 characters, like myPictureThatIAmGoingToOpenAfterThis are meaningful and easy to read, but are a pain to type.

These recipes probably aren't really useful as programs. Needing to pick the file over and over again is annoying if you want the same picture to appear. Now that we have the power to define recipes, we can define new ones to perform whatever tasks we want. Let's define one that will open a specific picture and another that opens a specific sound.

Use `pickAFile` to get the filename of the sound or picture you want. We're going to need the name in defining the recipe to play that specific sound or show that specific picture. We'll just set the value of `myFile` *directly*, instead of as a result of `pickAFile`, by putting the string between quotes directly in the recipe.

Program 3: Show a Specific Picture

Be sure to replace FILENAME below with the complete path to your own picture file; for example, "C:/ip-book/mediasources/barbara.jpg".

```
def showPicture():
  myFile = "FILENAME"
  myPict = makePicture(myFile)
  show(myPict)
```

How It Works

The variable `myFile` takes on the value of the filename—the same one that the function `pickAFile` would return if it were to pick that file. We then make a picture from the file and name it `myPict`. Finally, we show the picture in `myPict`.

Program 4: Play a Specific Sound

Be sure to replace FILENAME below with the complete path to your own sound file; for example, "C:/ip-book/mediasources/hello.wav".

```
def playSound():
  myFile = "FILENAME"
  mySound = makeSound(myFile)
  play(mySound)
```

Common Bug: Windows Filenames and Backslashes

Windows uses backslashes as file delimiters. Python gives special meanings to certain backslash-and-character combinations, as we'll talk more about later. For example, '\n' means the same thing as the ENTER or RETURN key. These combinations can occur naturally in Windows filenames. To avoid having Python misinterpret these characters, you can use forward slashes instead as in C:/ip-book/mediasources/barbara.jpg" or you can type your filenames with an "r" in front, like this:

```
>>> myFile = r"C:\ip-book\mediasources\barbara.jpg"
>>> print myFile
C:\\ip-book\\mediasources\\barbara.jpg
```

Making It Work Tip: Copying and Pasting

Text can be copied and pasted between the program and command areas. You can use `print pickAFile()` to print a filename, then select it and COPY it (from the EDIT menu), then click in the command area and PASTE it. Similarly, you can copy whole commands from the command area up to the program area. That's an easy way to test the individual commands and then put them all in a recipe once you have the order right and they're working. You can also copy text within the command area. Instead of retyping a command, select it, COPY it, PASTE it into the bottom line (make sure the cursor is at the end of the line!), and hit ENTER to execute it.

2.5.1   Variable Recipes: Real Math-Like Functions That Take Input

How do we create a real function, like a function in mathematics, that takes inputs, such as `ord` or `makePicture`? Why would you *want* to?

An important reason for using a variable to specify input to the recipe is to make a program more *general*. Consider Recipe 3, `showPicture`. That's for a specific filename. Would it be useful to have a function that could take *any* filename, then make and show the picture? That kind of function handles the *general* case of making and showing pictures. We call that kind of generalization **abstraction**. Abstraction leads to general solutions that work in lots of situations.

Defining a recipe that takes input is very easy. It continues to be a matter of *substitution* and *evaluation*. We'll put a name inside those parentheses on the def line. That name is sometimes called the **parameter** or **input variable**.

When you evaluate the function by specifying its name with an **input value** (also called the **argument**) inside parentheses (like makePicture(myFilename) or show(myPicture)), the input value is *assigned* to the input variable. We say that the input variable *takes on* the input value. During the execution of the function (recipe), the input value will be *substituted* for the variable.

Here's what a recipe would look like that takes the filename as an input variable:

Program 5: Show the Picture File Whose Filename Is Input
```
def showNamed(myFile):
  myPict = makePicture(myFile)
  show(myPict)
```

Click on the LOAD PROGRAM button to tell JES to read the function or functions in the PROGRAM AREA. If you have any errors in your function, you will need to fix them and click LOAD PROGRAM button again. Once you have successfully loaded your functions, you can use them in the COMMAND AREA.

When you type

```
showNamed("C:/ip-book/mediasources/barbara.jpg")
```

in the COMMAND AREA and hit enter, the variable myFile in the function showNamed takes on the value

```
"C:/ip-book/mediasources/barbara.jpg".
```

myPict will then refer to the picture resulting from reading and interpreting the file. Then the picture will be shown.

We can create a function to play a sound in the same way. We can type more than one function in the PROGRAM AREA. Just add the function shown below after the previous one and click LOAD PROGRAM again.

Program 6: Play the Sound File Whose Filename Is Input
```
def playNamed(myFile):
  mySound = makeSound(myFile)
  play(mySound)
```

Try this function by typing the following in the COMMAND AREA.

```
>>> playNamed("C:/ip-book/mediasources/croak.wav")
```

You can create functions that take more than one parameter. Just separate the parameters with commas.

Program 7: Play a Sound File While Showing a Picture
```
def playAndShow(sFile, pFile):
  mySound = makeSound(sFile)
  myPict = makePicture(pFile)
  play(mySound)
  show(myPict)
```

We can also write recipes that take pictures or sounds in as the input values. Here's a recipe that shows a picture but takes the picture object as the input value instead of the filename.

Program 8: Show the Picture Provided As Input
```
def showPicture(myPict):
  show(myPict)
```

At this point you may want to save your functions to a file so that you can use them again. Click on FILE and then SAVE PROGRAM. A file dialog window will appear that will allow you to specify where to save the file and what to call it. If you later exit JES and restart JES, you can use OPEN PROGRAM in the FILE menu to open the file again and click on Load Program to load the functions for use.

Now, what is the difference between the function showPicture and the built-in JES function show? Nothing at all. We can certainly create a function that provides a new name to another function. If that makes your code easier for you to understand, then it's a great idea.

What is the *right* input value for a function? Is it better to input a filename or a picture? And what does "better" mean here, anyway? You'll read more about all of these issues later, but here's a short answer: Write the function that is most useful to you. If defining showPicture is more readable for you than show, then that's useful. If what you really want is a function that takes care of making the picture and showing it to you, then you might find the showNamed function the most useful.

PROGRAMMING SUMMARY

In this chapter, we talk about several kinds of encodings of data (or objects).

Integers (e.g., 3)	Numbers without a decimal point—they can't represent fractions.
Floating-point numbers (e.g., 3.0, 3.01)	Numbers that can contain a decimal point —they can represent fractions.
Strings (e.g., "Hello!")	A sequence of characters (including spaces, punctuation, etc.) delimited on either end with a double quote.
Filename	A string whose characters represent a path and a base filename.
Pictures	Encodings of images, typically coming from a JPEG file.
Sounds	Encodings of sounds, typically coming from a WAV file.

Here are the program pieces introduced in this chapter:

print	Displays the value of an expression (variable, value, formula, etc.) in its text form.
def	Defines a function and its input variables (if any).
ord	Returns the equivalent numeric value (from the ASCII standard) for the input character.
abs	Takes a number and returns the absolute value of it.
pickAFile	Lets the user pick a file and returns the complete path name as a string. It doesn't take any input.
makePicture	Takes a path name as input, reads the file, and creates a picture from it. Returns the new picture.
show	Shows a picture provided as input. It doesn't return anything.
makeSound	Takes a path name as input, reads the file, and creates a sound from it. It returns the new sound.
play	Takes a sound and plays it. It doesn't return anything.

PROBLEMS

2.1 Computer science concept questions:

- What is an algorithm?
- What is an encoding?
- How can computers represent pictures as numbers?
- What is Moore's Law?

2.2 What does `def` mean? What does the statement `def someFunction(x,y):` do?

2.3 What does `print` mean? What does the statement `print a` do?

2.4 What is the output from `print 1 / 3`? Why do you get this output?

2.5 What is the output from `print 1.3 * 3`? Why do you get this output?

2.6 What is the output from `print 1.0 / 3`? Why do you get this output?

2.7 What is the output from `print 10 + 3 * 7`? Why do you get this output?

2.8 What is the output from `print (10 + 3) * 7`? Why do you get this output?

2.9 What is the output from `print "Hi" + "there"`? Why do you get this output?

2.10 What is the output from the following?

```
>>> a = 3
>>> b = 4
>>> x = a * b
>>> print x
```

2.11 What is the output from the following?

```
>>> a = 3
>>> b = -5
>>> x = a * b
>>> print x
```

2.12 What is the output from the following?

```
>>> a = 4
>>> b = 2
>>> x = a / b
>>> print x
```

2.13 What is the output from the following?

```
>>> a = 4
>>> b = 2
>>> x = b - a
>>> print x
```

2.14 What is the output from the following?

```
>>> a = -4
>>> b = 2
>>> c = abs(a)
>>> x = a * c
>>> print x
```

2.15 What is the output from the following?

```
>>> name = "Barb"
>>> name = "Mark"
>>> print name
```

2.16   What is the output from the following?

```
>>> a = ord("A")
>>> b = 2
>>> x = a * b
>>> print x
```

2.17   The following code gives the error message shown below. Fix the code.

```
>>> pickafile()
The error was:pickafile
Name not found globally.
A local or global name could not be found. You need
to define the function or variable before you try
to use it in any way.
```

2.18   The following code gives the error message shown below. Fix the code.

```
>>> a = 3
>>> b = 4
>>> c = d * a
The error was:d
Name not found globally.
A local or global name could not be found. You need
to define the function or variable before you try
to use it in any way.
```

2.19   What does show(p) do? (Hint: There's more than one answer to this question.)

2.20   Try some other operations with strings in JES. What happens if you multiply a number by a string, like 3 * "Hello"? What happens if you try to multiply a string by a string, "a" * "b"?

2.21   We evaluated the expression pickAFile() when we wanted to execute the function named pickAFile. But what is the name pickAFile anyway? What do you get if you print pickAFile? How about print makePicture? What prints, and what do you think it means?

TO DIG DEEPER

The best (deepest, most material, most elegant) computer science textbook is *Structure and Interpretation of Computer Programs* by Abelson, Sussman, and Sussman [2]. It's a challenging book to get through but definitely worth the effort. A newer book more aimed at the programming novice but in the same spirit is *How to Design Programs* [12].

Neither of these books is really aimed at students who want to program because it's fun or because they have something small they want to do. They're aimed at future professional software developers. The best books for the student exploring computing are by Brian Harvey. His *Simply Scheme* uses the same programming language as the Abelson *et al.* book, but is more approachable. Our favorite of this class of books, though, is Harvey's three-volume set *Computer Science Logo Style* [23], which combines good computer science with creative and fun projects.

3

Modifying Pictures Using Loops

Chapter Learning Objectives

The media learning goals for this chapter are:

- To understand how images are digitized by taking advantage of limits in human vision.
- To identify different models for color, including RGB, the most common one for computers.
- To manipulate color values in pictures, like increasing or decreasing red values.
- To convert a color picture to grayscale, using more than one method.
- To negate a picture.

The computer science goals for this chapter are:

- To use a matrix representation in finding pixels in a picture.
- To use the objects *pictures* and *pixels*.
- To use iteration (with a for loop) for changing the color values of pixels in a picture.
- To nest blocks of code within one another.
- To choose between having a function *return* a value and just providing a *side effect*.
- To determine the *scope* of a variable name.

3.1   HOW PICTURES ARE ENCODED

Pictures (images, graphics) are an important part of any media communication. In this chapter, we discuss how pictures are represented on a computer (mostly as *bitmap* images—each dot or *pixel* is represented separately) and how they can be manipulated. The chapters that follow this one will introduce alternative image representations, such as *vector* images.

Pictures are a two-dimensional array of *pixels*. Each of these terms will be described in this section.

For our purposes, a picture is an image stored in a JPEG file. **JPEG** is an international standard for how to store images with high quality but in little space. JPEG is a **lossy compression** format. That means that it is *compressed*, made smaller, but not with 100% of the quality of the original format. Typically, though, what gets thrown away is stuff that you don't see or don't notice anyway. For most purposes, a JPEG image works fine.

A one-dimensional array is a sequence of elements of the same type. You can assign a name to an array and then use index numbers to access elements of the array. The first element in an array is at index 0. In Figure 3.1 the value at index 0 is 15, the value at index 1 is 12, the value at index 2 is 13, and the value at index 3 is 10.

A two-dimensional array is also called a **matrix**. A matrix is a collection of elements arranged in both rows and columns. This means that both the row and column index can be specified in order to access a value in the matrix.

In Figure 3.2, you see an example matrix. At *coordinates* (0, 1) (horizontal, vertical), you'll find the matrix element whose value is 9. (0, 0) is 15, (1, 0) is 12, and (2, 0) is 13. We will often refer to these coordinates as (x, y) $(horizontal, vertical)$.

What's stored at each element in the picture is a **pixel**. The word "pixel" is short for "picture element." It's literally a dot, and the overall picture is made up of lots of

0	1	2	3
15	12	13	10

FIGURE 3.1
An example array.

	0	1	2	3
0	15	12	13	10
1	9	7	2	1
2	6	3	9	10

FIGURE 3.2
An example matrix.

these dots. Have you ever taken a magnifying glass to the pictures in a newspaper or magazine, or to a television or even your own monitor? When you look at the picture in the magazine or on the television, it doesn't look like it's broken up into millions of discrete spots, but it is.

You can get a similar view of individual pixels using the picture tool, as shown in Figure 3.3. This tool allows you to zoom in on a picture up to 500% so that each individual pixel is visible. One way to bring up the picture tool is to explore the picture as shown below.

```
>>> file = "c:/ip-book/mediasources/caterpillar.jpg"
>>> pict = makePicture(file)
>>> explore(pict)
```

Our human sensory apparatus can't distinguish (without magnification or other special equipment) the small bits in the whole. Humans have low visual *acuity*—we don't see as much detail as, say, an eagle. We actually have more than one kind of vision system in use in our brain and our eyes. Our system for processing color is different from our system for processing black-and-white (or **luminance**). We use luminance to detect motion and sizes of objects, for example. We actually pick up luminance detail better with the sides of our eyes than from the center of our eye. That's an evolutionary advantage, since it allows you to pick out the sabertooth tiger sneaking up on your right in those bushes over there.

The lack of resolution in human vision is what makes it possible to digitize pictures. Animals that perceive greater detail than humans (e.g., eagles or cats) may actually see the individual pixels. We break up the picture into smaller elements (pixels), but there are enough of them and they are small enough that the picture doesn't look choppy when one looks at it overall. If you *can* see the effects of the digitization (e.g., you can see little rectangles in some spots), we call that *pixelization*—the effect when the digitization process becomes obvious.

Picture encoding is more complex than sound encoding. A sound is inherently linear—it progresses forward in time. A picture has two dimensions, width and height.

FIGURE 3.3
Image shown in the JES picture tool: 100% image on left and 500% on right.

Visible light is continuous—visible light is any wavelength between 370 and 730 nanometers (0.00000037 and 0.00000073 meters). But our perception of light is limited by how our color sensors work. Our eyes have sensors that trigger (peak) around 425 nanometers (blue), 550 nanometers (green), and 560 nanometers (red). Our brain determines what a particular color is based on the feedback from these three sensors in our eyes. There are some animals with only two kinds of sensors, like dogs. These animals still perceive color, but not the same colors or in the same way as humans. One of the interesting implications of our limited visual sensory apparatus is that we actually perceive two kinds of orange. There is a *spectral* orange—a particular wavelength that is natural orange. There is also a mixture of red and yellow that hits our color sensors just right so that we perceive it as the same orange.

Based on how we perceive color, as long as we encode what hits our three kinds of color sensors, we're recording our human perception of color. Thus, we will encode each pixel as a triplet of numbers. The first number represents the amount of red in the pixel, the second is the amount of green, and the third is the amount of blue. We can make up any human-visible color by combining red, green, and blue light (Figure 3.4) Combining all three gives us pure white. Turning off all three gives us black. We call this the **RGB color model**.

There are other models for defining and encoding colors besides the RGB color model. There's the *HSV color model* which encodes Hue, Saturation, and Value (sometimes also called the *HSB* color model for Hue, Saturation, and Brightness). The nice thing about the HSV model is that some notions, like making a color "lighter" or "darker," map cleanly to it—for example, you simply change the saturation (Figure 3.5). Another model is the *CMYK color model*, which encodes Cyan, Magenta, Yellow, and blacK (using the "K" instead of the "B" since "B" could be confused with blue). The CMYK model is what printers use—those are the inks they combine to make colors. However, with four elements there is more to encode on a computer, so the model is less popular for media computation. RGB is the most popular model on computers.

Each color component (sometimes called a **channel**) in a pixel is typically represented with a single byte, eight bits. Eight bits can represent 256 patterns (2^8): 0000000, 00000001, up through 11111111. We typically use these patterns to represent the values 0 to 255. Each pixel, then, uses 24 bits to represent colors. There are 2^{24} possible patterns of 0s and 1s in those 24 bits, which means that the standard encoding for color using the RGB model can represent 16,777,216 colors. We can actually perceive more than 16 million colors, but it turns out that it just doesn't matter. There is no technology that comes even close to being able to replicate the whole color space that we can see.

FIGURE 3.4
Merging red, green, and blue to make new colors.

FIGURE 3.5
Picking colors using the HSB color model.

We do have devices that can represent 16 million distinct colors, but those 16 million colors don't cover the entire space of color (or luminance) that we can perceive. So the 24-bit RGB model is adequate until technology advances.

There are computer models that use more bits per pixel. For example, there are 32-bit models that use the extra eight bits to represent *transparency*, i.e. how much of the color "below" the given image should be blended with this color. These additional eight bits are sometimes called the **alpha channel**. There are other models that use more than eight bits for the red, green, and blue channels, but they are uncommon.

We actually perceive borders of objects, motion, and depth through a *separate* vision system. We perceive color through one system and *luminance* (how light/dark things are) through another system. Luminance is not actually the *amount* of light, but our *perception* of the amount of light. We can measure the amount of light (e.g., the number of photons reflected off the color) and show that a red spot and a blue spot are each reflecting the same amount of light, but we perceive the blue as darker. Our sense of luminance is based on comparisons with the surroundings. The optical illusion in Figure 3.6 highlights how we perceive gray levels. The two end quarters are actually the same level of gray but because the two mid-quarters end in a sharp contrast of lightness and darkness, we perceive one end as darker than the other.

Most tools for allowing users to pick out colors let the users specify the color as RGB components. The color chooser in JES (which is the standard Java Swing color

FIGURE 3.6
The ends of this figure are the same colors of gray but the middle two quarters contrast sharply, so the left looks darker than the right.

FIGURE 3.7
Picking a color using RGB sliders from JES.

chooser) offers a set of sliders for controlling the amount of each color (Figure 3.7). You can pick a color by typing the following in the command area.

```
>>> pickAColor()
```

As mentioned, a triplet of $(0, 0, 0)$ (red, green, blue components) is black, and $(255, 255, 255)$ is white. $(255, 0, 0)$ is pure red, but $(100, 0, 0)$ is red too—just darker. $(0, 100, 0)$ is a medium green, and $(0, 0, 100)$ is medium blue. When the red component is the same as the green and as the blue, the resultant color is gray. $(50, 50, 50)$ would be a fairly dark gray, and $(100, 100, 100)$ is lighter.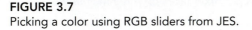

Figure 3.8 is a representation of pixel RGB triplets in a matrix representation. Thus, the pixel at $(1, 0)$ has color $(30, 30, 255)$, which means that it has a red value of 30, a

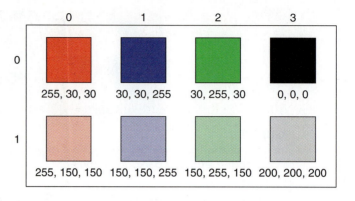

FIGURE 3.8
RGB triplets in a matrix representation.

TABLE 3.1 Number of bytes needed to store pixels at various sizes and formats

	320 × 240 image	640 × 480 image	1024 × 768 image
24-bit color	230,400 bytes	921,600 bytes	2,359,296 bytes
32-bit color	307,200 bytes	1,228,800 bytes	3,145,728 bytes

green value of 30, and a blue value of 255—it's a mostly blue color, but not pure blue. The pixel at (2, 1) has pure green but also more red and blue (150, 255, 150), so it's a fairly light green.

Images on disk and even in computer memory are usually stored in *compressed* form. The amount of memory needed to represent every pixel of even small images is pretty large (Table 3.1). A fairly small image of 320 pixels across by 240 pixels wide, with 24 bits per pixel, takes up 230,400 bytes—that's roughly 230 *kilobytes* (1000 bytes) or 1/4 *megabyte* (million bytes). A computer monitor with 1024 pixels across and 768 pixels vertically with 32 bits per pixel takes up three megabytes just to represent the screen.

3.2 MANIPULATING PICTURES

We manipulate pictures in JES by making a picture object out of a JPEG file, then changing the color of the pixels in the picture. To change a pixel's color, we manipulate the red, green, and blue components.

We make pictures using makePicture. We make the picture appear with show.

```
>>> file = pickAFile()
>>> print file
C:\ip-book\mediasources\beach.jpg
>>> myPict = makePicture(file)
>>> show(myPict)
>>> print myPict
```

```
Picture, filename C:\ip-book\mediasources\beach.jpg
    height 480 width 640
```

What makePicture does is to scoop up all the bytes at the input filename, bring them into memory, reformat them slightly, and place a sign on them announcing "This is a picture!" When you execute myPict = makePicture(filename), you are saying, "The name for that picture object (note the sign on it) is now myPict."

Pictures know their width and their height. You can query them with getWidth and getHeight.

```
>>> print getWidth(myPict)
640
>>> print getHeight(myPict)
480
```

We can get any particular pixel from a picture using getPixel with the picture, and the coordinates of the pixel desired. We can also get a one-dimensional array of all the pixels with getPixels. The one-dimensional array starts with all the pixels from the first row followed by all the pixels from the second row and so on. We reference the array elements using [index].

```
>>> pixel = getPixel(myPict,0,0)
>>> print pixel
Pixel red=2 green=4 blue=3
>>> pixels = getPixels(myPict)
>>> print pixels[0]
Pixel red=2 green=4 blue=3
```

Common Bug: Don't Try Printing the Pixels Array: Way Too Big!

getPixels literally returns an array of all the pixels. If you try to print the return value from getPixels, you'll get the printout of each pixel. How many pixels are there? Well, "beach.jpg" has a width of 640 and a height of 480. How many lines would print? $640 * 480 = 307{,}200$! A printout of 307,200 lines is very big. You probably don't want to wait for it to finish. If you do this accidentally, just quit JES and restart it.

Pixels know where they come from. You can ask them their x and y coordinates with getX and getY.

```
>>> print getX(pixel)
0
>>> print getY(pixel)
0
```

Each pixel knows how to getRed and setRed. (Green and blue work similarly.)

```
>>> print getRed(pixel)
2
>>> setRed(pixel,255)
>>> print getRed(pixel)
255
```

You can also ask a pixel for its color with `getColor`, and you can also set the color with `setColor`. Color objects know their red, green, and blue components. You can make new colors with the function `makeColor`.

```
>>> color = getColor(pixel)
>>> print color
color r=255 g=4 b=3
>>> newColor = makeColor(0,100,0)
>>> print newColor
color r=0 g=100 b=0
>>> setColor(pixel,newColor)
>>> print getColor(pixel)
color r=0 g=100 b=0
```

If you change the color of a pixel, the picture to which the pixel belongs is also changed.

```
>>> print getPixel(mypicture,0,0)
Pixel, color=color r=0 g=100 b=0
```

Common Bug: Seeing Changes in the Picture

If you show your picture, and then change the pixels, you may wonder why you don't see anything different. Picture displays don't automatically update. If you execute `repaint` with the picture, e.g., `repaint(picture)`, the picture will update.

You can also make colors from `pickAColor`, which gives you several ways to pick a color.

```
>>> color2=pickAColor()
>>> print color2
color r=255 g=51 b=51
```

When you have finished manipulating a picture, you can write it out with `writePictureTo`.

```
>>> writePictureTo(myPict,"C:/temp/changedPict.jpg")
```

Common Bug: End with .jpg

Be sure to end your filename with ".jpg" in order to get your operating system to recognize it as a JPEG file.

Common Bug: Saving a File Quickly—and How to Find It Again!

What if you don't know the whole path to a directory of your choosing? You don't have to specify anything more than the base name.

```
>>> writePictureTo(myPict,"new-picture.jpg")
```

The problem is finding the file again. In what directory was it saved? This is a pretty simple bug to resolve. The default directory (the one you get if you don't specify a path) is wherever JES is. If you have used `pickAFile()` recently, the default directory will be whatever directory you picked the file from. If you have a standard media folder (e.g., MEDIASOURCES) where you keep your media and pick files from, that's where your files will be saved if you don't specify a complete path.

We don't have to write new functions to manipulate pictures. We can do it from the Command Area using the functions just described.

```
>>> file="C:/ip-book/mediasources/caterpillar.jpg"
>>> pict=makePicture(file)
>>> show(pict)
>>> pixels = getPixels(pict)
>>> setColor(pixels[0],black)
>>> setColor(pixels[1],black)
>>> setColor(pixels[2],black)
>>> setColor(pixels[3],black)
>>> setColor(pixels[4],black)
>>> setColor(pixels[5],black)
>>> setColor(pixels[6],black)
>>> setColor(pixels[7],black)
>>> setColor(pixels[8],black)
>>> setColor(pixels[9],black)
>>> repaint(pict)
```

The result, showing a small black line at the top left of the picture, appears in Figure 3.9. This black line is 10 pixels long.

Making It Work Tip: Use JES HELP!

JES has a wonderful help system. Forget what function you need? Just choose an item from the JES HELP menu (Figure 3.10—it's all hyperlinked, so hunt around for what you need). Forget what a function you're already using does? Select it and choose EXPLAIN from the HELP menu and get an explanation of what you have selected (Figure 3.11).

FIGURE 3.9
Directly modifying the pixel colors via commands: note the small black line in the top left corner.

Table of Contents > Understanding Pictures in JES > Picture Objects in JES

Picture Objects in JES

To understand how to work with pictures in JES, you must first understand the objects (or encodings) that represent pictures.

You can imagine that each **picture** is made up of a collection of **pixels**, which is made up of **pixel** 1, pixel 2, pixel 3, etc, and that each pixel has it's own particular **color**.

Pictures	Pictures are encodings of images, typically coming from a JPEG file.
Pixels	Pixels are a sequence of Pixel objects. They flatten the two dimensional nature of the pixels in a picture and give you instead an arraylike sequence of pixels. **pixels[1]** returns the leftmost pixel in a picture.
Pixel	A pixel is a dot in the Picture. It has a color and an (x, y) position associated with it. It remembers its own Picture so that a change to the pixel changes the real dot in the picture.
Color	It's a mixture of red, green, and blue values, each between 0 and 255.

▲jump to top

FIGURE 3.10
An example JES HELP entry.

3.2.1 Exploring Pictures

At `http://mediacomputation.org`, you will find the MediaTools application with documentation for how to get it started. You will also find a MediaTools menu in JES. Both kinds of MediaTools have a set of image exploration tools that are really useful for studying a picture. The MediaTools application appears in Figure 3.12. The JES picture tool is shown in Figure 3.13.

The JES picture tool works from picture objects that you have defined *and named* in the Command Area. If you don't have the picture named, you can't view it with the JES picture tool. `p = makePicture(pickAFile())` will allow you to define a picture and name it p. You can then explore the picture using `explore(pict)` or you can choose PICTURE TOOL ... from the MEDIATOOLS menu, which will give you a pop-up menu of the available picture objects (by their variable names) and the opportunity to choose one of them by clicking OK (Figure 3.14).

The JES picture tool allows you to explore a picture. You can zoom in or out by choosing a level in the ZOOM menu. Press down with the mouse button as you move the cursor around the picture and you'll be shown the (x, y) (horizontal, vertical) coordinates and the RGB values of the pixel your mouse cursor is currently over (Figure 3.13).

Back | Forward | Go To: http://coweb.cc.gatech.edu/mediaCo | Go

setColor(pixel, color):
pixel: the pixel you want to set the color of
color: the Color you want to set the pixel to
Takes in a pixel and a Color, and sets the pixel to the provided color. **Example:**

```
def makeMoreBlue(pixel):
  myBlue = getBlue(pixel) + 60
  newColor = makeColor(getRed(pixel), getGreen(pixel), myBlue)
  setColor(pixel, newColor)
```

This will take in a pixel and increase its level of blue by 60.

Explain setColor | Line Number:1 Position: 1

FIGURE 3.11
An example JES Explain entry.

FIGURE 3.12
Using the MediaTools image exploration tools.

FIGURE 3.13
Selecting a pixel in the JES picture tool.

FIGURE 3.14
Picking a picture in the picture tool in JES.

The MediaTools application works from files on the disk rather than picture objects named in your Command Area. If you want to check out a file before loading into JES, use the MediaTools *application.* Click on the PICTURE TOOLS box in MediaTools and the tools will open. Use the OPEN button to bring up a file selection box—you click on directories you want to explore on the left, and on images you want on the right, then click OK. When the image appears, you have several different tools available. Move your cursor over the picture and press down with the mouse button.

- The red, green, and blue values will be displayed for the pixel you're pointing at. This is useful when you want to get a sense of how the colors in your picture map to numeric red, green, and blue values. It's also helpful if you're going to be doing some computation on the pixels and want to check the values.
- The x and y positions will be displayed for the pixel you're pointing at. This is useful when you want to figure out regions of the screen (e.g., if you want to process only part of the picture). If you know the range of x and y coordinates where you want to process, you can tune your for loop to reach just those sections.

- Finally, a magnifier is available to let you see the pixels blown up. (The magnifier can be clicked and dragged around.)

3.3   CHANGING COLOR VALUES

The easiest thing to do with pictures is to change the color values of their pixels by changing the red, green, and blue components. You can get radically different effects by simply tweaking these values. Some of Adobe Photoshop's *filters* do just what we're going to be doing in this section.

The way we're going to manipulate colors is by computing a *percentage* of the original color. If we want 50% of the amount of red in the picture, we're going to set the red channel to 0.50 times whatever it is right now. If we want to increase the red by 25%, we're going to set the red to 1.25 times whatever it is right now. Recall that the asterisk (*) is the operator for multiplication in Python.

3.3.1   Using Loops in Pictures

What we could do is to get each pixel in the picture and set it to a new value of red or green or blue. Let's say that we want to decrease the red by 50%. We can always write code like this:

```
>>> file="C:/ip-book/mediasources/barbara.jpg"
>>> pict=makePicture(file)
>>> show(pict)
>>> pixels = getPixels(pict)
>>> setRed(pixels[0],getRed(pixels[0]) * 0.5)
>>> setRed(pixels[1],getRed(pixels[1]) * 0.5)
>>> setRed(pixels[2],getRed(pixels[2]) * 0.5)
>>> setRed(pixels[3],getRed(pixels[3]) * 0.5)
>>> setRed(pixels[4],getRed(pixels[4]) * 0.5)
>>> setRed(pixels[5],getRed(pixels[5]) * 0.5)
>>> repaint(pict)
```

That's pretty tedious to write, especially for all the pixels even in a small image. What we need is a way of telling the computer to do the same thing over and over again. Well, not exactly the same thing—we want to change what's going on in a well-defined way. We want to take one step each time, or process one additional pixel.

We can do this with a `for` loop. A `for` loop executes some block of commands (that you specify) for each item in an *array* (that you provide), where each time the commands are executed, a particular variable (that you name) will have the value of a different element of the array. An array is an ordered collection of data. `getPixels` returns an array of all the pixel objects in an input picture.

We're going to write statements that look like this:

```
for pixel in getPixels(picture):
```

Let's talk through the pieces here.

- First comes the command name `for`.

- Next comes the variable name that you want to use in your code for addressing (and manipulating) the elements of the sequence. We're using the word `pixel` here because we want to process each of the pixels in the picture.
- The word `in` is **required**—you must type it! Typing `in` makes the command more readable than leaving it out, so there's a benefit to the extra four keystrokes (space-i-n-space).
- Then you need an *array*. The variable `pixel` is going to be assigned to each element of the array each time through the loop: one element of the array, one iteration through the loop, the next element of the array, the next iteration through the loop. We use the function `getPixels` to generate the array for us.
- Finally, you need a colon (":"). The colon is important—it signifies that what comes next is a *block* (you should recall reading about blocks in the last chapter).

What comes next are the commands that you want to execute for each pixel. Each time the commands are executed, the variable (in our example `pixel`) will be a different element from the array. The commands (called the *body*) are specified as a block. This means that they should follow the `for` statement, each on its own line, *and indented by two more spaces!* For example, here is the `for` loop that sets each pixel's red channel to half the original value.

```
for pixel in getPixels(picture):
  value = getRed(pixel)
  setRed(pixel,value * 0.5)
```

Let's talk through this code.

- The first statement says that we're going to have a `for` loop that will set the variable `pixel` to each of the elements of the array that is output from `getPixels(picture)`.
- The next statement is indented, so it's part of the body of the `for` loop—one of the statements that will be executed each time `pixel` has a new value (whatever the next pixel in the picture is). It gets the current red value at the current pixel and puts that in the variable `value`.
- The third statement is still indented, so it's still part of the loop body. Here we set the value of the red channel (`setRed`) of the pixel named `pixel` to the value of the variable `value` times 0.5. This will halve the original value.

Remember that what comes after a function definition `def` statement is *also* a block. If you have a `for` loop inside a function, then the `for` statement is indented two spaces already, so the body of the `for` loop (the statements to be executed) must be indented *four* spaces. The `for` loop's block is inside the function's block. That's called a **nested block**—one block is nested inside the other. Here's an example of turning a loop into a function.

```
def decreaseRed(picture):
  for pixel in getPixels(picture):
    value = getRed(pixel)
    setRed(pixel,value * 0.5)
```

You don't actually have to put loops into functions to use them. You can type them into the Command Area of JES. JES is smart enough to figure out that you need to type more than one command if you're specifying a loop, so it changes the prompt from >>> to .... Of course, it can't figure out when you're done, so you'll have to just hit ENTER without typing anything else to tell JES that you're done with the body of your loop. You probably realize that we don't really need the variable `value`—we can simply replace the variable with the function holding the same value. Here's how to do it at the command line:

```
>>> for pixel in getPixels(picture):
...    setRed(pixel,getRed(pixel) * 0.5)
```

Now that we see how to get the computer to do thousands of commands without writing thousands of individual lines, let's try it out.

3.3.2 Increasing/Decreasing Red (Green, Blue)

A common desire when working with digital pictures is to shift a picture's *redness* (or greenness or blueness—most often the redness). You can shift it higher to "warm" the picture, or reduce it to "cool" the picture or to deal with overly red digital cameras.

The recipe given below reduces the amount of color 50% in an input picture. It uses the variable p to stand for the current pixel. We used the variable `pixel` in the previous function. It doesn't matter—the name can be whatever we want.

Program 9: Reduce the Amount of Red in a Picture by 50%

```
def decreaseRed(picture):
  for p in getPixels(picture):
    value=getRed(p)
    setRed(p,value*0.5)
```

Go ahead and type the preceding code into your JES Program Area. Click LOAD PROGRAM to get Python to process the function (be sure to save it, something like DECREASERED.PY) and thus make the name `decreaseRed` stand for this function. Follow along the example below to get a better idea of how this all works.

This recipe takes a picture as input—the one that we'll use to get the pixels from. To get a picture, we need a filename, and then we need to make a picture from it. We can also open a JES picture tool on a picture using the function `explore(picture)`. This will make a copy of the current picture and show it in the JES picture tool. After we apply the function `decreaseRed` to the picture, we can explore it again and compare the two pictures side-by-side. Therefore, the recipe can be used like this:

```
>>> file="C:/ip-book/mediasources/Katie-smaller.jpg"
>>> picture=makePicture(file)
>>> explore(picture)
>>> decreaseRed(picture)
>>> explore(picture)
```

Common Bug: Patience—For Loops Always End

The most common bug with this kind of code is to give up and hit the STOP button before it ends on its own. If you're using a for loop, the program will *always* stop. But it might take a full minute (or two!) for some of the manipulations we'll do—especially if your source image is large.

The original picture and its red-reduced version appear in Figure 3.15. 50% is obviously a *lot* of red to reduce. The picture looks like it was taken through a blue filter. Notice that the first pixel's red value was 133 and has been changed to 66.

Tracing the Program: How Did That Work?

Computer Science Idea: The Most Important Skill Is Tracing

The most important skill that you can develop in programming is the ability to *trace* your program. (This is sometimes also called *stepping* or *walking through* your program.) To trace your program is to walk through it, line by line, and figure out what happens. Looking at a program, can you *predict* what it's going to do? You should be able to by thinking through what it does.

How It Works

Let's *trace* the function to decrease red and see how it worked. We want to break in at the point where we just called decreaseRed:

FIGURE 3.15
The original picture (*left*) and red-reduced version (*right*).

```
>>> file="C:/ip-book/mediasources/Katie-smaller.jpg"
>>> picture=makePicture(file)
>>> explore(picture)
>>> decreaseRed(picture)
>>> explore(picture)
```

What happens now? decreaseRed really stands for the function that we saw earlier, so it begins to execute.

```
def decreaseRed(picture):
  for p in getPixels(picture):
    value=getRed(p)
    setRed(p,value*0.5)
```

The first line we execute is def decreaseRed(picture):. This says that the function should expect some input and that the input will be named picture during the execution of the function.

Computer Science Idea: Names Inside of Functions Are Different from Names Outside of Functions

The names inside a function (like picture, p, and value in the decreaseRed example) are *completely* different from the names in the Command Area or any other function. We say that they have a different *scope*.

Inside the computer, we can imagine what it now looks like: there is some association between the word picture and the picture object that we gave it as input.

picture

Now we get to the line for p in getPixels(picture):. This means that all the pixels from the picture are lined up (within the computer) as a sequence (in the array), and that variable p should be assigned (associated with) the first one. We can imagine that inside the computer it now looks like this:

Each pixel has its own RGB values. p points at the first pixel. Note that the variable `picture` is still there—we may not use it anymore but it's still there.

Now we're at `value=getRed(p)`. This simply adds another name to the ones the computer is already tracking for us and gives it a simple numeric value.

Finally, we're at the bottom of the loop. The computer executes `setRed(p,value*` `0.5)` which changes the red channel of the pixel p to 50% of the `value`. The value of p is odd, so we would get 67.5 when we multiply by 0.5, but we are putting the result in an integer so that the fractional part of the number is simply thrown away. So the original red value of 135 changes to 67.

What happens next is very important: the loop starts over again! We go back to the `for` loop and take the *next* value in the array. The name p gets associated with that next value.

We get a new value for `value` at `value=getRed(p)`, so now `value` is 133, rather than the 135 it was from the first pixel.

And then we change *that* pixel's red channel.

Eventually, we get Figure 3.15. We keep going through all the pixels in the sequence and changing all the red values.

3.3.3   Testing the Program: Did That Really Work?

How do we know that what we did really worked? Sure, *something* happened to the picture, but did we really decrease the red? By 50%?

Making It Work Tip: Don't Just Trust Your Own Programs!
It's easy to mislead yourself into thinking that your program worked. After all, you told the computer to do something, so you shouldn't be surprised if the computer did what you wanted. But computers are really stupid—they can't figure out what you want. They only do what you tell them. It's pretty easy to get it *almost* right. Be sure to check. ■

We can check it several ways. One way is with the JES picture tool. You can check the RGB values at the same x and y coordinates in both the before and after picture using the picture tool. Click and drag the cursor to a location to check in the before-picture and then type in the same *x* and *y* coordinates in the after-picture tool and hit enter. This will show you the color values at the desired *x* and *y* location in both the before and after pictures (Figure 3.16).

We can also use the functions that we know in the Command Area to check the red values of individual pixels.

```
>>> file = pickAFile()
>>> pict = makePicture(file)
>>> pixel = getPixel(pict,0,0)
>>> print pixel
```

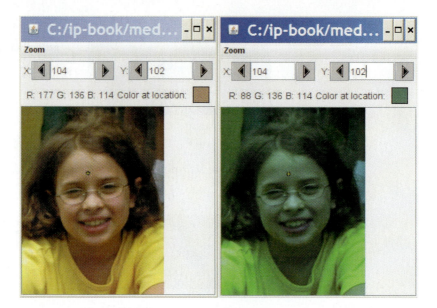

FIGURE 3.16
Using the JES picture tool to convince ourselves that the red was decreased.

```
Pixel, color=color r=168 g=131 b=105
>>> decreaseRed(pict)
>>> newPixel = getPixel(pict,0,0)
>>> print newPixel
Pixel, color=color r=84 g=131 b=105
>>> print 168 * 0.5
84.0
```

3.3.4   Changing One Color at a Time

Let's increase the red in the picture now. If multiplying the red component by 0.5 reduced it, multiplying it by something over 1.0 should increase it.

Program 10: Increase the Red Component by 20%
```
def increaseRed(picture):
  for p in getPixels(picture):
    value=getRed(p)
    setRed(p,value*1.2)
```

How It Works

We would use `increaseRed` using the same kind of Command Area statements as we did for `decreaseRed`. When we type something like `increaseRed(pict)`, the same kind of process occurs. We get all the pixels of the input picture `pict` (whatever that is) then assign the variable `p` to the first pixel in the list. We get its red value (say, 100) and name that `value`. We assign the red value of the pixel currently represented by the name p to 1.2 * 100 or 120. We then repeat the process for *every* pixel p in the input picture.

What happens if you increase the red in a picture that has lots of red in it and some of the resulting red values would go over 255? There are two options in this case. The value can be clipped to a maximum of 255 or you can wrap it around using the modulo (remainder) operator. For example if the value is 200 and you try to double it to 400, it can remain at 255 or wrap to 144 (400 − 256). Try it and see what happens.

JES provides an option to either clip color values to 255 or wrap them. To change this option click on EDIT in the menu and then on OPTIONS. The option to change is MODULO PIXEL COLOR VALUES BY 256.

We can even get rid of a color component completely. The next recipe erases the blue component from a picture

Program 11: Clear the Blue Component from a Picture

```
def clearBlue(picture):
    for p in getPixels(picture):
        setBlue(p,0)
```

3.4   CREATING A SUNSET

We can certainly do more than one picture manipulation at once. Once, Mark wanted to generate a sunset out of a beach scene. His first attempt was to increase the red but that doesn't work. Some of the red values in a given picture are pretty high. If you go past 255 for a channel value, the default is to *wrap-around*. If you setRed of a pixel to 256, you'll actually get *zero*. So increasing red created bright blue-green (no red) spots.

Mark's second thought was that maybe what happens in a sunset is that there is *less* blue and green, thus *emphasizing* the red, without actually increasing it. Here is the program that he wrote for that:

Program 12: Making a Sunset

```
def makeSunset(picture):
    for p in getPixels(picture):
        value=getBlue(p)
        setBlue(p,value*0.7)
        value=getGreen(p)
        setGreen(p,value*0.7)
```

How It Works

As in past examples, we take an input picture and make the variable p stand for each pixel in the input picture. We get each blue component and then set it again after multiplying its original value by 0.70. We then do the same to the green. Effectively, we're changing both the blue and green channels—reducing each by 30%. The effect works pretty well, as seen in Figure 3.17

FIGURE 3.17
Original beach scene (*left*) and at (fake) sunset (*right*).

3.4.1   Making Sense of Functions

You probably have lots of questions about functions at this point. Why did we write these functions in this way? How is it that we're reusing variable names like `picture` in both the function and the Command Area? Are there other ways to write these functions? Is there such a thing as a better or worse function?

Since we're always picking a file (or typing in a filename) and *then* making a picture before calling one of our picture manipulation functions and *then* showing or exploring the picture, it's natural to ask why we don't build those in. Why doesn't *every* function have `pickAFile()` and `makePicture` in it?

We use the functions in the way that makes them more *general* and *reusable*. We want each function to do one and only one thing, so that we can use the function again in a new context where we need that one thing done. An example may make this clearer. Consider the program to make a sunset (program 12). It works by reducing the green and blue, each by 30%. What if we rewrote this function so that it calls two *smaller* functions that just do the two pieces of the manipulation? We'd end up with something like program 13.

Program 13: Making a Sunset As Three Functions

```
def makeSunset2(picture):
  reduceBlue(picture)
  reduceGreen(picture)

def reduceBlue(picture):
  for p in getPixels(picture):
    value=getBlue(p)
    setBlue(p,value*0.7)

def reduceGreen(picture):
  for p in getPixels(picture):
    value=getGreen(p)
    setGreen(p,value*0.7)
```

How It Works

The first thing to realize is that this actually does work. `makeSunset` does the same thing here as in the previous recipe. The function `makeSunset` takes an input picture, then calls `reduceBlue` with the same input picture. `reduceBlue` makes p stand for each pixel in the input picture, and reduces the blue of each by 30% (by multiplying it by 0.7). `reduceBlue` then ends, and the *flow of control* (i.e., which statement executes next) returns to `makeSunset` and the *next* statement is executed. That is the call to the function `reduceGreen` with the same input picture. As before, `reduceGreen` walks each of the pixels and reduces the green value by 30%.

Making It Work Tip: Using Multiple Functions

It's perfectly okay to have multiple functions in one Program Area, saved in one file. It can make it easier to read and reuse functions.

It's perfectly okay to have one function (`makeSunset` in this case) use other functions written by the programmer in the same file (`reduceBlue` and `reduceGreen`). You use `makeSunset` just as you did before. It's the same recipe (it tells the computer to do the same thing), but with different functions. The earlier recipe did everything in one function and this one does it in three. In fact, you can also use `reduceBlue` and `reduceGreen`—make a picture in the Command Area and pass it as input to either of them. They work just like `decreaseRed`.

What's different is that the function `makeSunset` is somewhat simpler to read. It states pretty clearly, "To make a sunset means to reduce blue and reduce green." Being simple to read *is* important.

Computer Science Idea: Programs Are for People

Computers couldn't care less what a program looks like. Programs are written to communicate with *people*. Making programs easy to read and understand means that they are more easily changed and reused and they more effectively communicate process to other humans.

What if we had written `reduceBlue` and `reduceGreen` with `pickAFile` and `show` and `repaint` in it? We would be asked for the picture twice—once in each function. Because we wrote these functions to *only* reduce the blue and reduce the green ("one and only one thing"), we can use them in new functions like `makeSunset`.

Now let's say that we put `pickAFile` and `makePicture` into the `makeSunset`. The functions `reduceBlue` and `reduceGreen` are completely flexible and reusable again. But `makeSunset` is now less flexible and reusable. Is that a big deal? No, not if you only care about having the function to give a sunset look to a single frame. But what if you later want to build a movie with a few hundred frames, to each of which you want to add a sunset look? Do you really want to pick out each of those few hundred frames? Or would you rather make a loop to go through the frames (which we'll learn how to do in a few chapters) and send each of them as input to the *more general* form of makeSunset? That's why we make functions general and reusable—you never know when you're going to want to use a function again in a larger context.

Making It Work Tip: Don't Start by Trying to Write Applications

New programmers often want to write complete applications that a nontechnical user can use. You may want to write a makeSunset application that goes out and fetches a picture for a user and generates a sunset. Building good user interfaces that anyone can use is hard work. Start out more slowly. It's hard enough to make a reusable function that takes a picture as input. You can work on user interfaces later. ■

We could also write these functions with explicit filenames by saying at the beginning of one of the programs:

```
file="C:/ip-book/mediasources/bridge.jpg"
```

That way, we wouldn't be prompted for a file each time. But then the functions only work for the one file, and if we want them to work for some other file, we have to modify them. Do you really want to change the function each time you use it? It's easier to leave the function alone and change the picture that you hand to it.

Of course, we could change any of our functions to be handed a filename rather than a picture. For example, we could write:

```
def makeSunset3(filename):
  reduceBlue(filename)
  reduceGreen(filename)

def reduceBlue(filename):
  filename = makePicture(filename)
  for p in getPixels(picture):
    value=getBlue(p)
    setBlue(p,value*0.7)

def reduceGreen(filename):
  picture=makePicture(filename)
  for p in getPixels(picture):
    value=getGreen(p)
    setGreen(p,value*0.7)
```

Is this better or worse than the code we saw before? At some level, it doesn't matter—we can work with pictures or filenames, whichever makes more sense to us. The filename-as-input version does have several disadvantages, though. For one, it doesn't work! The picture is made in each of reduceGreen and reduceBlue, but then it isn't saved, so it gets lost at the end of the function. The earlier version of makeSunset2 (and its *subfunctions*, the functions it calls) works by *side effects*—the function doesn't return anything, but it changes the input object directly.

We could fix the loss-of-the-picture by saving the file to disk after we're done with each function, but then the functions are doing more than "one and only one thing."

There's also the inefficiency of making the picture twice, and if we were to add in the saving, saving the picture twice. Again, the best functions do "one and only one thing."

Even larger functions, like makeSunset2, do "one and only one thing." makeSunset2 makes a sunset-looking picture. It does so *by* reducing green and reducing blue. It calls two other functions to do that. What we end up with is a *hierarchy* of goals—the "one and only one thing" that is being done. makeSunset does its one thing by asking two other functions to do their one thing. We call this **hierarchical decomposition** (breaking down a problem into smaller parts, then breaking down the smaller parts until you get something that you can easily program) and it's very powerful for creating complex programs out of pieces that you understand.

Names in functions are *completely* separate from names in the Command Area. The *only* way to get any data (pictures, sounds, filenames, numbers) from the Command Area into a function is by passing it in as input to the function. Within the function, you can use any names you want. Names that you first define within the function (like picture in the last example) and names that you use to stand for the input data (like filename) *only* exist while the function is running. When the function is done, variable names literally do not exist anymore.

This is really an advantage. Earlier, we said that naming is very important to computer scientists: we name everything, from data to functions. But if each name could mean one and only one thing *forever*, we'd run out of names. In natural language, words mean different things in different contexts (e.g., "What do you mean?" and "You are being mean!"). A function is a different context—names can mean something different than they do outside of that function.

Sometimes you will compute something inside a function that you want to return to the Command Area or to a calling function. We've already seen functions that output a value, like pickAFile, which outputs a filename. If you did a makePicture inside a function, you might want to output the picture that you created inside the function. You can do this by using return, which we'll talk more about later.

The name you give to a function's input can be thought of as a *placeholder*. Whenever the placeholder appears, imagine the input data appearing instead. So in a function like

```
def decreaseRed(picture):
  for p in getPixels(picture):
    value=getRed(p)
    setRed(p,value*0.5)
```

we are going to call decreaseRed with a statement like decreaseRed(myPicture). Whatever picture is in myPicture *becomes known as* picture while decreaseRed is running. For those few seconds, picture in decreaseRed and myPicture in the Command Area *refer to the same picture*. Changing the pixels in one changes the pixels in the other.

We've now talked about different ways of writing the same function—some better, some worse. There are other ways that are pretty much equivalent and some that are much better. Let's consider a few more ways that we can write functions.

We can pass in more than one input at a time. Consider this version of `decreaseRed`:

```
def decreaseRed(picture, amount):
  for p in getPixels(picture):
    value=getRed(p)
    setRed(p,value*amount)
```

We would use this one by saying something like `decreaseRed(mypicture, 0.25)`. This use would reduce the red by 75%. We could say `decreaseRed (mypicture, 1.25)` and *increase* red by 25%. Perhaps this function should be better named `changeRed`, because that's what it is now—a general way of changing the whole amount of red in a picture. That's a pretty useful and powerful function.

Recall seeing this code in program 11:

```
def clearBlue(picture):
  for p in getPixels(picture):
    setBlue(p,0)
```

We could also write the same recipe like this:

```
def clearBlue(picture):
  for p in getPixels(picture):
    value = getBlue(p)
    setBlue(p,value*0)
```

It's important to note that this function achieves the *exact same* thing as the earlier recipe did. Both set the blue channel of all pixels to zero. An advantage of the latter function is that it has the same *form* as all the other color-changing functions we've seen. This may make it more understandable, which is useful. It is somewhat less efficient—it's not really necessary to *get* the blue value before setting it to zero nor is it necessary to multiply by zero when we just want the value of zero. The function is really doing more than it needs to do—it's not doing "one and only one thing."

3.5   LIGHTENING AND DARKENING

To lighten or darken a picture is pretty simple. It's the same pattern we saw previously, but instead of changing a color component, you change the overall color. Here are lightening and then darkening as recipes. Figure 3.18 shows the original and darker version of a picture.

Program 14: Lighten the Picture

```
def lighten(picture):
  for px in getPixels(picture):
    color = getColor(px)
    color = makeLighter(color)
    setColor(px,color)
```

FIGURE 3.18
The original picture (*left*) and a darker version (*right*).

How It Works

The variable px is used to represent each of the pixels in the input picture. (Not p! Does it matter? Not to the computer—if p means "pixel" to you, then use it, but feel free to use px or pxl or even pixel!) color takes on the color of the pixel px. The function makeLighter returns the new lighter color. The setColor method sets the color of the pixel to the new lighter color.

Program 15: Darken the Picture

```
def darken(picture):
  for px in getPixels(picture):
    color = getColor(px)
    color = makeDarker(color)
    setColor(px,color)
```

3.6   CREATING A NEGATIVE

Creating a *negative image* of a picture is much easier than you might at first imagine. Let's think it through. What we want is the opposite of each of the current values for red, green, and blue. It's easiest to understand at the extremes. If we have a red component of 0, we want 255 instead. If we have 255, we want the negative to have a 0.

Now let's consider the middle ground. If the red component is slightly red (say, 50), we want something that is almost completely red—where the "almost" is the same amount of redness in the original picture. We want the maximum red (255), but 50 less than that. We want a red component of $255 - 50 = 205$. In general, the negative should be $255 - original$. We need to compute the negative of each of the red, green, and blue components, then create a new negative color and set the pixel to the negative color.

FIGURE 3.19
Negative of the image.

Here's the recipe that does it, and you can see that it really does work (Figure 3.19).

Program 16: Create the Negative of the Original Picture

```
def negative(picture):
  for px in getPixels(picture):
    red=getRed(px)
    green=getGreen(px)
    blue=getBlue(px)
    negColor=makeColor( 255-red, 255-green, 255-blue)
    setColor(px,negColor)
```

How It Works

We use px to represent each of the pixels in the input picture. For each pixel px, we use the variables red, green, and blue to name the red, green, and blue components of the pixel's color. We make a *new* color with makeColor whose red component is 255-red, the green is 255-green, and the blue is 255-blue. This means that the new color is the *opposite* of the original color. Finally, we set the color of the pixel px to the new negative color (negColor) and move on to the next pixel.

3.7   CONVERTING TO GRAYSCALE

Converting to grayscale is a fun recipe. It's short, not hard to understand, and yet has such a nice visual effect. It's a really nice example of what one can do easily yet powerfully by manipulating pixel color values.

Recall that the resultant color is gray whenever the red component, green component, and blue component have the same value. This means that our RGB encoding supports 256 levels of gray, from (0, 0, 0) (black) to (1, 1, 1) through (100, 100, 100)

FIGURE 3.20
Color picture converted to grayscale.

and finally (255, 255, 255) (white). The tricky part is figuring out what the replicated value should be.

What we want is a sense of the *intensity* of the color, called the *luminance*. It turns out that there is a pretty easy way to compute it: we average the three component colors. Since there are three components, the formula we're going to use for intensity is:

$$\frac{(red + green + blue)}{3}$$

This leads us to the following simple recipe and Figure 3.20

Program 17: Convert to Grayscale

```
def grayScale(picture):
  for p in getPixels(picture):
    intensity = (getRed(p)+getGreen(p)+getBlue(p))/3
    setColor(p,makeColor(intensity,intensity,intensity))
```

This is actually an overly simple notion of grayscale. Below is a recipe that takes into account how the human eye perceives *luminance*. Remember that we consider blue to be darker than red, even if there's the same amount of light reflected off. So we *weight* blue lower, and red higher, when computing the average.

Program 18: Convert to Grayscale with Weights

```
def grayScaleNew(picture):
  for px in getPixels(picture):
    newRed = getRed(px) * 0.299
    newGreen = getGreen(px) * 0.587
    newBlue = getBlue(px) * 0.114
```

```
luminance = newRed+newGreen+newBlue
setColor(px,makeColor(luminance,luminance,luminance))
```

How It Works

We make px stand for each pixel in the picture. We then *weight* the redness, greenness, and blueness based on what empirical research shows about how we perceive the luminance of each of these colors. Note that $0.299 + 0.587 + 0.114$ is 1.0. We're still going to end up with a value between 0 and 255, but we're going to make *more* of the luminance value come from the green part, less from the red, and still less from blue (which, we have already established, is perceived to be darkest). We then add these three weighted values together to get our new luminance. We make the color and set the color of the pixel px to the new color we have made.

PROGRAMMING SUMMARY

In this chapter, we talk about several kinds of encodings of data (or objects).

Pictures	Encodings of images, typically created from a JPEG file.
Pixels	A one-dimensional array (sequence) of pixel objects. The code pixels[0] returns the top leftmost pixel in a picture.
Pixel	A dot in the picture. It has a color and an (x, y) position associated with it. It remembers its own picture so that a change to the pixel changes the real dot in the picture.
Color	A mixture of red, green, and blue values, each between 0 and 255.

PICTURE PROGRAM PIECES

getPixels	Takes a picture as input and returns a one-dimensional array of pixel objects in the picture with the pixels from the first row first and then the pixels from the second row and so on.
getPixel	Takes a picture, an x position, and a y position (two numbers), and returns the pixel object at that point in the picture.
getWidth	Takes a picture as input and returns its width in the number of pixels across the picture.
getHeight	Takes a picture as input and returns its length in the number of pixels top-to-bottom in the picture.
writePictureTo	Takes a picture and a filename (string) as input, then writes the picture to the file as a JPEG. (Be sure to end the filename in ".jpg" for the operating system to understand it properly.)

PIXEL PROGRAM PIECES

getRed, getGreen, getBlue	Each of these functions takes a pixel object and returns the value (between 0 and 255) of the amount of redness, greenness, and blueness (respectively) in that pixel.
setRed, setGreen, setBlue	Each of these functions takes a pixel object and a value (between 0 and 255) and sets the redness, greenness, or blueness (respectively) of that pixel to the given value.
getColor	Takes a pixel and returns the color object at that pixel.
setColor	Takes a pixel object and a color object and sets the color for that pixel.
getX, getY	Takes a pixel object and returns the *x* or *y* position (respectively) of where that pixel is at in the picture.

COLOR PROGRAM PIECES

makeColor	Takes three inputs for the red, green, and blue components (in order), and returns a color object.
pickAColor	Takes no input but puts up a color picker. Find the color you want and the function will return the color that you picked.
makeDarker, makeLighter	Each takes a color and returns a slightly darker or lighter version (respectively) of the color.

There are a bunch of **constants** that are useful in this chapter. These are variables with predefined values. These values are colors: black, white, blue, red, green, gray, darkGray, lightGray, yellow, orange, pink, magenta, and cyan.

PROBLEMS

3.1 Picture concept questions:

- Why don't we see red, green, and blue spots at each position in our picture?
- What is hierarchical decomposition? What is it good for?
- What is luminance?
- Why is the maximum value of any color component (red, green, or blue) 255?
- The color encoding we're using is RGB. What does this mean, in terms of the amount of memory required to represent color? Is there a limit to the number of colors that we can represent? Are there *enough* colors representable in RGB?

3.2 Program 9 (page 53) obviously reduces the red by too much. Write a version that only reduces the red by 10%, then one by 20%. Can you find pictures where each is most useful? Note that you can always repeatedly reduce the red in a picture but you don't want to have to do it *too* many times.

3.3 Write the blue and green versions of the reduce red function—Program 9 (page 53).

3.4 Each of the following is equivalent to the increase red function—Program 10 (page 58). Test them and convince yourself that they work. Which do you prefer and why?

```
def increaseRed2(picture):
   for p in getPixels(picture):
      setRed(p,getRed(p)*1.2)

def increaseRed3(picture):
   for p in getPixels(picture):
      redComponent = getRed(p)
      greenComponent = getGreen(p)
      blueComponent = getBlue(p)
      newRed=int(redComponent*1.2)
      newColor = makeColor
        (newRed,greenComponent,blueComponent)
      setColor(p,newColor)
```

3.5 If you keep increasing the red value and wrapping is on, eventually some pixels become *bright* green and blue. If you check those pixels with the picture tool, you'll find that the values of red are very *low*. What do you think is going on? How did they get so small? How does wrapping work?

3.6 Write a function to swap the values of two colors, e.g., swap the red value with the blue value.

3.7 Write a function to set the red, green, and blues values to zero. What is the result?

3.8 Write a function to set the red, green, and blue values to 255. What is the result?

3.9 What does the following function do?

```
def test1(picture):
    for p in getPixels(picture):
        setRed(p,getRed(p) * 0.3)
```

3.10 What does the following function do?

```
def test2(picture):
    for p in getPixels(picture):
        setBlue(p,getBlue(p) * 1.5)
```

3.11 What does the following function do?

```
def test3(picture):
    for p in getPixels(picture):
        setGreen(p,0)
```

3.12   What does the following function do?

```
def test4 (picture):
    for p in getPixels(picture):
        red = getRed(p)
        green = getGreen(p)
        blue = getBlue(p)
        color = makeColor
          (red + 10, green + 10, blue + 10)
        setColor(p,color)
```

3.13   What does the following function do?

```
def test5 (picture):
    for p in getPixels(picture):
        red = getRed(p)
        green = getGreen(p)
        blue = getBlue(p)
        color = makeColor
          (red - 20, green - 20, blue - 20)
        setColor(p,color)
```

3.14   What does the following function do?

```
def test6 (picture):
    for p in getPixels(picture):
        red = getRed(p)
        green = getGreen(p)
        blue = getBlue(p)
        color = makeColor(blue, red, green)
        setColor(p,color)
```

3.15   What does the following function do?

```
def test7 (picture):
    for p in getPixels(picture):
        red = getRed(p)
        green = getGreen(p)
        blue = getBlue(p)
        color = makeColor
          (red / 2, green / 2, blue / 2)
        setColor(p,color)
```

3.16   Write a function to change a picture to grayscale and then negate it.

3.17   Write three functions, one to clear blue (Program 11 [page 59]), and one to clear red, and one to clear green. For each of these, which would be the most useful in actual practice? How about combinations of them?

3.18   Rewrite the clear blue program (Program 11 [page 59]) to *maximize* blue (i.e., set it to 255) instead of clearing it. Is this useful? Would the red or green versions of the maximize function be useful? Under what conditions?

3.19 Write a function called `changeColor` that takes as input a picture *and* an amount to increase or decrease a color by *and* a number 1 (for red), 2 (for green), or 3 (for blue). The amount will be a number between −.99 and .99.

- `changeColor(pict,-.10,1)` should decrease the amount of red in the picture by 10%.
- `changeColor(pict,.30,2)` should increase the amount of green in the picture by 30%.
- `changeRed(pict,0,3)` should do nothing at all to the amount of blue (or red or green) in the picture.

TO DIG DEEPER

A wonderful book on how vision works, and how artists have learned to manipulate it, is *Vision and Art: The Biology of Seeing* by Margaret Livingstone [28].

4 Modifying Pixels in a Range

Chapter Learning Objectives

The media learning goals for this chapter are:

- To mirror pictures horizontally or vertically.
- To compose pictures into one another and create collages.
- To rotate pictures.
- To scale pictures smaller and larger.

The computer science goals for this chapter are:

- To use nested loops for addressing elements of a matrix.
- To loop through only part of an array.
- To develop some debugging strategies—specifically, to use `print` statements to explore executing code.

4.1   COPYING PIXELS

We can only get so far in our image processing with `getPixels` before we need to know *where* a pixel is. For example, if we want to reduce red on only half of a picture we have to have a way to specify which pixels to process. To do that, we'll need to start building our own `for` loops using `range`. Once we start doing this, we have more control over the exact *x* and *y* coordinates that we're processing, so we can start moving pixels where we want them. This is a very powerful feature.

Ask someone to clap her hands 10 times. How do you know if she did it right? You probably counted each clap. So the first time she clapped you thought 1, the second time 2 and so on till she stopped. If the count was 10 when she stopped, then she clapped 10 times. What value did the count start at? If you thought 1 after she clapped one time then the count was actually zero before the first clap.

A `for` loop is similar to this. It makes an index variable take on each value in turn from a sequence. We've used sequences of pixels generated from `getPixels` but it turns out that we can easily generate sequences of numbers using the Python function range. The function range takes two inputs: an integer starting point, and an integer ending point *that is not included in the sequence.*[1] Some examples will make this clear.

```
>>> print range(0,3)
[0, 1, 2]
>>> print range(0,10)
[0, 1, 2, 3, 4, 5, 6, 7, 8, 9]
>>> print range(3,1)
[]
```

You might be wondering what this square bracket stuff is (e.g., [0,3] in the first example above). That's the notation for an array—it's how Python prints out a series of numbers to show that this is an array.[2] If we use range to generate the array for the for loop, our variable will walk through each of the sequential numbers we generate.

Optionally, range can take a third input: how much to increment between elements of the sequence.

```
>>> print range(0,10,3)
[0, 3, 6, 9]
>>> print range(0,10,2)
[0, 2, 4, 6, 8]
```

Since most loops do start with zero (e.g., when indexing some data), providing only a *single* input to range *presumes* a zero starting point.

```
>>> print range(10)
[0, 1, 2, 3, 4, 5, 6, 7, 8, 9]
```

4.1.1 Looping Across the Pixels with range

If we want to know both the x and y values for a pixel we will have to use *two* for loops—one to move horizontally (x) across the pixels, and the other to move vertically (y) to get every pixel (Figure 4.1) . The function getPixels did this inside itself, to make it easier to write simple picture manipulations. The inner loop will be *nested* inside the outer loop, literally inside its block. At this point, you're going to have to be careful in how you indent your code to make sure that your blocks line up right.

Your loops will look something like this:

```
for x in range(0,getWidth(picture)):
    for y in range(0,getHeight(picture)):
        pixel=getPixel(picture,x,y)
```

For example, here's Program 14 (page 64), but using explicit x and y indices to access the pixel.

---

[1]This can be unexpected but is part of the definition of Python, so it's not something up for change if you want to learn how Python really works.
[2]Technically, range returns a *sequence*, which is a somewhat different collection of data than an array. For our purposes, we can think about it like an array.

FIGURE 4.1
The picture coordinates.

Program 19: Lighten the Picture Using Nested Loops

```
def lighten(picture):
  for x in range(0,getWidth(picture)):
    for y in range(0,getHeight(picture)):
      px = getPixel(picture,x,y)
      color = getColor(px)
      color = makeLighter(color)
      setColor(px,color)
```

How It Works

Let's walk through (trace) how it would work. Imagine that we have just executed `lighten(myPicture)`.

1. `def lighten(picture):` The variable `picture` becomes the new name for the picture in `myPicture`.

2. `for x in range(0,getWidth(picture)):` Variable x takes on the value 0.

3. `for y in range(0,getHeight(picture)):` Variable y takes on the value 0.

4. `px = getPixel(picture,x,y).` Variable px takes on the value of the pixel object at location (0, 0).

5. `setColor(px,color).` We set the pixel at (0, 0) to be the new lighter color.

6. `for y in range(0,getHeight(picture)):` Variable y now becomes 1. In other words, we're slowly moving down the first row of pixels, the column where x is 0.

7. `px = getPixel(picture,x,y)` px becomes the pixel at position (0, 1).

8. We lighten that color.

9. `for y in range(0,getHeight(picture)):` Variable y now becomes 2. And so on, until y becomes the height of the picture.

10. `for x in range(0,getWidth(picture)):` Variable x takes on the value 1.

11. Now y becomes 0 again, and we start down the next column where x is 1.

12. This continues until all the colors of all the pixels are lightened.

4.2 MIRRORING A PICTURE

Let's start out with an interesting effect that is only occasionally useful but is fun. Let's mirror a picture along its vertical axis. In other words, imagine that you have a mirror and you place it on a picture so that the left side of the picture shows up in the mirror. That's the effect we're going to implement. We'll do it in a couple of different ways.

First, let's think through what we're going to do. And let's simplify things a bit. Let's think about mirroring a two-dimensional array of numbers. We'll pick a horizontal `mirrorPoint`—halfway across the picture, `getWidth(picture)/2`.

When the width of the picture is even, we will copy half the picture from the left to the right, as shown in Figure 4.2. The width of this array is 2 so the mirrorPoint is 2 / 2 = 1. We need to copy from `x=0,y=0` to `x=1,y=0` and from `x=0,y=1` to `x=1,y=1`.

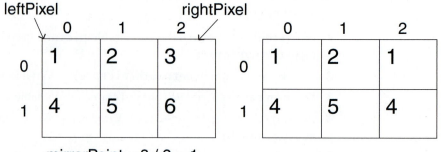

FIGURE 4.2
Copying pixels from left to right around a mirror point.

When the width of the picture is odd, we will not copy the middle column of pixels, as shown in Figure 4.2. We need to copy from x=0,y=0 to x=2,y=0 and from x=0,y=1 to x=2,y=1.

In each of these cases we started x at 0 and y at 0 and looped with x ranging from 0 to the mirrorPoint and y ranging from 0 to the height. The x value will range from 0 to just before the mirrorPoint. To mirror a picture, the color at the first column should be copied to the last column in the same row. The color at the second column should be copied to the second to last column in the same row and so on. So when x equals 0, we will copy the color from the pixel at x=0 and y=0 to x = width-1 and y = 0. When x equals 1, we will copy the color from the pixel at x=1 and y=0 to x=width-2 and y = 0. When x equals 2, we will copy the color from the pixel at x=2 and y=0 to x=width-3 and y = 0. Each time we are copying the color from the pixel on the left at the current x and y values to a pixel on the right at the width of the picture minus the current x value minus 1.

Take a look at Figure 4.2 to convince yourself that we'll actually reach every pixel using this scheme. Here's the actual recipe.

Program 20: Mirror Pixels in a Picture Along a Vertical Line

```
def mirrorVertical(source):
  mirrorPoint = getWidth(source) / 2
  width = getWidth(source)
  for y in range(0,getHeight(source)):
    for x in range(0,mirrorPoint):
      leftPixel = getPixel(source,x,y)
      rightPixel = getPixel(source,width - x - 1,y)
      color = getColor(leftPixel)
      setColor(rightPixel,color)
```

How It Works

mirrorVertical takes a source picture as input. We're using a vertical mirror halfway across the picture, so the mirrorPoint is the width of the picture divided by 2. We do the entire height of the picture, so the loop for y goes from 0 to the height of the picture. The x value goes from 0 to mirrorPoint (not including the mirrorPoint). Each time through the loop, we copy the color from another column of pixels from the left to the right.

We'd use it like this (and the result appears in Figure 4.3).

```
>>> file="C:/ip-book/mediasources/blueMotorcycle.jpg"
>>> print file
C:/ip-book/mediasources/blueMotorcycle.jpg
>>> picture=makePicture(file)
>>> explore(picture)
>>> mirrorVertical(picture)
>>> explore(picture)
```

Can we mirror horizontally? Sure!

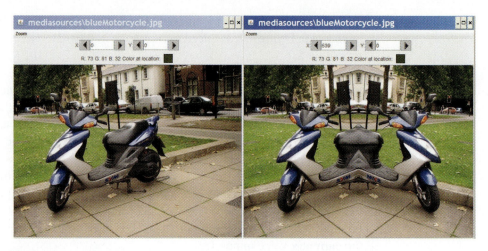

FIGURE 4.3
Original picture (*left*) and mirrored along the vertical axis (*right*).

Program 21: Mirror Pixels Horizontally, Top to Bottom

```
def mirrorHorizontal(source):
  mirrorPoint = getHeight(source) / 2
  height = getHeight(source)
  for x in range(0,getWidth(source)):
    for y in range(0,mirrorPoint):
      topPixel = getPixel(source,x,y)
      bottomPixel = getPixel(source,x,height - y - 1)
      color = getColor(topPixel)
      setColor(bottomPixel,color)
```

Now this last recipe copies from the top of the picture onto the bottom (see Figure 4.4). You can see that we're getting the color from topPixel, which is from the current x and y, which will always be *above* the mirrorPoint because smaller values of y are nearer the top of the picture. To copy from the bottom up, simply swap topPixel and bottomPixel (Figure 4.4).

Program 22: Mirror Pixels Horizontally, Bottom to Top

```
def mirrorBotTop(source):
  mirrorPoint = getHeight(source) / 2
  height = getHeight(source)
  for x in range(0,getWidth(source)):
    for y in range(0,mirrorPoint):
      topPixel = getPixel(source,x,y)
      bottomPixel = getPixel(source,x,height - y - 1)
      color = getColor(bottomPixel)
      setColor(topPixel,color)
```

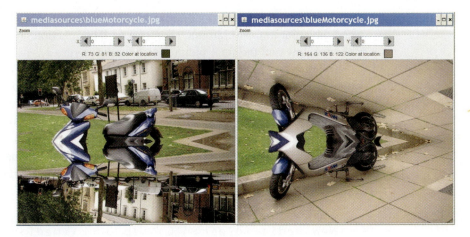

FIGURE 4.4
Mirroring horizontally, top to bottom (*left*) and bottom to top (*right*).

FIGURE 4.5
Temple of Hephaestus from the ancient agora in Athens.

Mirroring Usefully

While mirroring is mostly used for interesting effects, occasionally it has some more serious (but still fun) purposes. Mark took a picture of the Temple of Hephaestus in the ancient agora in Athens, Greece, when traveling to a conference (Figure 4.5). By sheer luck, he got the pediment dead horizontal. The pediment of the Temple of Hephaestus is damaged. He wondered if he could "fix" it by mirroring the good part onto the broken part.

To find the coordinates where we need to mirror, use the picture tool in JES to explore the picture.

```
>>> file = "C:/ip-book/mediasources/temple.jpg"
>>> templeP = makePicture(file)
>>> explore(templeP)
```

He explored the picture to figure out the range of values needed for the mirroring and the point to mirror around (Figure 4.6). The function he wrote to do the repair is given below and the final picture is shown in Figure 4.7—it worked pretty well! Of course, it is possible to tell that it was digitally manipulated. For example, if you check the shadows, you can see that the sun must have been on the left and the right at the same time.

We're going to use the *utility function* getMediaPath(baseName). It's particularly helpful when you want to deal with several pieces of media in the same directory but don't want to spell out the whole directory name. You just have to remember to use setMediaPath() first. All that getMediaPath does is to prepend the path found in setMediaPath to the input filename.

```
>>> setMediaPath()
New media folder: 'C:\\ip-book\\mediasources\\'
>>> getMediaPath("barbara.jpg")
'C:\\ip-book\\mediasources\\barbara.jpg'
>>> barb=makePicture(getMediaPath("barbara.jpg"))
```

Program 23: Mirror the Temple of Hephaestus

```
def mirrorTemple():
 source = makePicture(getMediaPath("temple.jpg"))
 mirrorPoint = 276
 for x in range(13,mirrorPoint):       * limit the Range
  for y in range(27,97):
   pleft = getPixel(source,x,y)
   pright = getPixel(source,mirrorPoint + mirrorPoint - 1 - x,y)
   setColor(pright,getColor(pleft))
 show(source)
 return source
```

Common Bug: Set the Media Folder First!

If you're to use code that uses getMediaPath(baseName), you'll need to execute setMediaPath() first.

How It Works

We found the mirrorPoint (276) by exploring the picture in JES. We don't really have to copy from 0 to 276, because the edge of the temple is at an x index of 13.

In this recipe, we're using getMediaPath. The function getMediaPath(baseName) is a shorthand. If you keep your media in one place, and you'd like to refer to it just by its base name, you can use getMediaPath(baseName), which actually generates a complete path for you. *However, you must use setMediaPath() first.* The function setMediaPath() lets you pick the place (directory) where you store your media. The function setMediaPath tells getMediaPath(baseName) how to construct the path. It returns the path for the media directory followed by the base name.

FIGURE 4.6
Coordinates where we need to do the mirroring.

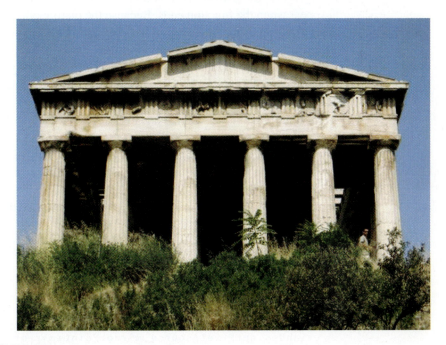

FIGURE 4.7
The manipulated temple.

This recipe is also one of the first ones we've written where we explicitly `return` a value. The keyword `return` sets the value that the function provides as output. In `mirrorTemple()`, the return value is the picture object `source` where the repaired temple is stored. If we invoked this function with `fixedTemple = mirrorTemple()`, the name `fixedTemple` would represent the picture returned from `mirrorTemple()`.

Common Bug: The Keyword `return` Is Always Last

The keyword `return` specifies what the return value is from the function but it also has the effect of *ending* the function. A common bug is to try to `print` or show *after* a return statement but that won't work. Once `return` is executed, no more statements in the function are executed.

Why do we `return` the fixed temple picture object? Why *haven't* we ever returned before? The functions we've written before this directly manipulate the input objects—this is called computation by *side effect*. We can't do it in this case because there are no inputs to `mirrorTemple()`. The rule of thumb on when to `return` is this: If you *create* the object of interest inside the function, you need to `return` it or else the object will just disappear when the function ends. Because the picture object `source` is created (using `makePicture`) inside the function `mirrorTemple()`, the object only exists within the function.

Why `return` anything at all? We do it for future use. Can you imagine *possibly* wanting to do something with the mirrored temple? Maybe composing it into a collage, or changing its color? You should `return` the object so that you will have that option later.

The temple example is a good one to ask ourselves about. If you really understand it, you can answer questions like, "What is the *first* pixel to be mirrored in this function?" and "How many pixels get copied anyway?" You should be able to figure out the answers by thinking through the program—pretend you're the computer and execute the program in your mind.

If that's too hard, you can insert `print` statements, like this:

```
def mirrorTemple():
 source = makePicture(getMediaPath("temple.jpg"))
 mirrorPoint = 276
 for x in range(13,mirrorPoint):
  for y in range(27,97):
   print"Copying color from",x,y,"to",mirrorPoint+mirrorPoint-1-x,y
   pleft = getPixel(source,x,y)
   pright = getPixel(source,mirrorPoint+mirrorPoint-1-x,y)
   setColor(pright,getColor(pleft))
 show(source)
 return source
```

When we run this version, it takes a *long* time to finish. Hit STOP after a little bit, since we only really care about the first few pixels. Here's what we got:

```
>>> p2=mirrorTemple()
Copying color from 13 27  to  538 27
Copying color from 13 28  to  538 28
Copying color from 13 29  to  538 29
```

It copies from (13, 27) to (538, 27) where the 538 is calculated from the `mirror`
Point (276) plus the `mirrorPoint` (552) minus 1 (551) then minus x (551 − 13
= 538).

How many pixels did we process? We can have the computer figure that one out too.
Before the loops, we say that our count is 0. Each time we copy a pixel, we add 1 to
our count.

```
def mirrorTemple():
  source = makePicture(getMediaPath("temple.jpg"))
  mirrorPoint = 276
  count = 0
  for x in range(13,mirrorPoint):
   for y in range(27,97):
    pleft = getPixel(source,x,y)
    pright = getPixel(source,mirrorPoint + mirrorPoint - 1 - x,y)
    setColor(pright,getColor(pleft))
    count = count + 1
  show(source)
  print "We copied",count,"pixels"
  return source
```

This comes back with `We copied 18410 pixels`. Where did this number come
from? We copy 70 rows of pixels (y goes from 27 to 97). We copy 263 columns of
pixels (x goes from 13 to 276). 70 × 263 is 18,410.

4.3   COPYING AND TRANSFORMING PICTURES

We can create wholly new pictures when we copy pixels *across* pictures. We're going
to end up keeping track of a *source* picture that we take pixels from and a *target* picture
that we're going to set pixels in. Actually, we don't copy the pixels—we simply make
the pixels in the target the same color as the pixels in the source. Copying pixels requires
us to keep track of multiple index variables: the (x, y) position in the source and the
(x, y) in the target.

What's exciting about copying pixels is that making some small changes in how we
deal with the index variables leads not only to *copying* the image but to *transforming*
it. In this section, we're going to talk about copying, cropping, rotating, and scaling
pictures.

Our target will be the paper-sized JPEG file in the MEDIASOURCES directory; this is
7 × 9.5 inches, which will fit on a 9 × 11.5 inch letter-size piece of paper with 1 inch
margins.

```
>>> paperFile=getMediaPath("7inx95in.jpg")
>>> paperPicture=makePicture(paperFile)
>>> print getWidth(paperPicture)
504
>>> print getHeight(paperPicture)
684
```

4.3.1 Copying

To copy a picture from one object to another, we simply make sure that we increment
sourceX and targetX variables (the source and target index variables for the *X* axis)
together, and the sourceY and targetY variables together. We could use a for loop,
but that only increments *one* variable. We have to make sure that we increment the *other*
variable (whichever one is *not* in the for loop) using an expression at the same time
(as close as we can) as when the for loop increments things. We'll do this by setting
initial values *just before* the loop starts, then adding to the index variable at the *bottom*
of the loop.

Here's a recipe for copying the picture of Barbara to the canvas.

Program 24: Copying a Picture to a Canvas

```
def copyBarb():
  # Set up the source and target pictures
  barbf=getMediaPath("barbara.jpg")
  barb = makePicture(barbf)
  canvasf = getMediaPath("7inX95in.jpg")
  canvas = makePicture(canvasf)
  # Now, do the actual copying
  targetX = 0
  for sourceX in range(0,getWidth(barb)):
    targetY = 0
    for sourceY in range(0,getHeight(barb)):
      color = getColor(getPixel(barb,sourceX,sourceY))
      setColor(getPixel(canvas,targetX,targetY), color)
      targetY = targetY + 1
    targetX = targetX + 1
  show(barb)
  show(canvas)
  return canvas
```

Computer Science Idea: Comments Are Good!

You see in Recipe 24 the use of lines with "#" at the start of them. This symbol says to
Python, "Ignore the rest of this line." What good is that? It allows you to put messages
in the program to be read by humans and not the computer—messages that explain how
things work, what sections of the program do, and why you did what you did. Remember
that programs are for humans, not computers. Comments make the programs better
suited to humans.

How It Works

This program copies the picture of Barbara to the canvas (Figure 4.8).

- The first few lines just set up the source (`barb`) and target (`canvas`) pictures.
- Next comes the loop for managing the *X* index variables, `sourceX` for the source picture and `targetX` for the target picture. Here are the key parts of the loop:

```
targetX = 0
for sourceX in range(0,getWidth(barb)):
  # Y LOOP GOES HERE
  targetX = targetX + 1
```

Because of the way these statements are arranged, from the point of view of the *Y* loop, `targetX` and `sourceX` are always incremented together. `targetX` becomes 0 just before `sourceX` becomes 0 in the `for` loop. At the end of the `for` loop, `targetX` is incremented by 1, and then the loop starts over again and `sourceX` is also incremented by 1 through the `for` statement.

The statement to increment `targetX` may look a little strange. `targetX = targetX + 1` isn't making a mathematical statement (which couldn't possibly be true). Instead it's giving directions to the computer. It says "Make the value of `targetX` to be (right side of =) whatever the *current* value of `targetX` is *plus* 1."

- Inside the loop for the *X* variables is the loop for the *Y* variables. It has a very similar structure, since its goal is to keep `targetY` and `sourceY` in sync in exactly the same way.

```
targetY = 0
for sourceY in range(0,getHeight(barb)):
  color = getColor(getPixel(barb,sourceX,sourceY))
```

FIGURE 4.8
Copying a picture to a canvas.

```
    setColor(getPixel(canvas,targetX,targetY), color)
    targetY = targetY + 1
```

It's inside the *Y* loop that we actually get the color from the source and set the corresponding pixel in the target to the same color.

Computer Science Idea: Copy Versus Reference

When we copy colors from the source picture to the target picture, the target picture contains just the color information. It does not know anything about the source picture. If we change the source picture, the target would not change. In computer science we can also make *references*. A reference is a pointer to another object. If the target picture contained a reference to the source picture, and we change the source picture, the target would also change.

■

It turns out that we can just as easily put the target variables in the `for` loops and set the source variables. The recipe that follows does the same as Recipe 24.

Program 25: Copying a Picture to a Canvas Another Way

```
def copyBarb2():
  # Set up the source and target pictures
  barbf=getMediaPath("barbara.jpg")
  barb = makePicture(barbf)
  canvasf = getMediaPath("7inX95in.jpg")
  canvas = makePicture(canvasf)
  # Now, do the actual copying
  sourceX = 0
  for targetX in range(0,getWidth(barb)):
    sourceY = 0
    for targetY in range(0,getHeight(barb)):
      color = getColor(getPixel(barb,sourceX,sourceY))
      setColor(getPixel(canvas,targetX,targetY), color)
      sourceY = sourceY + 1
    sourceX = sourceX + 1
  show(barb)
  show(canvas)
  return canvas
```

■

Of course, we don't have to copy from (0, 0) in the source to (0, 0) in the target. We can easily copy somewhere else in the canvas. All we have to do is to change where the target *X* and *Y* coordinates *start*. The rest stays exactly the same (Figure 4.9).

Program 26: Copy Elsewhere into the Canvas

```
def copyBarbMidway():
  # Set up the source and target pictures
  barbf=getMediaPath("barbara.jpg")
```

FIGURE 4.9
Copying a picture midway into a canvas.

```
barb = makePicture(barbf)
canvasf = getMediaPath("7inX95in.jpg")
canvas = makePicture(canvasf)
# Now, do the actual copying
targetX = 100
for sourceX in range(0,getWidth(barb)):
  targetY = 100
  for sourceY in range(0,getHeight(barb)):
    color = getColor(getPixel(barb,sourceX,sourceY))
    setColor(getPixel(canvas,targetX,targetY), color)
    targetY = targetY + 1
  targetX = targetX + 1
show(barb)
show(canvas)
return canvas
```

Similarly, we don't have to copy a *whole* picture. *Cropping* is taking only part of a picture out of the whole picture. Digitally, that's just a matter of changing your start and end coordinates. To grab just Barb's face out of the picture, we only have to figure out what the coordinates are where her face is located, then use them on the dimensions of sourceX and sourceY (Figure 4.10). We can do this by exploring the picture. The face is at (45, 25) to (200, 200).

Program 27: Cropping a Picture onto a Canvas
```
def copyBarbsFace():
  # Set up the source and target pictures
```

FIGURE 4.10
Copying part of a picture onto a canvas.

```
barbf=getMediaPath("barbara.jpg")
barb = makePicture(barbf)
canvasf = getMediaPath("7inX95in.jpg")
canvas = makePicture(canvasf)
# Now, do the actual copying
targetX = 100
for sourceX in range(45,200):        Cropp
  targetY = 100
  for sourceY in range(25,200):
    color = getColor(getPixel(barb,sourceX,sourceY))
    setColor(getPixel(canvas,targetX,targetY), color)
    targetY = targetY + 1
  targetX = targetX + 1
show(barb)
show(canvas)
return canvas
```

How It Works

The only difference between this program and the previous ones is the ranges on the source indices. We only want the x pixels between 45 and 200, so they are the inputs to range for sourceX. We only want the y pixels between 25 and 200, so they are the inputs to range that we use for sourceY. The rest is exactly the same.

We can still swap which variables are in the for loop and which are incremented. Computing the range for the target is a little complicated, though. If we want to start copying to (100, 100), then the length of the picture is $200 - 45$ and the height is $200 - 25$. Here's the recipe.

Program 28: Cropping the Face into the Canvas Differently

```
def copyBarbsFace2():
  # Set up the source and target pictures
  barbf=getMediaPath("barbara.jpg")
  barb = makePicture(barbf)
  canvasf = getMediaPath("7inX95in.jpg")
  canvas = makePicture(canvasf)
  # Now, do the actual copying
  sourceX = 45
  for targetX in range(100,100+(200-45)):
    sourceY = 25
    for targetY in range(100,100+(200-25)):
      color = getColor(getPixel(barb,sourceX,sourceY))
      setColor(getPixel(canvas,targetX,targetY), color)
      sourceY = sourceY + 1
    sourceX = sourceX + 1
  show(barb)
  show(canvas)
  return canvas
```

How It Works

Let's look at a small example to see what's going on in the copying recipe. We start out with a source and a target, and copy from the source to the target, pixel by pixel.

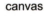

We then increment both `sourceY` and `targetY`, and copy again.

We continue down the column, incrementing both *Y* index variables.

When done with that column, we increment the *X* index variables and move on to the next column, until we have copied every pixel.

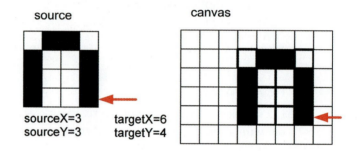

4.3.2 Creating a Collage

Here are a couple images of flowers (Figure 4.11), each 100 pixels wide and high. Let's make a *collage* of them by combining several of our effects to create different flowers. We'll copy them all into the blank image 640x480.jpg. All we really have to do is to copy the pixel colors to the right places.

Here's how we create the collage (Figure 4.12):

```
>>> flowers=createCollage()
```

FIGURE 4.11
Flowers to use in the collage.

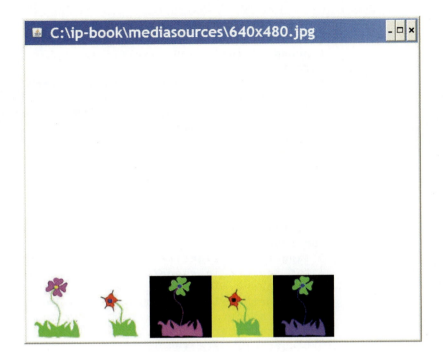

FIGURE 4.12
Collage of flowers.

Common Bug: Referenced Functions Must Be in the File!

This program uses functions that we wrote previously. These functions must be copied to the same file as the createCollage function in order for this to work. (Later we will see how to do this with an import instead.)

Program 29: Creating a Collage

```
def createCollage():
  flower1=makePicture(getMediaPath("flower1.jpg"))
  print flower1
  flower2=makePicture(getMediaPath("flower2.jpg"))
  print flower2
  canvas=makePicture(getMediaPath("640x480.jpg"))
  print canvas
  #First picture, at left edge
  targetX=0
  for sourceX in range(0,getWidth(flower1)):
    targetY=getHeight(canvas)-getHeight(flower1)-5
    for sourceY in range(0,getHeight(flower1)):
      px=getPixel(flower1,sourceX,sourceY)
      cx=getPixel(canvas,targetX,targetY)
      setColor(cx,getColor(px))
```

```
                    targetY=targetY + 1
                  targetX=targetX + 1
                #Second picture, 100 pixels over
                targetX=100
                for sourceX in range(0,getWidth(flower2)):
                  targetY=getHeight(canvas)-getHeight(flower2)-5
                  for sourceY in range(0,getHeight(flower2)):
                    px=getPixel(flower2,sourceX,sourceY)
                    cx=getPixel(canvas,targetX,targetY)
                    setColor(cx,getColor(px))
                    targetY=targetY + 1
                  targetX=targetX + 1
                #Third picture, flower1 negated
                negative(flower1)
                targetX=200
                for sourceX in range(0,getWidth(flower1)):
                  targetY=getHeight(canvas)-getHeight(flower1)-5
                  for sourceY in range(0,getHeight(flower1)):
                    px=getPixel(flower1,sourceX,sourceY)
                    cx=getPixel(canvas,targetX,targetY)
                    setColor(cx,getColor(px))
                    targetY=targetY + 1
                  targetX=targetX + 1
                #Fourth picture, flower2 with no blue
                clearBlue(flower2)
                targetX=300
                for sourceX in range(0,getWidth(flower2)):
                  targetY=getHeight(canvas)-getHeight(flower2)-5
                  for sourceY in range(0,getHeight(flower2)):
                    px=getPixel(flower2,sourceX,sourceY)
                    cx=getPixel(canvas,targetX,targetY)
                    setColor(cx,getColor(px))
                    targetY=targetY + 1
                  targetX=targetX + 1
                #Fifth picture, flower1, negated with decreased red
                decreaseRed(flower1)
                targetX=400
                for sourceX in range(0,getWidth(flower1)):
                  targetY=getHeight(canvas)-getHeight(flower1)-5
                  for sourceY in range(0,getHeight(flower1)):
                    px=getPixel(flower1,sourceX,sourceY)
                    cx=getPixel(canvas,targetX,targetY)
                    setColor(cx,getColor(px))
                    targetY=targetY + 1
                  targetX=targetX + 1
                show(canvas)
                return(canvas)
```

[handwritten margin note: Apply f(x) Before copying]

How It Works

While this program looks long, it's really just the same copying loop we've seen repeat-edly now, but one loop after the other.

- First we create the `flower1` and `flower2` picture objects that we're copying into the `canvas`.
- The first flower is just a plain copy of `picture1` at the leftmost edge of the canvas. We want the bottom of the flower to be five pixels from the edge, so `targetY` starts at the height of the canvas, minus the flower's height, minus 5. As `targetY` gets incremented (added to), it will grow *down* toward the bottom. It will get incremented for the number of pixels in the height of the flower (see the `sourceY` loop), so the maximum value `targetY` will take is the canvas height minus 5.
- We next copy the second picture in, starting `targetX` 100 pixels to the right, but the same loops really.
- Now we negate `flower1`, then copy it in, moving farther to the right (`targetX` is now starting at 300).
- Then we clear the blue from `flower2` and copy it into the canvas even farther to the right.
- The fifth flower decreases the red of `flower1`, *which is already negated* (from the third set of loops).
- We then `show` the canvas and `return` it. We need to return the canvas because we made it inside the collage function. If we don't return it, it simply disappears when the function ends and the function's context ends.

4.3.3   General Copying

The code to create the collage is very long and repetitive. Each time we copy a picture to the target, we calculate the `targetY` and set the `targetX`. We then loop through all the pixels in the source picture and copy them all to the target. Is there any way to make this shorter? What if we create a general copy function that takes in a picture to copy, the target, and specifies where to start the copy in the target?

Program 30: A General Copy Function

```
def copy(source, target, targX, targY):
  targetX = targX
  for sourceX in range(0,getWidth(source)):
    targetY = targY
    for sourceY in range(0,getHeight(source)):
      px=getPixel(source,sourceX,sourceY)
      tx=getPixel(target,targetX,targetY)
      setColor(tx,getColor(px))
      targetY=targetY + 1
    targetX=targetX + 1
```

Now we can rewrite the collage function to use this new general copy function.

Program 31: Improved Collage with the General Copy Function

```
def createCollage2():
    flower1=makePicture(getMediaPath("flower1.jpg"))
    print flower1
    flower2=makePicture(getMediaPath("flower2.jpg"))
    print flower2
    canvas=makePicture(getMediaPath("640x480.jpg"))
    print canvas
    #First picture, at left edge
    copy(flower1,canvas,0,getHeight(canvas)-getHeight(flower1)-5)
    #Second picture, 100 pixels over
    copy(flower2,canvas,100,getHeight(canvas)-getHeight(flower2)-5)
    #Third picture, flower1 negated
    negative(flower1)
    copy(flower1,canvas,200,getHeight(canvas)-getHeight(flower1)-5)
    #Fourth picture, flower2 with no blue
    clearBlue(flower2)
    copy(flower2,canvas,300,getHeight(canvas)-getHeight(flower2)-5)
    #Fifth picture, flower1, negated with decreased red
    decreaseRed(flower1)
    copy(flower1,canvas,400,getHeight(canvas)-getHeight(flower2)-5)
    return canvas
```

Now the code to create the collage is much easier to read, change, and understand. Writing functions so that they take parameters makes them easier to reuse. Repeating code several times in a function also can be a problem if the repeated code contains an error. You have to fix the error in several places instead of just one place.

Making It Work Tip: Reuse Functions Rather Than Copy

Try to write functions that can be reused by specifying parameters. Try to resist copying code to several places because it makes code longer and can make errors harder to fix.

4.3.4   Rotation

The image can be transformed by using the index variables differently or incrementing them differently but otherwise keeping the same copying algorithm. Let's rotate Barb to the left 90 degrees—at least that's the way it will seem. What we'll really do is to flip the image across the diagonal. We'll do that by simply swapping the *X* and *Y* variables in the target—we increment them the exact same way but we'll *use X* for *Y* and *Y* for *X* (Figure 4.13).

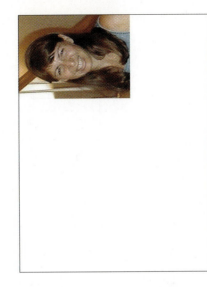

FIGURE 4.13
Copying a picture to a canvas.

Program 32: Rotating (Flipping) a Picture

```
def copyBarbSideways():
  # Set up the source and target pictures
  barbf=getMediaPath("barbara.jpg")
  barb = makePicture(barbf)
  canvasf = getMediaPath("7inX95in.jpg")
  canvas = makePicture(canvasf)
  # Now, do the actual copying
  targetX = 0
  for sourceX in range(0,getWidth(barb)):
    targetY = 0
    for sourceY in range(0,getHeight(barb)):
      color = getColor(getPixel(barb,sourceX,sourceY))
      setColor(getPixel(canvas,targetY,targetX), color)
      targetY = targetY + 1
    targetX = targetX + 1
  show(barb)
  show(canvas)
  return canvas
```

How It Works

Rotating (flipping across the diagonal) starts with the same source and target, and even the same variable values, but since we *use* the target *X* and *Y* differently, we get a different effect. To make this problem easier to understand, let's use a small matrix of numbers.

Now, as we increment the *Y* variables, we're moving *down* the source array, but *across* the target array.

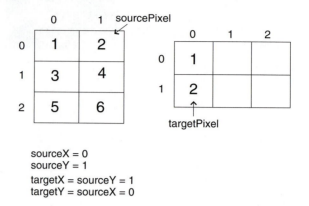

sourceX = 0
sourceY = 1
targetX = sourceY = 1
targetY = sourceX = 0

When we're done, we've done the same copy, but the result is completely different.

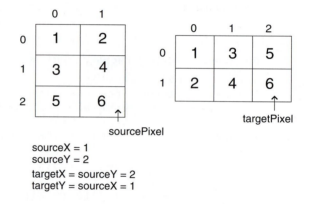

sourceX = 1
sourceY = 2
targetX = sourceY = 2
targetY = sourceX = 1

How would we *really* rotate 90 degrees? We need to think about where we want each pixel. The program below actually *does* a 90 degree rotation of the picture. The key difference is in the `setColor` function call. Note that we swap the `x` and `y` indices from previous examples but we use an equation for y: `width - targetX - 1`. Try tracing it to convince yourself that this does a real rotation.

Program 33: Rotating a Picture

```
def rotateBarbSideways():
  # Set up the source and target pictures
  barbf=getMediaPath("barbara.jpg")
  barb = makePicture(barbf)
  canvasf = getMediaPath("7inX95in.jpg")
  canvas = makePicture(canvasf)
  # Now, do the actual copying
  targetX = 0
  width = getWidth(barb)
```

```
for sourceX in range(0,getWidth(barb)):
 targetY = 0
 for sourceY in range(0,getHeight(barb)):
  color = getColor(getPixel(barb,sourceX,sourceY))
  setColor(getPixel(canvas,targetY,width - targetX - 1), color)
  targetY = targetY + 1
 targetX = targetX + 1
show(barb)
show(canvas)
return canvas
```

4.3.5   Scaling

A very common transformation for pictures is to scale them. Scaling up means to make them larger and scaling down makes them smaller. It's common to scale a 1-megapixel or 3-megapixel picture down to a smaller size to make it easier to place on the Web. Smaller pictures require less disk space, and less network bandwidth, and thus are easier and faster to download.

Scaling a picture requires the use of *sampling*, which we'll also use with sounds later. To scale a picture *smaller,* we are going to take *every other* pixel when copying from the source to the target. To scale a picture *larger*, we are going to take *every pixel twice*.

Scaling the picture down is the easier function. Instead of incrementing the source X and Y variables by 1, we simply increment by 2. We divide the amount of space by 2, since we'll fill half as much room–our length will be $(200 - 45)/2$ and the height will be $(200 - 25)/2$, still starting at $(100, 100)$. The result is a small face in the canvas (Figure 4.14).

FIGURE 4.14
Scaling the picture down.

Program 34: Scaling a Picture Down (Smaller)

```
def copyBarbsFaceSmaller():
  # Set up the source and target pictures
  barbf=getMediaPath("barbara.jpg")
  barb = makePicture(barbf)
  canvasf = getMediaPath("7inX95in.jpg")
  canvas = makePicture(canvasf)
  # Now, do the actual copying
  sourceX = 45
  for targetX in range(100,100+((200-45)/2)):
    sourceY = 25
    for targetY in range(100,100+((200-25)/2)):
      color = getColor(getPixel(barb,sourceX,sourceY))
      setColor(getPixel(canvas,targetX,targetY), color)
      sourceY = sourceY + 2
    sourceX = sourceX + 2
  show(barb)
  show(canvas)
  return canvas
```

How It Works

- We start out creating the picture objects: `barb` as our source, and `canvas` into which we'll compose Barb.

- Barb's face is in the rectangle (45,25) to (200,200). That means that the `sourceX` starts at 45 and the `sourceY` starts at 25. We don't specify the end of the range for the source indices because they're controlled by the `for` loops for the target indices.

- We're going to start `targetX` and `targetY` at 100 each. What are the end points for the ranges? We want to get *all* of Barb's face. The width of Barb's face is 200-45 (the maximum x index minus the minimum y index). Since we want to shrink Barb's face by half (in each direction), we'll be skipping every other pixel. That means that we'll have only half the width in the final composition: (200-45)/2 across. If we're starting `targetX` at 100, the end point for the range is 100 plus (200-45)/2. `targetY` works the same way.

- Because we want to skip every other pixel in the source, we increment `sourceX` and `sourceY` by 2 each time through the loop.

Scaling up the picture (making it larger) is a little trickier. We want to take every pixel twice. What we're going to do is to increment the source index variables by 0.5. Now we can't reference pixel 1.5. But if we reference *int*(1.5) (integer function) we'll get 1 again, and that will work. The sequence of 1, 1.5, 2, 2.5 ... will become 1,1, 2,2 ... The result is a larger form of the picture (Figure 4.15).

FIGURE 4.15
Scaling up a picture.

Program 35: Scaling the Picture Up (Larger)

```
def copyBarbsFaceLarger():
 # Set up the source and target pictures
 barbf=getMediaPath("barbara.jpg")
 barb = makePicture(barbf)
 canvasf = getMediaPath("7inX95in.jpg")
 canvas = makePicture(canvasf)
 # Now, do the actual copying
 sourceX = 45
 for targetX in range(100,100+((200-45)*2)):
  sourceY = 25
  for targetY in range(100,100+((200-25)*2)):
   color = getColor(getPixel(barb,int(sourceX),int(sourceY)))
   setColor(getPixel(canvas,targetX,targetY), color)
   sourceY = sourceY + 0.5
  sourceX = sourceX + 0.5
 show(barb)
 show(canvas)
 return canvas
```

You might want to be able to scale a picture to a particular size instead of always using the canvas pictures. There is a function called makeEmptyPicture that creates a picture of a desired width and height (both specified in pixels). makeEmptyPicture(640,480) would create a picture object that is 640 pixels wide by 480 pixels tall—just like the canvas.

How It Works

We start from the same place as the original copy.

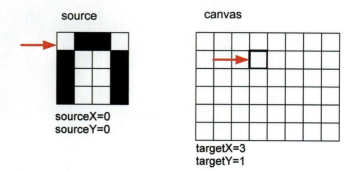

When we increment `sourceY` by 0.5, we end up referring to the same pixel in the source but the target has moved on to the next pixel.

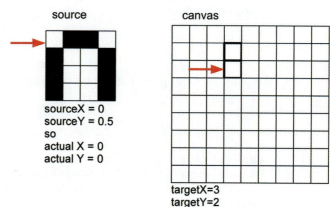

When we increment `sourceY` a second time by 0.5, we now move on to the next pixel, which we'll end up copying twice.

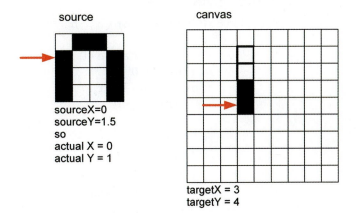

When we move to a new row in the target, we stay in the *same* row in the source. Thus, we end up copying every pixel twice, both horizontally and vertically. Eventually we end up doubling the picture in both directions, effectively quadrupling the area of the figure. Note that the end result is degraded a bit: it's choppier than the original.

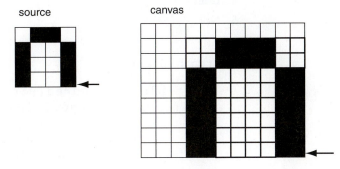

PROGRAMMING SUMMARY

`range`	Function that creates a sequence of numbers. Useful for creating indices for an array or matrix.
`setMediaPath()`	Lets you pick the media directory using a file chooser.
`setMediaPath(directory)`	Lets you specify the media directory.
`getMediaPath(baseName)`	Takes a base filename, then returns the complete path to that file (assuming it's in the media directory).
`makeEmptyPicture(width,height)`	Takes a height and width and returns an empty (all white) picture of the desired size.

PROBLEMS

4.1
```
def newFunction(a, b, c):
    print a
    list1 = range(0,4)
    value = 0
    for x in list1:
        print b
        value = value +1
    print c
    print value
```

If you call the function above by typing: newFunction("I", "you", "walrus"), what will print?

4.2   Which of the recipes below takes a picture and removes all the blue from every pixel that already has a blue value of more than 100?

1. A only

2. D only

3. B and C

4. C and D

5. None

6. All

What do the other ones do?

A.
```
def blueOneHundred(picture):
    for x in range(0,100):
        for y in range(0,100):
            pixel = getPixel(picture,x,y)
            setBlue(pixel,100)
```

B.
```
def removeBlue(picture):
    for p in getPixels(picture):
        if getBlue(p) > 0:
            setBlue(p,100)
```

C.
```
def noBlue(picture):
    blue = makeColor(0,0,100)
    for p in getPixels(picture):
        color = getColor(p)
        if distance(color,blue) > 100:
            setBlue(p,0)
```

D.
```
def byeByeBlue(picture):
    for p in getPixels(picture):
        if getBlue(p) > 100:
            setBlue(p,0)
```

4.3   We've seen that if you increment the source picture index by 2 while incrementing the target picture index by 1 for each copied pixel, you end up with the source being scaled down onto the target. What happens if you increment the target picture index by 2 as well? What happens if you increment both by 0.5 and use `int` to get just the integer part?

4.4   Write a function to mirror along the diagonal from (0, 0) to (*width, height*).

4.5   Write a function to mirror along the diagonal from (0, *height*) to (*width*, 0).

4.6   Write a function that will scale just part of the picture. Try making someone's nose longer.

4.7   Write a function that will scale down just a part of the picture. Make someone's head look smaller.

4.8   Write a function to flip a picture over so that if someone was looking right, they end of looking left.

4.9   Write a general crop function that takes a source picture, the start *X* value, the start *Y* value, the end *X* value, and the end *Y* value. Create and return the new picture and copy just the specified area into the new picture.

4.10   Write a function that copies different parts of a picture to different places in the target.

4.11   Write a general scaleUp function that takes in a picture and creates and returns a new picture twice as big using `makeEmptyPicture(width,height)`.

4.12   Write a general scaleDown function that takes in a picture and creates and returns a new picture half as big using `makeEmptyPicture(width,height)`.

4.13   Modify any of the functions from the last chapter to use a nested loop. Check the result to make sure it still does the same thing.

4.14   Write a function to copy a triangular area from one picture to another.

4.15   Write a function to mirror the input picture's leftmost 20 pixels to pixels 20 to 40.

4.16   Write a function that reduces red in the top third of a picture and clears blue in the bottom third.

4.17   What will be printed for this function if you executed each of these:

(a) `testMe (1, 2, 3)`

(b) `testMe (3, 2, 1)`

(c) `testMe (5, 75, 20)`

```
def testMe(p,q,r):
  if q > 50:
    print r
  value = 10
  for i in range(0,p):
    print "Hello"
    value = value - 1
  print value
  print r
```

4.18 Write a function named `makeCollage` to create a collage of the same image at least four times fit onto the 7x95in.jpg blank JPEG. (You are welcome to add additional images.) One of those four copies can be the original picture. The other three should be modified forms. You can scale, crop, or rotate the image, create a negative of the image, shift or alter colors on the image, and make it darker or lighter.

After composing your image, *mirror it*. You can do this vertically or horizontally (or otherwise), in any direction—just make sure that your four base images are still visible after mirroring.

Your single function should make all of this happen—all of the effects and compositing must occur from the single function `makeCollage`. Of course, it is perfectly okay to *use* other functions, but make it so that a tester of your program need only call `setMediaPath()`, put all your input pictures in a mediasources directory, and then execute `makeCollage()` in order to see a collage generated, shown, and returned.

*4.19 Think about how the grayscale algorithm works. Basically, if you know the *luminance* of anything visual (e.g., a small image, a letter), you can replace a pixel with that visual element in a similar way to create a collage image. Try implementing this. You'll need 256 visual elements of increasing lightness, all of the same size. You can create a collage by replacing each pixel in the original image with one of these visual elements.

TO DIG DEEPER

The "bible" of computer graphics is *Introduction to Computer Graphics* [14]. It's highly recommended.

CHAPTER 5

Advanced Picture Techniques

Chapter Learning Objectives

The media learning goals for this chapter are:

- To implement controlled color changes, like red-eye removal, sepia tones, and posterizing.
- To use blending to combine images.
- To use background subtraction to separate foreground from background images and to understand when and how it will work.
- To use chromakey to separate foreground from background images.
- To be able to add text and shapes to existing pictures.
- To use blurring to smooth degradation.

The computer science goals for this chapter are:

- To use conditionals.
- To be able to choose between using vector and bitmapped image formats.
- To be able to choose when one should write a program for a task versus using existing applications software.

5.1 REPLACING COLORS: RED-EYE, SEPIA TONES, AND POSTERIZING

Replacing colors with another color is pretty easy. We can do it broadly or just within a range. This approach allows us to create some interesting overall effects or tune the effect to do something like turn someone's teeth purple.

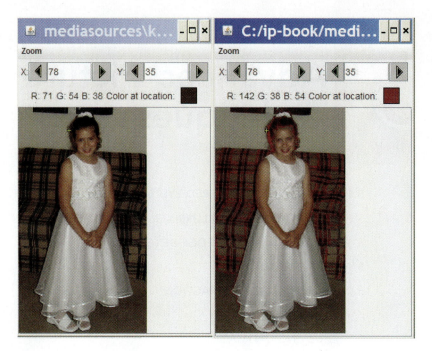

FIGURE 5.1
Changing brown to red.

Here's a recipe that replaces the brown color in Katie's hair with red. Mark used the JES picture tool to figure out roughly what the RGB values were for Katie's brown hair, then wrote a program to look for colors close to that and increase the redness of those pixels. Mark played a lot with the value that he used for distance (here, 50.0) and the amount to multiply the red value by (here, 2). The result is that the couch behind her gets increased too (Figure 5.1).

Program 36: Turn Katie into a Redhead

```
def turnRed():
  brown = makeColor(42,25,15)
  file="C:/ip-book/mediasources/katieFancy.jpg"
  picture=makePicture(file)
  for px in getPixels(picture):
    color = getColor(px)
    if distance(color,brown)<50.0:
      redness=int(getRed(px)*2)
      blueness=getBlue(px)
      greenness=getGreen(px)
      setColor(px,makeColor(redness,blueness,greenness))
  show(picture)
  return(picture)
```

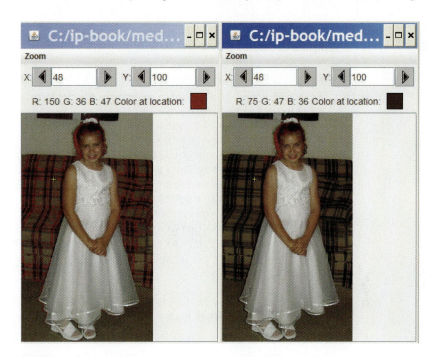

FIGURE 5.2
Double red in rectangular area range.

How It Works

This is actually quite similar to our increase-red recipe but uses an alternative method of setting the color.

- We create a `brown` color, which is what we found in Katie's hair using the picture tool in JES.
- We create the picture of Katie.
- For each of the pixels `px` in the picture, we get the color and then compare the color to the `brown` color we identified earlier. We want to know if the color at pixel `px` is *close enough* to `brown`. How do we define "close enough?" We say that it's within 50.0. Where did we get that number? We tried 10.0, but very little changed. We tried 100.0, and way too much matched (like the stripes in the couch behind Katie's head). We tried different numbers until we got the effect we wanted.
- If the color is "close enough," we get the red, green, and blue components of the color at `px`. We double the red by multiplying it by 2.
- We then set the color at `px` to a new color with the adjusted red and the same blue and green components. Then move on to the next pixel.

With the JES picture tool we can also figure out the coordinates just around Katie's face and then just do the browns near her face. The effect isn't too good, though it's clear that it worked. The line of redness is too sharp and rectangular (Figure 5.2).

Program 37: **Color Replacement in a Range**

```
def turnRedInRange():
  brown = makeColor(42,25,15)
  file="C:/ip-book/mediasources/katieFancy.jpg"
  picture=makePicture(file)
  for x in range(63,125):
    for y in range(6,76):
      px=getPixel(picture,x,y)
      color = getColor(px)
      if distance(color,brown)<50.0:
        redness=int(getRed(px)*2)
        blueness=getBlue(px)
        greenness=getGreen(px)
        setColor(px,makeColor(redness,blueness,greenness))
  show(picture)
  return(picture)
```

5.1.1   Reducing Red-Eye

"Red-eye" is the effect where the flash from the camera bounces off the back of the subject's eyes. Reducing red-eye is a really simple matter. We find the pixels that are "pretty close" (a distance from red of 165 works well) to red, then insert a replacement color.

We probably don't want to change the whole picture. In Figure 5.3, Jenny is wearing a red dress. We don't want to wipe out that red. We'll fix that by only changing the *range* where Jenny's eyes are. Using the JES picture tool, we find the upper left and lower right corners of her eyes. Those points were (109, 91) and (202, 107).

Program 38: **Reduce Red-Eye**

```
def removeRedEye(pic,startX,startY,endX,endY,
replacementcolor):
  red = makeColor(255,0,0)
  for x in range(startX,endX):
    for y in range(startY,endY):
      currentPixel = getPixel(pic,x,y)
      if (distance(red,getColor(currentPixel)) < 165):
        setColor(currentPixel,replacementcolor)
```

We call this function with:

```
>>> jenny = makePicture(getMediaPath("jenny-red.jpg"))
>>> explore(jenny)
>>> removeRedEye(jenny, 109, 91, 202, 107, makeColor(0,0,0))
>>> explore(jenny)
```

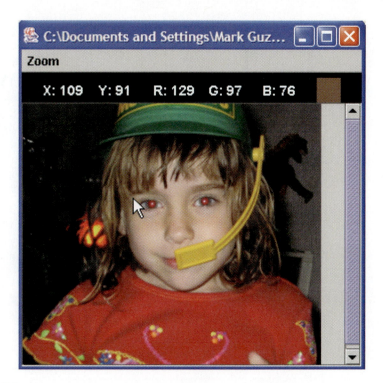

FIGURE 5.3
Finding the range of where Jenny's eyes are red.

to replace the red with black—certainly other colors could be used for the replacement color. The result was good, and we can check that the eye really does now have all-black pixels (Figure 5.4).

How It Works

This algorithm is really very similar to the one that we used for changing Katie's hair to red.

- This function was written to be useful for many different pictures, so it takes a lot of inputs (*parameters*) that the user can simply change for different programs. The function takes an input picture, then the rectangle coordinates where the color change should occur, then the color to replace the red with.
- We define red to be a pure, strong red—makeColor(255,0,0).
- For x and y within the rectangle provided as input, we get the currentPixel.
- We check whether the currentPixel is close enough to red. We determine "close enough" by looking for a distance within a *threshold value*. We tried different distances and settled on 165 as the distance that caught most of the eye redness that we cared about.
- We then swap the replacementColor for the "close enough" color at pixel currentPixel.

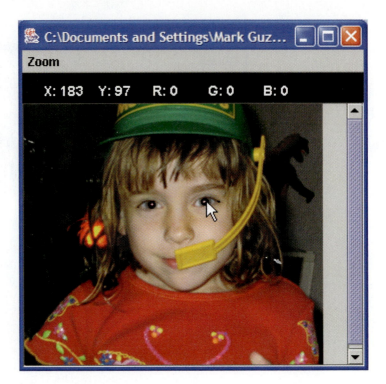

FIGURE 5.4
Finding the range of where Jenny's eyes are red.

5.1.2 Sepia-Toned and Posterized Pictures: Using Conditionals to Choose the Color

So far, we've done color subtraction by simply replacing one color with another. We can be more sophisticated in our color swapping. We can look for a range of colors by using if and choosing to replace some function of the original color or by changing to a specific color. The results are quite interesting.

For example, we might want to generate sepia-toned prints. Older prints sometimes have a yellowish tint. We could just do an overall color change but the end result isn't aesthetically pleasing. By looking for different kinds of colors—highlights, shadows—and treating them differently, we can get a better effect (Figure 5.5).

The way we do this is to first convert everything to grayscale, both because older prints were in a grayscale and because it makes it a little easier to work with. We then look for high, middle, and low ranges of color (really, luminance) and change them separately. (Why these particular values? Trial and error—tweaking them until we liked the effect.)

Program 39: Convert a Picture to Sepia Tones

```
def sepiaTint(picture):
  #Convert image to grayscale
  grayScaleNew(picture)
```

FIGURE 5.5
Original scene (*left*) and using our sepia-tone recipe (*right*).

```
#loop through picture to tint pixels
for p in getPixels(picture):
  red = getRed(p)
  blue = getBlue(p)

  #tint shadows
  if (red < 63):
    red = red*1.1
    blue = blue*0.9

 #tint midtones
  if (red > 62 and red < 192):
    red = red*1.15
    blue = blue*0.85

  #tint highlights
  if (red > 191):
    red = red*1.08
    if (red > 255):
      red = 255
    blue = blue*0.93

  #set the new color values
  setBlue(p, blue)
  setRed(p, red)
```

How It Works

The function starts by taking in a picture as input, then uses our grayScaleNew function
to convert it to grayscale. (We recommend that you copy the grayScaleNew function
into the program area along with sepiaTint—we just don't show it here.) For each of
the pixels, we grab the redness and blueness of the pixel. We know that the red and blue
will be the *same* values, since the picture is now all gray, but we'll want the redness and
blueness for *changing*. We look for specific ranges of colors and treat them differently.

Note that with tinting the highlights (where the light is brightest), we have an `if` inside an `if` block. The idea here is that we don't want the values to wrap around—if red gets too high, we want to cap it at 255. Finally, we set the blue and red values to the new red and blue values, and move on to the next pixel.

Posterizing is a very similar process that results in converting a picture to a smaller number of colors. We're going to do that by looking for a specific range of color, then setting the color to *one* value in that range. The result is that we reduce the number of colors in the picture (Figure 5.6). For example, in the recipe below, if red is 1, 2, 3, ... , or 64, we make it 31. We thus wipe a whole range of red variance and make it one specific red value. We tried this on a picture of a computing student, Anthony.

```
>>> file = "c:/ip-book/mediasources/anthony.jpg"
>>> student = makePicture(file)
>>> explore(student)
>>> posterize(student)
>>> explore(student)
```

FIGURE 5.6
Reducing the colors (*right*) from the original (*left*).

Program 40: Posterizing a Picture

```
def posterize(picture):

  #loop through the pixels
  for p in getPixels(picture):
    #get the RGB values
    red = getRed(p)
    green = getGreen(p)
    blue = getBlue(p)

    #check and set red values
    if(red < 64):
      setRed(p, 31)
    if(red > 63 and red < 128):
      setRed(p, 95)
    if(red > 127 and red < 192):
      setRed(p, 159)
    if(red > 191 and red < 256):
      setRed(p, 223)

    #check and set green values
    if(green < 64):
      setGreen(p, 31)
    if(green > 63 and green < 128):
      setGreen(p, 95)
    if(green > 127 and green < 192):
      setGreen(p, 159)
    if(green > 191 and green < 256):
      setGreen(p, 223)

    #check and set blue values
    if(blue < 64):
      setBlue(p, 31)
    if(blue > 63 and blue < 128):
      setBlue(p, 95)
    if(blue > 127 and blue < 192):
      setBlue(p, 159)
    if(blue > 191 and blue < 256):
      setBlue(p, 223)
```

■

An interesting effect comes from using both grayscale and posterize together. We do this by computing a luminance but then only set the pixel's color to either black or white—only two levels. The result is a picture that looks a bit like a stamped image or like a charcoal drawing (Figure 5.7).

Program 41: Posterize to Two Gray Levels

```
def grayPosterize(pic):
  for p in getPixels(pic):
    r = getRed(p)
```

FIGURE 5.7
Picture posterized to two gray levels.

```
g = getGreen(p)
b = getBlue(p)
luminance = (r+g+b)/3
if luminance < 64:
  setColor(p,black)
if luminance >= 64:
  setColor(p,white)
```

5.2   COMBINING PIXELS: BLURRING

When we make pictures larger (scaling them up), we usually get rough edges: sharp steps in lines that we call **pixelation**. We can reduce pixelation by *blurring* the image—purposefully making some of the hard edges "soft" (i.e., smoother and more curved).

There are *many* ways (algorithms) for blurring. We're going to use a really simple one here. What we do is set each pixel to a color that is an *average* of the colors of the pixels around it.

Program 42: A Simple Blur

```
def blur(filename):
  source=makePicture(filename)
  target=makePicture(filename)
  for x in range(1, getWidth(source)-2):
    for y in range(1, getHeight(source)-2):
      top = getPixel(source,x,y-1)
      left = getPixel(source,x-1,y)
      bottom = getPixel(source,x,y+1)
      right = getPixel(source,x+1,y)
      center = getPixel(target,x,y)
      newRed=(getRed(top)+ getRed(left) + getRed(bottom) + getRed(right)¬
+ getRed(center))/5
      newGreen=(getGreen(top) + getGreen(left) + getGreen(bottom)+¬
getGreen(right)+getGreen(center))/5
      newBlue=(getBlue(top) + getBlue(left) + getBlue(bottom) + getBlue¬
(right)+ getBlue(center))/5
      setColor(center, makeColor(newRed, newGreen, newBlue))
  return target
```

¬These lines of the program should continue with the next lines. A single command in Python may not break across multiple lines. ■

Making It Work Tip: Don't Break Lines Midway in Python

In examples like these, you may see lines "wrap." Lines that you would expect to be all on one line actually appear on two. That's a necessity to fit the code onto the page but we can't really break lines that way in Python. We can't break lines by hitting ENTER until the statement or expression is completed. ■

Figure 5.8 shows the flower from the collage made bigger, then blurred. You can see the pixelation in the bigger version—the sharp, blocky edges. With the blur, some of the pixelation goes away. More careful blurs take regions of colors into account (so that edges between colors are kept sharp) and thus are able to reduce pixelation without removing sharpness.

How It Works

We use this function with something like `newPic = blur (pickAFile())`. We then create two copies of the picture filename provided as input. We modify only the `target` so that we always average *original* colors from the `source`. We walk through the *x*

FIGURE 5.8
Making the flower bigger (*left*), then blurring it to reduce pixelation (*right*).

index values from 1 to the width minus 1—here we're explicitly taking advantage of the fact that `range` won't include the end values. We do the same with the y indices. The reason is that we're going to add 1 and subtract 1 from each x and y to compute the averages. We won't be averaging the edge pixels, then, but it'll be pretty hard to tell. For each (x, y), we get the pixel to the left $(x - 1, y)$, to the right $(x + 1, y)$, above $(x, y - 1)$, and below $(x, y + 1)$, as well as the pixel itself at the center (x, y) (from `target` because we can be sure that we haven't changed (x, y) yet). We compute the average of the reds of all five pixels, the greens, and the blues, then set color at (x, y) to the average color.

While this works surprisingly well (Figure 5.8), it's not quite as good as we might get. Some detail is lost when you simply blur like this. What if we blurred to get rid of pixelation but kept detail? How might we do that? What if we checked luminance values before we computed the average—perhaps we shouldn't blur across large luminance boundaries because that would reduce detail? That's just one idea—there are lots of good algorithms for blurring.

5.3 COMPARING PIXELS: EDGE DETECTION

Blurring is a process of computing an average across multiple pixels. *Edge detection* is a similar process where we compare pixels to determine what to put in a given pixel but we basically only set the pixel to black or white. The idea is to try to draw lines the way an artist might sketch a drawing.

It's really an amazing feature of our visual systems that we can look at a line drawing of someone and pick out a face or other features. Look at the world around you. There really aren't sharp lines defining features of the world. There are no clear lines around your nose or eyes, but any child can draw a face with a checkmark for a nose and two circles for eyes—and we will all recognize it as a face! Typically, we *see* a line where there is a difference in luminance.

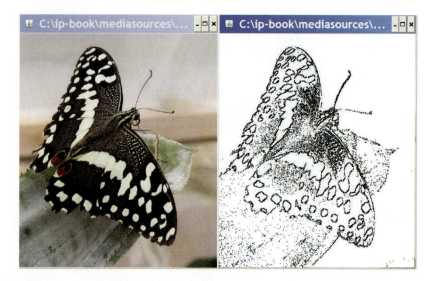

FIGURE 5.9
Butterfly (*left*) converted to a "line drawing" (*right*).

We can try to model this process (Figure 5.9). In the recipe below, we compare each pixel's luminance to the pixel *below* it and to the *right* of it. If there is a suitable difference in luminance below *and* to the right, then we make the pixel black. (Experimentation found that a threshold value of 10 worked pretty well.) Otherwise, we leave it white.

Program 43: Create a Simple Line Drawing Using Edge Detection

```
def lineDetect(filename):
  orig = makePicture(filename)
  makeBw = makePicture(filename)
  for x in range(0,getWidth(orig)-1):
    for y in range(0,getHeight(orig)-1):
      here=getPixel(makeBw,x,y)
      down=getPixel(orig,x,y+1)
      right=getPixel(orig,x+1,y)
      hereL=(getRed(here)+getGreen(here)+getBlue(here))/3
      downL=(getRed(down)+getGreen(down)+getBlue(down))/3
      rightL=(getRed(right)+getGreen(right)+getBlue(right))/3
      if abs(hereL-downL)>10 and abs(hereL-rightL)>10:
        setColor(here,black)
      if abs(hereL-downL)<=10 and abs(hereL-rightL)<=10:
        setColor(here,white)
  show(makeBw)
  return makeBw
```

How It Works

Like the gray-levels posterizing, the goal here is to set each pixel to either black or white, depending on whether there is a luminance difference or not.

- We call the function with something like `bwVersion = lineDetect (pickAFile())`. We make two copies of the picture from the input filename—the source `orig` (original) and the target `makeBw`.
- We use indices for *x* and *y* from 1 to the width minus 1 and height minus 1, but we're counting on the fact here that the `range` won't include the last value. We're going to be comparing the pixel at (x, y) to the pixels at $(x + 1, y)$ (right) and at $(x, y + 1)$ (down).
- We get the pixel in `here`, the pixel down `down`, and the pixel to the right `right`.
- We compute the luminance of all three pixels.
- If the *absolute value* (`abs`) of the difference between the luminance in the comparison pixel (`hereL`) and the luminance to the right (`rightL`) and below (`downL`) is greater than the threshold value of 10, then we make the pixel black. We use absolute value because we only care about the *difference* between the two luminance values. We don't really care which one is larger.
- If the difference between the luminance is *not* greater than the threshold value (less than or equal to it), then we set the pixel to white.

There are algorithms to do much better edge detection and line drawing. For example, here we're simply setting each pixel to black or white. We're not really considering the notion of a "line." We could use techniques like blurring to smooth the image and make the dots seem more like lines. We could also make pixels black only if we are going to make nearby pixels black; that is, create a line rather than simply make dots.

5.4   BLENDING PICTURES

In this chapter, we talk about techniques for creating pictures from other pieces. We'll compose pictures in new ways (e.g., pulling someone out from one background and putting them in a new setting) and create pictures from scratch without explicitly setting every pixel.

One of the ways that we can combine pictures to create new pictures is by mixing the colors of the pixels to reflect both pictures. When we create collages by copying, any overlap typically means that one picture shows *over* another. The last picture painted on is the one that appears on top of the other. But it doesn't have to be that way. We can *blend* pictures by multiplying their colors and adding them. This gives us the effect of *transparency*.

We know that 100% of something is the whole thing; 50% of one and 50% of another also is a whole. In the recipe below, we blend a picture of the mother and the daughter with an overlap of 70 (the width of Barbara minus 150) columns of pixels (Figure 5.10).

Program 44: Blending Two Pictures

```
def blendPictures():
    barb = makePicture(getMediaPath("barbara.jpg"))
    katie = makePicture(getMediaPath("Katie-smaller.jpg"))
    canvas = makePicture(getMediaPath("640x480.jpg"))
```

FIGURE 5.10
Blending the picture of mom and daughter.

```
#Copy first 150 columns of Barb
sourceX=0
for targetX in range(0,150):
  sourceY=0
  for targetY in range(0,getHeight(barb)):
    color = getColor(getPixel(barb,sourceX,sourceY))
    setColor(getPixel(canvas,targetX,targetY),color)
    sourceY = sourceY + 1
  sourceX = sourceX + 1
#Now, grab the rest of Barb
# at 50\% Barb and 50\% Katie
overlap = getWidth(barb)-150
sourceX=0
for targetX in range(150,getWidth(barb)):
  sourceY=0
  for targetY in range(0,getHeight(katie)):
    bPixel = getPixel(barb,sourceX+150,sourceY)
    kPixel = getPixel(katie,sourceX,sourceY)
    newRed= 0.50*getRed(bPixel)+0.50*getRed(kPixel)
    newGreen=0.50*getGreen(bPixel)+0.50*getGreen(kPixel)
    newBlue = 0.50*getBlue(bPixel)+0.50*getBlue(kPixel)
    color = makeColor(newRed,newGreen,newBlue)
    setColor(getPixel(canvas,targetX,targetY),color)
    sourceY = sourceY + 1
  sourceX = sourceX + 1
# Last columns of Katie
```

```
      sourceX=overlap
      for targetX in range(150+overlap,150+getWidth(katie)):
        sourceY=0
        for targetY in range(0,getHeight(katie)):
          color = getColor(getPixel(katie,sourceX,sourceY))
          setColor(getPixel(canvas,targetX,targetY),color)
          sourceY = sourceY + 1
        sourceX = sourceX + 1
      show(canvas)
      return canvas
```

How It Works

This function has three parts to it—the part where Barb is there without Katie, the part where there's some of each, and the part where there's just Katie.

- We start out by creating the picture objects for barb, katie, and the target canvas.
- For 150 pixel columns, we simply copy pixels from barb into the canvas.
- The next section is the actual blending. Our targetX index starts at 150, because we already have 150 columns from barb in the canvas. We're using sourceX and sourceY to index *both* barb and katie but we have to add 150 to sourceX when indexing barb because we've already copied 150 pixels of barb. Our *y* index will only go up to the height of the katie picture because it's shorter than the barb picture.
- The body of the loop is where the blending occurs. We get a pixel from barb and call it bPixel. We get one from katie and call it kPixel. We then compute the red, green, and blue for the target pixel (the one at targetX and targetY) by taking 50% of the red, green, and blue of each of the source pictures.
- Finally, we end up copying in the rest of the katie pixels.

5.5   BACKGROUND SUBTRACTION

Let's imagine that you have a picture of someone and a picture of where they stood without them there (Figure 5.11). Could you *subtract* the background of the person (i.e., figure out where the colors are exactly the same), and then replace another background? Say, of the moon (Figure 5.12)?

Program 45: Subtract the Background and Replace It with a New One

```
def swapBack(pic1, back, newBg):
  for x in range(0,getWidth(pic1)):
    for y in range(0,getHeight(pic1)):
      p1Pixel = getPixel(pic1,x,y)
      backPixel = getPixel(back,x,y)
      if (distance(getColor(p1Pixel),
        getColor(backPixel)) < 15.0):
        setColor(p1Pixel,getColor(getPixel(newBg,x,y)))
  return pic1
```

FIGURE 5.11
A picture of a child (Katie) and the background without her.

FIGURE 5.12
A new background: the moon.

How It Works

The function swapBack (swap background) takes a picture (with both foreground and background in it), a picture of the background, and a new background. For all the pixels in the input picture, we:

- Get the matching pixels (same coordinates) from both the picture and the background.

- Compare the distances between the colors. We use a threshold value here of 15.0, but do try it with others.

- If the distance is small (less than the threshold value), then assume that the pixel is part of the background. Take the color from the pixel at the same coordinates in the *new* background and set the pixel in the input picture to the new color.

You can do this but the effect isn't as good as you'd like (Figure 5.13). Our daughter's shirt color was too close to the color of the wall, so the moon bled into her shirt. Though the light was dim, a shadow is definitely having an effect here. The shadow wasn't in the background picture, so the algorithm treats the shadow as part of the foreground. This

FIGURE 5.13
Katie on the moon.

FIGURE 5.14
Two people in front of a wall (*left*) and a picture of the wall (*right*).

result suggests that the difference in color between the background and the foreground is important for making background subtraction work—and so is having good lighting!

Mark tried the same thing with a picture of two students in front of a tiled wall. Mark used a tripod (really critical to get the pixels to line up), but unfortunately left autofocus on, so the two original pictures (Figure 5.14) weren't all that comparable. The background swap (with the jungle scene) hardly did anything at all. Mark changed the threshold value to 50, and finally got *some* swapping (Figure 5.15).

Simply changing the threshold doesn't always improve things. It certainly makes more of the foreground get classified as background. But for problems like bleeding through of the new background into the clothing because of matching colors, the threshold value doesn't help much.

FIGURE 5.15
Swapping a jungle for the wall, using background subtraction, with a threshold of 50.

5.6   CHROMAKEY

Television weather forecasters wave to show a storm front coming in across a map. The reality is that they are being filmed standing before a background of a fixed color (usually blue or green) and then that background color is replaced digitally with pixels from the desired map. This is called **chromakey**. It's easier to replace a known color and isn't as sensitive to lighting problems. Mark took our son's blue sheet, attached it to the family entertainment center, then took a picture of himself in front of it using a timer on a camera (Figure 5.16).

Program 46: Chromakey: Replace All Blue with the New Background

```
def chromakey(source,bg):
  # source should have something in front of blue, bg is the
new background
  for x in range(0,getWidth(source)):
    for y in range(0,getHeight(source)):
      p = getPixel(source,x,y)
      # My definition of blue: If the redness
        + greenness < blueness
      if (getRed(p) + getGreen(p) < getBlue(p)):
      #Then, grab the color at the same spot from the new
background
        setColor(p,getColor(getPixel(bg,x,y)))
  return source
```

How It Works

Here we take in just a source (with both foreground and background in it) and a new background bg. *These must be the same size!* Mark used the JES picture tool to come up

FIGURE 5.16
Mark in front of a blue sheet.

with a rule for what would be "blue" for this recipe. He didn't want to look for equality or even a distance to the color (0, 0, 255) because he knew that very little of the blue would be *exactly* full-intensity blue. He found that pixels he thought of as blue tended to have smaller red and green values, and in fact, the blue values were greater than the sum of the red and the green. So that's what he looked for in this recipe. Wherever the blue was greater than the red and green, he swapped in the new background pixel's color instead.

The effect is really quite striking (Figure 5.17). Do note the "folds" in the lunar surface, though. The really cool thing is that this recipe works for any background that's the same size as the image (Figure 5.18).

There's another way of writing this code, which is shorter but does the same thing. It uses the getX and getY functions to figure out the coordinates. This leads to a somewhat messier setColor statement.

Program 47: Chromakey, Shorter

```
def chromakey2(source,bg):
  for p in pixels(source):
    if (getRed(p)+getGreen(p) < getBlue(p)):
      setColor(p,getColor(getPixel(bg,getX(p),getY(p))))
  return source
```

You don't really want to do chromakey with a common color like red—something that there's a lot of in your face. Mark tried it with the two pictures in Figure 5.19—one with the flash on and one with it off. He changed the test to if getRed(p) > (getGreen(p) + getBlue(p)):. The one without a flash was terrible—the student's face was "jungle-ified." The one with the flash was better but the flash is still visible after the swap (Figure 5.20). It's clear why moviemakers and weather people use blue

FIGURE 5.17
Mark on the moon.

FIGURE 5.18
Mark in the jungle.

or green backgrounds for chromakey—there's less overlap with common colors, like face colors.

The devices and software that implement chromakey professionally use a somewhat different process than this. Our algorithm looks for the color to be replaced, then does the replacement. In professional chromakey, a *mask* is produced. A mask is of the same size as the original image, where pixels to be changed are white in the mask, and those that should not be changed are black. The mask is then used to decide which pixels are

FIGURE 5.19
Student in front of a red background without the flash (*left*) and with flash on (*right*).

FIGURE 5.20
Using chromakey recipe with red background, flash off (*left*) and flash on (*right*).

to be changed. An advantage to using a mask is that we separate the processes of (a) detecting which pixels are to be changed and (b) making the changes to the pixels. By separating them, we can improve on each, and thus improve the whole effect.

5.7 DRAWING ON IMAGES

Sometimes you want to create your *own* images from scratch. We know that this is just a matter of setting pixel values to whatever we want but setting individual pixel values to draw a line or a circle or some letters is hard. One way of drawing on images is to simply set the pixels appropriately. Here's an example that creates horizontal and vertical lines over Carolina, a computing student at Georgia Tech (Figure 5.21). The program works by asking you to pick a file and then creates a picture from the file. Then it calls a function `verticalLines` that draws vertical lines on the picture 5 pixels apart. Then it calls a function `horizontalLines` that draws horizontal lines on the picture 5 pixels apart. It shows and returns the resulting picture.

FIGURE 5.21
Carolina normal (*left*) and with lines added (*right*).

Program 48: Draw Lines by Setting Pixels

```
def lineExample():
  img = makePicture(pickAFile())
  verticalLines(img)
  horizontalLines(img)
  show(img)
  return img

def horizontalLines(src):
  for x in range(0,getHeight(src),5):
    for y in range(0,getWidth(src)):
      setColor(getPixel(src,y,x),black)

def verticalLines(src):
  for x in range(0,getWidth(src),5):
    for y in range(0,getHeight(src)):
      setColor(getPixel(src,x,y),black)
```

Note that this program is using the color name black. You may remember that JES predefines a bunch of colors for you: black, white, blue, red, green, gray, lightGray, darkGray, yellow, orange, pink, magenta, and cyan. You can use any of these just as you would any other function or command.

We can imagine drawing anything we want like this by simply setting individual pixels to whatever colors we want. We could draw rectangles or circles simply by figuring out what pixels need to be what color. We could even draw letters—by setting the appropriate pixels to the appropriate colors, we could make any letter we want. While we could do it, it would involve a lot of work to do all the math for all the different shapes and letters. That's work that lots of people need, so basic drawing tools have been built into libraries for you.

5.7.1 Drawing with Drawing Commands

Most modern programming languages with graphics libraries provide functions that enable us to draw directly a variety of different kinds of shapes onto pictures and to draw text directly onto a picture. Here are some of those functions:

- `addText(pict,x,y,string)` puts the string starting at position (x, y) in the picture.
- `addLine(pict,x1,y1,x2,y2)` draws a line from position $(x1, y1)$ to $(x2, y2)$.
- `addRect(pict,x1,y1,w,h)` draws a rectangle with black lines with the upper-left-hand corner at $(x1, y1)$, a width of w, and a height of h.
- `addRectFilled(pict,x1,y1,w,h,color)` draws a rectangle filled with the `color` that you pick with the upper-left-hand corner at $(x1, y1)$, a width of w, and a height of h.

We can use these commands to add things to existing pictures. What would it look like if a mysterious red box washed up on the beach? We can make that scene appear with these kinds of commands (Figure 5.22).

FIGURE 5.22
A box washed up on the shore of the beach.

This is not a picture

FIGURE 5.23
A very small, drawn picture.

Program 49: Adding a Box to a Beach

```
def addABox():
  beach = makePicture(getMediaPath("beach-smaller.jpg"))
  addRectFilled(beach,150,150,50,50,red)
  show(beach)
  return beach
```

Below is another example of using these drawing commands (Figure 5.23).

Program 50: An Example of Using Drawing Commands

```
def littlepicture():
  canvas=makePicture(getMediaPath("640x480.jpg"))
  addText(canvas,10,50,"This is not a picture")
  addLine(canvas,10,20,300,50)
  addRectFilled(canvas,0,200,300,500,yellow)
  addRect(canvas,10,210,290,490)
  return canvas
```

5.7.2 Vector and Bitmap Representations

Here's a thought: Which of these is smaller, the picture (Figure 5.23) or the recipe? The picture, on the disk, is about 15 kilobytes (a *kilobyte* is 1000 bytes). Recipe 47 is less than 100 bytes. But for many uses, they are *equivalent*. What if you just saved the program and not the pixels? That's what a **vector representation** for graphics is about.

Vector-based graphical representations are executable programs that generate the picture when desired. Vector-based representations are used in Postscript, Flash, and AutoCAD. When you make a change to an image in Flash or AutoCAD, you are actually making a change to the underlying representation—essentially, you're changing the program, like the one in Recipe 47. The program is then executed again to make the image appear. But thanks to Moore's Law, the execution and new display occur so fast that it feels like you're changing the picture.

Font-definition languages like Postscript and TrueType actually define miniature programs (or equations) for each and every letter or symbol. When you want the letter or symbol at a particular size, the program is run to figure out which pixels should be set to what values. (Some specify more than one color to create the effect of smoother curves.) Because the programs are written to handle desired font size as an input, the letters and symbols can be generated at any size.

Bitmap graphical representations, on the other hand, store every individual pixel or a compressed representation of the pixels. Formats like BMP, GIF, and JPEG are essentially bitmap representations. GIF and JPEG are compressed representations— they don't represent each and every pixel with 24 bits. Instead, they represent the same information but with fewer bits.

What does **compression** mean? It means that various techniques have been used to make the file smaller. Some compression techniques are **lossy compression**—some detail is lost but hopefully the least significant detail (perhaps even invisible to the human eye, or ear). Other techniques, known as **lossless compression**, lose no detail but still scrunch the file. One lossless technique is **run length encoding** (RLE).

Imagine that you've got a long line of yellow pixels in a picture, surrounded by some blue pixels. Something like this:

B B Y Y Y Y Y Y Y Y Y B B

What if you encoded this, not as a long line of pixels, but as something like

B B 9 Y B B

In words, you encode "blue, blue, then nine yellows, then blue and blue." Since each of the yellow pixels takes 24 bits (3 bytes for red, green, and blue), but recording "nine" takes just a single byte, there's a huge savings. We say that we're encoding the *length* of the *run* of yellows—thus, encoding the run length. That's just one of the compression methods that is used to make pictures smaller.

There are several benefits to vector-based representations over bitmap representations. If you can represent the picture you want to send (say, over the Internet) using a vector-based representation, it's much smaller than sending all the pixels—in a sense, vector notation is already compressed. Essentially, you're sending the *instructions* for how to make the picture, rather than sending the picture itself. For very complex images, however, the instructions can be as long as the image (imagine sending all the directions on how to paint the *Mona Lisa*), so there is no benefit. But when the images are simple enough, representations like those used in Flash make for faster upload and download times than sending the same JPEG images.

The real benefit of vector-based notations comes when you want to change the image. Let's say that you're working on an architectural drawing, and you extend a line in your drawing tool. If your drawing tool is only working with bitmapped images (sometimes called a **painting tool**), then all you have are more pixels on the screen that are adjacent to the other pixels on the screen representing the line. There's nothing in the computer that says that all those pixels represent a line of any kind—they're just pixels. But if your drawing tool is working with vector-based representations (sometimes called a **drawing tool**), then extending a line means that you're changing an underlying representation of a line.

Why is that important? The underlying representation is actually a *specification* of the drawing, and it can be used anywhere that a specification is needed. Imagine taking the drawing of a part, then actually running the cutting and stamping machines based on that drawing. This happens regularly in many shops and it's possible because the drawing isn't just pixels—it's a specification of the lines and their relationships, which can then be scaled and used to determine the behavior of machines.

You might be wondering, "But how could we *change* the program? Can we write a program that would essentially retype the program or parts of the program?" Yes, we can, and we'll do it in the chapter on text.

5.8   PROGRAMS AS SPECIFYING DRAWING PROCESS

Drawing functions like these can be used to create pictures that are exactly specified—things that might be too hard to do by hand. Take, for example, Figure 5.24.

This is a rendering of a famous optical illusion and it's not as effective as the famous ones—but it's simple to understand how this version works. Our eyes tell us that the left half of the picture is lighter than the right half, even though the end quarters are exactly the same shade of gray. The effect is caused by the sharp boundary between the middle quarters, where one moves (left to right) from gray to white, and the other moves from black to gray.

The image in Figure 5.24 is a carefully defined and created picture. It would be very hard to do with pencil and paper. It would be possible with something like Photoshop,

FIGURE 5.24
A programmed grayscale effect.

but it wouldn't be easy. By using the graphics functions in this chapter, however, we can easily specify exactly what that picture should be.

Program 51: Draw the Gray Effect

```
def grayEffect():
  file = getMediaPath("640x480.jpg")
  pic = makePicture(file)
  # First, 100 columns of 100-gray
  gray = makeColor(100,100,100)
  for x in range(0,100):
    for y in range(0,100):
      setColor(getPixel(pic,x,y),gray)
  # Second, 100 columns of increasing grayness
  grayLevel = 100
  for x in range(100,200):
    gray = makeColor(grayLevel, grayLevel, grayLevel)
    for y in range(0,100):
      setColor(getPixel(pic,x,y),gray)
    grayLevel = grayLevel + 1
  # Third, 100 columns of increasing grayness, from 0
  grayLevel = 0
  for x in range(200,300):
    gray = makeColor(grayLevel, grayLevel, grayLevel)
    for y in range(0,100):
      setColor(getPixel(pic,x,y),gray)
    grayLevel = grayLevel + 1
  # Finally, 100 columns of 100-gray
  gray = makeColor(100,100,100)
  for x in range(300,400):
    for y in range(0,100):
      setColor(getPixel(pic,x,y),gray)
  return pic
```

Graphics functions are very good at drawings that are repeated where the positions of lines and shapes and the selection of colors can be made by mathematical relationships.

Program 52: Draw the Picture in Figure 5.25

```
def coolPic():
  canvas=makePicture(getMediaPath("640x480.jpg"))
  for index in range(25,0,-1):
    color = makeColor(index*10,index*5,index)
    addRectFilled(canvas,0,0,index*10,index*10,color)
  show(canvas)
  return canvas
```

FIGURE 5.25
Nested colored-rectangles image.

FIGURE 5.26
Nested blank-rectangles image.

Program 53: Draw the Picture in Figure 5.26

```
def coolPic2():
  canvas=makePicture(getMediaPath("640x480.jpg"))
  for index in range(25,0,-1):
    addRect(canvas,index,index,index*3,index*4)
    addRect(canvas,100+index*4,100+index*3,index*8,index*10)
  show(canvas)
  return canvas
```

5.8.1   Why Do We Write Programs?

Why do we write programs, especially programs that draw pictures? Could we draw pictures like these in Photoshop or Visio? Certainly we can, but we'd have to know *how*, and that's not easy knowledge to come by. Could we *teach* you how to do this in Photoshop? Probably, but that may take a lot of effort—Photoshop isn't simple.

But if we *give* you these programs, you can create the picture anytime you want. What's more, by giving you the program, I'm giving you the *exact* definition that you can go and change for yourself.

> **Computer Science Idea: We Write Programs to Encapsulate and Communicate Process**
>
> The reason why we write programs is to exactly specify a process and communicate it to others. ■

Imagine that you have some process to communicate. It doesn't have to be drawing—imagine that it's a financial process (such that you could do it in a spreadsheet or in a program like Quicken) or something that you do with text (such as laying out text for a book or a brochure). If you can do something by hand, you should just do it. If you need to *teach* someone else to do it, consider writing a program to do it. If you need to explain how to do it to *lots* of people, definitely use a program. If you want lots of people to be able to do the process themselves, without someone having to teach them something first, definitely write a program and give the people the program.

PROGRAMMING SUMMARY

Here are the functions introduced in this chapter:

`addText(pict,x,y,string)`	Puts the string starting at position (x, y) in the picture.
`addLine(picture,x1,y1,x2,y2)`	Draws a line from position $(x1, y1)$ to $(x2, y2)$.
`addRect(pict,x1,y1,w,h)`	Draws a rectangle with black lines with the upper-left-hand corner at $(x1, y1)$, a width of w, and a height of h.
`addRectFilled(pict,x1,y1,w,h,color)`	Draws a rectangle filled with the `color` that you pick with the upper-left-hand corner at $(x1, y1)$, a width of w, and a height of h.

PROBLEMS

5.1   Start with a picture of someone you know and make some specific color changes to it:

- Turn the teeth purple.
- Turn the eyes red.
- Turn the hair orange.

Of course, if your friend's teeth are already purple, or eyes red, or hair orange, choose a different target color.

5.2   Write a program `checkLuminance` that will input red, green, and blue values, and compute the luminance using the weighted average (as below). But then print out a warning to the user based on the computed luminance:

- If the luminance is less than 10, "That's going to be awfully dark."
- If the luminance is between 50 and 200, "Looks like a good range."
- Over 250, "That's going to be nearly white!"

5.3   Try doing chromakey in a range—grab something out of its background where the something is only in one part of a picture. For example, put a halo around someone's head but don't mess with the rest of the body.

5.4   Write a function to blend two pictures, starting with the top third of the first picture and then blend the two together in the middle third and then show the last third of the second picture. This works best if the two pictures are the same size.

5.5   Draw a black line on a picture when the difference between the colors of a pixel and the one to the right is greater than some passed amount.

5.6   Write a function to interleave two pictures. Take the first 20 pixels from the first picture and then 20 pixels from the second picture and then the next 20 pixels from the first picture and then the next 20 pixels from the second picture and so on till all the pixels have been used.

5.7   Write a function to take 25 percent of one picture blended with 75 percent of another.

5.8   Rewrite the encode function to use just one loop.

5.9   Create a movie poster by drawing text on a picture.

5.10 Create a comic strip by putting three to four pictures next to each other horizontally and adding text.

5.11 Using the drawing functions, draw a bull's eye.

5.12 Using the drawing tools presented here, draw a house—just go for the simple child's house with one door, two windows, walls, and a roof.

5.13 Draw horizontal and vertical lines on a picture with 10 pixels between the lines.

5.14 Draw diagonal lines on a picture from top left to bottom right.

5.15 Draw diagonal lines on a picture from top right to bottom left.

5.16 What is a vector-based image? How does it differ from a bitmapped image? When is it better to use a vector-based image?

5.17 Draw a house on the beach where we put the mysterious box previously.

5.18 Write a function to draw a simple face with eyes and a mouth.

5.19 Why do film makers use a green or blue screen for special effects instead of a red screen?

5.20 Get some green posterboard and take a picture of a friend in front of it. Now use chromakey to put her or him in the jungle or in Paris.

5.21 Now use your house function to draw a town with dozens of houses at different sizes. You'll probably want to modify your house function to draw at an input coordinate, then change the coordinate where each house is drawn.

5.22 Draw a rainbow—use what you know about colors, pixels, and drawing operations to draw a rainbow. Is this easier to do with our drawing functions or by manipulating individual pixels? Why?

TO DIG DEEPER

John Maeda is at the Aesthetics and Computation Group at the MIT Media Lab. Check out his processing environment (`http://www.processing.org`) for the development of interactive art, live video processing, and data visualization. Processing allows you to do some of the same effects as in this chapter.

PART 2 SOUND

6 Modifying Sounds Using Loops

Chapter Learning Objectives

The media learning goals for this chapter are:

- To understand how we digitize sounds, and the limitations of human hearing that allow us to digitize sounds.
- To use the Nyquist theorem to determine the sampling rate necessary for digitizing a desired sound.
- To manipulate volume.
- To create (and avoid) clipping.

The computer science goals for this chapter are:

- To understand and use arrays as a data structure.
- To use the formula that n bits result in 2^n possible patterns in order to figure out the number of bits needed to save values.
- To use the sound object.
- To debug sound programs.
- To use iteration (in for loops) for manipulating sounds.
- To use scope to understand when a variable is available for us.

6.1 HOW SOUND IS ENCODED

There are two parts to understanding how sound is encoded and manipulated.

- First, what are the physics of sound? How is it that we hear a variety of sounds?
- Next, how can we then map sounds into numbers on a computer?

6.1.1 The Physics of Sound

Physically, sounds are waves of air pressure. When something makes a sound, it makes ripples in the air just like stones or raindrops dropped into a pond cause ripples on the surface of the water (Figure 6.1). Each drop causes a wave of pressure to pass over the surface of the water, which causes visible rises in the water, and less visible but just as large depressions in the water. The rises are increases in pressure and the lows are decreases in pressure. Some of the ripples we see actually arise from *combinations* of ripples—some waves are the sums and interactions of other waves.

In the air, we call these increases in pressure *compressions* and decreases in pressure *rarefactions*. It's these compressions and rarefactions that allow us to hear sounds. The shape of the waves, their *frequency*, and their *amplitude* all impact what we perceive in the sound.

The simplest sound in the world is a **sine wave** (Figure 6.2). In a sine wave, the compressions and rarefactions arrive with equal size and regularity. In a sine wave, one compression plus one rarefaction is called a **cycle**. At some point in the cycle, there has to be a point where there is zero pressure, just between the compression and the rarefaction. The distance from the zero point to the greatest pressure (or least pressure) is called the **amplitude**.

In general, amplitude is the most important factor in our perception of *volume*: if the amplitude rises, we typically perceive the sound as being louder. When we perceive an increase in volume, we say that we're perceiving an increase in the *intensity* of sound.

Human perception of sound is not a direct mapping from the physical reality. The study of the human perception of sound is called *psychoacoustics*. One of the odd facts about psychoacoustics is that most of our perceptions of sound are *logarithmically* related to the actual phenomena.

We measure the change in intensity in **decibels** (dB). That's probably the unit that you most often associate with volume. A decibel is a logarithmic measure, so it matches the way we perceive volume. It's always a ratio, a comparison of two values. $10 * \log_{10}(I_1/I_2)$ is the change in intensity in decibels between two intensities, I_1 and I_2. If two amplitudes are measured under the same conditions, we can express the same definition as amplitudes: $20 * \log_{10}(A_1/A_2)$. If $A_2 = 2 * A_1$ (i.e., the amplitude doubles), the difference is roughly 6 dB.

FIGURE 6.1
Raindrops causing ripples on the surface of the water, just as sound causes ripples in the air.

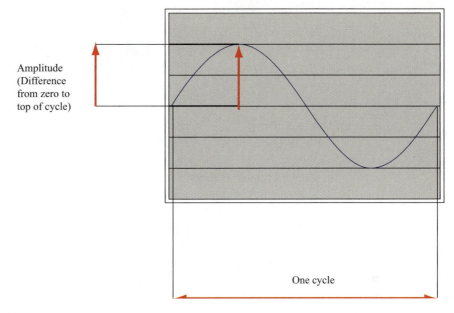

FIGURE 6.2
One cycle of the simplest sound: a sine wave.

When decibel is used as an absolute measurement, it's in reference to the threshold of audibility at *sound pressure level* (SPL): 0 dB SPL. Normal speech has an intensity of about 60 dB SPL. Shouted speech is about 80 dB SPL.

How often a cycle occurs is called the **frequency**. If a cycle is short, then there can be lots of them per second. If a cycle is long, then there are fewer of them. As the frequency increases we, perceive the **pitch** to increase. We measure frequency in *cycles per second* (cps) or *Hertz* (Hz).

All sounds are periodic—there is always some pattern of rarefaction and compression that leads to cycles. In a sine wave, the notion of a cycle is easy. In natural waves, it's not so clear where a pattern repeats. Even in the ripples in a pond, the waves aren't as regular as you might think. The time between peaks in waves isn't always the same—it varies. This means that a cycle may involve several peaks and valleys until it repeats.

Humans hear between 2 and 20,000 Hz (or 20 kilohertz, abbreviated 20 kHz). Again, as with amplitudes, that's an enormous range. To give you a sense of where music fits into that spectrum, the note A above middle C is 440 Hz in traditional *equal temperament* tuning (Figure 6.3).

Like intensity, our perception of pitch is almost exactly proportional to the log of the frequency. We don't perceive absolute differences in pitch but the *ratio* of the frequencies. If you heard a 100 Hz sound followed by a 200 Hz sound, you'd perceive the same pitch change (or *pitch interval*) as a shift from 1000 Hz to 2000 Hz. Obviously, a difference of 100 Hz is a lot smaller than a change of 1000 Hz, but we perceive it to be the same.

FIGURE 6.3
The note A above middle C is 440 Hz.

In standard tuning, the ratio in frequency between the same notes in adjacent octaves is 2 : 1. Frequency doubles each octave. We told you earlier that A above middle C is 440 Hz. You know, then, that the next A up the scale is 880 Hz.

How we think about music is dependent upon our cultural standards but there are some universals. Among them are the use of pitch intervals (e.g., the ratio between notes C and D remains the same in every octave), the constant relationship between octaves, and the existence of four to seven main pitches (not considering sharps and flats here) in an octave.

What makes the experience of one sound different from another? Why does a flute playing a note sound *so* different from a trumpet or a clarinet playing the same note? We still don't understand everything about psychoacoustics and what physical properties influence our perception of sound but here are some of the factors that lead us to perceive different sounds (especially musical instruments) as distinct:

- Real sounds are almost never single-frequency sound waves. Most natural sounds have *several* frequencies in them, often at different amplitudes. These additional frequencies are sometimes called *overtones*. When a piano plays the note C, for example, part of the richness of the tone is that the notes E and G are *also* in the sound, but at lower amplitudes. Different instruments have different overtones in their notes. The central tone, the one we're trying to play, is called the *fundamental*.

- Instrument sounds are not continuous with respect to amplitude and frequency. Some come slowly up to the target frequency and amplitude (like wind instruments), while others hit the frequency and amplitude very quickly and then the volume fades while the frequency remains pretty constant (like a piano).

- Not all sound waves are well represented by sine waves. Real sounds have funny bumps and sharp edges. Our ears can pick these up, at least in the first few waves. We can do a reasonable job of synthesizing with sine waves but synthesizers sometimes also use other kinds of wave forms to get different kinds of sounds (Figure 6.4).

6.1.2   Exploring How Sounds Look

At http://www.mediacomputation.org, you will find the MediaTools application with documentation for how to get it started. The MediaTools application contains tools for sound, graphics, and video. Using the sound tools, you can actually observe sounds as they come into your computer's microphone to get a sense of what louder and softer sounds look like, and what higher- and lower-pitched sounds look like.

You will also find a MediaTools menu in JES. The JES MediaTools also allow you to inspect sounds and pictures but you can't look at sounds in *real time*—as they hit your computer's microphone. You can see sounds in real time in the MediaTools application.

The MediaTools application sound editor looks like that in Figure 6.5. You can record sounds, open WAV files on your disk, and view the sounds in a variety of ways. (Of course, assuming that you have a microphone on your computer!)

To view sounds, click the Record Viewer button, then the RECORD button. (Hit the STOP button to stop recording.) There are three kinds of views that you can make of the sound.

The first is the **signal view** (Figure 6.6). In the signal view, you're looking at raw sound—each increase in air pressure results in a rise in the graph and each decrease in sound pressure results in a drop in the graph. Note how rapidly the wave changes. Try some softer and louder sounds so that you can see how their look changes. You can always get back to the signal view from another view by clicking the SIGNAL button.

FIGURE 6.4
Some synthesizers use triangular (or *sawtooth*) or square waves.

FIGURE 6.5
Sound editor main tool.

FIGURE 6.6
Viewing the sound signal as it comes in.

Spikes

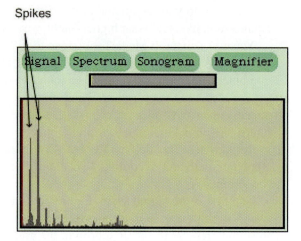

FIGURE 6.7
Viewing a sound in spectrum view with multiple spikes.

The second view is the **spectrum view** (Figure 6.7). The spectrum view is a completely different perspective on the sound. In the preceding section, you read that natural sounds are often actually composed of several different frequencies at once. The spectrum view shows these individual frequencies. This view is also called the *frequency domain*.

Frequencies increase in the spectrum view from left to right. The height of a column indicates the amount of energy (roughly, the volume) of that frequency in the sound. Natural sounds look like Figure 6.7 with more than one *spike* (rise in the graph). (The smaller rises around a spike are often seen as *noise*.)

The technical term for how a spectrum view is generated is called a **Fourier transform**. A Fourier transform takes the sound from the *time domain* (rises and falls in the sound over time) into the frequency domain (identifying which frequencies are in a sound, and the energy of those frequencies, over time). Frequencies increase in this view from left to right (leftmost are lower, rightmost are higher), and more energy at that frequency results in a taller spike.

The third view is the *sonogram view* (Figure 6.8). The sonogram view is very much like the spectrum view in that it describes the frequency domain but it presents these frequencies over time. Each column in the sonogram view, sometimes called a *slice* or *window (of time)*, represents all the frequencies at a given moment in time. The frequencies increase in the slice from lower (bottom) to higher (top). So, Figure 6.8 represents a sound that started off low and then got higher and then went lower again. The *darkness* of the spot in the column indicates the amount of energy of that frequency in the input sound at the given moment. The sonogram view is great for studying how sounds change over time (e.g., how the sound of a piano key being struck changes as the note fades, or how different instruments differ in their sounds, or how different vocal sounds differ).

FIGURE 6.8
Viewing the sound signal in a sonogram view.

Making It Work Tip: Explore Sounds!
You really should try these different views on real sounds. You'll get a much better understanding of sound and of what the manipulations we're doing in this chapter are doing to the sounds.

6.1.3   Encoding the Sound

You just read about how sounds work physically and how we perceive them. To manipulate sounds on a computer and play them back on a computer, we have to digitize them. To digitize sound means to take this flow of waves and turn it into numbers. We want to be able to capture a sound, perhaps manipulate it, and then play it back (through the computer's speakers) and hear what we captured as exactly as possible.

The first part of the process of digitizing sound is handled by the computer's hardware, the physical machinery of the computer. If a computer has a microphone and appropriate sound equipment (like a SoundBlaster sound card on Windows computers), then it's possible, at any moment, to measure the amount of air pressure against the microphone as a single number. Positive numbers correspond to rises in pressure, and negative numbers correspond to rarefactions. We call this an *analog-to-digital conversion (ADC)*—we've moved from an analog signal (a continuously changing sound wave) to a digital value. This means that we can get an instantaneous measure of the sound pressure, but it's only one step along the way. Sound is a continuously changing pressure wave. How do we store that in our computer?

FIGURE 6.9
Area under a curve estimated with rectangles.

By the way, playback systems on computers work essentially the same in reverse. Sound hardware does *digital-to-analog conversion (DAC)*, and the analog signal is then sent to the speakers. The DAC process also requires numbers representing pressure.

If you know calculus, you have some idea of how we might do this. You know that we can get close to measuring the area under a curve with more and more rectangles whose height matches the curve (Figure 6.9). With this idea, it's pretty clear that if we capture enough of those microphone pressure readings, we capture the wave. We call each pressure reading a *sample*—we are literally "sampling" the sound at that moment. But how many samples do we need? In integral calculus, you compute the area under the curve by (conceptually) having an infinite number of rectangles. While computer memories are growing larger and larger all the time, we can't capture an infinite number of samples per sound.

Mathematicians and physicists wondered about these kinds of questions long before there were computers and the answer to how many samples we need was actually computed long ago. The answer depends on the highest *frequency* you want to capture. Let's say that you don't care about any sounds higher than 8000 Hz. The **Nyquist theorem** says that we would need to capture 16,000 samples per second to completely capture and define a wave whose frequency is less than 8000 cycles per second.

Computer Science Idea: Nyquist Theorem

To capture a sound of at most *n* cycles per second, you need to capture 2*n* samples per second.

This isn't just a theoretical result. The Nyquist theorem influences applications in our daily life. It turns out that human voices don't typically get over 4000 Hz. That's why our telephone system is designed around capturing 8000 samples per second. That's why playing music through the telephone doesn't really work very well. The limit of (most) human hearing is around 22,000 Hz. If we were to capture 44,000 samples per second, we would be able to capture any sound that we could actually hear. CD's are created by capturing sound at 44,100 samples per second—just a little bit more than 44 kHz for technical reasons and for a fudge factor.

We call the rate at which samples are collected the *sampling rate*. Most sounds that we hear in daily life are at frequencies far below the limits of our hearing. You can capture and manipulate sounds in this class at a sampling rate of 22 kHz (22,000 samples per second) and they will sound quite reasonable. If you use too low a sampling rate to capture a high-pitched sound, you'll still hear something when you play the sound back, but the pitch will sound strange.

Typically, each of these samples are encoded in 2 bytes, or 16 bits. Though there are larger *sample size*, 16 bits works perfectly well for most applications. CD-quality sound uses 16-bit samples.

6.1.4   Binary Numbers and Two's Complement

In 16 bits, the numbers that can be encoded range from $-32,768$ to $32,767$. These aren't magic numbers—they make perfect sense when you understand the encoding. These numbers are encoded in 16 bits using a technique called **two's complement notation** but we can understand it without knowing the details of that technique. We've got 16 bits to represent positive and negative numbers. Let's set aside one of these bits (remember, it's just 0 or 1) to represent whether we're talking about a positive (0) or negative (1) number. We call this the *sign bit*. That leaves 15 bits to represent the actual value. How many different patterns of 15 bits are there? We could start counting:

```
000000000000000
000000000000001
000000000000010
000000000000011
. . .
111111111111110
111111111111111
```

This looks foreboding. Let's see if we can figure out a pattern. If we've got two bits, there are four patterns: 00, 01, 10, 11. If we've got three bits, there are eight patterns: 000, 001, 010, 011, 100, 101, 110, 111. It turns out that 2^2 is four, and 2^3 is eight. Play with four bits. How many patterns are there? $2^4 = 16$. It turns out that we can state this as a general principle.

Computer Science Idea: 2^n Patterns in *n* Bits

If you have *n* bits, there are 2^n possible patterns in those *n* bits.   ■

$2^{15} = 32,768$. Why is there one more value in the negative range than the positive? Zero is neither negative nor positive, but if we want to represent it as bits, we need to define some pattern as zero. We use one of the positive range values (where the sign bit is zero) to represent zero, so that it takes up one of the 32,768 patterns.

The way that computers often represent positive and negative integers is called *two's complement*. In two's complement, positive numbers are shown as usual in binary. The number 9 is 00001001 in binary. The two's complement of a negative number can be calculated by starting with the positive number in binary and inverting it so that all the

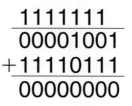

FIGURE 6.10
Adding 9 and −9 in two's complement.

1's become 0's and all the 0's become 1's. Finally, add 1 to the result. So −9 starts as 00001001 which after inversion is 11110110 and then adding 1 results in 11110111. One advantage to representing numbers in two's complement is that if you add a negative number (−3) to the positive number of the same value (3), the result is zero, since 1 plus 1 is 0, carry the 1 (Figure 6.10).

6.1.5 Storing Digitized Sounds

The sample size is a limitation on the amplitude of the sound that can be captured. If you have a sound that generates a pressure greater than 32,767 (or a rarefaction greater than −32,768), you'll only capture up to the limits of the 16 bits. If you were to look at the wave in the signal view, it would look like somebody had taken some scissors and *clipped* off the peaks of the waves. We call this effect *clipping* for that very reason. If you play (or generate) a sound that's clipped, it sounds bad—it sounds like your speakers are breaking.

There are other ways of digitizing sound but this is by far the most common. The technical term for this way of encoding sound is *pulse coded modulation (PCM)*. You may encounter this term if you read further in audio or play with audio software.

What this means is that a sound in a computer is a long list of numbers, each of which is a sample in time. There is an ordering in these samples: if you played the samples out of order, you wouldn't get the same sound at all. The most efficient way to store an ordered list of data items on a computer is with an **array**. An array is literally a sequence of bytes right next to one another in memory. We call each value in an array an **element**.

We can easily store the samples that make up a sound in an array. Think of each two bytes as storing a single sample. The array will be large—for CD-quality sounds, there will be 44,100 elements for every second of recording. A minute-long recording will result in an array with 26,460,000 elements.

Each array element has a number associated with it called its **index.** The index numbers increase sequentially. The first element of the array is at index 0, the second one is at index 1, and so on. The last element in the array is at an index equal to the number of elements in the array minus 1. You can think about an array as a long line of boxes, each one holding a value and each box having an index number (Figure 6.11).

Using the MediaTools, you can explore a sound (Figure 6.12) and get a sense of where the sound is quiet (small amplitudes) and loud (large amplitudes). This is important if you want to manipulate the sound. For example, the gaps between recorded words tend to be quiet—at least quieter than the words themselves. You can pick out where words end by looking for the gaps, as in Figure 6.12.

59	39	16	10	-1

0   1   2   3   4

FIGURE 6.11
A depiction of the first five elements in a real sound array.

FIGURE 6.12
A sound recording graphed in MediaTools.

You will soon read about how to read a file containing a recording of a sound into a *sound object*, view the samples in the sound, and change the values of the sound array elements. By changing the values in the array, you change the sound. Manipulating a sound is simply a matter of manipulating the elements in an array.

6.2 MANIPULATING SOUNDS

Now that we know how sounds are encoded, we can manipulate sounds using our Python programs. Here's what we'll need to do.

1. We'll need to get the filename of a WAV file and make a sound from it.

2. You will often get the samples of the sound. Sample objects are easy to manipulate, and they know that when you change them, they should automatically change the original sound. You'll read first about manipulating the samples to start with, then about how to manipulate the sound samples from within the sound itself.

3. Whether you get the sample objects out of a sound or just deal with the samples in the sound object, you will then want to do something to the samples.

4. You may want to explore both the original sound and the modified sound to check that the results match what you expected to happen.

5. You may want to write the sound back out to a new file for use elsewhere.

6.2.1 Open Sounds and Manipulating Samples

You can get the full pathname for a file by picking it with pickAFile and then make a sound object with makeSound. Here's an example of doing that in JES.

```
>>> filename=pickAFile()
>>> print filename
C:/ip-book/mediasources/preamble.wav
>>> aSound=makeSound(filename)
>>> print aSound
Sound file: C:\ip-book\mediasources\preamble.wav
    number of samples: 421110
```

What makeSound does is to scoop up all the bytes from the filename provided as input, dump them into memory, and place a big sign on them saying, "This is a sound!" When you execute aSound = makeSound(filename), you are saying, "Call that sound object over there aSound!" When you use the sound as input to functions, you are saying "Use that sound object over there (yeah, the one I named aSound) as input to this function."

You can get the samples from a sound using getSamples. The function getSamples takes a sound as input and returns an array of all the samples as sample objects. When you execute this function, it may take quite a while before it finishes—longer for longer sounds, shorter for shorter sounds.

The function getSamples makes an array of sample *objects* out of the basic sample array. An *object* is more than just a simple value like you read about earlier—for one difference, a sample object also knows what sound it came from and what its index is. You will read more about objects later but take it at face value now that getSamples provides you with a bunch of sample objects that you can manipulate—and in fact makes manipulation pretty easy. You can get the value of a sample object by using getSampleValue (with a sample object as input) and you set the sample value with setSampleValue (with a sample object and a new value as input).

But before we get to the manipulations, let's look at some other ways to get and set sample values. We can use the function getSampleValueAt to ask the sound to give us the values of specific samples at specific indices. The input values to getSampleValueAt are a sound and an index number.

```
>>> print getSampleValueAt(sound,0)
36
>>> print getSampleValueAt(sound,1)
29
```

Valid index values are any integer (0.1289 is not a good index value) between 0 and one less than the length of the sound in samples. We get the length with getLength(). Note the error that we get below if we try to get a sample past the end of the array.

```
>>> print getLength(sound)
421110
>>> print getSampleValueAt(sound,421110)
You are trying to access the sample at index: 421110,
but the last valid index is at 421109
The error was:
Inappropriate argument value (of correct type).
An error occurred attempting to pass an argument
to a function.
```

Debugging Tip: Getting More Information on Errors

If you're getting an error and want more information on it, go to the OPTIONS item in the EDIT menu of JES and choose EXPERT instead of NORMAL (Figure 6.13). Expert mode can sometimes give you more details—maybe more than you wanted, and probably more than once, but it can be helpful sometimes.

We can similarly change sample values by using setSampleValueAt. It takes a sound, an index, but also a new value for the sample at that index. We can check it again with getSampleValueAt.

```
>>> print getSampleValueAt(sound,0)
36
>>> setSampleValueAt(sound,0,12)
>>> print getSampleValueAt(sound,0)
12
```

FIGURE 6.13
Turning on Expert errors mode.

Common Bug: Mistyping a Name

You just saw a whole bunch of function names and some of them are pretty long. What happens if you type one of them wrong? JES will complain that it doesn't know what you mean, like this:

```
>>> writeSndTo(sound,"mysound.wav")
Name not found globally.
A local or global name could not be found. You need to
define the function or variable before you try to use
it in any way.
```

It's no big deal. Use the up arrow key on the keyboard to bring up the last thing you typed and use the left arrow to go to the spot to fix. Fix the error. Be sure to go back to the last character on the line using the right arrow key before you press enter.

What do you think would happen if we played this sound? Would it really sound different than it did before, now that we've turned the first sample from the number 36 to the number 12? Not really. To explain why not, let's find out what the sampling rate is for this sound, using the function `getSamplingRate`, which takes a sound as its input.

```
>>> print getSamplingRate(sound)
22050.0
```

The sound that we're manipulating in this example (a recording of Mark reading part of the U.S. Constitution's preamble) has a sampling rate of 22,050 samples per second. Changing one sample changes 1/22,050 of the first second of the sound. If you can hear that, you have amazingly good hearing—and we will have doubts about your truthfulness!

Obviously, to make a significant manipulation to the sound, we have to manipulate hundreds if not thousands of samples. We're certainly not going to do that by typing thousands of lines of

```
setSampleValueAt(sound,0,12)
setSampleValueAt(sound,1,24)
setSampleValueAt(sound,2,100)
setSampleValueAt(sound,3,99)
setSampleValueAt(sound,4,-1)
```

We need to take advantage of the computer executing our recipe, by telling it to go do something hundreds or thousands of times. That's the topic for the next section.

But we will end this section by talking about how to write your results back out to a file. Once you've manipulated your sound and want to save it out to use elsewhere, you use `writeSoundTo`, which takes a sound and a new filename as input. Be sure that your file ends with the extension ".wav" if you're saving a sound so that your operating system knows what to do with it.

```
>>> print filename
C:/ip-book/mediasources/preamble.wav
>>> writeSoundTo(sound,"C:/ip-book/mediasources/new-preamble.wav")
```

You'll probably figure out, when playing sounds a lot, that if you use `play` a couple of times in quick succession, you'll mix the sounds. The second `play` starts before the first one ends. How do you make sure that the computer plays only a single sound and then waits for it to end? You use `blockingPlay`. This works the same as `play` but it waits for the sound to end so that no other sound can interfere while it's playing.

6.2.2   Using the JES MediaTools

The JES MediaTools are available from the MEDIATOOLS menu in JES. When you choose the picture or sound tool, you will be offered a pop-up menu of *variable* names of pictures or sounds, appropriate to whichever tool you chose (Figure 6.14). Click OK and you'll enter the JES sound tool. You can also bring up the sound tool by exploring the sound, just like you did with pictures.

```
>>> explore(sound)
```

The sound tool lets you explore a sound.

- You can play the sound, then click anywhere in it to set a cursor point, then play it before or after the cursor.
- You can select a region (by clicking and dragging) and then play only that region (Figure 6.15).
- As you set a cursor, you're shown the sample index and sample value at that point.
- You can also zoom in to see every sound value (Figure 6.16); you will have to scroll to see all the values.

FIGURE 6.14
Exploring a sound in JES.

FIGURE 6.15
Exploring a sound in JES.

FIGURE 6.16
Zooming in to see every sound value.

Common Bug: Windows and WAV Files

The world of WAV files isn't as compatible and smooth as one might like. WAV files created with other applications (e.g., Windows Recorder) *may* not play in JES and JES WAV files may not play in all other applications (e.g., WinAmp 2). Apple QuickTime Player Pro (http://www.apple.com/quicktime) is good at reading *any* WAV file and exporting a new one that almost any other application can read.

6.2.3   Looping

The problem we're facing is a common one in computing: How do we get the computer to do something over and over again? We need to get the computer to **loop or iterate**. Python has commands especially for looping (or iterating). We're mostly going to use the command `for`. A `for` loop executes commands (that you specify) for a sequence (that you provide), where each time the commands are executed, a particular variable (that you name) will have the value of a different element of the sequence.

6.3   CHANGING THE VOLUME OF SOUNDS

Earlier, we said that the amplitude of a sound is the main factor in the volume. This means that if we increase the amplitude, we increase the volume. Or if we decrease the amplitude, we decrease the volume.

Don't get confused here—changing the amplitude doesn't reach out and twist up the volume knob on your speakers. If your speaker's volume (or computer's volume) is turned down, the sound will never get very loud. The point is getting the sound itself louder. Have you ever watched a movie on TV where, without changing the volume on the TV, the sound becomes so low that you can hardly hear it? (Marlon Brando's dialogue in the movie *The Godfather* comes to mind.) Or have you noticed how commercials are always louder than normal TV programs? That's what we're doing here. We can make sounds *shout* or *whisper* by tweaking the amplitude.

6.3.1   Increasing Volume

Let's increase the volume of a sound by doubling the value for each sample in the sound. We can use `getSamples` to get a sequence (array) of the samples in a sound. We can use a `for` loop to loop through all the samples in the sequence. For each sample, we will get the current value and then set it to the current value times 2.

Here's a function that doubles the amplitude of an input sound.

Program 54: Increase an Input Sound's Volume by Doubling the Amplitude

```
def increaseVolume(sound):
  for sample in getSamples(sound):
    value = getSampleValue(sample)
    setSampleValue(sample, value * 2)
```

Go ahead and type the above into your JES Program Area. Click LOAD PROGRAM to get Python to process the function and to allow us to use the name `increaseVolume`. Follow along the example below to get a better idea of how this all works.

To use this recipe, you have to create a sound first, then pass the sound to the function `increaseVolume` as input. In the example below, we get the filename by setting the variable f explicitly to a string that is a filename, as opposed to using `pickAFile`. Don't forget that you can't type this code in and have it work as-is: your pathnames will be different from mine.

```
>>> f="C:/ip-book/mediasources/test.wav"
>>> s=makeSound(f)
>>> explore(s)
>>> increaseVolume(s)
>>> explore(s)
```

We create a sound that we name s. We then explore the sound which will bring up the JES sound tool on a copy of the sound. Next we evaluate increaseVolume(s), the sound that is named s is *also* named sound but just within that function. This is a *very* important point. Both names refer to the same sound! The changes that take place in increaseVolume are really changing the *same* sound. You can think of each name as an *alias* for the other: they refer to the same *thing*.

There's a side point to mention here just in passing, but it becomes more important later: when the function increaseVolume ends, the name sound *has no value*. It only exists during the duration of that function's execution. We say that it only exists within the *scope* of the function increaseVolume. The scope of a variable is the area in which it is known. Variables that are defined in the command area have command area scope. They are only known in the command area. Variables that are defined in a function have function scope. They are only known in that function.

We can now play the file to hear that it's louder and write it to a new file.

```
>>> play(s)
>>> writeSoundTo(s,"c:/ip-book/mediasources/test-louder.wav")
```

Common Bug: Keep Sounds Short

Longer sounds take up more memory and will process more slowly.

6.3.2   Did That Really Work?

Now, is it really louder, or does it just seem that way? We can check this in several ways. You could always make the sound even louder by evaluating increaseVolume on our sound a few more times—eventually, you'll be totally convinced that the sound is louder. But there are ways to test even more subtle effects.

If we compared graphs of the two sounds using the JES MediaTools sound tool, you'd find that the graph of the sound does have greater amplitude after increasing it using our function. Check it out in Figure 6.17.

Maybe you're unsure that you're really seeing a larger wave in the second picture. You can use the JES sound tool to check the individual sample values. Click on a part of the wave that has a value other than 0 in one sound tool and then enter the index in the other sound tool and press enter. Compare the sample values. Notice in Figure 6.17 that the value at index 18375 was −1290 originally and after the volume was increased it is −2580, so the function did double the value.

Finally, you can always check for yourself from within JES. If you've been following along with the example,[1] then the variable s is now the louder sound. f should still be

---

[1] What? You haven't? You *should!* It'll make much more sense if you try it yourself.

FIGURE 6.17
Comparing the graphs of the original sound (*left*) and the louder one (*right*).

the filename of the original sound. Go ahead and make a new sound object which is the *original* sound—named below as sOriginal (for *sound original*). Check any sample value that you want. It's always true that the louder sound has twice the sample values of the original sound.

```
>>> print s
Sound file: C:/ip-book/mediasources/test.wav
    number of samples: 67585
>>> print f
C:/ip-book/mediasources/test.wav
>>> sOriginal=makeSound(f)
>>> print getSampleValueAt(s,0)
0
>>> print getSampleValueAt(sOriginal,0)
0
>>> print getSampleValueAt(s,18375)
-2580
>>> print getSampleValueAt(sOriginal,18375)
-1290
>>> print getSampleValueAt(s,1000)
4
>>> print getSampleValueAt(sOriginal,1000)
2
```

You can see that negative values become *more* negative. That's what's meant by "increasing the amplitude." The amplitude of the wave goes in *both* directions. We have to make the wave larger in both the positive and negative dimensions.

It's important to do what you just read in this chapter: *doubt* your programs. Did that *really* do what I wanted it to do? The way you check is by *testing*. That's what this section is about. You just saw several ways to test:

- By checking pieces of the results (using the JES sound tool).
- By writing additional code statements that check the results of the original program.

Figuring Out How It Worked

Let's walk through the code, slowly, and consider how this program works.

```
def increaseVolume(sound):
    for sample in getSamples(sound):
        value = getSampleValue(sample)
        setSampleValue(sample,value * 2)
```

Recall our picture of how the samples in a sound array might look. This shows the first values in the sound created from the file `gettysburg.wav`.

This is what `getSamples(sound)` would return: an array of sample values, each numbered. The `for` loop allows us to walk through each sample, one at a time. The name `sample` will be assigned to each sample in turn.

When the `for` loop begins, `sample` will be the name for the first sample.

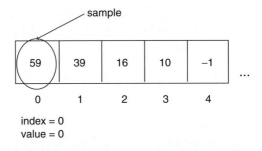

The variable `value` will take on the value of 59 when `value=getSampleValue-(sample)` is executed. The sample that the name `sample` references will then be doubled with `setSampleValue(sample,value*2)`.

That's the end of the first pass through the body of the `for` loop. Python will then start the loop again and move `sample` on to point at the *next* element in the array.

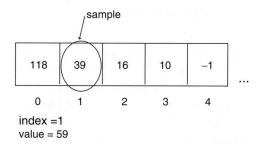

index =1
value = 59

The value is again set to the value of the sample, then the sample will be doubled.

index =1
value = 39

This is what it will look like after five times through the loop.

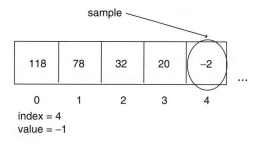

index = 4
value = −1

The for loop *keeps* going through all the samples—tens of thousands of them! Thank goodness it's the *computer* executing this recipe!

One way to think about what's happening here is that the for loop doesn't really *do* anything, in the sense of changing anything in the sound. Only the *body* of the loop does work. The for loop tells the computer *what* to do. It's a manager. What the computer actually does is something like this:

```
sample = sample #0
value = value of the sample, 59
change sample to 118
sample = sample #1
value = 39
change sample to 78
sample = sample #2
...
sample = sample #4
value = -1
```

```
change sample to -2
...
```

The for loop is only saying, "Do all of this for every element in the array." It's the *body* of the loop that contains the Python commands that are executed.

What you have just read in this section is called **tracing** the program. We slowly went through how each step in the program was executed. We drew pictures to describe the data in the program. We used numbers, arrows, equations, and even plain English to explain what was going on in the program. This is the single most important technique in programming. It's part of *debugging*. Your program will *not* always work. Absolutely, guaranteed, without a shadow of a doubt—you will write code that does not do what you want. But the computer *will* do *something*. How do you figure out what it *is* doing? You debug, and the most powerful way to do that is by tracing the program.

6.3.3 Decreasing Volume

Decreasing volume is the reverse of the process described above.

Program 55: Decrease an Input Sound's Volume by Halving the Amplitude
```
def decreaseVolume(sound):
  for sample in getSamples(sound):
    value = getSampleValue(sample)
    setSampleValue(sample,value * 0.5)
```

How It Works

- Our function takes a sound object as input. Within the function decreaseVolume, the input sound will be called sound—no matter what name it has in the Command Area.
- The variable sample will stand for each and every sample in the input sound.
- Each time sample is assigned a new sample, we will get the *value* of the sample. We put it in the variable value.
- We then set the sample value to 50% of its current value by multiplying value by 0.5, and setting the sample value to that.

We can use it like this.

```
>>> f=pickAFile()
>>> print f
C:/ip-book/mediasources/louder-test.wav
>>> sound=makeSound(f)
>>> explore(sound)
>>> play(sound)
>>> decreaseVolume(sound)
>>> explore(sound)
>>> play(sound)
```

We can even do it again, and lower the volume even further.

```
>>> decreaseVolume(sound)
>>> explore(sound)
>>> play(sound)
```

6.3.4   Making Sense of Functions, in Sounds

The lessons about how functions work in pictures (from Section 3.4.1) apply here in sounds as well. For example, we could put all the `pickAFile` and `makeSound` calls directly into our functions like `increaseVolume` and `decreaseVolume` but that would mean that the functions are doing more than *one and only one thing*. If we had to increase or decrease the volume to a bunch of sounds, we'd find it annoying to have to keep picking files.

We can write functions that take multiple inputs. For example, here's a recipe to `changeVolume`. It accepts a `factor` that is multiplied by each sample value. This function can be used to increase or decrease the amplitude (and thus, the volume).

Program 56: Change a Sound's Volume by a Given Factor

```
def changeVolume(sound, factor):
  for sample in getSamples(sound):
    value = getSampleValue(sample)
    setSampleValue(sample,value * factor)
```

This recipe is clearly more flexible than `increaseVolume` or `decreaseVolume`. Does that make it better? Certainly it is for some purposes (e.g., if you were writing software to do general audio processing), but for other purposes, having separate and clearly named functions for increasing and decreasing volume is better. Remember that software is written for humans—write software that is understandable for the people who will be reading and using your software.

We are reusing the name `sound` a lot. We use it to name sounds that we read from disk in the Command Area and we're using it to serve as a placeholder for inputs to functions. *That's okay.* Names can have different meanings depending on the context. Inside a function is a different context than the Command Area. If you create a variable in a function context (like `value` in Recipe 56), then that variable won't exist when you get back out to the Command Area. We can return values from a function context back out to the Command Area (or other calling function) by using `return`, which we'll talk more about later.

6.4   NORMALIZING SOUNDS

If you think about it, you may find it strange that the last two recipes work. We can multiply the numbers representing a sound—and the sound will seem (essentially) the same to our ears but louder. The way we experience a sound depends less on the specific numbers than on the *relationship* between them. Remember that the overall shape of the sound waveform is dependent on *many* samples. In general, if we multiply all the samples by the same multiplier, we only affect our sense of volume (intensity), not the sound itself. (We'll work to change the sound itself in future sections.)

A common operation that people want to do with sounds is to make them as **loud as possible**. This is called **normalizing**. It's not really hard to do but it takes a few more variables. Here's the recipe, in English, that we need to tell the computer to do.

- We have to figure out what the largest sample in the sound is. If it's already at the maximum value (32,767), then we can't really increase the volume and still get what seems like the same sound. Remember that we have to multiply all the samples by the same multiplier.

  It's an easy recipe (*algorithm*) to find the largest value—sort of a *subrecipe* within the overall normalizing recipe. Define a name (say, `largest`) and assign it a small value (0 works). Now check all the samples. If you find a sample larger than `largest`, change `largest` to have that larger value. Keep checking the samples, now comparing to the *new* largest. Eventually, the very largest value in the array will be in the variable `largest`.

  To do this, we'll need a way of figuring out the maximum value of two values. Python provides a built-in function called `max` that can do this.

  ```
  >>> print max(8,9)
  9
  >>> print max(3,4,5)
  5
  ```

- Next we need to figure out what value to multiply all the samples by. We want the largest value to become 32,767. Thus we want to figure out a *multiplier* such that (*multiplier*)(*largest*) = 32767.

  Solve for the multiplier:

  multiplier = 32767/*largest*. The multiplier will need to be a floating-point number (have a decimal component), so we need to convince Python that not everything here is an integer. Turns out that that's easy—use 32767.0. Simply stick on ".0".

- Now loop through all the samples, as we did for `increaseVolume`, and multiply the sample by the multiplier.

  Here's a recipe to normalize sounds.

Program 57: Normalize the Sound to a Maximum Amplitude

```
def normalize(sound):
    largest = 0
    for s in getSamples(sound):
        largest = max(largest,getSampleValue(s) )
    multiplier = 32767.0 / largest
    print "Largest sample value in original sound was",largest
    print "Multiplier is", multiplier

    for s in getSamples(sound):
        louder =  multiplier * getSampleValue(s)
        setSampleValue(s,louder)
```

There are several things to note about this program.

- There are blank lines in there! Python doesn't care about them. Adding blank lines can be useful to break up and improve the understandability of longer programs.

- There are `print` statements in there! `print` statements can be *really* useful. First, they give you some feedback that the program is running—a useful thing in long-running programs. Second, they show you what it's finding, which can be interesting. Third, it's a terrific testing method and a way to debug your programs. Let's imagine that the printout showed that the multiplier was less than 1.0. We know that this kind of multiplier *decreases* volume. You should probably suspect that something went wrong.

- Some of the statements in this recipe are pretty long, so they wrap around in the text. *Type them as a single line!* Python doesn't let you hit ENTER until the end of the statement—make sure that your print statements are all on one line.

Here's what the program looks like running.

```
>>> f = "c:/ip-book/mediasources/test.wav"
>>> s = makeSound(f)
>>> explore(s)
>>> normalize(sound)
Largest sample value in original sound was 11702
Multiplier is 2.8001196376687747
>>> explore(s)
>>> play(sound)
```

Exciting, huh? Obviously, the interesting part is hearing the much louder volume, which is awfully hard to demonstrate in a book.

6.4.1   Generating Clipping

Earlier, we talked about *clipping*, the effect when the normal curves of the sound are broken by the limitations of the sample size. One way of generating clipping is to keep increasing the volume. Another way is to explicitly force clipping.

What if you *only* had the largest and smallest possible sample values? What if all the positive values were the *maximum* values and all the negative values were the minimum values? Try this recipe, particularly on sounds with words in them.

Program 58: Set All Samples to Maximum Values

```
def onlyMaximize(sound):
  for sample in getSamples(sound):
    value = getSampleValue(sample)
    if value >= 0:
      setSampleValue(sample,32767)
    if value < 0:
      setSampleValue(sample,-32768)
```

The end result looks really strange (Figure 6.18). When you play the sound back, you'll hear some awful noises. That's clipping. The really amazing thing is that you

FIGURE 6.18
Original sound and the one with only maximum values.

can *still* make out the words in the sounds that you manipulate with this function. Our ability to decipher words from noise is incredibly powerful.

PROGRAMMING SUMMARY

In this chapter, we talk about several kinds of encodings of data (or objects).

Sounds	Encodings of sounds, typically coming from a WAV file.
Samples	Collections of sample objects, each indexed by a number (e.g., sample #0, sample #1). samples[0] is the first sample object. You can manipulate each sample in the samples like this: for s in samples:.
Sample	A value between −32,000 and 32,000 (roughly) representing the voltage that a microphone would generate at a given instant when recording a sound. The length of the instant is typically either 1/44,100 of a second (for CD-quality sound) or 1/22,050 of a second (for good-enough sound on most computers). A sample object remembers what sound it came from, so if you change its value, it knows to go back and change the right sample in the sound.

Here are the functions used or introduced in this chapter:

int	Returns the integer part of the input value.
max	Takes as many numbers as you want and returns the largest value.

SOUND FILE FUNCTIONS AND PIECES

pickAFile	Lets the user pick a file and returns the complete pathname as a string. No input.
makeSound	Takes a filename as input, reads the file, and creates a sound from it. Returns the sound.

SOUND OBJECT FUNCTIONS AND PIECES

`play`	Plays a sound provided as input. No return value.
`getLength`	Takes a sound as input and returns the number of samples in the sound.
`getSamples`	Takes a sound as input and returns the samples in the sound in a one-dimensional array.
`blockingPlay`	Plays the sound provided as input and makes sure that no other sound plays at the exact same time. (Try two `play`'s right after each other.)
`playAtRate`	Takes a sound and a rate (1.0 means normal speed, 2.0 is twice as fast, and 0.5 is half as fast) and plays the sound at that rate. The duration is always *the same* (e.g., if you play it twice as fast, the sound plays *twice* to fill the given time).
`playAtRateDur`	Takes a sound, a rate, and a duration as the number of samples to play.
`writeSoundTo`	Takes a sound and a filename (a string) and writes the sound to the file as a WAV file. (Make sure that the filename ends in ".wav" if you want the operating system to treat it right.)
`getSamplingRate`	Takes a sound as input and returns the number representing the number of samples in each second for the sound.
`getLength`	Returns the length of the sound as a number of samples.

SAMPLE-ORIENTED FUNCTIONS AND PIECES

`getSampleValueAt`	Takes a sound and an index (an integer value) and returns the value of the sample (between −32,000 and 32,000) for that object.
`setSampleValueAt`	Takes a sound, an index, and a value (should be between −32,000 and 32,000) and sets the value of the sample at the given index in the given sound to the given value.
`getSampleObjectAt`	Takes a sound and an index (an integer value) and returns the sample object at that index.
`getSampleValue`	Takes a sample object and returns its value (between −32,000 and 32,000). `getSampleValue` will also work.
`setSampleValue`	Takes a sample object and a value and sets the sample to the value. `setSampleValue` will also work.
`getSound`	Takes a sample object and returns the sound that it is part of.

PROBLEMS

6.1 What are each of the following:

1. Clipping

2. Normalize

3. Amplitude

4. Frequency

5. Rarefactions

6.2 Write the number −9 in two's complement. Write the number 4 in two's complement. Write the number −27 in two's complement.

6.3 Open up the SONOGRAM view and say some vowel sounds. Is there a distinctive pattern? Do "oh's" always sound the same? Do "ah's"? Does it matter whether you switch people: Are the patterns the same?

6.4 Get a couple of different instruments and play the same note on them in the MediaTools application's sound editor with the sonogram view open. Are all "C's" made equal? Using the MediaTools visualization, can you *see* the differences between the sounds?

6.5 Try out a variety of WAV files as instruments, using the piano keyboard in the MediaTools application sound editor. What kinds of recordings work best as instruments?

6.6 The increase volume recipe (Program 54 (page 155)) takes a sound as input. Write a function `increaseVolumeNamed` that takes a filename as input, then `plays` the louder sound.

6.7 Write a function to increase the volume for all the positive values and decrease the volume for all the negative values. Can you still understand any words in the sound?

6.8 Write a function to find the smallest value in a sound and print it out.

6.9 Write a function to count the number of times the value in a sound is 0 and print out the total.

6.10 Write a function to set values that are greater than 0 to the maximum positive value (32767) in a sound.

6.11 Rewrite increase volume (Program 54 (page 155)) so that it takes two inputs: the sound to increase in volume and a filename where the newly louder sound should be stored. Then increase the volume and write the sound out to the name file. You might also try rewriting it so that it takes an input filename instead of the sound, so that inputs are both filenames.

6.12 Rewrite increase volume (Program 54 (page 155)) so that it takes two inputs: a sound to increase in volume and a *multiplier*. Use the multiplier as *how much* to increase the amplitude of the sound samples. Can we use the same function to both increase and decrease the volume? Demonstrate commands that you would execute to do each.

6.13 In Section 6.3.2, we walked through how Program 54 (page 155) worked. Draw the pictures to show how Program 55 (page 160) works in the same way.

6.14 What happens if you increase a volume too far? Explore this by creating a sound object, then increasing the volume once, and again, and again. Does it always keep getting louder? Or does something else happen? Can you explain why?

6.15 Try sprinkling in some specific values into your sounds. What happens if you set the value of a few hundred samples in the middle of a sound to 32,767? Or a few hundred to −32,768? Or a bunch of zeroes? What happens to the sound?

6.16 Instead of multiplying samples by a multiplier (like 2 or 0.5), try *adding* a value to them. What happens to a sound if you add 100 to every sample? 1000?

TO DIG DEEPER

There are many wonderful books on psychoacoustics and computer music. One of Mark's favorites for understandability is *Computer Music: Synthesis, Composition, and Performance* by Dodge and Jerse [11]. The *"bible"* of computer music is Curtis Roads' massive *The Computer Music Tutorial* [35].

When you are using the MediaTools application, you are actually using a programming language called *Squeak*, developed initially and primarily by Alan Kay, Dan Ingalls, Ted Kaehler, John Maloney, and Scott Wallace [25]. Squeak is now open-source[2] and is an excellent cross-platform multimedia tool. There is a book that introduces Squeak including its sound capabilities [19] and another book on Squeak [20] that includes a chapter on *Siren*, a variation of Squeak by Stephen Pope especially designed for computer music exploration and composition.

[2]http://www.squeak.org

CHAPTER 7

Modifying Samples in a Range

Chapter Learning Objectives

The media learning goals for this chapter are:

- To splice sounds together to make sound compositions.
- To reverse sounds.
- To mirror sounds.

The computer science goals for this chapter are:

- To iterate an index variable for an array across a range.
- To use comments in programs and understand why.
- To identify some algorithms that cross media boundaries.

7.1 MANIPULATING DIFFERENT SECTIONS OF THE SOUND DIFFERENTLY

In the last chapter we described some useful things to do to sounds overall but really interesting effects come from chopping up sounds and manipulating each piece differently: some words this way, other sounds that way. How would you do that? We need to be able to loop through *portions* of the sample, without walking through the whole thing. Turns out to be an easy thing to do, but we need to manipulate samples somewhat differently (e.g., we have to use index numbers), and we have to use our for loop in a slightly different way.

Recall that each sample has a number and that we can get each individual sample with getSampleValueAt (with a sound and an index number as input). We can set any sample with setSampleValueAt (with inputs of a sound, an index number, and a new value). That's how we can manipulate samples without using getSamples and sample objects. But we still don't want to have to write code like:

```
setSampleValueAt(sound,1,12)
setSampleValueAt(sound,2,28) ...
```

Not for tens of thousands of samples!

Using `range`, we can do everything that we were doing with `getSamples`, but now directly referencing the index numbers. Here's Program 59 (page 169) written using `range`.

Program 59: Increase an Input Sound's Volume Using `range`
```
def increaseVolumeByRange(sound):
  for sampleIndex in range(0,getLength(sound)):
    value = getSampleValueAt(sound,sampleIndex)
    setSampleValueAt(sound,sampleIndex,value * 2)
```

Try it—you'll find that it performs just like the previous one.

But now we can do some really fun things with sounds because we can control which samples we're talking to. The next recipe *increases* the sound for the first half of the sound, then *decreases* it in the second half. See if you can trace how it's working.

Program 60: Increase the Volume, Then Decrease It
```
def increaseAndDecrease(sound):
  for sampleIndex in range(0,getLength(sound)/2):
    value = getSampleValueAt(sound,sampleIndex)
    setSampleValueAt(sound,sampleIndex,value * 2)
  for sampleIndex in range(getLength(sound)/2,getLength(sound)):
    value = getSampleValueAt(sound,sampleIndex)
    setSampleValueAt(sound,sampleIndex,value * 0.2)
```

How It Works

There are two loops in `increaseAndDecrease`, each of which deals with one half of the sound.

- The first loop deals with the samples from 0 to halfway through the sound. These samples all get multiplied by 2 to double their amplitude.

- The second loop goes from halfway through to the end of the sound. Here, we multiply each sample by 0.2, thus decreasing the volume by 80%.

Another Way of Writing Array References

It's worth pointing out that in many languages, square brackets (`[ ]`) are standard notation for accessing elements of arrays. It works that way in Python. For any array, `array[index]` returns the index-th element in the array. The number inside the square brackets is always an index variable but it's sometimes referred to as a *subscript* because of the way that mathematicians refer to the *i*-th element of a, e.g., a_i.

Let's do it here with samples to demonstrate.

```
>>> file = "C:/ip-book/mediasources/a.wav"
>>> sound = makeSound(file)
>>> samples = getSamples(sound)
>>> print samples[0]
Sample at 0 with value -90
>>> print samples[1]
Sample at 1 with value -113
>>> print getLength(sound)
9508
>>> samples[9507]
Sample at 9507 with value -147
>>> samples[9508]
The error was: 9508
Sequence index out of range.
The index you're using goes beyond the size of that
data (too low or high).
For instance, maybe you tried to access OurArray[10]
and OurArray only has 5 elements in it.
```

The first element in an array is at index 0. The last element in an array is at the length of the array minus 1.

Let's use range to make an array,[1] then reference it the same way.

```
>>> myArray = range(0,100)
>>> print myArray[0]
0
>>> print myArray[1]
1
>>> print myArray[99]
99
>>> mySecondArray = range(0,100,2)
>>> print mySecondArray[35]
70
```

The code range(0,100) creates an array with 100 elements in it. The first element is at index 0 and the last is at index 99. The array holds all the values from 0 to 99. Remember that when you specify a range using range(begin,end) the begin number is in the returned array but the end number is not.

7.2 SPLICING SOUNDS

Splicing sounds is a term that dates back to when sounds were recorded on tape—juggling the order of things on the tape involved literally cutting the tape into segments and then gluing it back together in the right order. That's "splicing." When everything is digital, it's *much* easier.

---

[1]Technically, a *sequence*, which can be indexed like an array but does not have all the characteristics of an array.

To splice sounds, we simply have to copy elements around in the array. It's easiest to do this with two (or more) arrays, rather than copy within the same array. If you copy all the samples that represent someone saying the word "the" up to the beginning of a sound (starting at index number 0), then you make the sound start with the word "the." Splicing lets you create all kinds of sounds, speeches, nonsense, and art.

The easiest kind of splice is when the sounds are in separate files. All that you need to do is to copy each sound, in order, into a target sound. Here's a recipe that creates the start of a sentence "Guzdial is . . .". (Readers are welcome to complete the sentence.)

Program 61: Merging Words into a Single Sentence

```
def merge():
  guzdialSound = makeSound(getMediaPath("guzdial.wav"))
  isSound = makeSound(getMediaPath("is.wav"))
  target = makeSound(getMediaPath("sec3silence.wav"))
  index = 0
  # Copy in "Guzdial"
  for source in range(0,getLength(guzdialSound)):
    value = getSampleValueAt(guzdialSound,source)
    setSampleValueAt(target,index,value)
    index = index + 1
  # Copy in 0.1 second pause (silence) (0)
  for source in range(0,int(0.1*getSamplingRate(target))):
    setSampleValueAt(target,index,0)
    index = index + 1
  # Copy in "is"
  for source in range(0,getLength(isSound)):
    value = getSampleValueAt(isSound,source)
    setSampleValueAt(target,index,value)
    index = index + 1
  normalize(target)
  play(target)
  return target
```

How It Works

There are three loops in the function merge, each of which copies one segment into the target sound—a segment being either a word or a silence between words.

- The function starts by creating sound objects for the word "Guzdial" (guzdial-Sound), the word "is" (isSound), and the target silence (target).

- Note that we set index (for the target) equal to 0 before the first loop. We then increment it in every loop, but we never again set it to a specific value. That's because index is always the index for the *next empty sample* in the target sound. Because each loop follows the previous one, we just keep tacking samples onto the end of the target.

- In the first loop, we copy each and every sample from guzdialSound into the target. We have the index source go from 0 to the length of guzdialSound. We get the sample value at source from guzdialSound, then set the sample value at `index` in the `target` sound to the value that we got from `guzdialSound`. We then increment `index` so that it points at the next empty sample index.

- In the second loop, we create 0.1 seconds of silence. Since `getSamplingRate` `(target)` gives us the number of samples in one second of `target`, 0.1 times tells us the number of samples in 0.1 seconds. We don't get any source value here—we simply set the `index`-th sample to 0 (for silence), then increment the `index`.

- Finally, we copy in all the samples from `isSound`, just like the first loop where we copied in `guzdialSound`.

- We `normalize` the sound to make it louder. This means that the function `normalize` *must* be in the Program Area with `merge`, even though we're not showing it here. We then `play` and `return` the sound.

  We return the target sound using `return target` because we created the sound in the function. The target sound wasn't handed in as input to the function. If we didn't return the sound we created in `merge`, it would disappear with the end of the `merge` function context (*scope*). By returning it, we allow another function to use the resulting sound.

Instead of using a 3 second silent sound as the target, we can make an empty sound of a particular length using `makeEmptySound(lengthInSamples)`. For example, we can create a sound that is just long enough to fit what we want to copy into it by doing the following:

```
guzLen = getLength(guzdialSound)
silenceLen = int(0.1 * 22050)
isLen = getLength(isSound)
target = makeEmptySound(guzLen + silenceLen + isLen)
```

The default sampling rate for a new sound is 22,050 samples per second. So if we want a tenth of a second of silence between the words, the length of that in samples is (0.1 ∗ 22050). We must convert that back to an integer using `int(0.1 * 22050)`. We can also create a new silent sound using `makeEmptySound(length,samplingRate)`.

The more common kind of splicing is when the words are in the middle of an existing sound and you need to pull them out from there. The first thing to do in splicing like that is to figure out the index numbers that delimit the pieces you're interested in. Using the JES sound tool, that's pretty easy to do.

- Open your WAV file in the JES sound tool. You can do this by creating the sound and exploring it.

- Scroll and move the cursor (by dragging in the graph) until you think that the cursor is before or after a sound of interest.

- Check your positioning by playing the sound before and after the cursor, using the buttons in the sound tool.

Using exactly this process, Mark found the ending points of the first few words in PREAMBLE10.WAV (Figure 7.1). He assumed that the first word started at index 0.

FIGURE 7.1
Exploring a sound to find the silence between words.

Word	Ending Index
We	15730
the	17407
People	26726
of	32131
the	33413
United	40052
States	55510

Writing a loop that copies things from one array to another requires a little bit of juggling. You need to think about keeping track of two indices: where you are in the array that you're copying *from* and where you are in the array that you're copying *to*. These are two different variables, tracking two different indexes. But they both increment in the same way.

The way that we're going to do it (another *subrecipe*) is to use one index variable to point at the right entry in the *target* array (the one we're copying *to*), use a `for` loop to have the second index variable move across the right entries in the *source* array (the one we're copying *from*), and (*very important!*) move the target index variable each time we do a copy. This is what keeps the two index variables synchronized.

We make the target index move by adding 1 to it. Very simply, we'll tell Python to do `targetIndex = targetIndex + 1`. Remember that this changes the value of `targetIndex` to be whatever it currently is *plus* 1, which moves (increases) the target index. If we put this in the body of the loop where we're changing the source index, we'll get them moving in synchrony.

The general form of the subrecipe is:

```
targetIndex = Where-the-incoming-sound-should-start
for sourceIndex in range(startingPoint,endingPoint)
  setSampleValueAt(target, targetIndex,
    getSampleValueAt(source, sourceIndex))
  targetIndex = targetIndex + 1
```

Below is the recipe that changes the preamble from "We the people of the United States" to "We the *united* people of the United States."

Program 62: Splice the Preamble to Have United People

Be sure to change the `file` variable before trying this on your computer.

```
# Splicing
# Using the preamble sound,
#  make "We the united people"
def splicePreamble():
    file = "C:/ip-book/mediasources/preamble10.wav"
    source = makeSound(file)
    # This will be the newly spliced sound
    target = makeSound(file)

    # targetIndex starts at just after
    # "We the" in the new sound
    targetIndex=17408
    # Where the word "United" is in the sound
    for sourceIndex in range(33414, 40052):
        value = getSampleValueAt(source, sourceIndex)
        setSampleValueAt(target, targetIndex, value)
        targetIndex = targetIndex + 1

    # Where the word "People" is in the sound
    for sourceIndex in range(17408, 26726):
        value = getSampleValueAt(source, sourceIndex)
        setSampleValueAt(target, targetIndex, value)
        targetIndex = targetIndex + 1

    #Stick some quiet space after that
    for index in range(0,1000):
        setSampleValueAt(target, targetIndex,0)
        targetIndex = targetIndex + 1

    #Let's hear and return the result
    play(target)
    return target
```

We'd use this function like this:

```
>>> newSound=splicePreamble()
```

How It Works

There's a lot going on in this recipe. Let's walk through it, slowly.

Note that there are lots of lines with "#" in them. The hash character signifies that what comes after that character on the line is a note to the programmer *and should be ignored by Python*. It's called a *comment*.

The function splicePreamble takes no parameters. Sure, it would be great to write a single function that can do any kind of splicing we want, in the same way as we've done generalized increasing volume and normalization. But how would you do this? How do you generalize all the start and end points? It's easier, at least to start, to create single recipes that handle specific splicing tasks.

We see here three of the copying loops like we set up earlier. Actually, there are only two. The first one copies the word "united" into place. The second one copies the word "people" into place. "But wait," you might be thinking. "The word 'people' was *already* in the sound!" That's true, but when we copy "united" in, we overwrite some of the word "people," so we copy it in again.

At the very end of the recipe, we return the target sound. The target sound was created in the function and not passed into it. If we didn't return it we wouldn't have any way to refer to it again. By returning it, it's possible to give it a name and play it (and even further manipulate it) after the function stops executing.

Here's the simpler form. Try it and listen to the result:

```
def spliceSimpler():
  file = "C:/ip-book/mediasources/preamble10.wav"
  source = makeSound(file)
  # This will be the newly spliced sound
  target = makeSound(file)
  # targetIndex starts at just after "We the" in the new sound
  targetIndex=17408
  # Where the word "United" is in the sound
  for sourceIndex in range(33414, 40052):
    value = getSampleValueAt(source, sourceIndex)
    setSampleValueAt(target, targetIndex, value)
    targetIndex = targetIndex + 1
  #Let's hear and return the result
  play(target)
  return target
```

Let's see if we can figure out what's going on mathematically. Recall the table back on page 173. We're going to start inserting samples at sample index 17,408. The word "united" has (40,052 − 33,414) 6,638 samples. (Exercise for the reader:

FIGURE 7.2
Comparing the original sound (*left*) to the spliced sound (*right*).

How long is that in seconds?) This means that we'll be writing into the target from 17,408 to (17,408 + 6,638) sample index 24,046. We know from the table that the word "people" ends at index 26726. If the word "people" is more than (26,726 − 24,046) 2,680 samples, then it will start earlier than 24,046, and our insertion of "united" is going to trample on part of it. If the word "united" is over 6,000 samples, we doubt that the word "people" is less than 2,000. That's why it sounds crunched. Why does it work with where the "of" is? The speaker must have paused in there. If you check the table again, you'll see that the word "of" ends at sample index 32,131 and the word before it ends at 26,726. The word "of" takes fewer than (32,131 − 26,726) 5,405 samples, which is why the original recipe works.

The third loop in the original Program 62 (page 174) looks like the same kind of copy loop but it's really only putting in a few 0's. Samples with a value of 0 represent silence. Putting a few in creates a pause that sounds better. (There's an exercise which suggests pulling them out and seeing what you hear.)

Figure 7.2 shows the original PREAMBLE10.WAV file in the top sound editor and the new spliced one (saved with `writeSoundTo`) on the bottom. The lines are drawn so that the spliced section lies between them, while the rest of the sounds are identical.

7.3 GENERAL CLIP AND COPY

The previous functions were a bit complicated. What would make them easier? It would be nice to have a general clip method that took a sound and a start and end index and returned a new sound clip with just that part of the original sound in it. Then it would be easy to create a clip with just "United" in it.

Program 63: Create a Sound Clip

```
def clip(source,start,end):
    target = makeEmptySound(end - start)
    targetIndex = 0
    for sourceIndex in range(start,end):
        sourceValue = getSampleValueAt(source,sourceIndex)
```

```
        setSampleValueAt(target,targetIndex,sourceValue)
        targetIndex = targetIndex + 1
    return target
```

Now we can create a sound clip with just the word "United" in it by doing the following:

```
>>> preamble = makeSound(getMediaPath("preamble10.wav"))
>>> explore(preamble)
>>> united = clip(preamble,33414,40052)
>>> explore(united)
```

It would also be nice to have a general copy method that would take a source sound and a target sound and copy all of the source into the target at a passed starting location in the target.

Program 64: General Copy

```
def copy(source,target,start):
    targetIndex = start
    for sourceIndex in range(0,getLength(source)):
        sourceValue = getSampleValueAt(source,sourceIndex)
        setSampleValueAt(target,targetIndex,sourceValue)
        targetIndex = targetIndex + 1
```

Now we can insert "United" into the preamble again using the new functions.

Program 65: Using the General Clip and Copy

```
def createNewPreamble():
    file = "C:/ip-book/mediasources/preamble10.wav"
    preamble = makeSound(file)
    united = clip(preamble,33414,40052)
    start = clip(preamble,0,17407)
    end = clip(preamble,17408,55510)
    len = getLength(start) + getLength(united) + getLength(end)
    newPre = makeEmptySound(len)
    copy(start,newPre,0)
    copy(united,newPre,17407)
    copy(end,newPre,getLength(start) + getLength(united))
    return newPre
```

Notice how this function calls the new general clip and copy. You can put all three of these in the same file. It would be nice if you could have a file of general sound functions that other functions can use, without having to have all the functions in the same file.

You can use do this by *importing* functions from other files. You will need to add from media import * as the first line in the file with the general sound functions, in order to use the multimedia functions that JES provides like `getMediaPath` or `getRed`. JES imports the media functions for you automatically, but now we won't be loading this general file through JES, so we must explicitly import the media functions. Let's call the general sound functions file MYSOUND.PY so that it doesn't conflict with other things in JES that use the name Sound.

```
from media import *

def clip(source,start,end):
  target = makeEmptySound(end - start)
  targetIndex = 0
  for sourceIndex in range(start,end):
    sourceValue = getSampleValueAt(source,sourceIndex)
    setSampleValueAt(target,targetIndex,sourceValue)
    targetIndex = targetIndex + 1
  return target

def copy(source,target,start):
  targetIndex = start
  for sourceIndex in range(0,getLength(source)):
    sourceValue = getSampleValueAt(source,sourceIndex)
    setSampleValueAt(target,targetIndex,sourceValue)
    targetIndex = targetIndex + 1
```

To use the new general sound functions, you must first use `setLibPath(path)`. This function tells Python where to look for the files that you are importing. The path is the full pathname to the directory with the file that contains the general functions.

```
>>> setLibPath("c:/ip-book/programs/")
```

To use the general sound functions `copy` and `clip` in another file, we add `from mySound import *` as the first line in the file. The `from mySound import *` is like copying the general functions into the same file as `createNewPreamble` but it is actually better than copying the functions. If we copy the general functions to lots of files, and *then* change the general functions, we have to change them everyplace that we copied them. But, if we import general functions and then change the general function file, the improved functions are the ones that are used everywhere.

```
from mySound import *

def createNewPreamble():
 file = "C:/ip-book/mediasources/preamble10.wav"
 preamble = makeSound(file)
 united = clip(preamble,33414,40052)
 start = clip(preamble,0,17407)
 end = clip(preamble,17408,55510)
 len = getLength(start) + getLength(united) + getLength(end)
 newPre = makeEmptySound(len)
 copy(start,newPre,0)
```

```
copy(united,newPre,17407)
copy(end,newPre,getLength(start) + getLength(united))
return newPre
```

General functions are also a form of *abstraction* like the general copy function that we used with pictures. By creating a file of general functions that we import, we are allowing others (including ourselves if we forget) to use the abstraction without understanding the details of how these functions are implemented. This is like how we have been using getRed and getMediaPath without knowing the details of how they work.

Making It Work Tip: A General Function Directory

If you put all the files that contain general functions in the same directory, you can use setLibPath once to allow you to access all of the general function files using import. You can have general function files for sounds, pictures, movies, etc.

7.4 REVERSING SOUNDS

In the splicing example, we copied the samples from the words just as they were in the original sound. We don't have to always go in the same order. We can reverse the words—or make them faster, slower, louder, or softer. As an example, here's a recipe that reverses a sound (Figure 7.3).

Program 66: Play the Given Sound Backwards (Reverse It)

```
def reverse(source):
    target = makeEmptySound(getLength(source))
    sourceIndex = getLength(source)-1
    for targetIndex in range(0,getLength(target)):
        sourceValue = getSampleValueAt(source,sourceIndex)
        setSampleValueAt(target,targetIndex,sourceValue)
        sourceIndex = sourceIndex - 1
    return target
```

FIGURE 7.3
Comparing the original sound (*left*) to the reversed sound (*right*).

You can try this out by typing the following in the command area:

```
>>> croak = makeSound(getMediaPath("croak.wav"))
>>> explore(croak)
>>> revCroak = reverse(croak)
>>> explore(revCroak)
```

How It Works

This recipe uses another variant of the array element copying subrecipe that we've already seen.

- It first creates the `target` sound as an empty sound the same length as the `source` sound.

- It starts the `sourceIndex` at the *end* of the array rather than the front (the length minus 1).

- The `targetIndex` moves from 0 to the length minus 1, during which time the recipe

  - gets the sample value in the source at the `sourceIndex`:

  - copies that value into the target at the `targetIndex`: and

  - *reduces* the `sourceIndex` by 1, meaning that the `sourceIndex` moves from the end of the array back to the beginning.

7.5 MIRRORING

Once we know how to play sounds forwards and backwards, *mirroring* a sound is the exact same process as mirroring a picture (Figure 7.4). Compare this to Program 20 (page 77). Do you agree that this is the same *algorithm* even though we're dealing with a different medium?

Program 67: Mirror a Sound Front to Back

```
def mirrorSound(sound):
  len = getLength(sound)
  mirrorpoint=len/2
  for index in range(0,mirrorpoint):
    left = getSampleObjectAt(sound,index)
    right = getSampleObjectAt(sound,len-index-1)
    value = getSampleValue(left)
    setSampleValue(right,value)
```

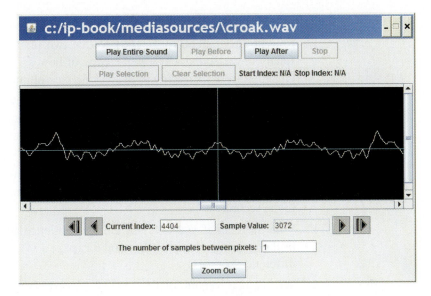

FIGURE 7.4
Mirroring a sound from front (*left*) to back (*right*).

PROGRAMMING SUMMARY

In this chapter, we talk about several kinds of encodings of data (or objects).

Sounds	Encodings of sounds, typically coming from a WAV file.
Samples	Collections of sample objects, each indexed by a number (e.g., sample #0, sample #1). `samples[0]` is the first sample object. You can manipulate each sample in the samples like this: `for s in samples:`.
Sample	A value between −32,000 and 32,000 (roughly) representing the voltage that a microphone would generate at a given instant when recording a sound. The length of the instant is typically either $1/44,1000$ of a second (for CD-quality sound) or $1/22,050$ of a second (for good-enough sound on most computers). A sample object remembers what sound it came from, so if you change its value, it knows to go back and change the right sample in the sound.

Here are the functions used or introduced in this chapter:

range	Takes two numbers and returns an array of all integers starting at the first number and stopping before the last number.
range	Can also take three numbers, and then returns an array of all the integers from the first, up to but not including the second, incrementing each time by the third.

PROBLEMS

7.1   Rewrite Program 60 (page 169) so that two input values are provided to the function: the sound and a *percentage* of how far into the sound to go before changing from increasing to decreasing the volume.

7.2   Rewrite Program 60 (page 169) so that you normalize the first second of a sound, then slowly decrease the sound in steps of 1/5 for each following second. (How many samples are in a second? getSamplingRate is the number of samples per second for the given sound.)

7.3   Try rewriting Program 60 (page 169) so that you have a linear increase in volume to halfway through the sound, then linearly decrease the volume down to zero in the second half.

7.4   What happens if you take out the bit of silence added in to the target sound in the splicing example (Program 62 (page 174))? Try it? Can you hear any difference?

7.5   Write a new version of Program 62 (page 174) to copy "We the" into a new sound and then copy in "united" and finally copy in "people." Be sure to add 2250 samples with a value of 0 in between the words. Return the new sound.

7.6   Write a new function clip that takes a sound, a starting index, and an ending index and returns a new sound with just that part of the original sound in it. The length of the new sound is ($endIndex - startIndex + 1$).

7.7   We think that if we're going to say "We the united people" in the splice (Program 62 (page 174)), "united" should be really emphasized—really loud. Change the recipe so that the word "united" is maximally loud (normalized) in the phrase "united people."

7.8   Try using a stopwatch to time the execution of the recipes in this chapter. Time from hitting return on the command until the next prompt appears. What is the relationship between execution time and the length of the sound? Is it a linear relationship (i.e., longer sounds take longer to process and shorter sounds take less time to process)? Or is it something else? Compare the individual recipes. Does normalizing a sound take longer than raising (or lowering) the amplitude a constant amount? How much longer? Does it matter whether the sound is longer or shorter?

7.9   Make an audio collage. Make it at least five seconds long, and include at least two different sounds (e.g., they come from different files). Make a copy of one of those different sounds and modify it using any of the techniques described in this chapter (e.g., mirroring, splicing, volume manipulations). Splice together the original two sounds and the modified sound to make the complete collage.

7.10   Compose a sentence that no one ever said by combining words from other sounds into a grammatically correct new sound. Write a function named audio-Sentence to generate a sentence out of individual words. Use at least three words in your sentence. You can use the words in the MEDIASOURCE folder from the Web site or record your own words. Be sure to include a tenth (1/10) of a second pause between the words. (*Hint 1:* Remember that zeroes for the sample values generate silence or pause. *Hint 2:* Remember that the sampling rate is the number of samples per second. From there, you should be able to figure out how many samples need to be made zero to generate a tenth of a second pause.) Be sure to access your sounds in your Media Folder using `getMediaPath` so that it will work for users of your program as long as they first execute `setMediaPath`.

7.11 Write a function to add 1 second of silence to the beginning of a sound. It should take the sound as input, create the new empty target sound, then copy the original sound starting after the first second in the target.

7.12 Search the Web for songs that have hidden messages that you can hear when you reverse the sound.

7.13 Write a function that splices together words and music.

7.14 Write a function that interleaves two sounds. It starts with 2 seconds of the first sound and then 2 seconds of the second sound. Then it continues with the next 2 seconds of the first sound and the next 2 seconds of the second sound and so on until both sounds have been fully copied to the target sound.

7.15 Write a function called `erasePart` to set all the samples in the second second of "thisisatest.wav" to 0's—essentially, making the second second go silent. (*Hint:* Remember that `getSamplingRate(sound)` tells you the number of samples in a single second in a sound.) Play and return the partially erased sound.

7.16 Can you write a function that finds the silence between words? What should it return?

7.17 Write a function to increase the volume on the passed sound just between the passed start and end index.

7.18 Write a function to reverse part of the passed sound just between the passed start and end index.

7.19 Write a function `mirrorBackToFront` that mirrors the second half of a sound into the first half.

7.20 Write a function called `reverseSecondHalf` that takes a sound as input, then reverses just the second half of the sound and returns the result. For example, if the sound said "MarkBark," the returned sound should say "MarkkraB."

CHAPTER 8

Making Sounds by Combining Pieces

Chapter Learning Objectives

The media learning goals for this chapter are:

- To blend sounds so that one fades into another.
- To create echoes.
- To change the frequency (pitch) of a sound.
- To create sounds that don't exist in nature by composing more basic sounds (sine waves).
- To choose between sound formats such as MIDI and MP3 for different purposes.

The computer science goals for this chapter are:

- To use file paths to reference files at different places on the disk.
- To explain blending as an algorithm that crosses media boundaries.
- To build programs from multiple functions.

8.1 COMPOSING SOUNDS THROUGH ADDITION

Creating sounds digitally that didn't exist previously is lots of fun. Rather than simply copying sample values around or multiplying them, we actually change their values and add waves together. The result are sounds that never existed until you made them.

In physics, adding sounds involves issues of canceling waves out and enforcing other factors. In math, it's about matrices. In computer science, it's one of the easiest processes one can imagine. Let's say that you've got a sound, `source`, that you want to add in to the `target`. *Simply add the values at the same index numbers* (as in Figure 8.1). That's it!

FIGURE 8.1
The top and middle waves are added together to create the bottom wave.

```
for sourceIndex in range(0,getLength(source)):
  targetValue=getSampleValueAt(target,sourceIndex)
  sourceValue=getSampleValueAt(source,sourceIndex)
  setSampleValueAt(target,targetIndex,sourceValue+targetValue)
```

The function `setSampleValueAt` takes a sound, the index of the sample to change in the sound, and the new value to set the sample to. It is similar to `setSampleValue` except that you don't have to first pull out the sample from the sound.

To make some of our manipulations easier, we're going to be using `setMediaPath` and `getMediaPath`. JES knows how to *set* a media directory (folder) and then reference media files within the folder. This makes it much easier to reference media files—you don't have to spell out the whole path. The functions we'll use are `setMediaPath` and `getMediaPath`. The function `setMediaPath()` will allow you to select the media directory using a file chooser. The function `getMediaPath(baseName)` takes a base file name and will prepend the media directory in front of the base name and return it.

```
>>> setMediaPath()
New media folder: C:/ip-book/mediasources/
>>> print getMediaPath("barbara.jpg")
C:/ip-book/mediasources/barbara.jpg
>>> print getMediaPath("sec1silence.wav")
C:/ip-book/mediasources/sec1silence.wav
```

Common Bug: It's Not a File, It's a String

Just because getMediaPath returns something that looks like a path doesn't mean that a file really exists there. You have to know the right base name, and if you do, it's easier to use in your code. But if you use a name that doesn't exist, you'll get a path to a nonexistent file and getMediaPath will warn you.

```
>>> print getMediaPath("blah-blah-blah")
Note: There is no file at C:/ip-
book/mediasources/blah-blah-blah
C:/ip-book/mediasources/blah-blah-blah
```

8.2   BLENDING SOUNDS

In this example, we take two sounds—someone saying "Aah!" and a bassoon instrument sound of C in the fourth octave—and *blend* them. To do this we copy part of the "Aah!," then add 50% of each, and then copy the C. This is very much like mixing 50% of each at a sound mixing board. It's also very much like the way we blended pictures in Program 44 (page 118).

Program 68: Blending Two Sounds

```
def blendSounds():
 bass = makeSound(getMediaPath("bassoon-c4.wav"))
 aah = makeSound(getMediaPath("aah.wav"))
 canvas = makeSound(getMediaPath("sec3silence.wav"))
 #Each of these is over 40K samples
 for index in range(0,20000):
  setSampleValueAt(canvas,index,getSampleValueAt(aah,index))
 for index in range(0,20000):
  aahSample = getSampleValueAt(aah,index+20000)
  bassSample=getSampleValueAt(bass,index)
  newSample = 0.5*aahSample + 0.5 * bassSample
  setSampleValueAt(canvas,index+20000,newSample)
 for index in range(20000,40000):
  setSampleValueAt(canvas,index+20000,getSampleValueAt(bass,index))
 play(canvas)
 return canvas
```

How It Works

Like blending the picture (Program 44 (page 118)), there are loops in this function for each segment of the blended sound.

- We start by creating the `bass` and `aah` sounds for blending and a silent sound `canvas` that we're blending into. The length of these sounds is over 40,000 samples but we're just going to use the first 40,000 as an example.

- In the first loop, we simply get 20,000 samples from `aah` and copy them into `canvas`. Note that we're not using a separate index variable for the `canvas`—instead, we're using the same index variable, `index`, for both sounds.

- In the next loop, we copy 20,000 samples from both `aah` and `bass` blended into `canvas`. We use the index variable, `index`, to index all three sounds—we use the basic `index` for accessing `bass` and add 20,000 to `index` to access `aah` and `canvas` (since we have already copied 20,000 samples from `aah` into `canvas`). We get a sample from each of `aah` and `bass`, then multiply each by 0.5 and add the results together. The result is a sample that represents 50% of each.

- Finally, we copy another 20,000 samples from `bass`. The resultant sound is returned (since it would disappear otherwise), which sounds like "Aah," a little of each, then just a bassoon note.

8.3   CREATING AN ECHO

Creating an echo effect is similar to the splicing recipe (Program 62 (page 174)) that we saw in the last chapter but involves creating sounds that didn't exist before. We do this by *adding* wave forms. What we're doing here is adding samples from a `delay` number of samples away into the sound but multiplied by 0.6 so that they're fainter.

Program 69: Make a Sound and a Single Echo of It

```
def echo(delay):
  f = pickAFile()
  s1 = makeSound(f)
  s2 = makeSound(f)
  for index in range(delay, getLength(s1)):
    # set delay value to original value + delayed value * .6
    echoSample = 0.6*getSampleValueAt(s2, index-delay)
    comboSample = getSampleValueAt(s1,index) + echoSample
    setSampleValueAt(s1, index,comboSample)
  play(s1)
  return s1
```

How It Works

The `echo` function takes as input the amount of delay between echoes and returns the echoed sound. Try this with different amounts of delay. With low values of delay, the echo will sound more like *vibrato*. Higher values (try 10,000 or 20,000) will give you a real echo.

- This function prompts you for a filename to echo (not a great idea if we want to use the echo-generating function for other purposes), then creates two copies of the sound. s1 is where we'll create the echoed sound. s2 is where we'll get the original, unadulterated samples for creating the echo. (You could try this with just a single sound to get some interesting layered echoes.)

- Our index loop skips over the delay samples, then goes to the end of the sound.

- The echoed sound is delay samples back, so index-delay is the sample we need. We multiply it by 0.6 to make it softer in volume.

- We then add the echoed sample to the current sample in comboSample, then store it at index.

- At the end, we play the sound and return it.

8.3.1   Creating Multiple Echoes

This recipe lets you set the number of echoes you get. You can generate some amazing effects with it.

Program 70: Creating Multiple Echoes

```
def echoes(sndFile, delay,num):
  # Create a new snd, that echoes the input soundfile
  # num number of echoes, each delay apart
  s1 = makeSound(sndFile)
  ends1 = getLength(s1)
  ends2 = ends1 + (delay * num)
  #ends2 is in samples -- must covert to seconds
  s2 = makeEmptySound(1+int(ends2/getSamplingRate(s1)))

  echoAmplitude = 1.0
  for echoCount in range(1,num):
    # 60\% smaller each time
    echoAmplitude = echoAmplitude * 0.6
    for posns1 in range(0,ends1):
      posns2 = posns1+(delay*echoCount)
      values1 = getSampleValueAt(s1,posns1)*echoAmplitude
      values2 = getSampleValueAt(s2,posns2)
      setSampleValueAt(s2,posns2,values1+values2)
  play(s2)
  return s2
```

8.3.2   Creating Chords

A musical chord is three or more notes that create a harmonious sound when played together. A C major chord is a combination of the notes C, E, and G. To create the chord, we can just add the values together at the same index. The directory MEDIASOURCES contains sound files for the notes C, E, and G each played on a bassoon.

Program 71: Creating a Chord

```
def createChord():
  c = makeSound(getMediaPath("bassoon-c4.wav"))
  e = makeSound(getMediaPath("bassoon-e4.wav"))
  g = makeSound(getMediaPath("bassoon-g4.wav"))
  chord = makeEmptySound(c.getLength())
  for index in range(0,c.getLength()):
    cValue = getSampleValueAt(c,index)
    eValue = getSampleValueAt(e,index)
    gValue = getSampleValueAt(g,index)
    total = cValue + eValue + gValue
    setSampleValueAt(chord,index,total)
  return chord
```

8.4 HOW SAMPLING KEYBOARDS WORK

Sampling keyboards are keyboards that use recordings of sounds (e.g., pianos, harps, trumpets) to create music by playing them in the desired pitch. Modern music and sound keyboards (and synthesizers) allow musicians to record sounds in their daily lives and turn them into "instruments" by shifting their original frequencies. How do the synthesizers do this? It's not really complicated. The interesting part is that it allows you to use any sound you want as an instrument.

Sampling keyboards use huge amounts of memory to record lots of different instruments at different pitches. When you press a key on the keyboard, the recording *closest* (in pitch) to the note you pressed is selected and then is shifted to exactly the pitch you requested.

This first recipe works by creating a sound that *skips* every other sample. You read that right—after being so careful to treat all the samples the same, we're now going to skip half of them! In the mediasources directory, you'll find a sound named c4.wav. This is the note C, in the fourth octave of a piano, played for one second. It makes a good sound to experiment with, but any sound will work.

Program 72: Double the Frequency of a Sound

```
def double(source):
  len = getLength(source) / 2 + 1
  target = makeEmptySound(len)
  targetIndex = 0
  for sourceIndex in range(0, getLength(source), 2):
    sourceValue = getSampleValueAt(source,sourceIndex)
    setSampleValueAt(target, targetIndex, sourceValue)
    targetIndex = targetIndex + 1
  play(target)
  return target
```

Here's how to use it:

```
>>> file = pickAFile()
>>> print file
C:/ip-book/mediasources/c4.wav
>>> c4 = makeSound(file)
>>> play(c4)
>>> c4doubled=double(c4)
```

This recipe looks like it's using the array-copying subrecipe we saw earlier, but note that the `range` uses the third parameter—we're incrementing by 2. If we increment by 2, we only fill half the samples in the target, so the second loop just fills the rest with zeroes.

Try it![1] You'll see that the sound really does double in frequency.

How did that happen? It's not really all that complicated. Think of it this way: the frequency of the basic file is really the number of cycles that pass by in a certain amount of time. If you skip every other sample, the new sound has just as many cycles, but has them in half the amount of time.

Now let's try the other way. Let's take every sample twice. What happens then?

To do this, we need to use the Python function `int` to return the integer portion of the input.

```
>>> print int(0.5)
0
>>> print int(1.5)
1
```

Here's the recipe that *halves* the frequency. We're using the array-copying subrecipe again but we're sort of reversing it. The `for` loop moves the `targetIndex` along the length of the sound. The `sourceIndex` is now being incremented—but only by 0.5. The effect is that we'll take every sample in the source twice. The `sourceIndex` will be 1, 1.5, 2, 2.5, and so on, but because we're using the `int` of that value, we'll take samples 1, 1, 2, 2, and so on.

Program 73: Halve the Frequency

```
def halve(source):
    target = makeEmptySound(getLength(source) * 2)
    sourceIndex = 0
    for targetIndex in range(0, getLength(target)):
        value = getSampleValueAt(source, int(sourceIndex))
        setSampleValueAt(target, targetIndex, value)
        sourceIndex = sourceIndex + 0.5
    play(target)
    return target
```

---

[1]You are now trying this out as you read, aren't you?

How It Works

The function `halve` takes the source sound as input. It creates a target sound that is twice as long as the source sound. The `sourceIndex` is set to 0 (that's where in the source we're copying from) and we have a loop for `targetIndex` from 0 to the end of the `target` sound. We get a sample value from `source` at the *integer* value (`int`) of the `sourceIndex`. We set the sample value at `targetIndex` to the value that we got from the `source` sample. We then add 0.5 to the `sourceIndex`. This means that the `sourceIndex`, each time through the loop, will take on the values 0, 0.5, 1, 1.5, 2, 2.5, and so on. But the integer part of this sequence is 0, 0, 1, 1, 2, 2, and so on. The result is that we take each sample from the `source` sound *twice*.

Think about what we're doing here. Imagine that the number 0.5 above was actually 0.75, or 2, or 3. Would this work? The `for` loop would have to change but essentially the idea is the same in all these cases. We are *sampling* the source data to create the target data. Using a *sample index* of 0.5 slows down the sound and halves the frequency. A sample index larger than 1 speeds up the sound and increases the frequency.

Let's try to generalize this sampling with the recipe that follows. (Note that this one *won't* work right.)

Program 74: Shifting the Frequency of a Sound: BROKEN!

```
def shift(source,factor):
  target = makeEmptySound(getLength(source))
  sourceIndex = 0

  for targetIndex in range(0, len):
    sourceValue = getSampleValueAt(source,sourceIndex)
    setSampleValueAt(target, targetIndex, sourceValue)
    sourceIndex = sourceIndex + factor

  play(target)
  return target
```

Here's how we could use this:

```
>>> cF=getMediaPath("c4.wav")
>>> print cF
c:/ip-book/mediasources/c4.wav
>>> c4 = makeSound(testF)
>>> lowerC4=shift(c4,0.75)
```

That seems to work. But, what if the `factor` for sampling is *more* than 1.0?

```
>>> higherTest=shift(c4,1.5)
You are trying to access the sample at index: 67585,
but the last valid index is at 67584
The error was:
Inappropriate argument value (of correct type).
An error occurred attempting to pass an argument to a
```

```
function. Please check line 218 of C:\ip-book\
programs\mySound.py
```

Why? What's happening? Here's how you could see it: print out the `sourceIndex` just before the `setSampleValueAt`. You'd see that the `sourceIndex` becomes *larger* than the length of the source sound. Of course, that makes sense. If each time through the loop we increment the `targetIndex` by 1, but increment the `sourceIndex` by *more than 1*, we'll get past the end of the source sound before we reach the end of the target sound. But how do we avoid this?

Here's what we want to happen: if the `sourceIndex` ever gets larger than the length of the source, we want to reset the `sourceIndex` back to zero. In Python we use an `if` statement to only execute the code in the following block if the test is true.

Program 75: Shifting the Frequency of a Sound

```
def shift(source,factor):
    target = makeEmptySound(getLength(source))
    sourceIndex = 0

    for targetIndex in range(0, len):
        sourceValue = getSampleValueAt(source,sourceIndex)
        setSampleValueAt(target, targetIndex, sourceValue)
        sourceIndex = sourceIndex + factor
        if (sourceIndex >= sourceLen)
            sourceIndex = 0

    play(target)
    return target
```

We can actually set the factor so that we get whatever frequency we want. We call this factor the *sampling interval*. For a desired frequency f_0, the sampling interval should be:

$$samplingInterval = (sizeOfSourceSound)\frac{f_0}{samplingRate}$$

This is how a keyboard synthesizer works. It has recordings of pianos, voices, bells, drums, whatever. By *sampling* those sounds at different sampling intervals, it can shift the sound to the desired frequency.

The last recipe in this section plays a single sound at its original frequency, then at two times, three times, four times, and five times.

Program 76: Playing a Sound in a Range of Frequencies

```
def playASequence(file):
    # Play the sound five times, increasing the frequency
    for factor in range(1,6):
        sound = makeSound(file)
        target = shift(sound,factor)
        blockingPlay(target)
```

8.4.1   Sampling as an Algorithm

You should recognize a similarity between the halving recipe, Program 73 (page 190), and the recipe for scaling a picture up (making it larger), Program 35 (page 99). To halve the frequency, we take each sample twice by incrementing by 0.5 and using the `int()` function to get the integer part of that. To make the picture larger, we take each pixel twice, adding 0.5 to our index variables and using the `int()` function on them. These are using the same *algorithm*—the same basic process is being used in each. The details of pictures vs. sounds aren't critical. The point is that the same basic process is being used in each.

We have seen other algorithms that cross media boundaries. Obviously, our increasing-red and increasing-volume functions (and the decreasing versions) are essentially doing the same thing. The way we blend pictures or sounds is the same. We take the component color channels (pixels) or samples (sounds) and add them using percentages to determine the amount from each that we want in the final product. As long as the percentages total 100%, we'll get a reasonable output that reflects the input sounds or pictures at the correct percentages.

Identifying algorithms like these is useful for several reasons. If we understand the algorithm in general (e.g., when it's slow and when it's fast, what it works for and what it doesn't, what the limitations are), then the lessons learned apply in the specific picture or sound instances. Knowing the algorithms is also useful for designers. When you are designing a new program, keep the algorithms in mind so that you can use them when they apply.

When we double or halve the sound frequency, we are also shrinking or doubling the length of the sound. You might want a target sound whose length is *exactly* the length of the sound rather than have to clear out extra stuff from a longer sound. You can do that with `makeEmptySound`. The function `makeEmptySound(22050 * 10)` returns a new empty sound of 10 seconds in length with a sampling rate of 22,050.

8.5   ADDITIVE SYNTHESIS

Additive synthesis creates sounds by adding sine waves together. We saw earlier that it's really pretty easy to add sounds together. With additive synthesis, you can shape the waves yourself, set their frequencies, and create "instruments" that have never existed.

8.5.1   Making Sine Waves

Let's figure out how to produce a set of samples to generate a sound at a given frequency and amplitude. An easy way to do this is to create a sine wave. A whistle, for example, is almost a perfect sine wave. The trick is to create a sine wave with the desired frequency.

If you took values from 0 to 2π, computed the sine of each value, and graphed the computed values, you'd get a sine wave. From your really early math courses, you know that there's an infinity of numbers between 0 and 1. Computers don't handle infinity very well, so we'll actually only take *some* values between 0 and 2π.

To create the graph shown below, Mark filled 20 rows (a totally arbitrary number) of a spreadsheet with values from 0 to 2π (about 6.28). Mark added about 0.314 (6.28/20) to each preceding row. In the next column, he took the sine of each value in the first column, then graphed it.

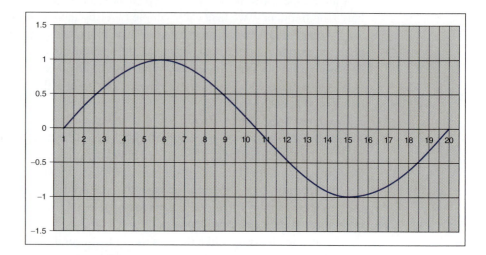

If we want to create a sound at a given frequency, say 440 Hz, we have to fit an entire cycle like the one in the graph into 1/440 of a second (440 cycles per second, meaning that each cycle fits into 1/440 second, or 0.00227 seconds). Mark made the graph using 20 values. Call it 20 *samples*. How many samples do we have to chop up the 440 Hz cycle into? That's the same as asking how many samples must go by in 0.00227 seconds. We know the sampling rate—that's the number of samples in one second. Let's say that it's 22,050 samples per second (our default sampling rate). Each sample is then 1/22050 which equals 0.0000453 seconds. How many samples fit into 0.00227? That's 0.00227/0.0000453, or about 50. What we just did here mathematically is:

$$interval = 1/frequency$$

$$samplesPerCyle = \frac{interval}{1/samplingRate} = (samplingRate)(interval)$$

Now let's spell this out as Python. To get a waveform at a given frequency, say 440 Hz, we need 440 of these waves in a single second. Each one must fit into the interval of 1/*frequency*. The number of samples that needs to be produced during the interval is the sampling rate divided by the frequency, or interval $(1/f) * (sampling\ rate)$. Call that the *samplesPerCycle*.

At each entry of the sound *sampleIndex*, we want to:

- Get the fraction of *sampleIndex/samplesPerCycle*.
- Multiply that fraction by 2π. That's the number of radians we need. Take the *sine* of (*sampleIndex/samplesPerCycle*) $* 2\pi$.
- Multiply the result by the desired amplitude and put it in the `sampleIndex`.

To build sounds, there are some *silent* sounds in the media sources. Our sine wave generator will use one second of silence to build a sine wave of one second. We'll provide an amplitude as input—that will be the *maximum* amplitude of the sound. (Since sine generates between −1 and 1, the range of amplitudes will be between −*amplitude* and *amplitude*.)

Program 77: Generate a Sine Wave at a Given Frequency and Amplitude

```
def sineWave(freq,amplitude):

    # Get a blank sound
    mySound = getMediaPath('sec1silence.wav')
    buildSin = makeSound(mySound)

    # Set sound constant
    sr = getSamplingRate(buildSin)          # sampling rate

    interval = 1.0/freq     # Make sure it's floating point
    samplesPerCycle = interval * sr    # samples per cycle
    maxCycle = 2 * pi

    for pos in range (0,getLength(buildSin)):
        rawSample = sin((pos / samplesPerCycle) * maxCycle)
        sampleVal = int(amplitude*rawSample)
        setSampleValueAt(buildSin,pos,sampleVal)

    return buildSin
```

Note that we used 1.0 divided by `freq` to calculate the interval. We used 1.0 instead of 1 to make sure that the result is a floating point and not an integer. If Python sees us only using integers it will give us an integer result by throwing away anything after the decimal. By using at least one floating point number (1.0) it will give us the result as a floating point.

Here we are building a sine wave of 880 Hz at an amplitude of 4,000.

```
>>> f880=sineWave(880,4000)
>>> play(f880)
```

8.5.2 Adding Sine Waves Together

Now let's add sine waves together. As we said at the beginning of the chapter, that's pretty easy: just add the samples at the same indices together. Here's a function that adds one sound into a second sound.

Program 78: Add Two Sounds Together

```
def addSounds(sound1,sound2):
  for index in range(0,getLength(sound1)):
    s1Sample = getSampleValueAt(sound1,index)
    s2Sample = getSampleValueAt(sound2,index)
    setSampleValueAt(sound2,index,s1Sample+s2Sample)
```

Let's add together 440 Hz, 880 Hz (twice 440), and 1,320 Hz (880 + 440) but we'll have the amplitudes increase. We'll double the amplitude each time: 2,000, then 4,000, then 8,000. We'll add them all up into the name f440 and explore the result. At the end, we will generate a 440 Hz sound so that we can listen to them both and compare.

```
>>> f440=sineWave(440,2000)
>>> f880=sineWave(880,4000)
>>> f1320=sineWave(1320,8000)
>>> addSounds(f880,f440)
>>> addSounds(f1320,f440)
>>> play(f440)
>>> explore(f440)
>>> just440=sineWave(440,2000)
>>> play(just440)
>>> explore(f440)
```

Common Bug: Beware of Adding Amplitudes Past 32,767

When you add sounds, you add their amplitudes also. A maximum of 2,000 + 4,000 + 8,000 will never be greater than 32,767 but don't worry about that. Remember what happened when the amplitude got too high in the last chapter...

8.5.3 Checking Our Result

How do we know if we really got what we wanted? If we explore the original f440 sound and the modified f440 sound, which is really the combination of the three sounds, you will notice that the wave forms look very different (Figure 8.2). That tells you that we did *something* to the sound...but what?

We can test our code by using the sound tools in MediaTools. First, we save out a sample wave (just 400 Hz) and the combined wave.

```
>>> writeSoundTo(just440,"C:/ip-book/mediasources/just440.wav")
>>> writeSoundTo(f440,"C:/ip-book/mediasources/combined440.wav")
```

FIGURE 8.2
The raw 440 Hz signal (*left*) and the 440 + 880 + 1,320 Hz signal (*right*).

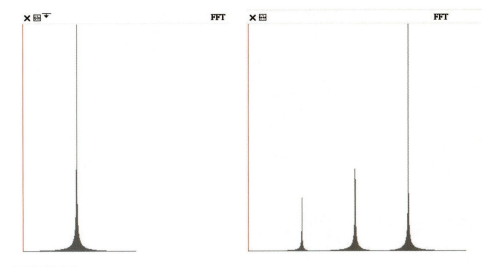

FIGURE 8.3
FFT of the 440 Hz sound (*left*) and the combined sound (*right*).

The way you can really check your additive synthesis is with an FFT (fast fourier transform). Generate the FFT for each signal by using the MediaTools application. You'll see that the 440 Hz signal has a single spike (Figure 8.3). That's what you'd expect—it's supposed to be a single sine wave. Now look at the combined wave form's FFT. It's what it's supposed to be. You see three spikes there and each succeeding one is double the height of the last one.

8.5.4   Square Waves

We don't have to just add sine waves. We can also add *square waves*. These are literally square-shaped waves, moving between +1 and −1. The FFT will look very different, and the *sound* will be very different. It can actually be a much richer sound.

Try swapping this recipe in for the sine wave generator and see what you think. Note the use of an if statement to swap between the positive and negative sides of the wave halfway through a cycle.

Program 79: Square Wave Generator for a Given Frequency and Amplitude

```
def squareWave(freq,amplitude):

    # Get a blank sound
    mySound =  getMediaPath("sec1silence.wav")
    square = makeSound(mySound)

    # Set music constants
    samplingRate = getSamplingRate(square)     # sampling rate
    seconds = 1   # play for 1 second

    # Build tools for this wave
    # seconds per cycle: make sure floating point
```

```
interval = 1.0 * seconds / freq
# creates floating point since interval is fl point
samplesPerCycle = interval * samplingRate
# we need to switch every half-cycle
samplesPerHalfCycle = int(samplesPerCycle / 2)
sampleVal = amplitude
s = 1
i = 1

for s in range (0, getLength(square)):
  # if end of a half-cycle
  if (i > samplesPerHalfCycle):
    # reverse the amplitude every half-cycle
    sampleVal = sampleVal * -1
    # and reinitialize the half-cycle counter
    i = 0
  setSampleValueAt(square,s,sampleVal)
  i = i + 1

return(square)
```

Use it like this:

```
>>> sq440=squareWave(440,4000)
>>> play(sq440)
>>> sq880=squareWave(880,8000)
>>> sq1320=squareWave(1320,10000)
>>> writeSoundTo(sq440,getMediaPath("square440.wav"))
Note: There is no file at C:/ip-book/mediasources/
square440.wav
>>> addSounds(sq880,sq440)
>>> addSounds(sq1320,sq440)
>>> play(sq440)
>>> writeSoundTo(sq440,getMediaPath("squarecombined440.wav"))
Note: there is no file at C:/ip-book/pmediasources/
squarecombined440.wav
```

How It Works

This recipe creates sine waves that are square in shape and all the sample values are either the passed amplitude or −1 times the amplitude. Let's walk through what happens when sq440 = squareWave(440,4000) is executed.

- First we create a silent sound that is 1 second long called square.
- Next we calculate the number of samples per cycle based on the sampling rate, frequency, and length in seconds. This is $(1.0 * 1/440) * 22050$, which is about 50.11363.
- We calculate the number of samples in half of a cycle as an integer (25) so that half of the values in a cycle will be positive and half negative. We use i to track

how many values have been set in `square` in order to check if we have done half a cycle. We set the `sampleVal` to be the passed `amplitude`.

- If we reach the end of a half cycle (`i == samplesPerHalfCycle`) we multiply the `sampleVal` by −1 to negate it. If `sampleVal` was positive, it will become negative. And if it was negative, it will become positive. We also reset `i` to zero to start counting the next half cycle.

- We set the sample value in `square` to `sampleVal`. We increment `i`.

- After the loop finishes, we return the `square` sound.

You'll find that the waves really do look square (Figure 8.4) but the most amazing thing is all the additional spikes in FFT (Figure 8.5). Square waves really do result in a much more complex sound.

8.5.5 Triangular Waves

You can create triangular waves instead of square waves with this recipe.

FIGURE 8.4
The 440 Hz square wave (*left*) and additive combination of square waves (*right*).

FIGURE 8.5
FFTs of the 440 Hz square wave (*left*) and additive combination of square waves (*right*).

Program 80: Generate Triangular Waves

```
def triangleWave(freq, theAmplitude):

  # Get a blank sound
  mySoundF = getMediaPath("sec1silence.wav")
  triangle = makeSound(mySoundF)

  # Set music constants
  # use the passed amplitude
  amplitude = theAmplitude
  # sampling rate (samples per second)
  samplingRate = 22050
  # play for 1 second
  seconds = 1

  # Build tools for this wave
  # seconds per cycle: make sure floating point
  interval = 1.0 * seconds / freq
  # creates floating point since interval is fl point
  samplesPerCycle = interval * samplingRate
  # we need to switch every half-cycle
  samplesPerHalfCycle = int(samplesPerCycle / 2)
  # value to add for each subsequent sample; must be integer
  increment = int(amplitude / samplesPerHalfCycle)
  # start at bottom and increment or decrement as needed
  sampleVal = -amplitude
  i = 0

  # create 1 second sound
  for s in range (0, samplingRate):

    # if end of a half-cycle
    if (i == samplesPerHalfCycle):
      # reverse the increment every half-cycle
      increment = increment * -1
      # and reinit the half-cycle counter
      i = 0

    sampleVal = sampleVal + increment
    setSampleValueAt(triangle,s,sampleVal)
    i = i + 1

  play(triangle)
  return triangle
```

Use it like this (Figure 8.6):

```
>>> tri440=triangleWave(440,4000)
>>> explore(tri440)
```

FIGURE 8.6
Exploring a triangular wave.

How It Works

This recipe is similar to the one that creates square waves but these waves are triangular in shape. The `sampleValue` will be initialized to the negation of the passed amplitude. An increment is added to the `sampleValue` each time through the loop. The variable `i` tracks where we are in the cycle and when we reach halfway through a cycle it negates the `increment` and resets the value of `i` to zero.

8.6   MODERN MUSIC SYNTHESIS

Additive synthesis is how early music synthesizers worked. Nowadays, additive synthesis isn't too common because the sounds it generates don't sound natural. Synthesizing from recorded sounds is quite common.

The most common synthesis technique today is probably **frequency modulation synthesis or FM synthesis**. In FM synthesis, an oscillator (a programmed object that generates a regular series of outputs) controls (modulates) frequencies with other frequencies. The result is a richer sound, less tinny or computer-sounding.

Another common technique is **subtractive synthesis**. In subtractive synthesis, *noise* is used as the input, and then *filters* are applied to remove unwanted frequencies. The result is, again, a richer sound, though typically not as rich as FM synthesis.

Why would we want to create sounds or music with computers anyway? What's the point when there are lots of great sounds, music, and musicians in the world? The point is that if you want to tell someone else *how* you got that sound, so that they could replicate the process or even modify the sound in some way (perhaps making it better), a program is the way to do it. A program succinctly captures and communicates a process—how a sound or a piece of music is generated.

8.6.1 MP3

Nowadays, the audio files on your computer are most commonly MP3 files (or perhaps MP4 or one of its related or descendant file types). MP3 files are sound (and video, in some cases) encodings based on the MPEG-3 standard. They are audio files but compressed in special ways.

One way in which MP3 files are compressed is called **lossless compression**. As we know, there are techniques for storing data that use fewer bits. For example, we know that every sample is typically two bytes wide. What if we didn't store every sample but instead stored the *difference* from the last sample to this sample? The difference between samples is usually much smaller than 32,767 to −32,768—it might be +/− 1000. That takes fewer bits to store.

But MP3 also uses **lossy compression**. It actually throws away some of the sound information. For example, if there's a really soft sound immediately after or simultaneous with a really loud sound, you won't be able to hear the soft sound. An *analog* recording (the type used in records) keeps all those frequencies. MP3 throws away the ones you can't actually hear. Analog recordings are different than digital recordings in that they continuously record the sound while digital recordings take samples at time intervals.

WAV files are compressed, but not as much as MP3, and they only use lossless techniques. MP3 files tend to be much smaller than the same sound in a WAV format. AIFF files are similar to WAV files.

8.6.2 MIDI

MIDI is the *Musical Instrument Digital Interface*. It's really a set of agreements between manufacturers of computer music devices (sequencers, synthesizers, drum machines, keyboards, etc.) for how their devices will work together. Using MIDI, you can control various synthesizers and drum machines from different keyboards.

MIDI is not used for encoding sound as much as encoding music. MIDI doesn't record what something sounds like, but how it is played. Literally, MIDI encodes information like "Press the key down on synthesized instrument X at pitch Y," then later "Release the key Y on instrument X." The quality of MIDI sound depends entirely on the synthesizer, the device generating the synthesized instrument.

MIDI files tend to be very small. Instructions like "Play key #42 on track 7" are only some five bytes long. This makes MIDI attractive in comparison with large sound files. MIDI has been particularly popular for karaoke machines.

MIDI has an advantage over MP3 or WAV files in that it can specify a lot of music in very few bytes. But MIDI can't record sounds. For example, if you want to record a specific person's style of playing an instrument, or record *anyone* singing, you don't want to use MIDI. To capture actual sounds, you need to record the actual samples, so you'll need MP3 or WAV.

Most modern operating systems have pretty good synthesizers built into them. We can use them from Python. JES has built into it a function `playNote` that takes as input a MIDI note, a duration (how long to play the sound) in milliseconds, and an intensity (how hard to strike the key) from 0 to 127. `playNote` will always use a piano-sounding instrument. MIDI notes correspond to keys, not to frequencies. C in the first octave is 1, C# is 2. C in the fourth octave is 60, D is 62, and E is 64.

Here's a simple example of playing some MIDI notes from JES. We can use `for` loops to specify loops in the music.

Program 81: Playing MIDI Notes (Example)

```
def song():
    playNote(60,200,127)
    playNote(62,500,127)
    playNote(64,800,127)
    playNote(60,600,127)
```

PROGRAMMING SUMMARY

`if`	Allows Python to make decisions. `if` takes an expression to test for true or false (basically, anything that evaluates to 0 is false, and everything else is true). The block that follows is executed if the test is true.
`int`	Returns the integer part of the input value, throwing away anything after the decimal.
`setMediaPath()`	Lets you pick a folder where you get and store media.
`getMediaPath(baseFileName)`	Takes an input of a base file name, then returns the complete path to that file (assuming it's in the media folder that you set using `setMediaPath()`).
`playNote`	Takes as input the note, duration, and intensity. Each note is represented as an integer value from 0 to 127 and middle C is 60. The duration is specified in milliseconds. The intensity can also range from 0 to 127. If you leave this out JES will use 64 for the intensity.

PROBLEMS

8.1   What are each of the following:

1. MIDI

2. MP3

3. Analog

4. Amplitude

5. Sampling rate

8.2   What is the difference between lossless compression and lossy compression? Which type of sound files use what type of compression?

8.3   Rewrite the echo function (Program 69 (page 187)) to generate *two* echoes back, each `delay` samples previous. *Hint:* Start your index loop at `2*delay + 1`, then access one echo sample at `index-delay` and another at `index - 2*delay`.

8.4   Write a general blend function that takes the two sounds to blend as input and returns a new sound. It can also take the number of samples to use from the first sound before the blend begins and the number of samples to blend.

8.5   How long is a sound compared to the original when it's been frequency doubled (Program 72 (page 189))? How long is a sound compared to the original when only every fourth sound value is copied into the target sound?

8.6   Write a function that will create a new sound with one half of one sound and then add the two sounds together and then add the second half of the second sound. This is easiest to do if the sounds have the same length.

8.7   Write a function that will blend three sounds together. Start with part of the first sound, then a blend of sound1 and sound2, and then a blend of sound2 and sound3, and end with the rest of sound3.

8.8   Blend in some words over some music. Start with the music at 75% and the words at 25% and gradually make the words 75% and the music 25%.

8.9   Write a function to create a pyramid sound wave.

8.10   Write a function to create a sawtooth sound wave.

8.11   Write a function to change the frequency of a sound 10 times.

8.12   Create another version of the shift function that creates the target to be as big as the resulting sound should be. So if the factor is less than one it would create a larger sound and if greater than one a smaller sound.

8.13   Does the shift function work with a factor of 0.3? If it doesn't, can you fix it to copy each source value 3 times into the target?

8.14   Hip-hop DJ's spin turntables back and forth so that sections of sound are played forwards and backwards quickly. Try combining backwards play (Program 66 (page 179)) and frequency shifting (Program 72 (page 189)) to get the same effect. Play a second of a sound quickly forward, then quickly backward, two or three times. (You might have to move faster than just double the speed.)

8.15   Consider changing the `if` block in the frequency shift recipe (Program 75 (page 192)) to `sourceIndex = sourceIndex - getLength(source)`. What's the difference from just setting the `sourceIndex` to 0? Is this better or worse? Why?

8.16   If you use the shifting recipe (Program 75 (page 192)) with a factor of 2.0 or 3.0, you'll get the sound repeated or even triplicated. Why? Can you fix it? Write `shiftDur` that takes a number of samples (or even seconds) to play the sound.

8.17   Using the sound tools, figure out the characteristic pattern of different instruments. For example, pianos tend to have a pattern the opposite of what we created—the amplitudes *decrease* as we get to higher sine waves. Try creating a variety of patterns and see how they sound and how they look.

8.18   When musicians work with additive synthesis, they will often wrap *envelopes* around the sounds, and even around each added sine wave. An envelope *changes* the amplitude over time—it might start out small, then grow (rapidly or slowly), then hold at a certain value during the sound, and then drop before the sound ends. That kind of pattern is sometimes called the *attack-sustain-decay (ASD) envelope*. Pianos tend to attack quickly, then decay quickly. Flutes tend to attack slowly and sustain as long as you want. Try implementing that for the sine and square wave generators.

8.19   Create a function to play a song using MIDI.

TO DIG DEEPER

Good books on computer music say a lot about creating sounds from scratch, as in this chapter. One of Mark's favorites for understandability is *Computer Music: Synthesis, Composition, and Performance* by Dodge and Jerse [11]. The "bible" of computer music is Curtis Roads's massive *The Computer Music Tutorial* [35].

One of the most powerful tools for playing with this level of computer music is *CSound*. It's a software music synthesis system, free, and totally cross-platform. The book by Richard Boulanger [7] has everything you need for playing with CSound.

CHAPTER 9

Building Bigger Programs

Chapter Learning Objectives

- To demonstrate two different design strategies: top-down and bottom-up.
- To demonstrate different testing strategies, such as black box and glass box.
- To demonstrate several debugging strategies to use when figuring out programming problems.

The computer science goals for this chapter are:

- To use methods for accepting user input and generating output for the user.
- To use a new iteration structure, the `while` loop.

For many problems that you might solve with a program, the kinds of programs we have been writing so far in this book will work just fine. Relatively small programs with maybe a dozen lines of code can solve many interesting problems and make many interesting creations. There are many, many more problems and creations, though, that *could* be solved with larger and more complex programs. That's what this chapter is about. These are the issues that are addressed by the field of *software engineering*.

Writing larger programs involves solving problems that have to do with managing the activity of programming itself.

- What program lines are you going to write? How are you going to decide what functions you need? This is the process of *design*. There are many approaches to design, but the two most common are **top-down** and **bottom-up**. In top-down design, you figure out what has to be done, refine the *requirements* until you think you can identify the pieces, and then you write the pieces (typically from the highest level first). In bottom-up design, you start with what you know, and keep adding to it until you've got your program.

- Things won't work the first time. Programming has been defined as "the art of debugging a blank sheet of paper."[1] Debugging is figuring out what *doesn't* work, why, and how to fix it. The activity of programming and the activity of *debugging* are intricately connected. Learning to debug is an important skill that leads to figuring out how to make programs that actually *run*.

- Even if things work the first time, it's unlikely that you got it completely right. Big programs have lots of parts to them. You need to use *testing* techniques to make sure that you got all (or even most) of the mistakes (*bugs*) in the program.

- Even after testing and debugging, most large programs are not "done." Many large programs get used over a long period of time to solve problems that come up often (like bookkeeping or tracking inventory). These large programs are *never* finished. Instead, new features are added, or newly discovered bugs have to be squashed. The *maintenance* stage of program development goes on for as long as the program is in use. Overall, over the course of a lifetime of a program, maintenance is *by far* the most expensive part.

9.1   DESIGNING PROGRAMS TOP-DOWN

Top-down design is how most engineering disciplines recommend designing. You start out by developing a list of *requirements*: what needs to be done, using English or math, that can be iteratively refined. Refining requirements means making them clearer and more specific. The goal of refining requirements in top-down design is to get to the point where the statements of the requirements can be directly implemented as program code.

The top-down process is preferred because it's understandable and you can plan for it—it's really what makes the business of software possible. Imagine working with a customer who wants you to program something. You are given a problem statement and then work with the customer to refine it into to a set of requirements. You go build the program. If the customer is not happy with it, you can test to see if the software meets the requirements. If it does, and the customer agreed to the requirements, then you've met your agreement. If it doesn't, then you need to make it meet the requirements—but not necessarily meet the customer's changed needs.

In detail, the process looks something like this:

- Start out with the problem statement. If you don't have one, write one. What are you trying to do?

---

[1] http://foldoc.doc.ic.ac.uk/foldoc/index.html.

- Start refining the problem statement. Are there parts to the program? Perhaps you should use **hierarchical decomposition** to define subfunctions? Do you know that you have to open some pictures or set some constant values? And then are there some loops? How many do you need?

- Keep refining the problem statement until you get to statements or commands or functions that you know (or know how to write).

- When you are working on a large program, you are almost certainly going to use functions that call other functions (*subfunctions*). Start by writing the functions you might call from the Command Area, then the lower level functions, until you get to the subfunctions.

9.1.1 A Top-Down Design Example

If we followed this process and defined functions (*procedures*) instead of lines of code, we would be using **procedural abstraction**. In procedural abstraction, you define high-level functions that call lower-level functions. The lower-level functions are easy to write and test, and the higher-level functions become easy to read, because they're simply calling lower-level functions.

We have seen some procedural abstraction earlier in the book. An example is when we redefined the collage in terms of lower-level functions that did copying of pixels for us. These lower-level functions are a form of abstraction. By naming those lines of code with a function name, we can stop thinking in terms of those individual lines, and instead use a meaningful name for those lines. By providing parameters to the function, we make the function reusable.

Let's build a simple *adventure game*. An adventure game is a kind of video game where the player explores a world, moving between rooms and spaces in the game using commands like "go north" and "take the key." Often there are puzzles to solve and battles to wage. The original adventure game was written in the 1970's by William Crowther and then extended by Don Woods. It was based on exploration of a set of caves. The genre was made popular in the 1980's with the Infocom games like *Zork* and *Hitchhiker's Guide to the Galaxy*. Modern adventure games tend to be graphical, like *Myst*. The original text-based adventure games blended gaming with storytelling, which is what we'll aim for.

At this point, we need to define our problem. What kind of adventure game are we going to build? What size? What will the user be able to do? We want to define the problem within the limitations of what we can develop.

Let's build an adventure game where the user can walk between rooms and that's it. No puzzles and no real game play. We want just a simple example. Here's a sketch of how a simple set of rooms might be laid out. Just to make it interesting, let's pretend it's a setting for a horror or thriller story.

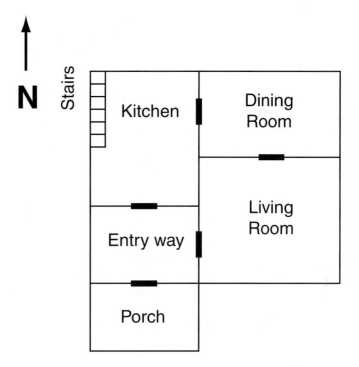

9.1.2   Designing the Top-Level Function

How will our program work? We can come up with an outline for how it might run:

1. We start out by telling the player the basics of how to play the game.

2. We describe the room to the player. Let's put the player in a particular room to start.

3. We get the player's command ("north" or "quit") typed in.

4. We figure out which room the user goes into next, because of their command (direction) choice.

5. We repeat from step 2 on until the user says to quit.

We can actually write the function that will do these things right now. We need to know a couple of additional functions in Python that we haven't seen yet.

- `printNow` is a function[2] that takes a string as input then prints it to the Command Area *as soon as it executes*. That's in contrast to `print` which doesn't display anything to the Command Area until the program is done running. `printNow` is useful for displaying things during the game.

- To get input from the user we can use `requestString`. The function `request String` takes as input a prompt that will appear in the window requesting user

---

[2]In Python 3.0, even `print` is a function, so it's not as strange as it might seem.

What is your name?

Mark

OK   Cancel

FIGURE 9.1
What the requestString dialog looks like.

input (Figure 9.1). (In Python, the ability to read a string input from the user is called raw_input.) The function returns the string that the user types in.

```
>>> print requestString("What is your name?")
Mark
```

• The bigger challenge is how to just keep repeating some lines of code *indefinitely* until something specific happens. We can't do that with a for loop.

Instead, we'll use a new kind of loop called a while loop. A while loop takes a test (like an if). What's different, compared with if, is that the while loop repeats the body of the loop *indefinitely* until the test becomes true.

```
>>> x = 0
>>> while (x < 3):
...             print "Counting..."
...             x = x + 1
...
Counting...
Counting...
Counting...
```

With these three new pieces, we can write the function that corresponds to the outline that appeared earlier.

Program 82: Top-Level Function of Adventure Game
```
def playGame():
  location = "Porch"
  showIntroduction()
  while not (location == "Exit") :
    showRoom(location)
    direction = requestString("Which direction?")
    location = pickRoom(direction, location)
```

This function is pretty close to the outline we presented earlier, line-for-line. What may be strange here is that we have not seen or written some of these functions, like showIntroduction, showRoom, and pickRoom. That is one of the points of top-down design—we can make the *plan* for how the whole program should work, and what functions we will need in the full program, long before we write all the parts.

How It Works

- We will use the variable `location` to store the room where the player currently is. We'll start out on the "Porch."
- The function `showIntroduction` will display the instructions to the user.
- We will use the location "Exit" to represent the player's request to leave the game. While the location is *not* "Exit," we will keep playing the game.
- At the start of each turn, we show the description of the current room. The function `showRoom` will display the room's description, using the player's `location` as the input for which room to show.
- We get the user's request for a new `direction` via `requestString`.
- We pick a new room for the user via the `pickRoom` function, based on the inputs of the requested `direction` and the current room `location`.

Notice that we know *nothing* about how these subfunctions will work. We cannot possibly know how they will work right now, since we have not written them yet. What this means is that this top-level function, `playGame`, is *decoupled* from the lower-level subfunctions. We define them in terms of the inputs, outputs, and what they should do. Somebody else could write these functions for us now. That's another reason why top-level design is so commonly used for engineering.

- It makes it easier to maintain, since the different pieces can change without changing the whole thing.
- We plan functions before we write them.
- We can allow different programmers to work together on the same program, working from the plan.

9.1.3   Writing the Subfunctions

Now that we have the plan, we can just go ahead and write the rest of the subfunctions to make this work. For right now, we will put all these functions in the file together to make it work right. We could also put useful functions in a separate file and `import` the functions. For now, let's just complete our design and implementation of the adventure game.

Program 83: showIntroduction for the Adventure Game

```
def showIntroduction():
  printNow("Welcome to the Adventure House!")
  printNow("In each room, you will be told which directions
    you can go.")
  printNow("You can move north, south, east, or west by typing
    that direction.")
  printNow("Type help to replay this introduction.")
  printNow("Type quit or exit to end the program.")
```

How It Works

Showing the introduction simply displays information for the user/player, via the printNow function. We tell the player how to move (by typing a direction), and how to get help or quit. Notice that, in so doing, we are further defining the later functions. In our pickRoom function, we will have to manage inputs like "help," "quit," and "exit."

Program 84: showRoom for the Adventure Game

```
def showRoom(room):
  if room == "Porch":
    showPorch()
  if room == "Entryway":
    showEntryway()
  if room == "Kitchen":
    showKitchen()
  if room == "LivingRoom":
    showLR()
  if room == "DiningRoom":
    showDR()
```

How It Works

We could make showRoom into a long function with lots of printNow function calls. However, that would be tedious to write and challenging to maintain. What if you wanted to change the description of the living room? You could wade through a long function and find the right printNow to change. Or, you could simply change the showLR function. That's how we set it up here.

Program 85: pickRoom for the Adventure Game

```
def pickRoom(direction, room):
  if (direction == "quit") or (direction == "exit"):
    printNow("Goodbye!")
    return "Exit"
  if direction == "help":
    showIntroduction()
    return room
  if room == "Porch":
    if direction == "north":
      return "Entryway"
  if room == "Entryway":
    if direction == "north":
      return "Kitchen"
    if direction == "east":
      return "LivingRoom"
    if direction == "south":
      return "Porch"
  if room == "Kitchen":
```

```
    if direction == "east":
       return "DiningRoom"
    if direction == "south":
       return "Entryway"
 if room == "LivingRoom":
    if direction == "west":
       return "Entryway"
    if direction == "north":
       return "DiningRoom"
 if room == "DiningRoom":
    if direction == "west":
       return "Kitchen"
    if direction == "south":
       return "LivingRoom"
```

How It Works

This function is defined by the map. Given a current room and the desired direction, this function returns the name of the new room for the player to be located in.

Program 86: Showing Rooms in the Adventure Game

```
def showPorch():
 printNow("You are on the porch of a frightening looking house.")
 printNow("The windows are broken. It's a dark and stormy night.")
 printNow("You can go north into the house. If you dare.")

def showEntryway():
 printNow("You are in the entry way of the house. There are cobwebs in the corner.")
 printNow("You feel a sense of dread.")
 printNow("There is a passageway to the north and another to the east.")
 printNow("The porch is behind you to the south.")

def showKitchen():
 printNow("You are in the kitchen. All the surfaces are covered with pots, pans,¬
 food pieces, and pools of blood.")
 printNow("You think you hear something up the stairs that go up the west side of¬
 the room.")
 printNow("It's a scraping noise, like something being dragged along the floor.")
 printNow("You can go to the south or east.")

def showLR():
 printNow("You are in a living room. There are couches, chairs, and small tables.")
 printNow("Everything is covered in dust and spider webs.")
 printNow("You hear a crashing noise in another room.")
 printNow("You can go north or west.")
```

¬These lines of the program should continue with the next lines. A single command in Python may not break across multiple lines.

```
def showDR():
 printNow("You are in the dining room.")
 printNow("There are remains of a meal on the table.  You can't tell what it is,¬
 and maybe don't want to.")
 printNow("Was that a thump to the west?")
 printNow("You can go south or west")
```

¬These lines of the program should continue with the next lines. A single command in Python may not break across multiple lines.

How It Works

For each room, there are simply some printNow invocations to describe that room. From a programming sense, these are very simple functions. From the author's perspective, this is where the fun and creative stuff is.

We now have enough to play our game. We start it by invoking our top-level function, by typing playGame(). Descriptions show up in the Command Area and prompts appear in a dialog box above the game (Figure 9.2). A run of the program might look like this:

```
>>> playGame()
Welcome to the Adventure House!
In each room, you will be told which directions you
   can go.
You can move north, south, east, or west by typing that
   direction.
Type help to replay this introduction.
Type quit or exit to end the program.
You are on the porch of a frightening looking house.
```

FIGURE 9.2
Screenshot of adventure game play.

The windows are broken. It's a dark and stormy night.
You can go north into the house. If you dare.
You are in the entry way of the house. There are
  cobwebs in the corner.
You feel a sense of dread.
There is a passageway to the north and another to
  the east.
The porch is behind you to the south.
You are in a living room. There are couches, chairs,
  and small tables.
Everything is covered in dust and spider webs.
You hear a crashing noise in another room.
You can go north or west.
Goodbye!

9.2   DESIGNING PROGRAMS BOTTOM-UP

Bottom-up is a different process, that can end up in essentially the same place. You start with some idea of what you want to do—you could call it a problem statement. But instead of refining the problem, you focus on building the solution program. You want to reuse code from other programs as much as possible.

The most important thing you do with bottom-up design is to *try* your program *very* often. Does it do what you want? Does it do what you *expect*? Does it make sense? If not, add `print` statements and explore the code until you understand what it's doing. If you don't know what it does, you can't change it into what you want.

Here's what the bottom-up process typically looks like, starting from a problem statement:

- How much of the problem do you already know how to do? How much of it can you get from other programs that you've written? For example, does the problem say that you have to manipulate sound? Try a couple of sound recipes in the book to remember how to do that. Does it say that you have to change red levels? Can you find a recipe that does that and try it?

- Now, can you add some of these pieces (that you can write or can steal from other programs) together? Can you put together a couple of recipes that do *part* of what you want?

- Keep growing the program. Is it closer to what you need? What else do you need to add?

- Run your program *often*. Make sure it works and that you understand what you have so far.

- Repeat until you're satisfied with the result.

9.2.1   An Example Bottom-Up Process

Most of the examples in this book are developed in a bottom-up process. The way we did background subtraction and chromakey is a good example. We started out with the idea of removing the background of someone and putting them in a new picture. Where do we start?

We can imagine that part of the problem is finding all the pixels that are part of the person or part of the background. We've done things like that before, as when we found all the brown in Katie's hair in order to turn it red (Program 36 (page 106)). That tells us that we're going to want to check if there's a large enough distance between a person color and a background color, and if so, we want to bring in a new background's pixel's color—the pixel at the same point. We've done things like that, too, as when we copied pictures into the canvas.

At this point, we could probably write something like:

```
if distance(personColor,bgColor)<someThresholdValue:
    bgColor = getColor(getPixel(newBackground,x,y))
    setColor(getPixel(personPicture,x,y),bgColor)
```

That's the guts of the background subtraction recipe. The rest of it is simply setting up the variables (Program 45 (page 120)). But then, when we tried it, we found that it didn't work very well, for a variety of reasons. That's what led us to chromakey (Program 46 (page 123)). Chromakey is a better way of figuring out which pixels are part of the background and which are part of the foreground but the basic process is the same as swapping the background—so most of the program is reusable in the new context.

The key process here is to take ideas (or even lines of code) from other projects, and combine them, *testing* what you're doing all the time. Bottom-up programming is quite close to "debugging a blank sheet of paper." Debugging is a critical skill in bottom-up design or programming.

9.3   TESTING YOUR PROGRAM

It is really hard to test your programs well, especially for a new programmer. You wrote the code, so you assume that it does what you wrote! Becoming a good tester requires a large helping of humility. You have to accept the fact that you may have written something incorrectly or that you may not have completely understood *what* to write.

There are two main approaches to testing programs. One is called *glass-box testing*, which is where you test every possible path through your program. The approach is called "glass-box" because you actually look at your program and think through how to test each and every line of your program. You know what the structure of your program is, so you test according to that structure.

To use glass-box testing of our adventure game, we would traverse every door, in both directions. For example, go from the Porch north to the Entryway, then south back to the Porch. Did you go to the right place each time? Did the rooms display correctly? We would test what happens in response to the commands "help," "quit," and "exit." That would make sure that we test each and every line of our program.

The second approach is called *black-box testing*, where you do not consider how the program is written. Instead, you consider how the program is supposed to behave, and in particular, in response to both valid and *invalid* inputs. The player will not necessarily type the right commands. The player might make a mistake and mistype something or may try a command that she thinks is reasonable but you did not consider.

For example, let's use black-box testing with the `pickRoom` function. First we should test all the correct inputs to `pickRoom`, like this:

```
>>> pickRoom('north','Porch')
'Entryway'
>>> pickRoom('north','Entryway')
'Kitchen'
```

Now, let's try some invalid inputs—some misspellings and incorrect ideas.

```
>>> pickRoom('nrth','Porch')
>>> pickRoom('Entryway','Porch')
```

That's a real problem. In response to invalid input, `pickRoom` does not return anything. When we try to set the variable `location` from the response, we will not be able to get a valid room. The variable `location` will be empty. Further, the player won't get any response that something has gone wrong.

We need to change `pickRoom` so that, if no other response matches, some reasonable reply is made, and a reasonable value is returned. Probably the most reasonable return is simply to return the same room—leave the player where she is.

Program 87: Improved `pickRoom` for the Adventure Game

```
def pickRoom(direction, room):
  if (direction == "quit") or (direction == "exit"):
    printNow("Goodbye!")
    return "Exit"
  if direction == "help":
    showIntroduction()
    return room
  if room == "Porch":
    if direction == "north":
      return "Entryway"
  if room == "Entryway":
    if direction == "north":
      return "Kitchen"
    if direction == "east":
      return "LivingRoom"
    if direction == "south":
      return "Porch"
  if room == "Kitchen":
    if direction == "east":
      return "DiningRoom"
    if direction == "south":
      return "Entryway"
  if room == "LivingRoom":
    if direction == "west":
      return "Entryway"
    if direction == "north":
      return "DiningRoom"
```

```
    if room == "DiningRoom":
      if direction == "west":
        return "Kitchen"
      if direction == "south":
        return "LivingRoom"
    printNow("You can't (or don't want to) go in that direction.")
  return room
```

Now, our program will work a bit more reasonably in response to incorrect input.

```
>>> pickRoom('nrth','Porch')
You can't (or don't want to) go in that direction.
'Porch'
>>> pickRoom('Entryway','Porch')
You can't (or don't want to) go in that direction.
'Porch'
```

The first sentence here is just saying that the input direction is not allowed and that the second line ('Porch') is the room that the player is now in.

9.3.1 Testing the Edge Conditions

Professional programmers test every program extensively to make sure that it works the way they expect. One of the black-box items they focus on is testing the *Edge conditions*. What's the smallest input that the program should work with? What's the largest input that the program should work with? Make sure that the program can work with both the smallest and largest possible inputs is what we mean by testing the edge conditions.

You can also use this strategy for testing your programs that manipulate media. Let's say that your picture-manipulation program fails (generates an error or doesn't seem to stop) with a particular picture and you've tried to trace the program but can't figure out why it's failing. Try it with a different picture. Does it work with a smaller picture? How about with an empty (all white or all black) picture? Maybe you'll find that your program works but is just so slow that you didn't think it was working with the larger picture.

Sometimes functions that manipulate indices (e.g., scaling programs) may fail on programs of one size but not another. For example, mirroring programs may work with odd-number indices but not even-number indices. Try inputs with different kinds of sizes to see which succeed or fail.

9.4 TIPS ON DEBUGGING

How do you figure out what your program is doing if it runs but isn't doing what you want? This is the process of *debugging*. Debugging is figuring out what your program is doing, how that differs from what you *want* it to be doing, and how to get the program from where it is to where you need it to be.

Starting from an error message is the *easiest* kind of debugging. You have some indication from Python about what the error is, and you have some idea (a line number) about where the error is. That tells you where to look to fix the problem and make the error go away.

The much harder kind of debugging is where the program works but doesn't do what you want. Now you have to figure out what the program is doing and what you want it to be doing.

The first step is *always* to **figure out what the program is doing**. Whether you have explicit error messages or not, this is always the first thing to do. If you get an error, the important question is why the program worked up to there, and what variable values were present at that point such that the error occurred.

> ### Computer Science Idea: Learn to Trace Code!
> The most important thing you can do when debugging your programs is to be able to trace your code. Think about your program the way the computer does. Walk each line and figure out what it does.

Start out debugging by walking the code, at least the lines around where the error is occurring. What does the error say? What might be causing the error? What are the values of the variables before and after that point? The interesting question is why the error occurred *now*. Why didn't it happen earlier in the program?

If you can, run the program. It's always easier to have the computer *tell* you what's happening instead of having to figure it out yourself. That said, simply executing your functions won't give you the answer. Add `print` statements to your code to show you the values of the variables.

> ### Debugging Tip: Print Statements Are Your Friends!
> Print out what's going on in your programs. Do this when you can't figure out what's going on from tracing the program. Print out the values of equations that are too complex. Print out simple statements like "I'm in this function now!" to let you know that you are reaching the functions you think you're calling. Let the computer *tell* you what it's doing.

Sometimes, especially in a loop, you'll want to use `printNow`. Since `printNow` prints the input string to the Command Area *as soon as it occurs*, it is more useful than `print` for debugging. You want to be able to see what's happening *when* it's happening.

> ### Debugging Tip: Don't Be Afraid to Change the Program
> Save a new copy of your program, then edit out all the parts you're confused about. Can you get the rest to run? Now start adding pieces back in (copy–paste) from the original copy of your program. Changing the program so that you're only running part of it at a time is a great way to figure out what's going on.

9.4.1 Finding Which Statement to Worry About

The bugs that are often hardest to figure out are the ones that *look* just fine. Spacing errors and mismatched parentheses fall into this category. These are particularly hard to find in large programs, where the error just says that there's a problem "somewhere" around a given line, but Python isn't exactly sure where.

A time-honored strategy for figuring out what's wrong is to get rid of all the statements that you're sure about. Simply put a "#" in front of the statements that you think are okay. If you comment out an if or for, make sure that you also comment out the block after the statement. Now try again.

If the error goes away, then you were wrong—you actually commented out the statements where the problem is. Uncomment a few and try again. When the error message comes back, the error is in one of the lines that you just uncommented.

If the error is still there, you now have only a few statements to check—the ones that are still uncommented. Eventually, the error either goes away or you have a single line that's uncommented. Either way, you can now figure out where the error is.

9.4.2 Seeing the Variables

Besides printing, there are other tools built into JES to help you figure out what your programs are doing. The showVars function will show you all the variables and their values at the point when it's executed (Figure 9.3). It will show you both the variables in the current *context* and the variables in the *global* context (accessible even from the Command Area). You can use showVars() in the Command Area to see the variables you've created there—perhaps you'd forgotten their names or wanted to see what the values were in several variables at once.

The other powerful tool in JES is the *Watcher*. The Watcher allows you to see which lines are being executed *as* they are executed. Figure 9.4 shows the Watcher running the code given below—the makeSunset() function from Program 13 (page 60). We simply open the Watcher (from the debug menu or from the WATCHER button), then use the Command Area as normal. Whenever we execute our own functions, the Watcher will run.

```
def makeSunset(picture):
  reduceBlue(picture)
  reduceGreen(picture)

def reduceBlue(picture):
  for p in getPixels(picture):
    value=getBlue(p)
    setBlue(p,value*0.7)

def reduceGreen(picture):
  for p in getPixels(picture):
    value=getGreen(p)
    setGreen(p,value*0.7)
```

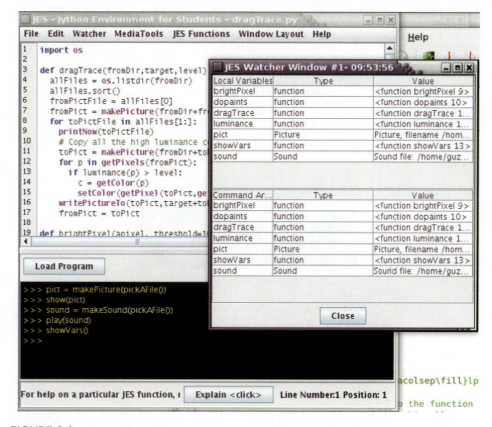

FIGURE 9.3
Showing variables in JES.

We can PAUSE execution, then STEP through it from there. We can also STOP execution, go FULL SPEED, or even set a speed from slow to fast. When you have the Watcher open, the program *will* run more slowly. The faster the program runs, the less information will be displayed (i.e., not every line executed will show up in the Watcher).

Besides stepping through execution and seeing which statements get executed when, you can also observe particular variables. After clicking ADD VARIABLE, you will be prompted for the name of the variable. Then, when the Watcher runs, the value of the variable will be displayed along with the line. When the variable doesn't have a value yet, you'll see that too (Figure 9.5).

9.4.3   Debugging the Adventure Game

Let's use some of these techniques with the adventure game. The problem that we have with the adventure game is that it basically works! There are no obvious error messages generated. By going through our testing process, we were able to figure out that we were not handling invalid input correctly. What else could be a problem?

FIGURE 9.4
Stepping through the makeSunset() function with the Watcher.

FIGURE 9.5
Watching the variable value in the makeSunset() function with the Watcher.

Let's look at what happens when we run the program:

```
>>> playGame()
Welcome to the Adventure House!
In each room, you will be told which directions you
    can go.
You can move north, south, east, or west by typing
    that direction.
Type help to replay this introduction.
```

Type quit or exit to end the program.
You are on the porch of a frightening looking house.
The windows are broken. It's a dark and stormy night.
You can go north into the house. If you dare.
You are in the entry way of the house. There are
  cobwebs in the corner.
You feel a sense of dread.
There is a passageway to the north and another to
  the east.
The porch is behind you to the south.
You are in a living room. There are couches, chairs,
  and small tables.
Everything is covered in dust and spider webs.
You hear a crashing noise in another room.
You can go north or west.
You are in the dining room.
There are remains of a meal on the table. You can't
  tell what it is, and maybe don't want to.
Was that a thump to the west?
You can go south or west
You are in the kitchen. All the surfaces are covered
  with pots, pans, food pieces, and pools of blood.
You think you hear something up the stairs that go up
  the west side of the room.
It's a scraping noise, like something being dragged
  along the floor.
You can go to the south or east.
Goodbye!

What's wrong with that? Here are two problems that we have with that printout:

1. It's really hard to look back and figure out which room was which. The room descriptions all blur together.

2. We can't go back and figure out what we typed where. If this was a big map with lots of rooms, we would want to be able to scroll back and figure out what we typed to get to different rooms.

Let's deal with the first one. We need some kind of space or separator to appear between room descriptions. Where would we put that statement? Certainly, it has to be *inside* the main top-level loop. It could go inside the showRoom function, maybe as the first line. Or it could go in the top-level function, just before or after we show the room. On the grounds that it's better to make detail changes in the subfunctions, let's change showRoom.

Program 88: Improved showRoom for the Adventure Game

```
def showRoom(room):
  printNow("===========")
  if room == "Porch":
```

```
      showPorch()
if room == "Entryway":
    showEntryway()
if room == "Kitchen":
    showKitchen()
if room == "LivingRoom":
    showLR()
if room == "DiningRoom":
    showDR()
```

■

Now, let's deal with the second one. We should print out what the player typed. We have to do this *after* the call to requestString. This change could, again, be in the top-level loop, or could be at the start of pickRoom. Both could work. This time, let's take the opposite choice. The function pickRoom is pretty complicated already. Let's respond right after the player makes a choice.

Program 89: Improved playGame for the Adventure Game

```
def playGame():
  location = "Porch"
  showIntroduction()
  while not (location == "Exit") :
    showRoom(location)
    direction = requestString("Which direction?")
    printNow("You typed: "+direction)
    location = pickRoom(direction, location)
```

■

Now we can try our debugged program.

```
>>> playGame()
Welcome to the Adventure House!
In each room, you will be told which directions you
    can go.
You can move north, south, east, or west by typing
    that direction.
Type help to replay this introduction.
Type quit or exit to end the program.
===========
You are on the porch of a frightening looking house.
The windows are broken. It's a dark and stormy night.
You can go north into the house. If you dare.
You typed: north

===========
You are in the entry way of the house. There are
    cobwebs in the corner.
You feel a sense of dread.
There is a passageway to the north and another to
    the east.
```

```
The porch is behind you to the south.
You typed: east
===========
You are in a living room. There are couches, chairs,
  and small tables.
Everything is covered in dust and spider webs.
You hear a crashing noise in another room.
You can go north or west.
You typed: north
===========
You are in the dining room.
There are remains of a meal on the table.  You can't
  tell what it is, and maybe don't want to.
Was that a thump to the west?
You can go south or west
You typed: west
===========
You are in the kitchen. All the surfaces are covered
  with pots, pans, food pieces, and pools of blood.
You think you hear something up the stairs that go up
  the west side of the room.
It's a scraping noise, like something being dragged
  along the floor.
You can go to the south or east.
You typed: south
===========
You are in the entry way of the house. There are
  cobwebs in the corner.
You feel a sense of dread.
There is a passageway to the north and another to
  the east.
The porch is behind you to the south.
You typed: exit
Goodbye!
```

9.5   ALGORITHMS AND DESIGN

Algorithms are general descriptions of processes that can be implemented in any specific programming language. Knowledge of algorithms is one of the tools in professional programmers' toolboxes. We've seen several algorithms so far:

- The *sampling algorithm* is a process that can be used to shift a sound's frequency up or down or to scale a picture smaller or larger. We don't have to talk about loops or incrementing source or target indices to describe the sampling algorithm. The sampling algorithm works by changing how we copy samples or pixels from a source to a target—instead of taking every sample or pixel, we can take every other sample/pixel, or every sample/pixel twice, or some other pattern of sampling.

- We've also seen how we copy pixels or samples from a source to a target. We simply keep track of where we are in both the source and target.
- We've seen that blending is essentially the same for both pixels and samples. We apply a weighting to each of the pixels or samples being summed, then add the weighted values to create a blended sound or a blended picture.

The role of algorithms in design is to allow us to *abstract* a description of the program to be designed, above the basic program code. Professional programmers know lots of algorithms and this allows them to think through program design problems at a higher level. We can talk about negating pictures and mirroring the negated pictures *without* talking about loops or source and target indices. We can focus on more abstract names like "mirroring" without focusing on code.

Programmers also know a lot *about* the algorithms they know. They know how to make the algorithms efficient, and when they're not useful, and what the hitches about them might be. For example, we know that when scaling sound, we have to be careful not to go beyond the bounds of the sound. There are better and worse algorithms, in terms of how quickly they execute and how much memory they require. We will say more about speed of algorithms in Chapter 13.

9.6 RUNNING PROGRAMS OUTSIDE OF JES

Python programs can be run in many ways. If you build larger and more complex programs, you will want to run them outside of JES. What you are learning in this book is *directly* usable in Python (or Jython). Commands like `for` and `print` work in both Python and Jython. System libraries like `ftplib` and `urllib` are exactly the same in Python and Jython.

However, the media tools we're using are not built-in to Python or Jython. It's possible to do it in Python. There are Python implementations like Myro (`http://www.roboteducation.org`) that include the same image functions as in JES. There is also the *Python Imaging Library (PIL)* which provide similar functionality, with differently named functions.

You can use the libraries that we provide in Jython. Jython is available at `http://www.jython.org` for most computer systems. Our media libraries works in Jython with only a few extra commands (see Figure 9.6).

Here's how we make the media functions work in traditional Jython.

- To find modules to `import`, Python uses a variable called `sys.path` (from the built-in system library `sys`) to list all the directories where it should look for modules. If you want to use the JES media library in Jython, you need to put the location of those module files in your `sys.path`. (This is what `setLibPath` does for you in JES.)

    You need to `import sys` to get access to the `sys.path` variable. To manipulate that variable, we use the method `insert` to put the JES SOURCES directory in your path (see Figure 9.6). On the Macintosh, you will need to reference the Java and

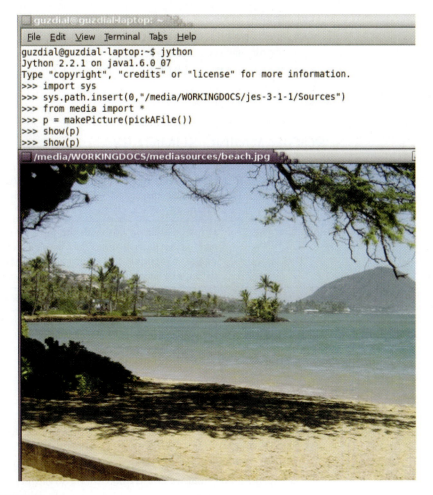

FIGURE 9.6
Using Jython to do media functions outside of JES.

Jython code inside the JES application, typing something like `sys.path.insert`
`(0,"/users/guzdial/JES.app/Contents/Resources/Java")`.

- You then use `from media import *` to make things like `pickAFile` and
  `makePicture` available in Jython.

  The statement `from media import *` is actually inserted (invisibly to you,
  the student programmer) into your Program Area each time you press the LOAD
  button. That's how the special media features of JES are made available to your
  programs.

Here's how it works to generate the image Figure 9.6 from Linux:

```
guzdial@guzdial-laptop:~\$ jython
Jython 2.2.1 on java1.6.0_07
Type "copyright", "credits" or "license" for more
  information.
```

```
>>> import sys
>>> sys.path.insert(0,"/media/MyUSB/jes-4-0/Sources")
>>> from media import *
>>> p = makePicture(pickAFile())
>>> show(p)
```

PROGRAMMING SUMMARY

printNow	Prints the input to the function *immediately*, while the program is still running. Whereas print doesn't print the input until the program finishes executing.
requestString	Displays a dialog box with the input prompt, accepts a string from the user, and returns that string. The analogous functions requestNumber, requestInteger, and even requestIntegerInRange (which restricts the entered integer to being between two input values) also exist in JES.
showVars	Displays all the existing variables and their values.
while	Loops through the statements in the block of statements following the while statement as long the test specified in the while statement is true.

PROBLEMS

9.1 Typically, one does not *optimize* a program (make it run faster or with less use of memory) until after it is running, well-debugged, and well-tested. (Of course, you still have to test again after each optimizing modification.) Here is an optimization that we could make to the adventure game. Currently, showRoom compares the room variable to each possible room—even if it matched earlier. Python gives us a way of only testing once, by using an elif instead of later if statements. The statement elif means "else if." You only test the elif statement if the earlier if was false. You may have as many elif statements as you like after an if. You might use it like this:

```
if (room == ''Porch''):
    showPorch()
elif (room == ''Kitchen''):
    showKitchen()
```

Rewrite the showRoom method more optimally by using elif.

9.2 A function like pickRoom is hard to read with all the nested if statements. It can be made clearer with appropriate use of comments to explain what each section of code is doing—checking the room, then checking the possible directions in the room. Add comments to pickRoom to make it easier to read.

9.3 Add comments to *all* the methods, to make it easier for someone else to read the function.

9.4   Add another variable for the player, called a `hand`. Make the hand initially empty. Change the description so that there is a "key" in the Living Room. If the player types the command `key` while in the Living Room, the key gets put in the hand. Now, if the player has the key when entering the Kitchen, the stairs become accessible, allowing the player to go "west" and up the stairs. You will have to add some rooms to the game to make this work.

9.5   Create the ability to go `down` from the porch, to explore a secret underground world.

9.6   Add additional secret items to have in the player's hand to allow different rooms to be accessed, such as a lantern to allow access to a tunnel under the porch.

9.7   Add a "bomb" in the Dining Room. If the player types `bomb` in the Dining Room, the bomb goes in the hand. If the player types `bomb` in the upstairs where the Ogre is, the bomb is dropped and the Ogre is blasted to smithereens.

9.8   Add the ability for the player to *lose* the game (perhaps die). When the player loses, the game should print what happened, and then the game exits. Perhaps finding the Ogre *without* the bomb in the player's hand will make the player lose the game.

9.9   Add the ability for the player to *win* the game. When the player wins, the game should print what happened and exit the game. Perhaps finding the secret treasure room under the Porch would make the player win the game.

9.10 Room descriptions do not have to be wholly verbal. Play a relevant sound when the player enters a particular room. Use `play`, so that game play can continue while the sound is playing.

9.11 Room descriptions can be visual, as well as textual and auditory. Display a picture relevant to the room when the room is entered. For extra credit, only `show` a picture once, and if the room is reentered, `repaint` the picture to bring it back to the front again.

9.12 A source of possible error in this adventure game is that the names for the rooms appear in several places. If the Dining Room is spelled "DiningRoom" in one place and "DinngRoom" (missing the second "i") in another place, the game won't work correctly. The more rooms you add, and the more places where you have the room names typed, the odds increase that the error will be made.
      There are a couple of ways of making this error less likely to occur:

   - Do not name the rooms with strings of characters. Instead, use numbers. It's easier to type and check "4" than "DiningRoom."

   - Use a *variable* for `DiningRoom` and use that one variable for checking the location. Then it doesn't matter if you're using numbers or strings (and strings are much easier to read and understand).

   Use one of these techniques to rewrite the adventure game with fewer potential errors.

9.13 The function `printNow` is not the only way to present information to the user during the running of a program. We might also use the function `showInformation` which takes a string as input, then displays it in a dialog box. Currently, our showRoom subfunctions presume that we will display the room information via printNow. If functions like showPorch *returned a string* with the description, then the function showRoom could either use printNow to display the room description or showInformation.

Rewrite the room showing functions to return a string, then modify showRoom to easily change between printing the room information and showing it in a dialog box.

9.14 Consider this program:

```
def testMe(p,q,r):
  if q > 50:
    print r
  value = 10
  for i in range(1,p):
    print "Hello"
    value = value - 1
  print value
  print r
```

If we execute testMe(5,51,"Hello back to you!"), what will print?

9.15
```
def newFunction(a, b, c):
    print a
    list1 = range(1,5)
    value = 0
    for x in list1:
        print b
        value = value +1
    print c
    print value
```

If you call the preceding function by typing
newFunction("I", "you", "walrus")
what will the computer print?

TO DIG DEEPER

Textual adventure games today are typically called *interactive fiction*. There are Web sites and archives where you can download and play interactive fiction. Even better, there are programming languages especially designed for building video games, like *Inform 7*.

Probably the best book ever written on software engineering is *The Mythical Man-Month: Essays on Software Engineering, Anniversary Edition (2nd Edition)* by Frederick P. Brooks (Addison-Wesley, 1995). Brooks points out that many of the issues of developing software are organizational issues. We highly recommend this book.

PART 3 TEXT, FILES, NETWORKS, DATABASES, AND UNIMEDIA

CHAPTER 10
Creating and Modifying Text

Chapter Learning Objectives

The media learning goals for this chapter are:

- To generate text in a form-letter style.
- To manipulate structured text, such as phone and address listings.
- To generate random structured text.

The computer science goals for this chapter are:

- To access object components using dot notation.
- To manipulate strings.
- To read and write files.
- To understand file structures like trees.
- To write programs that manipulate programs, which leads to powerful ideas like interpreters and compilers.
- To use the modules in the Python Standard Library, such as the random and os utilities.
- To get a sense of the functionality available in the Python Standard Library.
- To broaden the understanding of import capability.

10.1   TEXT AS UNIMEDIA

Nicholas Negroponte, founder of the MIT Media Lab, said that what makes computer-based multimedia possible is the fact that the computer is actually **unimedia**. The computer really understands only one thing: zeros and ones. We can use the computer for multimedia because any medium can be encoded as zeros and ones.

He might as well have been talking about *text* as the unimedia. We can encode any medium to text. What's even better than using zeros and ones, we can *read* the text. Later in this chapter, we map sounds to text and then back to sounds, and we do the same with pictures. But once we have our media in text, we don't have to go back to the original medium: we can map sounds to text and then to pictures, and thus create *visualizations* of sounds.

The World Wide Web is primarily text. Visit any Web page, then go to the menu of your Web browser and choose to "View the source." What you will see is text. Every Web page is actually text. The text references the pictures, sounds, and animations that appear when you view the page, but the page itself is defined as text. The words in the text are in a notation called *HyperText Markup Language (HTML)*.

Until now, we've been able to get by with a relatively few programming-language ideas. JES was designed so that we can do all our sound and picture work using only assignment, `for`, `if`, `print`, `return`, and functions. But programming languages have more features and capabilities than just these. In this chapter, we start to show you what's under the hood of JES to give you more capability in your programming.

10.2 STRINGS: MAKING AND MANIPULATING STRINGS

Text is typically manipulated as **strings**. A string is a sequence of characters. Strings are stored in memory as an array, just like sounds. Strings are a contiguous sequence of our memory mailboxes—the mailboxes right next to one another. The string "Hello" would be stored in five mailboxes right next to one another: one mailbox holding the binary code representing "H," the next one holding "e," the next one holding "l," and so on.

Strings are defined with sequences of characters inside quote marks. Python is unusual in that it allows several different kinds of quoting. We can use single quotes, double quotes, or even triple quotes. We can *nest* quotes. If we start a string with double quotes, then we can use single quotes inside the string because the string isn't ended until the next set of double quotes. If you start a string with single quotes, you can put all the double quotes you want inside the string, because Python is waiting for the single quotes to end.

```
>>> print 'This is a single-quoted string'
This is a single-quoted string
>>> print "This is a double-quoted string"
This is a double-quoted string
>>> print """This is a triple-quoted string"""
This is a triple-quoted string
```

Why triple quote? Because it allows us to embed new lines and spaces and tabs in our strings. We can't use it easily from the Command Area, but we can in the Program Area.

```
def sillyString():
  print """This is using triple quotes.  Why?
Notice the different lines.


Because we can do this."""
```

```
>>> sillyString()
This is using triple quotes.   Why?
Notice the different lines.
```

```
Because we can do this.
```

The value of having so many different kinds of quotes is to make it easy to put quotes *inside* of strings. For example, HTML uses double quotes as part of its notation. If you want to write a Python function that creates HTML pages (a common use for Python), then you will need strings that contain quotes. Since any of these quotes work, you can embed double quotes by simply using single quotes to start and end the string.

```
>>> print " " "
Your code contains at least one syntax error, meaning
it is not legal jython.
>>> print ' " '
 "
```

A string can be thought of as an array or sequence of characters. It really is a sequence—you can use `for` to walk along all the characters.

```
>>> for i in "Hello":
...       print i
...
H
e
l
l
o
```

In memory, a string is a series of consecutive mailboxes (to continue our metaphor of memory as a mailroom), each containing the binary code for the corresponding character. The function `ord()` gives us the ASCII (American Standard Code for Information Interchange) encoding for each character. Thus, we find that the string "Hello" is five mailboxes, the first containing 72, and then 101, and then 108, and so on.

```
>>> str = "Hello"
>>> for char in str:
...       print ord(char)
...
72
101
108
108
111
```

In JES, that's a slight simplification. The version of Python we're using, Jython, is built on Java, which is actually *not* using ASCII to encode its strings. It's using *Unicode*, which is an encoding for characters where two bytes are used for each character. Two bytes gives us 65,536 possible combinations. All those extra possible codes allow us to go beyond a simple Latin alphabet, numbers, and punctuation. We can represent Hiragana, Katakana, and other *glyph* (graphic depictions of characters) systems.

What this should tell you is that there are many more possible characters than can be typed at the keyboard. Not only are there special symbols but there are invisible characters like tabs and pressing the return/enter key. We type these in Python strings (and in many other languages, such as Java and C) using *backslash escapes*. Backslash escapes are the backslash key \ followed by a character.

- \t is the same as typing the tab key.
- \b is the same as typing the backspace key (which is not a particularly useful character to put in a string, but you can). When you print \b, it shows up as a box on most systems—it's not actually printable (see below).
- \n is the same as typing the enter/return key.
- \uXXXX where XXXX is a code made up of 0–9 and A–F (known as a *hexadecimal* number) represents the Unicode character with that code. You can look up the codes at http://www.unicode.org/charts.

Here is an image of an interaction, so that you can see the unicode glyphs.

```
>>> print "hello\tthere.\nMark"
hello     there.
Mark
>>> print u"\uFEED"
ﻭ
>>> print u"\u03F0"
ϰ
>>> print "This\bis\na\btest"
This☐ is
a☐ test
```

Remember that we used an 'r' at the start of a filename string earlier in this book for example,

```
r"C:\ip-book\mediasources\barbara.jpg"
```

An 'r' tells Python to read the string in *raw mode*. All the backslash escapes are ignored. That's important in Windows paths because Windows uses backslashes as *delimiters*. If your filename begins with a 'b,' for example, Python would view that \b as a backspace character, not as a delimiter-b.

We can easily add strings together using + (also called **concatenation** of strings) and get strings' lengths using the function len().

```
>>> hello = "Hello"
>>> print len(hello)
5
```

```
>>> mark = ", Mark"
>>> print len(mark)
6
>>> print hello+mark
Hello, Mark
>>> print len(hello+mark)
11
```

10.3 MANIPULATING PARTS OF STRINGS

We use the square bracket notation ([]) to reference parts of strings.

- `string[n]` returns the *n*th character in the string, where the first character in the string is zero.
- `string[n:m]` returns a *slice* of the string starting at the *n*th character and up to *but not including* the *m*th (similar to how the `range()` function works). You can optionally leave out *n* or *m*. If *n* is missing, it's assumed to be zero (the start of the string). If *m* is missing, it's assumed to be the end of the string. We can also use negative numbers at either end to trim off that much from that side.

We can think about the characters of the string as being in boxes, each with its own index number.

H	e	l	l	o
0	1	2	3	4

```
>>> hello = "Hello"
>>> print hello[1]
e
>>> print hello[0]
H
>>> print hello[2:4]
ll
>>> print hello
Hello
>>> print hello[:3]
Hel
>>> print hello[3:]
lo
>>> print hello[:]
Hello
>>> print hello[-1:]
o
>>> print hello[:-1]
Hell
```

10.3.1   String Methods: Introducing Objects and Dot Notation

Everything in Python is actually more than just a value—it's an *object*. An object combines data (like a number or a string or a list) with the *methods* that can act upon that object. Methods are like functions except that they're not globally accessible. You can't execute a method the way you can execute `pickAFile()` or `makeSound()`. A method is a function that can only be accessed *through* an object.

Strings in Python are objects. They are not only sequences of characters—they also have methods that are not globally accessible but are known only to strings. To execute a method of a string, you use *dot notation*. You type `object.method()`.

An example method known only to strings is `capitalize()`. It capitalizes the string it's called upon. It will not work on a function or on a number.

```
>>> test="this is a test."
>>> print test.capitalize()
This is a test.
>>> print capitalize(test)
A local or global name could not be found. You need
to define the function or variable before you try to
use it in any way.
NameError: capitalize
>>> print 'this is another test'.capitalize()
This is another test
>>> print 12.capitalize()
Your code contains at least one syntax error, meaning
it is not legal jython.
```

There are *many* useful string methods.

- `startswith(prefix)` returns true if the string starts with the given prefix. Remember that `true` in Python is anything 1 or greater and `false` is zero.

```
>>> letter = "Mr. Mark Guzdial requests the pleasure of your company..."
>>> print letter.startswith("Mr.")
1
>>> print letter.startswith("Mrs.")
0
```

- `endswith(suffix)` returns true if the string ends with the given suffix. `endswith` is particularly useful for checking whether a filename is the right kind for a program.

```
>>> filename="barbara.jpg"
>>> if filename.endswith(".jpg"):
...         print "It's a picture"
...
It's a picture
```

- `find(str)` and `find(str,start)` and `find(str,start,end)` all find the `str` in the object string and return the index number where the string starts. In the optional forms, you can tell it what index number to start from, and even where to stop looking.

  This is very important: the `find()` method returns −1 if it fails. Why −1? Because any value 0 to whatever *could* be a valid index where a search string might be found.

  ```
  >>> print letter
  Mr. Mark Guzdial requests the pleasure of your company...
  >>> print letter.find("Mark")
  4
  >>> print letter.find("Guzdial")
  9
  >>> print len("Guzdial")
  7
  >>> print letter[4:9+7]
  Mark Guzdial
  >>> print letter.find("fred")
  -1
  ```

  There also exists `rfind(findstring)` (and the same variations with optional parameters) that searches from the end of the string toward the front.

- `upper()` translates the string to uppercase.
- `lower()` translates the string to lowercase.
- `swapcase()` makes all uppercase into lowercase and vice versa.
- `title()` makes just the first characters uppercase and the rest lower.

  These methods can be *cascaded*—one modifying the result of another.

  ```
  >>> string="This is a test of Something."
  >>> print string.swapcase()
  tHIS IS A TEST OF sOMETHING.
  >>> print string.title().swapcase()
  tHIS iS a tEST oF sOMETHING.
  ```

- `isalpha()` returns true if the string is not empty and is all letters—no numbers and no punctuation.
- `isdigit()` returns true if the string is not empty and all numbers. You might use this if you were checking the results of some search you were doing. Say that you were writing a program to look for stock prices. You want to parse out a current *price*, not a stock name. If you get it wrong, maybe your program might make buys or sells that you don't want. You could use `isdigit()` to check your result automatically.
- `replace(search,replace)` searches for the `search` string and replaces it with the `replace` string. It returns the result but doesn't change the original string.

```
>>> print letter
Mr. Mark Guzdial requests the pleasure of your company...
>>> letter.replace("a","!")
'Mr. M!rk Guzdi!l requests the ple!sure of your comp!ny...'
>>> print letter
Mr. Mark Guzdial requests the pleasure of your company...
```

10.3.2   Lists: Powerful, Structured Text

Lists are very powerful structures that we can think about as a kind of *structured text*. Lists are defined with square brackets with commas between their elements but they can contain just about anything—including sublists. Like strings, you can reference parts with square bracket notations, and you can add them together with +. Lists are also sequences, so you can use a for loop on them to walk through their pieces.

```
>>> myList = ["This","is","a", 12]
>>> print myList
['This', 'is', 'a', 12]
>>> print myList[0]
This
>>> for i in myList:
...         print i
...
This
is
a
12
>>> print myList + ["Really!"]
['This', 'is', 'a', 12, 'Really!']
>>> anotherList=["this","has",["a",["sub","list"]]]
>>> print anotherList
['this', 'has', ['a', ['sub', 'list']]]
>>> print anotherList[0]
this
>>> print anotherList[2]
['a', ['sub', 'list']]
>>> print anotherList[2][1]
['sub', 'list']
>>> print anotherList[2][1][0]
sub
>>> print anotherList[2][1][0][2]
b
```

Lists have a set of methods that they understand but strings do not.

- append(something) puts something in the list at the end.
- remove(something) removes something from the list if it's there.

- `sort()` puts the list in alphabetical order.
- `reverse()` reverses the list.
- `count(something)` tells you the number of times that something is in the list.
- `max()` and `min()` are functions we've seen before that take a list as input and give you the maximum and minimum values in the list.

```
>>> list = ["bear","apple","cat","elephant","dog","apple"]
>>> list.sort()
>>> print list
['apple', 'apple', 'bear', 'cat', 'dog', 'elephant']
>>> list.reverse()
>>> print list
['elephant', 'dog', 'cat', 'bear', 'apple', 'apple']
>>> print list.count('apple')
2
```

One of the most important string methods, `split(delimiter)`, converts a string into a list of substrings, separating on a delimiter string that you provide. This allows us to convert strings into lists.

```
>>> print letter.split(" ")
['Mr.', 'Mark', 'Guzdial', 'requests', 'the',
'pleasure', 'of', 'your', 'company...']
```

Using `split()` we can process **formatted text**—text where the separation between parts is a well-defined character, like **tab-delimited text** or **comma-delimited text** from a spreadsheet. Here's an example using structured text to store a phone book. The phone book has lines separated by newlines and parts separated by colons. We can split on the newlines, then the colons, to get a list of sublists. Searches through this can be made with a simple `for` loop.

Program 90: A Simple Phone Book Application

```
def phonebook():
  return """
Mary:893-0234:Realtor:
Fred:897-2033:Boulder crusher:
Barney:234-2342:Professional bowler:"""

def phones():
  phones = phonebook()
  phonelist = phones.split('\n')
  newphonelist = []
  for list in phonelist:
    newphonelist = newphonelist + [list.split(":")]
  return newphonelist
```

```
def findPhone(person):
  for people in phones():
    if people[0] == person:
      print "Phone number for",person,"is",people[1]
```

■

How It Works

There are three functions here: one to provide the phone text, the other to create the phone list, and the third to look up a phone number.

- The first function, phonebook, creates the structured text and returns it, using triple quotes so that the lines can be formatted with newline characters. The format is name, colon, phone number, colon, and job, then colon and end of the line.

  ```
  >>> print phonebook()

  Mary:893-0234:Realtor:
  Fred:897-2033:Boulder crusher:
  Barney:234-2342:Professional bowler:
  ```

- The second function, phones, returns a list of all the phones. It accesses the phone list through phonebook, then splits it into lines. The result of split is a list comprising a string with colons in it. The loop in phones then chops up each list using split on the colons. What phones returns, then, is a list of lists.

  ```
  >>> print phones()
  [[''], ['Mary', '893-0234', 'Realtor', ''],
  ['Fred', '897-2033', 'Boulder crusher', ''],
  ['Barney', '234-2342', 'Professional bowler', '']]
  ```

- Finally, the third function, findPhone, takes a name as input and finds the corresponding phone number. It loops over all the sublists that phones returns and finds the one where the first item in the sublist (index number 0) is the input name. It then prints the result

  ```
  >>> findPhone('Fred')
  Phone number for Fred is 897-2033
  ```

10.3.3   Strings Have No Font

Strings have no **font** (characteristic look of the letters) or **style** (typically the boldface, italics, underline, and other effects applied to the string) associated with them. Font and style information is added to strings using word-processors and other programs. Typically, these are encoded as **style runs**.

A style run is a separate representation of the font and style information with indices into the string to show where the changes should take place. For example, **The old** *brown* fox runs might be encoded as [[bold 0 6][italics 8 12]].

Think about strings with style runs. What do you call this combination of related information? It's clearly not a single value. Could we encode the string with the style runs in a complex list? Sure—we can do just about *anything* with lists!

Most software that manages formatted text will encode strings with style runs as an **object**. Objects have data associated with them, perhaps in several parts (like strings and style runs). Objects know how to act upon their data, using *methods* that may be known only to objects of that type. If the same method name is known to multiple objects, it probably does the same thing, but probably not in the same way.

This is foreshadowing. Objects will be discussed later.

10.4   FILES: PLACES TO PUT YOUR STRINGS AND OTHER STUFF

Files are large, named collections of bytes on your hard disk. Files typically have a **base name** and a **file suffix**. The file BARBARA.JPG has the base name of "barbara" and a file suffix of "jpg" that tells you that the file is a JPEG picture.

Files are clustered into **directories** (sometimes called **folders**). Directories can contain other directories as well as files. There is a base directory on your computer which is referred to as the **root directory**. On a computer using the Windows operating system, the base directory will be something like C:\. A complete description of what directories to visit to get to a particular file from the base directory is called a **path**.

```
>>> file=pickAFile()
>>> print file
C:\ip-book\mediasources\640x480.jpg
```

The path that is printed tells us how to go from the root directory to the file 640X480.JPG. We start at C:\, choose the directory IP-BOOK, then the directory MEDIASOURCES.

We call this structure a **tree** (Figure 10.1). We call C:\ the **root** of the tree. The tree has **branches** where there are subdirectories. Any directory can contain more directories (branches) or files, which are referred to as **leaves**. Except for the root, each **node** of the tree (branch or leaf) has a single **parent** branch node, though a parent can have multiple **children** branches and leaves.

We need to know about directories and files if we're going to manipulate files, especially lots of files. If you're dealing with a big Web site, you are going to be

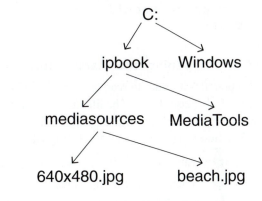

FIGURE 10.1
Diagram of a directory tree.

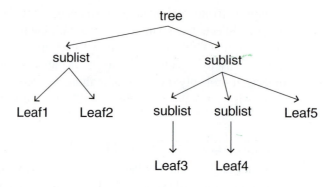

FIGURE 10.2
Diagram for a list.

working with a lot of files. If you are going to be dealing with video, you will have about 30 files (individual frames) for each second of video. You don't really want to write a line of code to open each frame. You want to write programs that will walk directory structures to process Web or video files.

We can also represent trees in lists. Because lists can contain sublists, just as directories can contain subdirectories, it's a pretty easy encoding. The important point is that lists allow us to represent complex, hierarchical relationships, like trees (Figure 10.2).

```
>>> tree = [["Leaf1","Leaf2"],[["Leaf3"],["Leaf4"],
"Leaf5"]]
>>> print tree
[['Leaf1', 'Leaf2'], [['Leaf3'], ['Leaf4'], 'Leaf5']]
>>> print tree[0]
['Leaf1', 'Leaf2']
>>> print tree[1]
[['Leaf3'], ['Leaf4'], 'Leaf5']
>>> print tree[1][0]
['Leaf3']
>>> print tree[1][1]
['Leaf4']
>>> print tree[1][2]
Leaf5
```

10.4.1   Opening and Manipulating Files

We open files in order to read or write them. We use a function named (not surprisingly) open(filename,how). The filename can be a complete path or just a base filename and suffix. If you don't provide a path, the file will be opened in the current JES directory.

The how input is a string describing what you want to do with the file.

- "rt" means "read the file as text—translate the bytes into characters for me."
- "wt" means "write the file as text."
- "rb" and "wb" mean "read and write bytes" (respectively). You use these if you are going to manipulate **binary files** (like JPEG, WAV, Word, or Excel files).

The function `open()` returns a file object that you then use to manipulate the file. The file object understands a set of methods.

- `file.read()` reads the whole file as a giant string. (If you opened the file for writing, don't try to read from it.)
- `file.readlines()` reads the whole file into a list where each element is a single line. You can only use `read()` or `readlines()` once per file opening.
- `file.write(somestring)` writes `somestring` to the file. (If you opened the file for reading, don't try to write to it.)
- `file.close()` closes the file. If you were writing to the file, closing it makes sure that all the data gets written out on the disk. If you were reading from the file, it releases the memory that's used for manipulating the file. In either case, it's a good idea to close your files when you're done with them. Once you close a file, you can't read or write the file again until you reopen it.

Here are examples of opening a program file that we wrote earlier and of reading it in as a string and as a list of strings.

```
>>> program=pickAFile()
>>> print program
C:\ip-book\programs\littlePicture.py
>>> file=open(program,"rt")
>>> contents=file.read()
>>> print contents
def littlePicture():
  canvas=makePicture(getMediaPath("640x480.jpg"))
  addText(canvas,10,50,"This is not a picture")
  addLine(canvas,10,20,300,50)
  addRectFilled(canvas,0,200,300,500,yellow)
  addRect(canvas,10,210,290,490)
  return canvas
>>> file.close()
>>> file=open(program,"rt")
>>> lines=file.readlines()
>>> print lines
['def littlePicture():\n', '
canvas=makePicture(getMediaPath("640x480.jpg"))\n', '
addText(canvas,10,50,"This is not a picture")\n', '
addLine(canvas,10,20,300,50)\n', '
addRectFilled(canvas,0,200,300,500,yellow)\n', '
addRect(canvas,10,210,290,490)\n', '  return canvas']
>>> file.close()
```

Here's an example of writing a silly file. The \n creates the new lines in the file.

```
>>> writeFile = open("myfile.txt","wt")
>>> writeFile.write("Here is some text.")
>>> writeFile.write("Here is some more.\n")
>>> writeFile.write("And now we're done.\n\nTHE END.")
```

```
>>> writeFile.close()
>>> writeFile=open("myfile.txt","rt")
>>> print writeFile.read()
Here is some text.Here is some more.
And now we're done.

THE END.
>>> writeFile.close()
```

10.4.2 Generating Form Letters

Not only can we write programs to take apart structured text, we can write programs that *assemble* structured text. One of the classic structured texts that we're all too familiar with is spam or form letters. The really good spam writers (if that's not a contradiction in terms) fill in details that actually refer to *you* in the message. How do they do this? It's pretty easy—they have a function that takes in the relevant input and plugs it into the right places.

Program 91: A Form Letter Generator
```python
def formLetter(gender,lastName,city,eyeColor):
 file = open("formLetter.txt","wt")
 file.write("Dear ")
 if gender=="F":
  file.write("Ms. "+lastName+":\n")
 if gender=="M":
  file.write("Mr. "+lastName+":\n")
 file.write("I am writing to remind you of the offer ")
 file.write("that we sent to you last week. Everyone in ")
 file.write(city+" knows what an exceptional offer this is!")
 file.write("(Especially those with lovely eyes of"+eyeColor+"!)")
 file.write("We hope to hear from you soon.\n")
 file.write("Sincerely,\n")
 file.write("I.M. Acrook, Attorney at Law")
 file.close()
```

How It Works

This function takes a gender, a last name (family name), city, and eye color as input. It opens a FORMLETTER.TXT file, then writes out an opening, tuned to the gender of the recipient. It writes out a bunch of text, inserting the input into the right places. Then closes the file.

When this is executed with formLetter("M","Guzdial","Decatur", "brown"), it generates:

```
Dear Mr. Guzdial:
I am writing to remind you of the offer that we
sent to you last week. Everyone in Decatur knows what
```

```
an exceptional offer this is!(Especially those with
lovely eyes of brown!)We hope to hear from you soon.
Sincerely,
I.M. Acrook,
Attorney at Law
```

10.4.3   Writing Out Programs

Now let's start *using* files. Our first program will do something pretty interesting—let's write a program to *change* another program. We'll read the LITTLEPICTURE.PY file and change the text string that's inserted into the picture. We'll find() the addText() function, then search for each of the double quotes. Then we'll write out a new file with everything from LITTLEPICTURE.PY up to the first double quote, insert our new string, and put in the rest of the file from the second double quote to the end.

Program 92: A Program to Change the littlePicture Program

```
def changeLittle(filename,newString):
  # Get the original file contents
  programFile="littlePicture.py"
  file = open(programFile,"rt")
  contents = file.read()
  file.close()
  # Now, find the right place to put our new string
  addPos= contents.find("addText")
  #Double quote after addText
  firstQuote = contents.find('"',addPos)
  #Double quote after firstQuote
  endQuote = contents.find('"',firstQuote+1)
  # Make our new file
  newFile = open(filename,"wt")
  newFile.write(contents[:firstQuote+1]) # Include the quote
  newFile.write(newString)
  newFile.write(contents[endQuote:])
  newFile.close()
```

How It Works

This program opens up the file *littlePicture.py* (the name assumes that it's in the JES directory, since no path is provided). It reads the whole thing in as a big string, then closes the file. Using the find method, it finds where the addText is, where the first double quote is, and where the last double quote is. It then opens up a new file (for writable text: "wt") and writes out all of the little program up to the first double quote. Then it writes out the input string. Then it writes out the rest of the little program from the last double quote on. Thus, it replaces the string that's added. Finally, it closes the new file.

When we run this with changeLittle("sample.py","Here is a sample of changing a program"), we get in SAMPLE.PY:

```
def littlePicture():
    canvas=makePicture(getMediaPath("640x480.jpg"))
    addText(canvas,10,50,"Here is a sample of changing a program")
    addLine(canvas,10,20,300,50)
    addRectFilled(canvas,0,200,300,500,yellow)
    addRect(canvas,10,210,290,490)
    return canvas
```

This is how vector-based drawing programs work. When you change a line in Auto-CAD or Flash or Illustrator, you're actually changing the underlying representation of the picture—in a real sense, a little program whose execution results in the picture you're working with. When you change the line, you're actually changing the program, which is then re-executed to show you the updated picture. Is this process slow? Computers are fast enough that we just don't notice.

Being able to manipulate text is quite important for gathering data on the Internet. Most of the Internet is just text. Go to your favorite Web page, then use the VIEW SOURCE (or something like this) option in the menu. That's the text that defines the page you're seeing in the browser. Later, we'll learn how to download pages directly from the Internet, but for now, let's assume that you've saved (*downloaded*) pages or files from the Internet onto your disk, and then we'll do searches from there.

For example, there are places on the Internet where you can grab sequences of nucleotides associated with things like parasites. I found a file of this type that looks like this:

```
>Schisto unique AA825099
gcttagatgtcagattgagcacgatgatcgattgaccgtgagatcgacga
gatgcgcagatcgagatctgcatacagatgatgaccatagtgtacg
>Schisto unique mancons0736
ttctcgctcacactagaagcaagacaatttacactattattattattatt
accattattattattattactattattattattactattattta
ctacgtcgcttttttcactccctttattctcaaattgtgtatccttccttt
```

Let's say that we had a subsequence (like "ttgtgta") and wanted to know which parasite it was part of. If we read in this file into a string, we could search for the subsequence. If it's there (i.e., the find result is not equal <> to −1), we search *backwards* from there to find the ">" that starts each parasite name, then *forward* to the end of line (newline character) to get the name of the file. If we don't find the subsequence (find() returns a −1), the subsequence isn't there.

Program 93: Finding a Subsequence in Parasite Nucleotide Sequences

```
def findSequence(seq):
    sequencesFile = getMediaPath("parasites.txt")
    file = open(sequencesFile,"rt")
    sequences = file.read()
    file.close()
    # Find the sequence
    seqLoc = sequences.find(seq)
```

```
#print "Found at:",seqLoc
if seqLoc <> -1:
  # Now, find the ">" with the name of the sequence
  nameLoc = sequences.rfind(">",0,seqLoc)
  #print "Name at:",nameLoc
  endline = sequences.find("\n",nameLoc)
  print "Found in ",sequences[nameLoc:endline]
if seqLoc == -1:
  print "Not found"
```

How It Works

The function findSequence takes a part of a sequence as an input. It opens the PARA-SITES.TXT file (in the media folder specified with setMediaPath) and reads the whole thing into the string sequences. We look for the sequence in the string sequences using find. If it's found (i.e., the result isn't −1), then we look *backwards* from where we found the sequence (seqLoc) to the beginning of the string (0) to find the ">" which starts the sequence. We then search forward from the greater-than sign to the end of the line ("\n"). This gives us where in the original sequences string we can find the name of the parasite that our input subsequence is from.

We have been reading the entire contents of a file into one big string and then processing the string. But, if you have very large files it might be better to process the contents one line at a time. You can do this using the readlines function which returns a list of strings with one string per line of the file. For example if you want to change every occurrence of a string in a file you could use the following function.

Program 94: Replacing All Occurrences of a Word in a File

```
def replaceWord(fileName,origWord,repWord):
  file = open(fileName,"rt")
  outFile = open("out-" + fileName,"wt")
  for line in file.readlines():
    newLine = line.replace(origWord,repWord);
    outFile.write(newLine)
  file.close()
  outFile.close()
```

There are programs that wander the Internet, gathering information from Web pages. For example, Google's news page (http://news.google.com) isn't written by reporters. Google has programs that go out and snag headlines out of *other* news sites. How do these programs work? They simply download pages from the Internet and chop out the desired pieces.

For example, let's say that you wanted to write a function that would give you the current temperature by reading it off a local weather page. In Atlanta, a good weather page is http://www.ajc.com/weather—the weather page of the *Atlanta Journal-Constitution*. By viewing the source, we can find where the current temperature appears on the page, and what the key features of the text are around it to grab just the temperature. Here's the relevant part of the page that Mark found one day:

```
<td ><img src="/shared-local/weather/images/ps.gif"
width="48" height="48" border="0"><font size=-2><br>
  </font>
<font size="-1"
face="Arial, Helvetica, sans-serif"><b>Currently
  </b><br>
Partly sunny<br> <font size="+2">54<b>&deg;</b><
  /font>
<font face="Arial, Helvetica, sans-serif" size="+1">
F</font></font></td> </tr>
```

You can see the word `Currently` in there, then the temperature just before the characters <b>°. We can write a program to chop out those pieces and return the temperature, given that the weather page is saved in a file named AJC-WEATHER.HTML. Now this program won't *always* work with the current AJC weather page. The page format may change, and the key text we're looking for might move or disappear. But as long as the format is the same, this recipe will work.

Program 95: Get the Temperature off a Weather Page

```
def findTemperature():
  weatherFile = getMediaPath("ajc-weather.html")
  file = open(weatherFile,"rt")
  weather = file.read()
  file.close()
  # Find the Temperature
  currLoc = weather.find("Currently")
  if currLoc <> -1:
    # Now, find the "<b>&deg;" following the temp
    temploc = weather.find("<b>&deg;",currLoc)
    tempstart = weather.rfind(">",0,temploc)
    print "Current temperature:",weather[tempstart+1:temploc]
  if currLoc == -1:
    print "They must have changed the page format--can't find the temp"
```

How It Works

This function assumes that the file AJC-WEATHER.HTML is stored in the media folder specified with `setMediaPath`. The function `findTemperature` opens and reads the file as text, then closes it. We look for the word "Currently." If we find it (the result is not -1), we look for the degree marker after the "Currently" (stored in `currLoc`). We then search backwards for the end of the previous tag, ">." The temperature is between these points. If `currLoc` is −1, we give up because we couldn't find the word "Currently."

10.5   THE PYTHON STANDARD LIBRARY

In every programming language, there's a way of extending the basic functions of the language with new ones. In Python, this functionality is referred to as **importing a module**. As we saw earlier, a **module** is simply a Python file with new capabilities defined in it. When you `import` a module, it's as if you typed that Python file in at that point and all the objects, functions, and variables in it become defined at once.

Python comes with an extensive library of modules that you can use to do a wide range of things, such as accessing the Internet, generating random numbers, and accessing files in a directory—a useful thing to do when developing Web pages or working with video.

Let's use that as our first example. The module we'll use is the `os` module. The function in the `os` module that knows how to list the files in a directory is `listdir()`. We access the piece of the module using dot notation.

```
>>> import os
>>> print os.listdir("C:\ip-book\mediasources\pics")
['students1.jpg', 'students2.jpg', 'students5.jpg',
'students6.jpg', 'students7.jpg', 'students8.jpg']
```

We can use `os.listdir()` to title pictures in a directory or to insert a statement, such as a copyright claim. Now `listdir()` just returns the base filename and suffix. That's enough to make sure that we have pictures and not sounds or something else. But it doesn't give us complete paths for `makePicture`. To get a complete path, we can combine the input directory with the base filename from `listdir()`—but we need a path delimiter between the two pieces. Python has a standard that if a filename has a "//" in it, that will be replaced with whatever the right path delimiter is for the operating system you're using.

Program 96: Title a Set of Pictures in a Directory

```
import os

def titleDirectory(dir):
  for file in os.listdir(dir):
    print "Processing:",dir+"//"+file
    if file.endswith(".jpg"):
      picture = makePicture(dir+"//"+file)
      addText(picture,10,10,"Property of CS1315 at Georgia Tech")
      writePictureTo(picture,dir+"//"+"titled-"+file)
```

How It Works

The function `titleDirectory` takes a directory (path name, as a string) as input. It then walks through each filename `file` in the directory. If the filename ends with ".jpg," it's probably a picture. So we make the picture from the `file` in the given `dir` directory. We add text to the picture, then write the picture back out as "titled-" plus the filename, in the given `dir` directory.

10.5.1 More on Import and Your Own Modules

There are actually several forms of the `import` statement. The one we're using here, `import module,` makes all of the module available through dot notation. These are several other options:

- We can import just a few things from a module, but then access them without using dot notation. This form is `from module import name`.

  ```
  >>> from os import listdir
  >>> print listdir(r"C:\Documents and Settings")
  ['Default User', 'All Users', 'NetworkService',
  'LocalService', 'Administrator', 'Driver',
  'Mark Guzdial']
  ```

  We can use the form `from module import *` to import *everything* from the module and access it without using dot notation at all.

- We can `import module as newname` if we'd like to import a module but then use `newname` to reference the module. You can use this to make it easier to access Java libraries from Jython. Java libraries sometimes have long names like `java.awt.event`. We can use this syntax to create a shorthand, e.g.

  ```
  import java.awt.event as event
  ```

  Then you can reference elements in `java.awt.event` as `event`.

A module is just a Python file. As we saw earlier in this book, you can import your own code as a module. If you have the function `findTemperature` in the file FINDTEMPERA-TUREFILE.PY in the JES directory, you can simply execute `import findTemperature from findTemperatureFile` and then use `findTemperature` as if it were typed into your Program Area.

10.5.2 Another Fun Module: Random

Another fun and sometimes useful module is `random`. The base function `random.random()` generates random numbers (evenly distributed) between 0 and 1.

```
>>> import random
>>> for i in range(1,10):
...         print random.random()
...
0.8211369314193928
0.6354266779703246
0.9460060163520159
0.904615696559684
0.33500464463254187
0.08124982126940594
0.0711481376807015
0.7255217307346048
0.2920541211845866
```

Random numbers can be fun when they're applied to tasks like picking random words from a list. The function random.choice() does that.

```
>>> for i in range(1,5):
...         print random.choice(["Here", "is", "a",
"list", "of", "words", "in", "random", "order"])
...
list
a
Here
list
```

From there, we can generate random sentences by randomly picking nouns, verbs, and phrases from lists.

Program 97: Randomly Generate Language

```
import random

def sentence():
  nouns = ["Mark","Adam","Angela","Larry","Jose","Matt","Jim"]
  verbs = ["runs", "skips", "sings", "leaps", "jumps", "climbs",¬
  "argues", "giggles"]
  phrases = ["in a tree", "over a log", "very loudly", "around¬
  the bush", "while reading the newspaper"]
  phrases = phrases + ["very badly", "while skipping", "instead¬
  of grading", "while typing on the CoWeb."]
  print random.choice(nouns), random.choice(verbs),
  random.choice(phrases)
```

¬These lines of the program should continue with the next lines. A single command in Python may not break across multiple lines. ■

How It Works

We simply create lists for nouns, verbs, and phrases—taking care that all the combinations make sense in terms of number. The print statement defines the desired structure: a random noun, then a random verb, then a random phrase.

```
>>> sentence()
Jose leaps while reading the newspaper
>>> sentence()
Jim skips while typing on the CoWeb.
>>> sentence()
Matt sings very loudly
>>> sentence()
Adam sings in a tree
>>> sentence()
Adam sings around the bush
>>> sentence()
Angela runs while typing on the CoWeb.
```

```
>>> sentence()
Angela sings around the bush
>>> sentence()
Jose runs very badly
```

The basic process here is common in simulation programs. What we have is a structure defined in the program: a definition of what counts as a noun, a verb, and a phrase, and a statement that what we want is a noun, then a verb, then a phrase. The structure gets filled in with random choices. The interesting question is how much can be simulated with a structure and randomness. Could we simulate intelligence this way? And what's the difference between a *simulation* of intelligence and a really thinking computer?

Imagine a program that reads input from the user and then generates a random sentence. Maybe there are a few *rules* in the program that search for keywords and respond to them, like:

```
if input.find("Mother") <> -1:
    print "Tell me more about your Mother"
```

Joseph Weizenbaum wrote a program like this many years ago, called *Doctor* (later known as *Eliza*). His program would act like a Rogerian psychotherapist, echoing back whatever you said, with some randomness, but searching for keywords so that it would seem to really be "listening." The program was meant as a joke, not as a real effort to create a simulation of intelligence. To Weizenbaum's dismay, people took it seriously. They started treating it like a therapist. Weizenbaum changed his research direction from *artificial intelligence* to concern over the ethical use of technology and how easily people can be fooled by technology.

10.5.3   A Sampling of Python Standard Libraries

We have seen some of the Python standard modules like os, sys, and random so far. There are *lots* of modules in the Python Standard Library. There are lots of reasons for using these modules.

- They are written very well—fast, well-documented, and well-tested. You can trust them and save yourself effort.
- It is always a good idea to reuse program code. It's a good practice to get into.
- In a bottom-up design process, starting from existing modules is a great way to start on a new project.

Some of the modules that you might want to explore include:

- datetime and calendar modules know how to manipulate dates, time, and calendars. For example, you can find out what day of the week it was when the US Declaration of Independence was signed in 1776.

```
>>> from datetime import *
>>> independence = date(1776,7,4)
>>> independence.weekday()
3
>>> #0 is Monday, so 3 is Thursday
```

- The `math module` knows lots of important mathematical functions, like `sin` (sine) and `sqrt` (square root).
- The `module zipfile` knows how to read and write compressed "zip" files.
- The module `email` provides facilities for writing your own program to manipulate email (e.g., like a spam filter).
- `SimpleHTTPServer` is actually a Web server all by itself—programmable in Python, to boot!

PROGRAMMING SUMMARY

GENERAL PROGRAM PIECES

`random`	Module for generating random numbers or making random choices.
`os`	Module for manipulating the operating system.

STRING FUNCTIONS, FUNCTIONS, AND PIECES

`string[n]`, `string[n:m]`	Returns the character in the string at position n ([n]) or the substring from n to $m - 1$. Remember that these start at index 0.
`startswith`	Returns true if the string starts with the input string.
`endswith`	Returns true if the string ends with the input string.
`find`	Returns the index if the input string is found in the string; -1 otherwise.
`upper`, `lower`	Returns a new string converted to the specified case.
`isalpha`, `isdigit`	Returns true if the whole string is alphabetic or numeric (digits), respectively.
`replace`	Takes two input substrings—replaces all instances of the first with the second in the given string.
`split`	Bursts a string into a list of substrings using the input string as the delimiter.

LIST FUNCTIONS AND PIECES

`append`	Appends the input to the end of the list.
`remove`	Removes the input from the list.

sort	Sorts the list.
reverse	Reverses the list.
count	Counts the number of times the input appears in the list.
max, min	Given a list of numbers as input, returns the maximum or minimum (respectively) value in the list.

PROBLEMS

10.1   Create a string variable that contains the sentence "Don't do that!" in it. Create a string variable that contains double quotes in it. Create a string variable that has a tab in it. Create a string variable that has a filename in it with backslashes.

10.2   Write a function that prints every other letter in a string.

10.3   Write a function that takes a string and prints out the letters in the string in reverse order.

10.4   Write a function that finds and removes the second occurrence of a given string in a passed string.

10.5   Write a function to uppercase every other word in a passed sentence. So given "The dog ran a long way," it would output "The DOG ran A long WAY."

10.6   Write a function that takes a passed sentence and an index and returns the sentence with the word at the index uppercased. For example, if the function takes in a sentence "I love the color red" and the index 4 it returns "I love the color RED."

10.7   Write a function that takes a sentence as input and returns it scrambled (the order of the words all mixed up). For example if it is passed "Does anything rhyme with orange?" it might return "Orange with does anything rhyme?".

10.8   Write a function that can find the zip code for a person from a delimited string for an address. For example it might read a string that has in it "name:line1:line2: city:state:zipCode" and return the zip code.

10.9   Modify the changeLittle function to use readLines instead of read.

10.10   Create a function that makes smaller pictures (thumbnails) of every picture in a directory. The user should input the directory path and the scale factor.

10.11   Create a secret message by encoding each character of a string into a number using ord.

10.12   Create a function that reverses the items in a list.

10.13   Create a function that replaces a passed string in a list of strings with a new string.

10.14   Are the numbers returned from the random.random() function really random? How are they generated?

10.15   Look up Joseph Weizenbaum's Eliza program. Can you write something similar but restricted to questions about school?

10.16   Write short essay responses to these questions.

(a) Give me one example of a task for which you would not write a program and give me another example of a task for which you would write a program.

(b) What's the difference between an array, a matrix, and a tree? Give an example where we have used each to represent some data of interest to us.

(c) What is dot notation and when do you use it?

(d) Why is red a bad color to use for chromakey?

(e) What's the difference between a function and a method?

(f) Why is a tree a better representation than an array for files on a disk? Why do you have many directories on your disk, and not just one gigantic one?

(g) What are some advantages that vector-based graphics have over bitmap graphical representations (like JPEG, BMP, GIF)?

10.17   You've seen code to mirror pictures in Program 20 (page 77) and you've seen code to mirror sounds in Program 67 (page 180). It should be pretty easy to use the same algorithm to mirror *text*. Write a function to take a string, then return the mirrored string with the front half copied over the second half.

10.18   Extend the form letter recipe to take an input of a pet's name and type, and reference the pet in the form letter. `"Your pet "+petType+","+petName+"` `will love our offer!"` might generate `"Your pet poodle, Fifi,` `will love our offer!"`.

10.19   Imagine that you have a list of the genders (as single characters) of all the students in your class, in order of their last name. The list will look something like "MFFMMMFFMFMMFFFM" where M is male and F is female. Write a function (below) `percentageGenders(string)` to accept a string that represents the genders. You are to count all of the M's and F's in the string and print out the ratio (as a decimal) of the each gender. For example, if the input string were "MFFF," then the function should print something like "There are 0.25 males, 0.75 females" (*Hint:* Better multiply something by 1.0 to make sure that you get floats not integers.)

10.20   You worked late into the night on an assignment and didn't realize that you wrote a huge section of your term paper with your fingers on the wrong home keys.

Where you meant to type: "This is an unruly mob." You actually typed: "Ty8s 8s ah 7hr7o6 j9b."

Basically you swapped: 7 for U, 8 for I, 9 for O, 0 for P, U for J, I for K, O for L, H for N, and J for M. (Those were the only keystrokes you got wrong—you caught yourself before you got much further.) You also never touched the shift key, so it's only lowercase letters that you care about.

Knowing Python as you do, you decide to write a quick program to fix your text. Write a function `fixItUp` that takes a string as input and returns a string with the characters put the way that they ought to have been.

*10.21   Write a function `doGraphics` that will take a list as input. The function `doGraphics` will start by creating a canvas from the 640x480.JPG file in the mediasources folder. You will draw on the canvas according to the commands in the input list. Each element of the list will be a string. There will be two kinds of strings in the list:

- "b 200 120" means to draw a black dot at x position 200 and y position 120–(200, 120). The numbers, of course, will change, but the command will always be a "b." You can assume that the input numbers will always have three digits.

- "l 000 010 100 200" means to draw a line from position (0, 10) to position (100, 200).

So an input list might look like: ["b 100 200","b 101 200","b 102 200","l 102 200 102 300"] (but have any number of elements).

TO DIG DEEPER

The book that Mark uses for making his way through the Python modules is Frederik Lundh's *Python Standard Library* [29]. You can find the listing of library modules, with their documentation, at `http://docs.python.org/library/`.

Advanced Text Techniques: Web and Information

11.1 NETWORKS: GETTING OUR TEXT FROM THE WEB

11.2 USING TEXT TO SHIFT BETWEEN MEDIA

11.3 HIDING INFORMATION IN A PICTURE

Chapter Learning Objectives

The media learning goals for this chapter are:

- To write programs to directly access and use text information from the Internet.
- To translate a sound or picture to text and translate text back to a sound or picture.
- To hide a message in a picture.

The computer science goals for this chapter are:

- To use a program to access the Internet.
- To show that information can be encoded in many ways.

11.1 NETWORKS: GETTING OUR TEXT FROM THE WEB

A *network* is formed whenever computers communicate with one another. Rarely does the communication take place with voltages over wires, the way that a computer encodes 0's and 1's internally. It's too hard to maintain specific voltages over distances. Instead, 0's and 1's are encoded in some other way. For example, a **modem** (literally *modulator-demodulator*) maps 0's and 1's to different audio frequencies. When we hear these different tones, it sounds like a bunch of buzzing bees to us, but to modems, it's pure binary.

Like onions and ogres, networks have layers. At the bottom level is the physical substrate. How are the signals being passed? Higher levels define how data is encoded. What makes up a zero? A one? Do we send one bit at a time? A **packet** of bytes at a time? Even higher levels define the **protocol** for communication. How does one computer tell another computer that it wants to talk and what it wants to talk about? How do we address your computer at all? By thinking about these distinct layers, and keeping them distinct, we can easily swap out one part without changing the others. For example, most people with a direct connection to a network use a wired connection to an **Ethernet** network, but Ethernet is actually a mid-level protocol that works over wireless networks.

Humans also have protocols. If Mark walks up to you, holds out his hand, and says, "Hi, my name is Mark," you will most certainly hold out your hand and say something like "My name is Carolina" (assuming that your name is Carolina—if it wasn't, that would be pretty funny). In each culture, there's a protocol about how people greet one another. Computer protocols are about the same things but they're written down to communicate the process exactly. What's said isn't too different. One computer may send the message 'HELO' to another to start a conversation (We don't know why the protocol writers couldn't spare the extra 'L' to spell it right), and a computer may send 'BYE' to end the conversation. (We even sometimes call the start of a computer protocol the "*handshake*.") It's all about establishing a connection, and making sure that both sides understand what's going on.

The **Internet** is a network of networks. If you have a device in your home so that your computers can talk to one another (e.g., a **router**), then you have a network. With just that, you can probably copy files around between computers and print. When you connect your network to the wider Internet (through an **Internet Service Provider (ISP)**), your network becomes part of the Internet.

The Internet is based on a set of agreements about a whole bunch of things:

- *How computers are addressed*: Currently, each computer on the Internet has a 32-bit number associated with it—four byte values that are usually written like this separated by periods "101.132.64.15." These are called **IP addresses** (for Internet Protocol addresses).

  There is a system of **domain names** by which people can refer to specific computers without knowing their IP addresses. For example, when you access `http://www.cnn.com`, you are actually accessing `http://157.166.226.26/`. That worked for us last time we tried it but it could change. There is a network of *domain name servers* that keep track of names like "www.cnn.com" and map them to addresses like "157.166.226.26." The fact that the numbers can change is one of the advantages of the domain name server—the name stays the same and can point at any address. You can be connected to the Internet and still not be able to get to your favorite Web sites if your domain name server is broken. You might be able to get to it if you type in the IP address directly.

- *How computers communicate*: Data is placed in *packets* that have a well-defined structure, including the sender's IP address, the receiver's IP address, and a number of bytes per packet.

- *How packets are routed around the Internet*: The Internet was designed in the time of the *Cold War*. It was designed to withstand a nuclear attack. If a section of the Internet is destroyed (or damaged, or blocked as a form of censorship), the packet-routing mechanism of the Internet will simply find a route around the damage.

But the topmost layers of the network define what the data being passed around *means*. One of the first applications placed on top of the Internet was electronic mail.

Over the years, the mail protocols have evolved to standards today like **POP** (post office protocol) and **SMTP** (simple mail transfer protocol). Another old and important protocol is **FTP** (file transfer protocol), which allows us to transfer files between computers.

These protocols aren't super-complicated. When the communication ends, one computer will probably say 'BYE' or 'QUIT' to the other. When one computer tells another computer to accept a file via FTP, it literally says "STO filename" (again, early computer developers didn't want to spare the two more bytes to say "STORE").

The *World Wide Web* is yet another set of agreements, developed mostly by Tim Berners-Lee. The Web is based on top of the Internet, simply adding more protocols on top of the existing ones.

- *How to refer to things on the Web*: Resources on the Web are referenced using **URL**s, **(uniform resource locators)**. A URL specifies the protocol to use to address the resource, the domain name of the **server** that can provide the resource, and the **path** to the resource on that server. For example, a URL like `http://www.cc.gatech.edu/index.html` says "Use the HTTP protocol to talk to the computer at `www.cc.gatech.edu` and ask it for the resource index.html."

  Not every file on every computer attached to the Internet is accessible via a URL. There are some preconditions before a file is accessible via a URL. First, an Internet-accessible computer has to be running a piece of software that understands a protocol that Web browsers understand, typically HTTP (hypertext transfer protocol) or FTP. We call a computer that is running such a piece of software a *server*. A browser that accesses a server is called a **client**. Second, a server typically has a *server directory* accessible via that server. Only files in the directory, or subdirectories within the directory, are available.

- *How to serve documents*: The most common protocol on the Web is **HTTP. It defines how resources are served on the Web**. HTTP is really simple—your browser literally says to a server things like "GET index.html" (just those letters!).

- *How documents will be formatted*: Documents on the Web are formatted using **HTML, HyperText Markup Language**.

You'll notice the term **HyperText** showing up frequently in reference to the Web. HyperText is literally nonlinear text. Ted Nelson invented the term hypertext to describe the kind of reading that we all do on the Web but that didn't exist before computers: read a little on one page, then click a link and read a little over there, then click BACK and continue reading where you left off. The basic idea of HyperText dates back to Vannevar Bush, who was one of President Franklin Roosevelt's science advisers, but it wasn't until the computer came along that we could envision implementing Bush's model of a *Memex*—a device for capturing flows of thought. Tim Berners-Lee invented the Web and its protocols as a way of supporting rapid publication of research findings with connections between documents. The Web is certainly not the ultimate HyperText system. Systems like the ones that Ted Nelson worked on wouldn't allow "dead links" (links that are no longer accessible). But for all its warts, the Web *works*.

A browser (e.g., Internet Explorer, Netscape Navigator, Mozilla, Opera) understands a lot about the Internet. It usually knows several protocols, such as HTTP, FTP, *gopher* (an early HyperText protocol), or *mailto* (SMTP). It knows HTML, how to format it, and how to grab resources referenced within the HTML, like JPEG pictures. It is also possible to access the Internet without nearly that much overhead. Mail clients (e.g., Outlook and Eudora) know some of these protocols without knowing all of them. Even JES understands a little bit about SMTP and HTTP to support turnin of assignments.

Python, like other modern languages, provides modules to support access to the Internet without all the overhead of a browser. Basically, you can write small programs that are clients. Python's module urllib allows you to open URLs and read them as if they were files.

```
>>> import urllib
>>> connection = urllib.urlopen("http://www.ajc.com/weather")
>>> weather = connection.read()
>>> connection.close()
```

Using this example, we can fix our temperature-reading program (Program 95 (page 250)) to read the weather page directly from the Internet.

Program 98: Get the Temperature from a Live Weather Page

```
def findTemperatureLive():
  # Get the weather page
  import urllib #Could go above, too
  connection=urllib.urlopen("http://www.ajc.com/weather")
  weather = connection.read()
  connection.close()
  #weatherFile = getMediaPath("ajc-weather.html")
  #file = open(weatherFile,"rt")
  #weather = file.read()
  #file.close()
  #Find the Temperature
  currLoc = weather.find("Currently")
  if currLoc <> -1:
    # Now, find the "<b>&deg;" following the temp
    temploc = weather.find("<b>&deg;",currLoc)
    tempstart = weather.rfind(">",0,temploc)
    print "Current temperature:",weather[tempstart+1:temploc]
  if currLoc == -1:
    print "They must have changed the page format -- can't
find the temp"
```

How It Works

The function findTemperatureLive is nearly identical to the last one, except that we're reading the string weather from the AJC Web site *live*. We use the module urllib to gain the ability to read the Web page as a string and then search the string in the same way that we did the file previously.

We can use FTP via the `ftplib` in Python.

```
>>> import ftplib
>>> connect = ftplib.FTP("cleon.cc.gatech.edu")
>>> connect.login("guzdial","mypassword")
'230 User guzdial logged in.'
>>> connect.storbinary("STOR barbara.jpg",open(getMediaPath("barbara.jpg")))
'226 Transfer complete.'
>>> connect.storlines("STOR JESintro.txt",open("JESintro.txt"))
'226 Transfer complete.'
>>> connect.close()
```

To create interaction on the Web, we need programs that actually generate HTML. For example, when you type a phrase into a text area and then click the SEARCH button, you are actually causing a program to execute on the server that executes your search and then *generates* the HTML (Web page) that you see in response. Python is a common language for this kind of programming. Its modules, ease of quoting, and ease of writing make it excellent for writing interactive Web programs.

11.2   USING TEXT TO SHIFT BETWEEN MEDIA

As we said at the beginning of this chapter, we can think about text as *unimedia*. We can map from sound to text and back again and the same with pictures. And more interestingly, we can go from sound to text ... to pictures.

Why would we want to do any of this? Why should we care about transforming media in this way? For the same reasons that we care about digitizing media at all. Digital media transformed into text can be more easily transmitted from place to place, checked for errors, and even corrected for errors. It turns out that very often when you are attaching binary files to an e-mail message, your binary file is actually converted to text first. In general, *choosing a new representation allows you to do new things.*

Mapping sound to text is easy. Sound is just a series of samples (numbers). We can easily write these out to a file.

Program 99: Write a Sound to a File as Text Numbers

```
def soundToText(sound,filename):
  file = open(filename,"wt")
  for s in getSamples(sound):
    file.write(str(getSampleValue(s))+"\n")
  file.close()
```

How It Works

We're taking an input sound and a filename as input, then opening the filename for writable text. We then loop through each sample and write it to the file. We're using the function str() here to convert a number into its string representation so that we can add a newline to it and write it to a file.

What do we do with sound as text? Manipulate it as a series of numbers, as with Excel (Figure 11.1). We can quite easily do modifications, such as multiplying each sample by 2.0 here. We can even graph the numbers, and see the same kind of sound graph as we've seen in MediaTools (Figure 11.2). (You will get an error, though—Excel doesn't like to graph more than 32,000 points, and at 22,000 samples per second, 32,000 samples is not a long sound.)

How do we convert a series of numbers back into a sound? Say that you do some modification to the numbers in Excel and now you want to hear the result. How do you do it? The mechanics of Excel are easy: simply copy the column you want into a new worksheet, save it as text, then get the pathname of the text file to use in Python.

The program itself is a little more complicated. When going from sound to text, we knew that we could use getSamples to write out all the samples. But how do we know how many lines are in the file? We can't really use getLines—it doesn't exist. We have to watch out for two problems: (a) having more lines in the file than we can fit into

FIGURE 11.1
Sound-as-text file read into Excel.

FIGURE 11.2
Sound-as-text file graphed in Excel.

the sound that we're using to read into, and (b) running out of lines before we reach the end of the sound.

To do this, we're going to use a `while loop`, which we did see briefly in an earlier chapter. A `while` loop, like an `if`, takes an expression and executes its block if the expression proves to be true. It differs from an `if` because *After* executing the block, a `while` loop *retests* the expression. If it's still true, the whole block is executed again. Eventually, you expect that the expression will become false, and then the line after the `while`'s block will execute. If it doesn't, you get something called an *infinite loop*—the loop continues forever (hypothetically).

```
while 1==1:
    print "This will keep printing until the computer is turned off."
```

For our text-to-sound example, we want to keep reading samples from the file and storing them into the sound *as long as* we have numbers in the file *and as long as* there is still room in the sound. We use the function `float()` to convert the string number into a real number. (`int` would work, too, but this gives us the chance to introduce `float`.)

```
>>> print 2*"123"
123123
>>> print 2 * float("123")
246.0
```

Program 100: Convert a File of Text Numbers into a Sound

```
def textToSound(filename):
  #Set up the sound
  sound = makeSound(getMediaPath("sec3silence.wav"))
  soundIndex = 0
  #Set up the file
  file = open(filename,"rt")
  contents=file.readlines()
  file.close()
  fileIndex = 0
  # Keep going until run out of sound space or run out of file contents
    while (soundIndex < getLength(sound)) and (fileIndex < len(contents)):
    sample=float(contents[fileIndex])
    #Get the file line
    setSampleValueAt(sound,soundIndex,sample)
    fileIndex = fileIndex + 1
    soundIndex = soundIndex + 1
  return sound
```

How It Works

The function `textToSound` takes a filename as input that contains the samples as numbers. We open up a silent three-second sound to hold the sound. `soundIndex` stands for the next sample to read, and `fileIndex` stands for the next number to read for the file list `contents`. The `while` loop says to keep going until *either* the `soundIndex` goes past the length of the sound *or* the `fileIndex` goes past the end of the file (in the list `contents`). In a loop we convert the next string in the list to a float, set the sample value to that, then increment both `fileIndex` and `soundIndex`. When we're done (by either condition in the `while`), we return the input sound.

But we don't *have* to map from sounds to text and back to sounds. We could decide to go to a picture instead. The program below takes a sound and maps each sample to a pixel. All we have to do is to define our mapping, how we want to represent the samples. We chose a very simple one: if the sample is greater than 1000, the pixel is red; if less than −1000 it is blue, and everything else is green (Figure 11.3).

We now have to deal with the case where we run out of samples before we run out of pixels. To do this, we use yet another new programming construct: a `break`. A break statement stops our current loop and goes to the line below it. In this example, if we run out of samples, we stop the `for` loop that is processing the pixels.

Program 101: Visualizing Sound

```
def soundToPicture(sound):
  picture = makePicture(getMediaPath("640x480.jpg"))
  soundIndex = 0
  for p in getPixels(picture):
    if soundIndex > getLength(sound):
      break
```

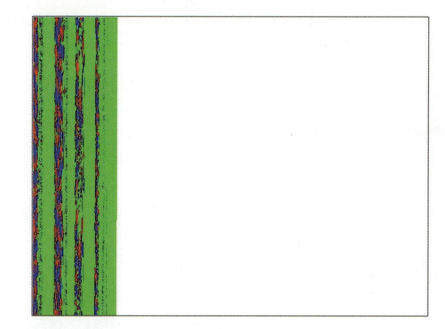

FIGURE 11.3
A visualization of the sound "This is a test".

```
    sample = getSampleValueAt(sound,soundIndex)
    if sample > 1000:
      setColor(p,red)
    if sample < -1000:
      setColor(p,blue)
    if sample <= 1000 and sample >= -1000:
      setColor(p,green)
    soundIndex = soundIndex + 1
  return picture
```

How It Works

In soundToPicture, we open up a 640 × 480 blank picture and take a sound as input. For each of the pixels in the picture, we get a sample value at soundIndex and figure out a mapping to a color, then set the pixel p to that color. We then increment the soundIndex. If the soundIndex ever goes past the end of the sound, we simply break and bail out of the loop. We return the created picture at the end.

Think about how WinAmp does its visualizations, or how Excel or MediaTools graph, or how this program does its visualization. Each is just deciding a different way of mapping from samples to colors and space. It's just a mapping. It's all just bits.

Computer Science Idea: It's All Just Bits

Sound, pictures, and text are all just "bits." They're just information. We can map from media to the other any way we wish, and even convert back to the original media. We merely have to define our representation.

11.2.1 Using Lists as Structured Text for Media Representations

Lists, as we have already said, are very powerful. It's pretty easy to go from sound to lists.

Program 102: Map Sounds to Lists

```
def soundToList(sound):
  list = []
  for s in getSamples(sound):
    list = list + [getSampleValue(s)]
  return list

>>> list = soundToList(sound)
>>> print list[0]
6757
>>> print list[1]
6852
>>> print list[0:100]
```

```
[6757, 6852, 6678, 6371, 6084, 5879, 6066, 6600,
7104, 7588, 7643, 7710, 7737, 7214, 7435, 7827,
7749, 6888, 5052, 2793, 406, -346, 80, 1356, 2347,
1609, 266, -1933, -3518, -4233, -5023, -5744,
-7394, -9255, -10421, -10605, -9692, -8786, -8198,
-8133, -8679, -9092, -9278, -9291, -9502, -9680,
-9348, -8394, -6552, -4137, -1878, -101, 866, 1540,
2459, 3340, 4343, 4821, 4676, 4211, 3731, 4359, 5653,
7176, 8411, 8569, 8131, 7167, 6150, 5204, 3951, 2482,
818, -394, -901, -784, -541, -764, -1342, -2491,
-3569, -4255, -4971, -5892, -7306, -8691, -9534,
-9429, -8289, -6811, -5386, -4454, -4079, -3841,
-3603, -3353, -3296, -3323, -3099, -2360]
```

Going from pictures to lists is similarly easy—we simply have to define our representation. How about mapping each pixel as its *X* and *Y* positions, then its red, green, and blue channels? We have to use double square brackets because we want these five values as sublists inside the big list.

Program 103: Map Pictures to Lists

```
def pictureToList(picture):
  list = []
  for p in getPixels(picture):
    list = list + [[getX(p),getY(p),getRed(p),getGreen(p),getBlue(p)]]
  return list

>>> picture = makePicture(pickAFile())
>>> piclist = pictureToList(picture)
```

```
>>> print piclist[0:5]
[[1, 1, 168, 131, 105], [1, 2, 168, 131, 105], [1, 3, 169,
132, 106], [1, 4, 169, 132, 106], [1, 5, 170, 133, 107]]
```

Going back again is also easy. We simply have to make sure that our X and Y positions are within the bounds of our canvas.

Program 104: Map Lists to Pictures

```
def listToPicture(list):
  picture = makePicture(getMediaPath("640x480.jpg"))
  for p in list:
    if p[0] <= getWidth(picture) and p[1]<= getHeight(picture):
      setColor(getPixel(picture,p[0],p[1]),makeColor(p[2],p[3],p[4]))
  return picture
```

We can figure out that this will work because we can see how the mapping works both ways and then consider just the mapping from lists to pictures. The numbers don't *have* to have come from a picture. We could just as easily have mapped from weather data or stock ticker data or just about anything into a list of numbers that we then visualize. It's all bits . . .

All we're really doing here is changing the encoding. We're not changing the base information at all. Different encodings offer us different capabilities.

A really smart mathematician, Kurt Gödel, used the notion of encodings to come up with one of the most brilliant proofs of the 20th century. He proved the **Incompleteness theorem**, thereby demonstrating that any powerful mathematical system cannot prove all mathematical truths. He figured out a mapping from mathematical statements of truth to numbers. This was long before we had ASCII, where such mappings are commonplace. Once these statements were numbers, he was able to show that there are numbers representing true statements that could not be derived from the mathematical system. In this way, he showed that no system of logic can prove all true statements. By changing his encoding, he gained new capabilities, and thus was able to prove something that no one knew before.

Claude Shannon was an American engineer and mathematician who developed *information theory*. Information theory describes how information can be represented in different media. When we map a picture into text or sounds, we are applying information theory.

11.3   HIDING INFORMATION IN A PICTURE

Steganography is about hiding information in ways that can't be easily detected. If we have a text message displayed in black on a white picture, we can hide it inside another picture. We will do this by first changing all the red values in the original picture to even. Then we will loop through the pixels of the text we want to hide and if the pixel color is close to black, then we will make the red value odd in the modified picture.

Program 105: Encoding the Message

```
def encode(msgPic,original):
  # Assume msgPic and original have same dimensions
  # First, make all red pixels even
  for pxl in getPixels(original):
    # Using modulo operator to test oddness
    if (getRed(pxl) % 2) == 1:
      setRed(pxl, getRed(pxl) - 1)
  # Second, wherever there's black in msgPic
  # make odd the red in the corresponding original pixel
  for x in range(0,getWidth(original)):
    for y in range(0,getHeight(original)):
      msgPxl = getPixel(msgPic,x,y)
      origPxl = getPixel(original,x,y)
      if (distance(getColor(msgPxl),black) < 100.0):
        # It's a message pixel! Make the red value odd.
        setRed(origPxl, getRed(origPxl)+1)
```

Now we can hide a message in the picture of the beach by doing the following.

```
>>> beach = makePicture(getMediaPath("beach.jpg"))
>>> explore(beach)
>>> msg = makePicture(getMediaPath("msg.jpg"))
>>> encode(msg,beach)
>>> explore(beach)
>>> writePictureTo(beach,getMediaPath("beachHidden.png"))
```

You should save the picture using either the png or bmp format. Don't save the picture using the JPEG (jpg) format. The JPEG standard is lossy, which means that it doesn't save the picture exactly as originally specified. It throws away detail (like specific red values) that you normally wouldn't notice but in this case we want to save the picture exactly as it is so that we can decode it later.

Can you detect any difference between the original picture of the beach and the one with the message hidden in it (Figure 11.4)? We doubt it.

Now let's get back out the hidden message. Here is the function to do that.

Program 106: Decoding the Message

```
def decode(encodedImg):
  # Takes in an encoded image. Return the original message
  message = makeEmptyPicture(getWidth(encodedImg),getHeight(encodedImg))
  for x in range(0,getWidth(encodedImg)):
    for y in range(0,getHeight(encodedImg)):
      encPxl = getPixel(encodedImg,x,y)
```

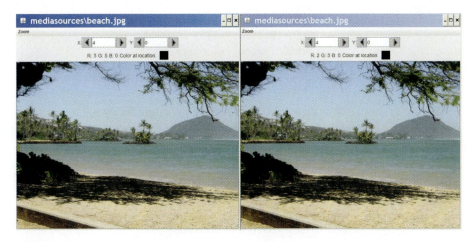

FIGURE 11.4
The original picture (*left*) and the picture with the hidden message (*right*).

FIGURE 11.5
The decoded message.

```
        msgPxl = getPixel(message,x,y)
        if (getRed(encPxl) % 2) == 1:
          setColor(msgPxl,black)
    return message
```

We can decode the message using the following code. You should be able to read the resulting message (Figure 11.5).

```
>>> origMsg = decode(beach)
>>> explore(origMsg)
```

PROGRAMMING SUMMARY
GENERAL PROGRAM PIECES

while	Creates a loop. Executes the body iteratively as long as the provided logical expression is true (i.e., not zero).
break	Breaks a loop immediately—jumps to the end of the for or while.
urllib, ftplib	Module for using URLs or FTP access.
str	Converts numbers (or other objects) to their string representations.
float	Converts a number or string to its floating-point equivalent representation.

PROBLEMS

11.1   Go to a page with a lot of text in it, like http://www.cnn.com and use your browser's menus to SAVE the file as something like MYPAGE.HTML. Edit the file using JES or even an editor like Windows Notepad. Find some text in the page that you can see when you view the page, like a headline or article text. *Change it!* Instead of "protesters" rioting, make it "College students" or even "kindergarteners." Now OPEN that file in your browser. You've just rewritten the news!

11.2   Create a function that pulls data from several Web sites and puts it all together on one Web page.

11.3   Create a function that pulls a sound from a URL and creates a sound clip saved on your local machine.

11.4   Create a function that pulls a picture from a URL and creates a thumbnail saved on your local machine.

11.5   Match the letter of the definition next to the appropriate phrase below. *(Yes, you will have one unused definition.)*

___ `Domain Name Server` ___ `Web Server` ___ `HTTP` ___ `HTML`
___ `Client` ___ `IP Address` ___ `FTP` ___ `URL`

(a) A computer that matches names like *www.cnn.com* to their addresses on the Internet.

(b) A protocol used to move files between computers (e.g., from your personal computer to a larger computer that acts as a Web server).

(c) A string that explains how (what protocol) and on what machine (domain name) and where on the machine (path) a particular file can be found on the Internet.

(d) A computer that offers files through HTTP.

(e) The protocol on which most of the Web is built, a very simple form aimed at rapid transmission of small bits of information.

(f) What a browser (like Internet Explorer) is when contacting a server like *yahoo.com*

(g) The tags that go into Web pages to identify parts of the page and how they should be formatted.

(h) A protocol used for transmitting electronic mail between computers.

(i) The numeric identifier of a computer on the Internet—four numbers between 0 and 255, like *120.32.189.12*

11.6   For each of the following, see if you can figure out the representation in terms of bits and bytes.

(a) Internet addresses are four numbers, each between 0 and 255. How many bits are in an Internet address?

(b) In the programming language Basic, lines can be numbered, each one between 0 and 65535. How many bits are needed to represent a line number?

(c) Each pixel's color has three components, red, green, and blue, each of which can be between 0 and 255. How many bits are needed to represent a pixel's color?

(d) A string in some systems can only be up to 1,024 characters. How many bits are needed to represent the length of a string?

11.7   What is a domain name server? What does it do?

11.8   What are FTP, SMTP, and HTTP? What are they each used for?

11.9   What is HyperText? Who invented it?

11.10   What is the difference between a client and a server?

11.11   How does knowing how to manipulate text help you in gathering and creating information on the Internet?

11.12 What is the Internet?

11.13 What is an ISP? Can you give an example of one?

11.14 Write a function to map a picture to a sound.

11.15 Is it possible to hide a color picture in another picture? Why or why not?

11.16 Write a function to translate text into a picture.

11.17 Write a function to translate text into a sound.

11.18 Write a function to encrypt text by replacing each letter with the following letter in the alphabet. Write a function to decrypt such a message as well.

11.19 Write a function to encrypt text by changing the order of the characters in the message. Write a function to decrypt such a message as well.

11.20 Write a function to encrypt text by using positions of the letters in some other document. Write a function to decrypt such a message as well.

TO DIG DEEPER

The book that Mark uses for making his way through the Python modules is Frederik Lundh's *Python Standard Library* [29]. You can find the listing of library modules, with their documentation, at `http://docs.python.org/library/`.

CHAPTER
12 Making Text for the Web

Chapter Learning Objectives

The media learning goals for this chapter are:

- To gain some basic skill with HTML.
- To automatically generate HTML for input data, like an index page for a directory of images.
- To use databases to generate Web content.

The computer science goals for this chapter are:

- To use another number base, hexadecimal, for specifying RGB colors.
- To distinguish between XML and HTML.
- To explain what SQL is, and what it has to do with relational databases.
- To create and use subfunctions (utility functions).
- To demonstrate one use for hash tables (dictionaries).

12.1   HTML: THE NOTATION OF THE WEB

The World Wide Web is mostly text and most of the text is in the specification language **HTML** (hypertext markup language). HTML is based on **SGML** (Standard Generalized Markup Language), which is a way of adding additional text to one's text to identify logical parts of the document: "This here is the title," "This here is a heading," and "This is just a plain ol' paragraph." Originally, HTML (like SGML) was supposed to just identify logical parts of a document—how it *looked* was up to the browser. Documents were *expected* to look different from one browser to another. But as the Web evolved, two separate goals developed: being able to specify *lots* of logical parts (e.g., prices, part numbers, stocker ticker codes, temperatures), and being able to control formatting very carefully.

For the first goal, **XML** (extensible markup language) evolved. This allows you to define new tags like <partnumber>7834JK</partnumber>. For the second goal, things like **cascading style sheets** were developed. Yet another markup language, **XHTML**, was developed, which is HTML in terms of XML.

For most of this chapter, we'll be introducing XHTML, but we're not going to distinguish it from the original HTML. We'll just talk about it as HTML.

We're not going to have a complete tutorial for HTML here. There are many of these available, both in print and on the Web, and many are highquality. Enter "HTML tutorial" into your favorite search engine and take your pick. Instead, we'll talk here about some general notions of HTML, and mention the tags that you should really know.

A markup language means that text is inserted into the original text to identify the parts. In HTML, the inserted text (called **tags**) is delimited with angle brackets: less-than and greater-than signs. For example, <p> starts a paragraph, and </p> ends a paragraph.

Web pages have several parts, and the parts nest within each other. The first is a **doctype** right at the top of the page that announces the *kind* of page this is (i.e., whether the browser should try to interpret it as HTML, XHTML, CSS, or something else). Following the doctype comes a heading (<head>...</head>) and a body (<body>...</body>). The heading can contain information like the title *nested* within it—the ending of the title comes before the ending of the head. The body has many pieces nested within it, such as headings (h1 starts and ends before the body ends) and paragraphs. All of the body and head nests within an <html>...</html> set of tags. Figure 12.1 shows a simple Web page's source and Figure 12.2 shows how the page appears in Internet Explorer. Try this yourself. Simply type it in with JES, save it with an HTML file suffix, and then open it in a Web browser. The only difference between this file and any Web page is that this file lives on your disk. If it were on a Web server, it would be a Web page.

Common Bug: Browsers Are Forgiving but Usually Wrong

Browsers are very forgiving. If you forget the DOCTYPE or make mistakes in the HTML, a browser will literally guess at what you meant and then try to show it. Murphy's Law, though, says that it will guess *wrong*. If you want your Web page to look just the way you want, get the HTML right.

FIGURE 12.1
Simple HTML page source.

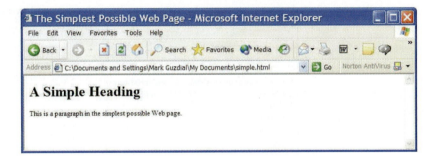

FIGURE 12.2
Simple HTML page open in Internet Explorer.

Here are some of the tags that you should know well:

- The <body> tag can take parameters to set the background, text, and link colors. These colors can be simple color names like "red" or "green" or they can be specific RGB colors.

  You specify colors in **hexadecimal**. Hexadecimal is a number system, whereas the decimal number system is base 10, hexadecimal is base 16. The decimal numbers 1 to 20 translate to hexadecimal 1, 2, 3, 4, 5, 6, 7, 8, 9, A, B, C, D, E, F, 10, 11, 12, 13, and 14. Think of hexadecimal "14" as one 16 plus 4 ones, which gives a result of 20.

  The advantage of hexadecimal is that each digit corresponds to four bits. Two hexadecimal digits correspond to a byte. Thus, the three bytes of RGB colors are six hexadecimal digits, in RGB order. Hexadecimal FF0000 is red—255 (FF) for red, 0 for green, and 0 for blue. 0000FF is blue. 000000 is black, and FFFFFF is white.

- Headings are specified using tags <h1>...</h1> through <h6>...</h6>. Smaller numbers are more prominent.

- There are lots of tags for different kinds of styles: emphasis ..., italics <i>...</i>, boldface ..., bigger <big>...</big> and smaller <small>...</small> fonts, typewriter font <tt>...</tt>, preformatted text <pre>...</pre>, block quotes <blockquote>...</blockquote>, and subscripts _{...} and superscripts ^{...} (Figure 12.3). You can also control things like font and color using the <font>...</font> tags.

- You can insert breaks without new paragraphs using <br />.

- You use the <image src="image.jpg"/> tag to insert images (Figure 12.4). The image tag takes an image as an src= parameter. What comes after that is an image specification, in one of several forms.

  - If it's just a filename (like "flower1.jpg"), then it's assumed to be an image in the same directory as the HTML file referencing it.

  - If it's a path, it's assumed to be a path *from the same directory as the HTML page* to that image. So if there was an HTML page in "MY DOCUMENTS" that referenced an image in the MEDIASOURCES directory, we might have a reference to "mediasources/flower1.jpg". You can use UNIX conventions here

FIGURE 12.3
HTML styles.

```
<!DOCTYPE HTML PUBLIC"-//W3C//DTD HTML 4.01
    Transition//EN"
    "http://wwww.w3.org/TR/html4/loose.dtd">
<html>

    <head>
      <title>The Simplest Possible Web Page</title>
    </head>

    <body>

      <h1>A Simple Heading</h1>

      <p>This is a paragraph in the simplest<br/>
      poissible Web page.</p>

      <img src="mediasources/flower1.jpg"/>

    </body>

</html>
```

FIGURE 12.4
Inserting an image into an HTML page.

(e.g., ".." references the parent directory, so "../images/flower1.jpg"
would say to go to the parent directory, then down to IMAGES to grab image
FLOWER1.JPG).

- It can also be a complete URL—you can reference images entirely on other
  servers.

You can also manipulate the width and height of images with options to the image
tag (e.g., `<image height="100" src="flower.jpg">` to limit the height to 100
pixels) and adjust the width so that the picture keeps its height: width ratio. Using
the option `alt` you can specify text to be displayed if the image can't be displayed
(e.g., for audio or Braille browsers).

- You use the *anchor tag* `<a href="someplace.html">anchor text</a>` to create links from anchor text somewhere else. In this example, `someplace.html` is

the *target* for the anchor—it's where you go when you click on the *anchor*. The *anchor* is what you click on. It can be text, like anchor text, or it can be an image. As seen in Figure 12.5, the target can also be a complete URL.

Note, too, in Figure 12.5, that line breaks in the source file don't show up in the browser. We can even have line breaks in the middle of an anchor tag and they don't affect the view. The breaks that *matter* (i.e., that show up in the browser view) are generated by tags like <br /> and <p>.

- You create bullet lists (*unordered lists*) and numbered lists (*ordered lists*) using the <ul>...</ul> and <ol>...</ol> tags, respectively. Individual items are specified using tags <li>...</li>.

- Tables are created using <table>...</table> tags. Tables are constructed out of table rows using <tr>...</tr> tags, and each row consists of several table data items identified with <td>...</td> tags (Figure 12.6). Tables contain rows and rows contain table data items.

There is *lots* more to HTML, such as frames (having subwindows within one's HTML page window), divisions (<div />), horizontal rules (<hr />), and applets and JavaScript. The items listed above are the most critical for understanding the rest of this chapter.

```
<body>
<h1>A Simple Heading</h1>
<p>This is a paragraph in the simplest
<br/>
possible Web page.</p>
<img src="mediasources/flower1.jpg"
    alt="A Flower" />
<p>Here is a link to
<a href =
    "http://www.cc.gatech.edu/~mark.guz
    dial/">Mark Guzdial</a>
</p>

</body>
```

FIGURE 12.5
An HTML page with a link in it.

```
<table border="5">
<tr><td>Column
    1</td><td>Column
    2</td></tr>
<tr><td>Element in column
    1</td><td>Element in
    column 2</td></tr>
</table>
```

FIGURE 12.6
Inserting a table into an HTML page.

12.2   WRITING PROGRAMS TO GENERATE HTML

HTML itself is not a programming language. HTML can't specify loops, conditionals, variables, data types, or anything else we've learned about specifying process. HTML is used to describe structure, not process.

That said, we can easily write programs to generate HTML. Python's multiple ways of quoting strings come in *really* handy here!

Program 107: **Generating a Simple HTML Page**

```
def makePage():
    file=open("generated.html","wt")
    file.write("""<!DOCTYPE HTML PUBLIC "-//W3C//DTD HTML 4.01
Transition//EN" "http://wwww.w3.org/TR/html4/loose.dtd">

<html>
<head> <title>The Simplest Possible Web Page</title>
</head>
<body>
<h1>A Simple Heading</h1>
<p>Some simple text.</p>
</body>
</html>""")
    file.close()
```

This works but it's really boring. Why would you write a program to write what you can do with a text editor? You write programs for replicability, communicating process, and tailoring. Let's make a home page creator.

Program 108: **Initial Home Page Creator**

```
def makeHomePage(name, interest):
    file=open("homepage.html","wt")
    file.write("""<!DOCTYPE HTML PUBLIC "-//W3C//DTD HTML 4.01
Transition//EN" "http://wwww.w3.org/TR/html4/loose.dtd">
<html>
<head>
<title>"""+name+"""'s Home Page</title>
</head>
<body>
<h1>Welcome to """+name+"""'s Home Page</h1>
<p>Hi!  I am """+name+""".  This is my home page!
I am interested in """+interest+"""</p>
</body>
</html>""")
    file.close()
```

Thus, executing makeHomePage("Barb","horses") will create:

```
<!DOCTYPE HTML PUBLIC "-//W3C//DTD HTML 4.01
```

```
Transition//EN" "http://wwww.w3.org/TR/html4/
  loose.dtd">
<html>
<head>
<title>Barb's Home Page</title>
</head>
<body>
<h1>Welcome to Barb's Home Page</h1>
<p>Hi!  I am Barb.  This is my home page!
I am interested in horses</p>
</body>
</html>
```

Debugging Tip: Write the HTML First

Programs to generate HTML can be confusing. Before you start trying to write one, write the HTML. Make up a sample of what you want the HTML to look like. Make sure that it works in your browser. *Then* write the Python function that generates that kind of HTML.

Modifying this program is painful, though. There is so much detail in the HTML and all that quoting is hard to get around. We're better off using *subfunctions* to break up the program into pieces that are easier to manipulate. This is, again, an example of using **procedural abstraction**. Here's a version of the recipe where we confine the parts that we'll change most often to the top.

Program 109: Improved Home Page Creator

```python
def makeHomePage(name, interest):
  file=open("homepage.html","wt")
  file.write(doctype())
  file.write(title(name+"'s Home Page"))
  file.write(body("""
<h1>Welcome to """+name+"""'s Home Page</h1> <p>Hi!  I am
"""+name+""".  This is my home page! I am interested in
"""+interest+"""</p>"""))
  file.close()

def doctype():
  return '<!DOCTYPE HTML PUBLIC "-//W3C//DTD HTML 4.01
Transition//EN" "http://wwww.w3.org/TR/html4/loose.dtd">'

def title(titlestring):
  return "<html><head><title>"+titlestring+"</title></head>"

def body(bodystring):
  return "<body>"+bodystring+"</body></html>"
```

We can grab content for our Web pages from anywhere we want. Here is a recipe that can pull information out of a directory provided as input and generates an index

```
<!DOCTYPE HTML PUBLIC "-//W3C//DTD
   HTML 4.01 Transition//EN"
   "http://wwww.w3.org/TR/html4/loose.dtd"
   ><html><head><title>Samples from
C:\Documents and Settings\Mark
Guzdial\My
Documents\mediasources\pics</title></hea
d><body><h1>Samples from
C:\Documents and Settings\Mark
Guzdial\My Documents\mediasources\pics
</h1>
<p>Filename: students1.jpg<image
   src="students1.jpg" height="100" /></p>
<p>Filename: students2.jpg<image
   src="students2.jpg" height="100" /></p>
<p>Filename: students5.jpg<image
   src="students5.jpg" height="100" /></p>
<p>Filename: students6.jpg<image
   src="students6.jpg" height="100" /></p>
<p>Filename: students7.jpg<image
   src="students7.jpg" height="100" /></p>
<p>Filename: students8.jpg<image
   src="students8.jpg" height="100" /></p>
</body></html>
```

FIGURE 12.7
Creating a thumbnail page.

page of those images (Figure 12.7). We're not going to list the doctype() and other *utility functions* here—we'll just focus on the part we care about. And that is how we should think about it—just the part we care about; we write doctype() once, then forget about it!

Program 110: Generate a Thumbnail Page

```
import os

def makeSamplePage(directory):
 samplesFile=open(directory+"//samples.html","wt")
 samplesFile.write(doctype())
 samplesFile.write(title("Samples from "+directory))
 # Now, let's make up the string that will be the body.
 samples="<h1>Samples from "+directory+" </h1>"
 for file in os.listdir(directory):
  if file.endswith(".jpg"):
   samples=samples+"<p>Filename: "+file
   samples=samples+'<image src="'+file+'"height="100"/></p>'
 samplesFile.write(body(samples))
 samplesFile.close()
```

We can pull information off the Web to create new Web content. That's how sites like *Google News* work.[1] Here's a version of our home page creator that gathers the temperature live (designed especially for Atlanta).

[1] http://news.google.com

Program 111: Generate Home Page with Temperature Information

```
import urllib

def makeHomePage(name, interest):
  file=open("homepage.html","wt")
  file.write(doctype())
  file.write(title(name+"'s Home Page"))
  file.write(body("""
<h1>Welcome to """+name+"""'s Home Page</h1> <p>Hi!  I am
"""+name+""".   This is my home page! I am interested in
"""+interest+"""</p> <p>Right here and right now it's
"""+findTemperatureLive()+""" degrees. (If you're in
the North, nyah-nyah!)"""))
  file.close()

def findTemperatureLive():
  # Get the weather page
  import urllib
  connection=urllib.urlopen("http://www.ajc.com/weather")
  weather = connection.read()
  connection.close()
  #weatherFile = getMediaPath("ajc-weather.html")
  #file = open(weatherFile,"rt")
  #weather = file.read()
  #file.close()
  # Find the Temperature
  curLoc = weather.find("Currently")
  if curLoc <> -1:
    # Now, find the "<b>&deg;" following the temp
    tempLoc = weather.find("<b>&deg;",curLoc)
    tempStart = weather.rfind(">",0,tempLoc)
    return weather[tempStart+1:tempLoc]
  if curLoc == -1:
    return "They must have changed the page format--can't find the temp"
```

Remember the random sentence generator? We can add that, too.

Program 112: Home Page Generator with Random Sentences

```
import urllib
import random

def makeHomePage(name, interest):
  file=open("homepage.html","wt")
  file.write(doctype())
  file.write(title(name+"'s Home Page"))
  file.write(body("""
<h1>Welcome to """+name+"""'s Home Page</h1> <p>Hi!  I am
"""+name+""".   This is my home page! I am interested in
```

```
"""+interest+"""</p> <p>Right here and right now it's
"""+findTemperatureLive()+""" degrees. (If you're in the
North, nyah-nyah!).</p> <p>Random thought for the day:
"""+sentence()+"</p>"))
    file.close()

def sentence():
    nouns = ["Mark", "Alicia", "Maria", "Latrice", "Jose", "Corey",¬
    "Teshaun"]
    verbs = ["runs", "skips", "sings", "leaps", "jumps", "climbs",¬
    "argues", "giggles"]
    phrases = ["in a tree", "over a log", "very loudly", "around the¬
    bush", "while reading the news"]
    phrases = phrases + ["very badly", "while skipping", "instead of¬
    grading", "while typing on the CoWeb."]
    return random.choice(nouns)+" "+random.choice(verbs)+" "+random.¬
    choice(phrases)+"."

def findTemperatureLive():
    # Get the weather page
    import urllib
    connection=urllib.urlopen("http://www.ajc.com/weather")
    weather = connection.read()
    connection.close()
    #weatherFile = getMediaPath("ajc-weather.html")
    #file = open(weatherFile,"rt")
    #weather = file.read()
    #file.close()
    # Find the Temperature
    curLoc = weather.find("Currently")
    if curLoc <> -1:
        # Now, find the "<b>&deg;" following the temp
        tempLoc = weather.find("<b>&deg;",curLoc)
        tempStart = weather.rfind(">",0,tempLoc)
        return weather[tempStart+1:tempLoc]
    if curLoc == -1:
        return "They must have changed the page format--can't find the temp"
```

¬These lines of the program should continue with the next lines. A single command in Python may not break across multiple lines.   ◾

How It Works

Let's walk through the whole large example.

- We are going to need both `urllib` and `random` in this function, so we `import` both of them at the top of our Program Area.
- Our main function is `makeHomePage`. We call it with a name and an interest to mention.
- At the top of `makeHomePage`, we open the HTML file we're writing, then write out the `doctype` using the utility function (it's not listed here, but would have to

be in the Program Area). We write out the title (using the `title` function) with the input `name` inserted, and then the body (using the `body` function).

- The input to the `body` function is a long string, whose construction is where we're actually invoking `findTemperatureLive()` and `sentence()`. We use triple-quoting so that we can put in returns wherever we want them. We write out the `name` and the `interest` by concatenating them into the middle of the HTML string.

- We call `findTemperatureLive()` midway through the body string. Note that this version is somewhat different from the one we built last chapter. Here we `return` the result strings rather than simply use `print`. By returning them, we can use the result and insert it into our HTML body string.

- We call `sentence()` as our `"Random thought for the day:"`. Again, `sentence()` is slightly different in that it is using `return` instead of `print` so that we can use the output in our HTML body string.

- Finally, back at `makeHomePage`, we close the HTML file, and we're done.

Where do you think large Web sites get all their information? There are *so* many pages in those Web sites. Where do they get it all? Where do they store it all?

12.3 DATABASES: A PLACE TO STORE OUR TEXT

Large Web sites use **databases** to store their text and other information. Sites like EBay.com, Amazon.com, and CNN.com have large databases with lots of information in them. The pages at these sites aren't generated by somebody typing in information. Instead, programs walk over the database gathering all the information and generating HTML pages. They may do this on a timed basis, to keep updating the page. (See the "last generated" information at CNN.com or Google News.)

Why databases rather than simple text files? There are four reasons:

- Databases are fast. Databases store *indices* that keep track of where key information (like last name or ID number) is in a file, so that you can find "Guzdial" right away. Files are indexed on filename but not on the content *in* the file.

- Databases are standardized. You can access the Microsoft Access, Informix, Oracle, Sybase, and MySQL databases from any number of tools or languages.

- Databases can be **distributed**. A great many users, on different computers across a network, can put information into a database and pull information out of it.

- Databases store **relations**. When we used lists to represent pixels, we had to keep in our heads which number meant what. Databases store names for *fields* of data. When a database knows which fields are important (e.g., which ones you're going to search on most often), it can be indexed on those fields.

Python has built-in support for several different databases, and provides a general support for any kind of database called `anydbm` (Figure 12.8). **Keys** go in square brackets and those are the fields that you get the fastest access through. Both keys and values can only be strings using `anydbm`. Here's an example of retrieving information from `anydbm`.

FIGURE 12.8
Using the simple database.

```
>>> db = anydbm.open("mydbm","r")
>>> print db.keys()
['barney', 'fred']
>>> print db['barney']
My wife is Betty.
>>> for k in db.keys():
...          print db[k]
...
My wife is Betty.
My wife is Wilma.
>>> db.close()
```

Another Python database, shelve, allows you to put strings, lists, numbers, or just about anything in the value.

```
>>> import shelve
>>> db=shelve.open("myshelf","c")
>>> db["one"]=["This is",["a","list"]]
>>> db["two"]=12
>>> db.close()
>>> db=shelve.open("myshelf","r")
>>> print db.keys()
['two', 'one']
>>> print db['one']
['This is', ['a', 'list']]
>>> print db['two']
12
```

12.3.1 Relational Databases

Most modern databases are relational databases. In relational databases, information is stored in tables (Figure 12.9). Columns in a relational table are named and rows of data are assumed to be related.

Complex relationships are stored across multiple tables. Let's say that you have a bunch of pictures of students and you want to keep track of which students are in which pictures—where there is more than one student in a given picture. You might record a structure like that in a collection of tables for recording students and student IDs,

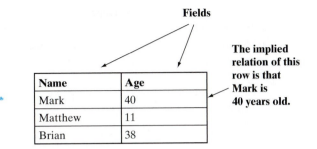

FIGURE 12.9
An example relational table.

Picture	PictureID
Class1.jpg	P1
Class2.jpg	P2

StudentName	StudentID
Katie	S1
Brittany	S2
Carrie	S3

PictureID	StudentID
P1	S1
P1	S2
P2	S3

FIGURE 12.10
Representing more complex relationships across multiple tables.

pictures and picture IDs, then the mapping between student IDs and picture IDs, as in Figure 12.10.

How would you use tables like the one in Figure 12.10 to figure out which picture Brittany is in? You start up by looking up Brittany's ID in the student table, then look up the picture ID in the picture-student table, then look up the picture name in the picture table, to result in CLASS1.JPG. How about figuring out who's in that picture? You look up the ID in the picture table, then look up which student IDs are related to that picture ID, and then look up the student names.

This use of multiple tables to answer a **query** (a request for information from a database) is called a **join**. Database joins work best if the tables are kept simple, with only a single relation per row.

12.3.2   An Example Relational Database Using Hash Tables

To explain relational database ideas, this section builds a relational database using a simpler structure in Python. In this way, we can describe how some database ideas, like joins, work. This section is optional.

We can use a structure called a **hash table** or **dictionary** (other languages sometimes call them *associative arrays*) to create rows for database relational tables using shelve. Hash tables allow us to relate keys and values, like databases, but only in memory.

```
>>> row={'StudentName':'Katie','StudentID':'S1'}
>>> print row
{'StudentID': 'S1', 'StudentName': 'Katie'}
>>> print row['StudentID']
S1
>>> print row['StudentName']
Katie
```

Besides defining all of the hash table at once, we can fill in the hash table in pieces.

```
>>> pictureRow = {}
>>> pictureRow['Picture']='Class1.jpg'
>>> pictureRow['PictureID']='P1'
>>> print pictureRow
{'Picture': 'Class1.jpg', 'PictureID': 'P1'}
>>> print pictureRow['Picture']
Class1.jpg
```

Now we can create a relational database by storing each table in a separate `shelve` database and representing each row as a hash table.

Program 113: Creating a Relational Database Using `shelve`

```
import shelve
def createDatabases():
  #Create Student Database
  students=shelve.open("students.db","c")
  row = {'StudentName':'Katie','StudentID':'S1'}
  students['S1']=row
  row = {'StudentName':'Brittany','StudentID':'S2'}
  students['S2']=row
  row = {'StudentName':'Carrie','StudentID':'S3'}
  students['S3']=row
  students.close()
  #Create Picture Database
  pictures=shelve.open("pictures.db","c")
  row = {'Picture':'Class1.jpg','PictureID':'P1'}
  pictures['P1']=row
  row = {'Picture':'Class2.jpg','PictureID':'P2'}
  pictures['P2']=row
  pictures.close()
  #Create Picture-Student Database
  pictures=shelve.open("pict-students.db","c")
  row = {'PictureID':'P1','StudentID':'S1'}
  pictures['P1S1']=row
  row = {'PictureID':'P1','StudentID':'S2'}
  pictures['P1S2']=row
  row = {'PictureID':'P2','StudentID':'S3'}
  pictures['P2S3']=row
  pictures.close()
```

How It Works

The function `createDatabases` actually creates three different database tables.

- The first one is STUDENTS.DB. We create dictionaries (hash tables) representing Katie, who is "S1," then store that in the database `students` using the student ID "S1" as the index. We do the same for Brittany and Carrie—it's okay to use the same `row` variable for each of them, because we simply create the hash table and then store it to the database.

- Next we create the PICTURES.DB database. We set up the relationship between the "Picture" CLASS1.JPG and its ID "P1." Then we store that in the `pictures` database. We repeat the process for the picture CLASS2.JPG. Could we have used a variable `database` for each database? Since we only open one at a time, then close it before the next one, we certainly could have. But it would have been less readable.

- Finally, we open and fill the PICT-STUDENTS.DB database. We create rows relating the picture IDs to the student IDs, store them in the database, then close the database.

Using the databases we just created, we can do a *join*. Obviously, the idea is that we would be doing this lookup sometime after creating the database, and maybe after adding lots more entries to it. (If we only had two pictures and three students in the database, this would be a pretty silly exercise in programming.) We have to loop through the data to find the values we need to match across databases.

Program 114: Doing a Join with Our `shelve` Database

```
def whoInClass1():
  # Get the pictureID
  pictures=shelve.open("pictures.db","r")
  for key in pictures.keys():
    row = pictures[key]
    if row['Picture'] == 'Class1.jpg':
      id = row['PictureID']
  pictures.close()
  # Get the students' IDs
  studentslist=[]
  pictures=shelve.open("pict-students.db","c")
  for key in pictures.keys():
    row = pictures[key]
    if row['PictureID']==id:
      studentslist.append(row['StudentID'])
  pictures.close()
  print "We're looking for:",studentslist
  # Get the students' names
  students = shelve.open("students.db","r")
  for key in students.keys():
    row = students[key]
```

```
    if row['StudentID'] in studentslist:
      print row['StudentName'],"is in the picture"
students.close()
```

How It Works

Each of the parts of the join requires a different loop through our database.

- First, we open PICTURES.DB and name it `pictures`. We loop through all the `keys`, getting each `row` (hash table), and checking if the 'Picture' entry is CLASS1.JPG. When we find it, we store the picture ID in `id`. We close the database because we're done with it.

- Next, we open PICT-STUDENTS.DB in `pictures` (it's okay to reuse the name). We know that there may be more than one student in a picture, so we create a list to store all the student IDs that we find, `studentslist`. For each key in `pictures`, we look for 'PictureID' entries in the hash table that match our `id`. When we find one, we `append` the 'StudentID' part of the hash table onto our `studentslist`.

- Finally, we open the STUDENTS.DB database in `students`. We loop through all the `keys` and get the hash table `row`. We use a neat feature of lists that we haven't seen previously: we can ask whether a string is `in` the list `studentslist`. If the given 'StudentID' is one of those that we're looking for (in `studentslist`), then we print the corresponding 'StudentName' from the `row` hash table. Finally, we close the `students` database to clean up.

Running this looks like this:

```
>>> whoInClass1()
We're looking for: ['S2', 'S1']
Brittany is in the picture
Katie is in the picture
```

12.3.3   Working with SQL

Real databases don't make you do loops to do joins. Instead, you typically use **SQL (structured query language)** to manipulate and query databases. There are actually several languages in the SQL database language family but we're not going to make distinctions here. SQL is a large and complex programming language and we're not going to even attempt to go over all of it. But we are going to touch on enough of it to give you a sense of what SQL is like and how it's used.

SQL can be used with many different databases, including Microsoft Access. Python can talk to virtually all of them in the way that we'll be using it here. There are also freely available databases like **MySQL** that use SQL and can be controlled from Python. If you want to play with the examples we'll be doing here, you can install *MySQL* from http://www.mysql.com into JES. You need to set up MySQL, and you need to download the *JAR file* that allows Java to access MySQL and put that in your JYTHON LIB folder.

To manipulate a MySQL database from JES, you need to create a *connection* that will provide you with a *cursor* to manipulate via SQL. We use MySQL from JES with a function like this, so that we can execute `con = getConnection()`.

Program 115: Getting a MySQL Connection from Jython

We find all these details hard to remember, so we hide them in a function and just say con = getConnection() with this in the Program Area: com.ziclix.python.sql import zxJDBC def getConnection(): db =zxJDBC.connect("jdbc:mysql://localhost/test", "root", None, "com.mysql.jdbc.Driver") con = db.cursor() return con ∎

To execute SQL commands from here, we use an `execute` method on the connection like this:

```
con.execute("create table Person (name VARCHAR(50), age INT)")
```

Here's a very brief taste of SQL:

- To create a table in SQL, we use `create table tablename (columnname datatype,...)`. So in the example above, we're creating a *Person* table with two columns: a name with a variable number of characters up to 50, and an integer age. Other datatypes include numeric, float, date, time, year, and text.

- We insert data into SQL using `insert into tablename values (column-value1, columnvalue2,...)`. Here's where our multiple kinds of quotes come in handy.

  ```
  con.execute('insert into Person values
    ("Mark",40)')
  ```

- Think about selecting data in a database as literally selecting, as you would in a word-processor or a spreadsheet, the rows that you want in the table. Some examples of selection commands in SQL are:

  ```
  Select * from Person
  Select name,age from Person
  Select * from Person where age>40
  Select name,age from Person where age>40
  ```

  We can do all of this from Python. Our connection has an **instance variable** (like a method, but known only to objects of that type), rowcount, that tells you the number of rows selected. The method fetchone() gives you the next selected row, as a **tuple** (think of this as a special kind of list—we can use it just like a list for most purposes).

  ```
  >>> con.execute("select name,age from Person")
  >>> print con.rowcount
  3
  >>> print con.fetchone()
  ('Mark', 40)
  ```

```
>>> print con.fetchone()
('Barb', 41)
>>> print con.fetchone()
('Brian', 36)
```

We can also select using a condition.

Program 116: Selecting and Showing Data with a Conditional Select

```
def showSomePersons(con, condition):
  con.execute("select name, age from Person "+condition)
  for i in range(0,con.rowcount):
    results=con.fetchone()
    print results[0]+" is "+str(results[1])+" years old"
```

How It Works

The function showSomePersons takes the input of a database connection con and a condition, which is meant to be a string containing an SQL where clause. We then ask the connection to execute a select SQL command. We concatenate the condition onto the end of our select command. We then have a loop for each of the rows returned from the selection (using con.rowcount to get that number of rows). We use fetchone to get each response and print it. Note the use of normal list indexing on the returned tuple.

Here's an example of using showSomePersons:

```
>>> showSomePersons(con,"where age >= 40")
Mark is 40 years old
Barb is 41 years old
```

We can now think about doing one of our joins using a conditional select. The next code snippet says "Return a picture and student name, from these three tables, where the student name is 'Brittany', where the students' ID is the same as the student ID in the student-picture IDs table, and the picture ID from the IDs table is the same as the ID in the picture table."

```
Select
    p.picture,
    s.studentName
From
    Students as s,
    IDs as i,
    Pictures as p
Where
    (s.studentName="Brittany") and
    (s.studentID=i.studentID) and
    (i.pictureID=p.pictureID)
```

12.3.4   Using a Database to Build Web Pages

Now let's get back to our Web page creator. We can store information in our database, retrieve it, then put it in our Web page—just like Amazon, CNN, and eBay.

```
>>> import anydbm
>>> db=anydbm.open("news","c")
>>> db["headline"]="Katie turns 8!"
>>> db["story"]="""Our daughter, Katie, turned 8 years
old yesterday. She had a great birthday. Grandma and
Grandpa came over. The previous weekend, she had
three of her friends over for a sleepover then a
morning run to Dave and Buster's."""
>>> db.close()
```

Program 117: **Building a Web Page with Database Content**

```
def makeHomePage(name, interest):
  file=open("homepage.html","wt")
  file.write(doctype())
  file.write(title(name+"'s Home Page"))
  # Import the database content
  db=anydbm.open("news","r")
  file.write(body("""
<h1>Welcome to """""+name+""""'s Home Page</h1> <p>Hi!  I am
"""+name+""".  This is my home page! I am interested in
"""+interest+"""
</p> <p>Right here and right now it's
"""+findTemperatureLive()+""" degrees. (If you're in the
North, nyah-nyah!).</p>
<p>Random thought for the day:
"""+sentence()+"""</p>
<h2>Latest news:
"""+db["headline"]+"""</h2>
<p>"""+db["story"]+"</p>"))
  file.close()
  db.close()

#Rest, like findTemperatureLive(), from previous examples
```

Now we can think about how a large Web site like CNN.com works. Reporters enter stories into a database that are distributed all over the world. Editors (also distributed or all in one place) retrieve stories from the database, update them, then store them back. On a regular basis (perhaps more often when a hot story emerges) the Web page generation program runs, gathers up the stories, and generates the HTML. "POOF! You have a large Web site!" Databases are really critical to how large Web sites run.

PROBLEMS

12.1   What are the differences between SGML, HTML, XML, and XHTML?

12.2   Convert the following hexadecimal numbers to decimal: 2A3, 321, 16, 24, F3.

12.3   Convert the following decimal numbers to hexadecimal: 113, 64, 129, 72, 3.

12.4   Convert the following colors to hexadecimal: gray, yellow, pink, orange, and magenta. You can get the red, green, and blue values for each color using `print color`.

12.5   Write a function to create a simple home page with your name, your picture, and a table with the titles of your courses and teacher names.

12.6   Write a function to read and return the current headline from `http://www.cnn.com`. Modify the function that creates a home page to use this function.

12.7   Write a function to read and return the status from your friend's Facebook page. Modify the function that creates a home page to use this function to display the status messages from five of your friends facebook home pages.

12.8   Use a hash table to store texting shortcuts and their definitions. For example, "lol" means "laugh out loud." Use this hash table to decode a text message.

12.9   Given a relational database with a person table that contains an id, name, and age. What do each of the following return?

- Select * from person.
- Select age from person.
- Select id from person.
- Select name,age from person.
- Select * from person where age > 20.
- Select name from person where age < 20.

12.10   Why should you use a relational database? Are there other kinds of databases? Who invented relational databases?

12.11   Relational database questions:

- What is a database table?
- What is a join?
- What is a query?
- What is a connection?

12.12   Relational database questions:

- What is SQL?
- How do you create a table in SQL?
- How do you insert a row in a table in SQL?
- How do you get data from a table in SQL?

12.13   Your father calls you. "My tech support people are saying that the company Web site is down because the database program is broken. What does the database have to do with our company Web site?" You explain to him how databases can be integral to running large Web sites. Explain both (a) how the Web site comes to be authored through the database, and (b) how the HTML is actually created.

12.14 You have a new computer that seems to connect to the Internet but when you try to go to `http://www.cnn.com` you get a "Server Not Found" error. You call tech support and they tell you to try to go to `http://64.236.24.20`. That works. Now both you and the tech know what's wrong with your computer's settings. What isn't working properly, since you can get to a site via the Internet but can't get the domain name `www.cnn.com` to be recognized?

12.15 Given a folder with images in it, create an index HTML page with links to each image. Write a function that takes a string which is the path to a directory. You will create a page in the folder named INDEX.HTML that should be an HTML page containing a link to every JPEG file in the directory.

You will also generate a thumbnail (half the size) copy of each image. Use `makeEmptyPicture` to create a blank picture of the right size, then scale down the original picture into the blank picture. Name the new image "half-" + the original file name (e.g., if the original file name was "fred.jpg," save the half-size image as "half-fred.jpg"). The anchor in the link to each full-size picture should be the half-size image.

12.16 Add something to your HTML home page generator that will make random, relevant comments about the weather depending on the temperature.

- If it's going to be less than 32, you want to insert either "Watch out for ice!" or "Is it going to snow?"
- If it's going to be between 32 and 50, you want to insert either "I can't wait for winter to be over!" or "Come on, Spring!"
- If it's over 50 but less than 80, you want to insert either "It's getting warmer!" or "Light jacket weather."
- If it's over 80, you want to insert either "FINALLY! Summer!" or "Time to go swimming!"

Write a function named `weathercomment` that will take a temperature as input and return one of the phrases randomly. In other words, you want to use the temperature to decide which are the relevant phrases, then pick one randomly from there.

12.17 Write a function that reads delimited strings from a file with names and phone numbers and uses a database to store the names as the keys and the phone numbers as the values. Take as input the file name and the name of the person who's phone number you are looking for. How would you look up the phone number to find the name it belongs to?

12.18 Create a relational database that has a person table, a picture table, and a person-picture table. In the person table store an id, the person name, and the person's age. In the picture table store a picture id and filename. In the person-picture table keep track of the people in each picture. Write a function that let you find all the pictures for people over a certain age.

12.19 Create a relational database that has a product table, a customer table, an order table, and an order item table. In the product table store an id, name, picture, description, and price. In the customer table store the id, name, and address. In the order table store the order id and customer id. In the order item table store the order id, product id, and quantity. Write a function to let you find all orders for a given customer. Write a function to let you find all orders with a total cost greater than some specified value.

12.20 Go to www.half.com and look up a popular movie that they sell as a DVD. What database tables and fields do you think are needed to represent the data for a DVD?

TO DIG DEEPER

There are several good books on using Python and Jython for Web development and programming. We particularly recommend the books by Gupta [18] and Hightower [24] for their discussions of the use of Java in database contexts.

4 MOVIES

13.1   GENERATING ANIMATIONS

13.2   WORKING WITH VIDEO SOURCE

13.3   BUILDING A VIDEO EFFECT BOTTOM-UP

Chapter Learning Objectives

The media learning goals for this chapter are:

- To understand how a series of still images can be perceived as motion.
- To create animations with different motions and effects.
- To use video sources for animations and processing.
- To work out how a digital effect is implemented.

The computer science goals for this chapter are:

- To understand another example of using multiple functions to make coding easier.
- To understand a detailed example of bottom-up design and implementation.
- To use optional and named arguments to Python functions.

Movies (video) are actually very simple to manipulate. They are arrays of pictures (**frames**). You need to be concerned with the **frame rate** (the number of frames per second) but it's mostly just things you've seen before. We're going to use the term *movies* to refer generically to **animations** (motion generated entirely by graphical drawings) and **video** (motion generated by some kind of photographic process).

What makes movies work is a feature of our visual system called **persistence of vision**. We do not see every change that happens in the world. For example, you don't typically see your eyes blink, even though they do it quite often (typically 20 times a minute). But each time we blink, we don't panic and think, "Where'd the world go?" Instead, our eyes retain an image for a short time and keep telling the brain that the same image is there.

If we see one *related* picture after another fast enough, our eye retains the image and our brain sees continuous motion. "Fast enough" is about 16 frames per second—we see the 16 related pictures within a second, we think continuous motion. If the pictures aren't related, our brain reports a *montage*, a collection of disparate (though perhaps thematically connected) images. We refer to this 16 *frames per second* (*fps*) as the lower bound for the sensation of motion.

Early silent pictures were 16 fps. Motion pictures standardized on 24 fps to make sound smoother—16 fps didn't provide enough physical space on the film to encode enough sound data. (Ever wonder why silent pictures often look fast and jerky? Think about what happens when you scale up a picture or sound—that's exactly what happens if you play a 16 fps movie at 24 fps.) Digital video (e.g., video cameras) captures at 30 fps. How high is useful? There are some U.S. Air Force experiments suggesting that pilots can recognize a blurb of light in the shape of an aircraft (and figure out what kind it is) in 1/200 of a second. Video game players say that they can discern a difference between 30 fps video and 60 fps video.

Movies are challenging to work with because of the amount and speed of the data involved. **Real-time processing** of video (e.g., doing some modification to each frame as it comes in or goes out) is hard because whatever processing you do has to fit into 1/30 of a second. Let's do the math for how many bytes are needed to record video:

- One second of 640 × 480 frame size images at 30 fps means 30(*frames*) ∗ 640 ∗ 480(*pixels*) = 9,216,000 pixels.
- At 24-bit color (one byte for each of R, G, and B), that's 27,648,000 bytes, or 27 megabytes *per second.*
- For a 90-minute feature film, that's 90 ∗ 60 ∗ 27,648,000 = 149,299,200,000 bytes—149 gigabytes.

Digital movies are almost always stored in a compressed format. A DVD only stores 6.47 gigabytes, so even on a DVD the movie is compressed. Movie format standards like *MPEG, QuickTime,* and *AVI* are all compressed movie formats. They don't record every frame—they record *key frames* and then record the differences between one frame and the next. The *JMV* format is slightly different—it's a file of JPEG images, so every frame is there, but every frame is compressed.

Movies can use some different compression techniques than pictures or sounds. Think about watching someone walk across a frame of a camera. Between two successive frames, only a little bit changes—where the person just was and where they now are. If we recorded only those differences, and not all the pixels for the whole frame, then we save a lot of space.

An MPEG movie is really just an MPEG image sequence merged with an MPEG (like MP3) audio file. We're going to follow that lead and *not* deal with sound here. The tools described in the next section *can* create movies with sound, but the real trick of processing movies is handling all the images. That's what we're going to focus on here.

13.1   GENERATING ANIMATIONS

To make movies, we're going to create a series of JPEG frames and then reassemble them. We'll place all of our frames in a single directory and number them so that the tools know how to reassemble them into a movie in the right order. We'll literally name

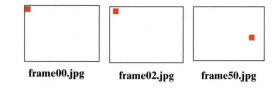

frame00.jpg   **frame02.jpg**   **frame50.jpg**

FIGURE 13.1
A few frames from the first movie: moving a rectangle down and right.

our files FRAME0I.JPG, FRAME02.JPG, and so on. It's important to include the leading zeroes, so that the files are listed in numeric order when placed in alphabetical order.

Here's our first movie-generating program, which simply moves a red rectangle from top left to bottom right (Figure 13.1).

Program 118: Create a Movie with a Moving Rectangle

```
def makeRectMovie(directory):
  for num in range(1,30): #29 frames (1 to 29)
    canvas = makeEmptyPicture(300,200)
    addRectFilled(canvas,num * 10, num * 5, 50,50, red)
    # convert the number to a string
    numStr=str(num)
    if num < 10:
      writePictureTo(canvas,directory+"\\frame0"+numStr+".jpg")
    if num >= 10:
      writePictureTo(canvas,directory+"\\frame"+numStr+".jpg")
  movie = makeMovieFromInitialFile(directory+"\\frame00.jpg");
  return movie
```

You can try this out by creating a directory called `rect` in the `Temp` directory and then executing the following.

```
>>>    rectM = makeRectMovie("c:\\Temp\\rect")
>>>    playMovie(rectM)
```

When you execute `playMovie(movie)` it will display all the frames of the movie in a movie player. Once the movie has finished displaying, you can use the PREV button to see the previous frame and the NEXT button to see the next frame in the movie. The PLAY MOVIE button will play the entire movie again. The DELETE ALL PREVIOUS button will delete all frames before the displayed frame in the directory. The DELETE ALL AFTER button will delete all the frames after the displayed frame in the directory. The WRITE QUICKTIME button will write out a QuickTime movie from all the frames in the directory. The WRITE AVI button will write out an AVI movie from all the frames in the directory. The movies will be in the directory with the frames and will have the same name as the directory.

FIGURE 13.2
The movie player showing the rectangle movie.

FIGURE 13.3
A ticker tape movie.

How It Works

The key part of this recipe are the lines right after `makeEmptyPicture`. We have to compute a different position for the rectangle depending on the current frame number. The equations in the `addRectFilled()` functions compute different positions for different frames of the movie (Figure 13.2).

While `setPixel()` gets upset if you try to set a pixel outside the bounds of the picture, the graphics functions like `addText()` and `addRect()` don't generate errors for going beyond the borders. They'll simply *clip* the image for the picture (show only what they can), so you can create simple code to make animations and not worry about going out of bounds. This makes creating a tickertape movie really pretty easy (Figure 13.3).

Program 119: Generate a Tickertape Movie

```
def tickertape(directory,string):
  for num in range(1,100): #99 frames
    canvas = makeEmptyPicture(300,100)
    #Start at right, and move left
    addText(canvas,300-(num*10),50,string)
    # Now, write out the frame
    # Have to deal with single digit vs. double digit frame numbers¬
    differently
    numStr=str(num)
    if num < 10:
      writePictureTo(canvas,directory+"//frame0"+numStr+".jpg")
```

¬These lines of the program should continue with the next lines. A single command in Python may not break across multiple lines.

```
if num >= 10:
   writePictureTo(canvas,directory+"//frame"+numStr+".jpg")
```

How It Works

The function `tickertape` takes a directory in which the frames of the movie will be stored and a string to write out. For each of 99 frames (from 1 to 100, but not including 100), we make an empty picture of size (300, 100) and put the string into it as text. The y position is always at 50 (same position vertically), and the x position (horizontally) is at 300-(num*10). As the frame number, num, increases, this equation gets smaller. So each frame has the string drawn closer to the left side (smaller x values) of the frame. We convert the frame number, num, number to a string `numStr` and use that to make a filename with the right number of leading zeroes.

Can we move more than one thing at once? Sure! Our drawing code just gets a little more complicated. We could just move things with linear motion like all the examples up until now, but let's try something different. Here's a recipe that uses *sine* and *cosine* to create circular motion to match our linear motion of Program 118 (page 301) (Figure 13.4).

Program 120: Move Two Objects at Once

```
def movingRectangle2(directory):
  for num in range(1,30): #29 frames
    canvas = makeEmptyPicture(300,250)
    #add a filled rect moving linearly
    addRectFilled(canvas,num*10,num*5, 50,50,red)

    # Let's have one just moving around
    blueX = 100+ int(10 * sin(num))
    blueY = 4*num+int(10* cos(num))
    addRectFilled(canvas,blueX,blueY,50,50,blue)

    # Now, write out the frame
    # Have to deal with single digit vs. double digit
    numStr=str(num)
```

FIGURE 13.4
Moving two rectangles at once.

```
if num < 10:
  writePictureTo(canvas,directory+"//frame0"+numStr+".jpg")
if num >= 10:
  writePictureTo(canvas,directory+"//frame"+numStr+".jpg")
```

How It Works

We know that `sin` and `cos` generate values between −1 and 1. (You remember that, right?) The x position of the blue box is set by `100 + int(10 * sin(num))`. This means that the x position of the blue box will be around 100, plus or minus 10 pixels. It'll shift left to right and right to left as the values of `sin` change. The y position is determined by `4 * num + int(10 * cos(num))`. The y position, then, is always increasing (the box is falling), but plus or minus 10, so there's a slight up-and-down motion while it's falling.

We don't have to create our animations only out of things that we can do with graphics primitives. We can use the same kinds of images we've used previously through `setColor()`. This kind of code runs pretty slowly.

Debugging Tip: `PrintNow()` to Print `NOW`

There is a JES function called `printNow()` that takes a string and prints it *immediately*—it doesn't wait until the function is done to print the line to the Command Area. That's useful when you want to know what frame number a function is on. You might want to go look at the first few frames from the operating system by double-clicking on them once they are generated.

The recipe below moves Mark's head around on the screen. This function took over a minute to complete on our computer. Frames from running the program can be seen in Figure 13.5.

FIGURE 13.5
A couple of frames from moving the head movie.

Program 121: Move Mark's Head

```
def moveHead(directory):
  markF=getMediaPath("blue-mark.jpg")
  mark = makePicture(markF)
  head = clip(mark,275,160,385,306)
  for num in range(1,30): #29 frames
    printNow("Frame number: "+str(num))
    canvas = makeEmptyPicture(640,480)
    # Now, do the actual copying
    copy(head,canvas,num*10,num*5)
    # Now, write out the frame
    # Have to deal with single digit vs. double digit frame
      numbers differently
    numStr=str(num)
    if num < 10:
      writePictureTo(canvas,directory+"//frame0"+numStr+".jpg")
    if num >= 10:
      writePictureTo(canvas,directory+"//frame"+numStr+".jpg")

def clip(picture,startX,startY,endX,endY):
  width = endX - startX + 1
  height = endY - startY + 1
  resPict = makeEmptyPicture(width,height)
  resX = 0
  for x in range(startX,endX):
    resY=0 # reset result y index
    for y in range(startY,endY):
      origPixel = getPixel(picture,x,y)
      resPixel = getPixel(resPict,resX,resY)
      setColor(resPixel,(getColor(origPixel)))
      resY=resY + 1
    resX=resX + 1
  return resPict
```

How It Works

We've created a new method clip that creates and returns a new picture with just the pixels in the rectangle defined by the passed startX, startY, endX, and endY. We use this clip function to create a picture with just Mark's head in it. Then we use the general copy function (Program 30 (page 93)) to copy Mark's head to different locations in the canvas based on the frame number num.

Our movie programs are getting more complicated now. We might want to be able to write them in parts, with the frame-writing part kept separate. This means that we can focus in the main body of the function on what we want in the frame, not on writing the frame. This is an example of **procedural abstraction**.

Program 122: Move Mark's Head, Simplified

```
def moveHead2(directory):
  markF=getMediaPath("blue-mark.jpg")
  mark = makePicture(markF)
  face = clip(mark,275,160,385,306)
  for num in range(1,30): #29 frames
    printNow("Frame number: "+str(num))
    canvas = makeEmptyPicture(640,480)
    # Now, do the actual copying
    copy(face,canvas,num*10,num*5)
    # Now, write out the frame
    writeFrame(num,directory,canvas)

def writeFrame(num,dir,pict):
    # Have to deal with single digit vs. double digit
    numStr=str(num)
    if num < 10:
      writePictureTo(pict,dir+"//frame0"+numStr+".jpg")
    if num >= 10:
      writePictureTo(pict,dir+"//frame"+numStr+".jpg")
```

But this `writeFrame()` function assumes two-digit maximum frame numbers. We could want more frames. Here's a version that allows for three-digit frame numbers.

Program 123: Writeframe() for Over 100 Frames

```
def writeFrame(num,dir,pict):
    # Have to deal with single digit vs. double digit
    numStr=str(num)
    if num < 10:
      writePictureTo(pict,dir+"//frame00"+numStr+".jpg")
    if num >= 10 and num<100:
      writePictureTo(pict,dir+"//frame0"+numStr+".jpg")
    if num >= 100:
      writePictureTo(pict,dir+"//frame"+numStr+".jpg")
```

We can use the image manipulations that we created in Chapter 3 over multiple frames to create quite interesting movies. Remember the sunset-generating program (Program 12 (page 59))? Let's modify it to *slowly* generate a sunset across many frames. We modify it so that the difference between each frame is only 1%. This version actually goes too far, and generates a supernova, but the effect is still pretty interesting (Figure 13.6).

Program 124: Make a Slow-Sunset Movie

```
def slowSunset(directory):
  #outside the loop!
  canvas = makePicture(getMediaPath("beach-smaller.jpg"))
```

FIGURE 13.6
Frames from the slow-sunset movie.

```
for num in range(1,100): #99 frames
  printNow("Frame number: "+str(num))
  makeSunset(canvas)
  # Now, write out the frame
  writeFrame(frame,directory,canvas)

def makeSunset(picture):
  for p in getPixels(picture):
    value=getBlue(p)
    setBlue(p,value*0.99) #Just 1% decrease!
    value=getGreen(p)
    setGreen(p,value*0.99)
```

How It Works

The key to this movie is that we create the `canvas` *before* the loop that creates each frame. Within the loop, we simply keep using the same base `canvas`. This means that each call to `makeSunset` increases the "sunsetness" (no, it's not a word) by 1%. (We're not going to show `writeFrame()` anymore, since we assume that you'll include it in your Program Area and file.)

The `swapBack()` recipe that we made a while ago can also be used to good effect for generating movies. We modify the function in Program 45 (page 120) to take a threshold as input, then we pass in the frame number as the threshold. The effect is a slow fade into the background image (Figure 13.7) .

Program 125: **Fade Out Slowly**

```
def swapBack(pic1, back, newBg, threshold):
  for x in range(0,getWidth(pic1)):
    for y in range(0,getHeight(pic1)):
      p1Pixel = getPixel(pic1,x,y)
      backPixel = getPixel(back,x,y)
      if (distance(getColor(p1Pixel),getColor(backPixel))
        < threshold):
        setColor(p1Pixel,getColor(getPixel(newBg,x,y)))
  return pic1
```

FIGURE 13.7
Frames from the slow-fade-out movie.

```
def slowFadeout(directory):
  origBack = makePicture(getMediaPath("bgframe.jpg"))
  newBack = makePicture(getMediaPath("beach.jpg"))
  for num in range(1,60): #59 frames
    # do this in the loop
    kid = makePicture(getMediaPath("kid-in-frame.jpg"))
    swapBack(kid,origBack,newBack,num)
    # Now, write out the frame
    writeFrame(num,directory,kid)
```

How It Works

The frame number here is the threshold value for when we decide to swap in the new background instead of keeping the original pixels in swapBack. As the threshold increases, we replace more and more of the pixels of the original picture with new background pixels. As the frame number increases, then, we end up having more new background and less of both the old background and the old foreground. Note that here we create the kid picture *inside* the frame loop. We want the effect to be new for each frame, with the frame differences computed in swapBack with the changing threshold.

13.2 WORKING WITH VIDEO SOURCE

As we said earlier, dealing with real video, in real-time, is very hard. We're going to cheat by saving the video as a sequence of JPEG images, manipulate the JPEG images, then convert back into a movie. This lets us use video as a source (e.g., for background images).

To manipulate movies that already exist, we have to break them into frames. The MediaTools application can do this for you for MPEG movies (Figure 13.8). The MENU button in the MediaTools application lets you save any MPEG movie as a series of JPEG frame pictures. Tools like Apple's QuickTime Pro can do the same for QuickTime and AVI movies.

FIGURE 13.8
Saving a MPEG movie as a series of frames in the MediaTools application.

FIGURE 13.9
Frames from the Mommy watching Katie movie.

13.2.1   Video Manipulating Examples

In MEDIASOURCES is a brief movie of our daughter Katie dancing around. Let's create a movie of Mommy (Barb) watching her daughter—we'll simply composite Barb's head onto the frames of Katie dancing (Figure 13.9).

Program 126: Make Movie of Mommy Watching Katie

```
import os

def mommyWatching(directory):
  kidDir=r"C://ip-book//mediasources//kid-in-bg-seq"
  barbF=getMediaPath("barbaraS.jpg")
  barb = makePicture(barbF)
  face = clip(barb,22,9,93,97)
  num = 0
  for file in os.listdir(kidDir):
    if file.endswith(".jpg"):
      num = num + 1
```

```
printNow("Frame number: "+str(num))
framePic = makePicture(kidDir+"//"+file)
# Now, do the actual copying
copy(face,framePic,num*3,num*3)
# Now, write out the frame
writeFrame(num,directory,framePic)
```

How It Works

The directory where the video source images are stored is `C:/ip-book/mediasources/kid-in-bg-seq/`. We put that in a variable and get Barb's picture. We then make a picture of just Barb's face using the `clip` method. The frame number, `num`, is incremented in the loop, because we're actually going to read each frame individually as a video source via `os.listdir` on the `kidDir` (directory where the kid video frames are). We're lucky that `os.listdir` returns the frames in alphabetical order, which (with leading zeroes) is also numeric order. We read the file, make sure it's one of our JPEG frames, then open it and copy Barb's head onto it. We then write out the frame using `writeFrame`.

We can certainly do more sophisticated image processing than simple composing or sunsets. For example, we can do *chromakey* on movie frames. That's how many computer-generated effects in real movies are made. To try this out, we took a simple video of our three children (Matthew, Katie, and Jenny) crawling in front of a blue screen (Figure 13.10). We didn't do the lighting right, so the background turned out to be black instead of blue. That turned out to be a critical error. As a result, the chromakey also modified Matthew's pants, Katie's hair, and Jenny's eyes, so that you can see the moon right through them (Figure 13.11). Like red, black is a color that one should *not* use for the background when doing chromakey.

FIGURE 13.10
Frames from the original kids crawling in front of a blue screen.

FIGURE 13.11
Frames from the kids on the moon movie.

Program 127: Using Chromakey to Put Kids on the Moon

```
import os

def kidsOnMoon(directory):
  kids="C://ip-book//mediasources//kids-blue"
  moon=getMediaPath("moon-surface.jpg")
  back=makePicture(moon)
  num = 0
  for frameFile in os.listdir(kids):
    num = num + 1
    printNow("Frame: "+str(num))
    if frameFile.endswith(".jpg"):
      frame=makePicture(kids+"//"+frameFile)
      for p in getPixels(frame):
        if distance(getColor(p),black) <= 100:
          setColor(p,getColor(getPixel(back,getX(p),getY(p))))
      writeFrame(num,directory,frame)
```

Mark took video of fish underwater. Water filters out red and yellow light, so the video looks too blue (Figure 13.12). Let's increase the red and green in the video (yellow is a mixture of red and green light). Let's also create a new function that multiplies the red and green values in a picture by some input factor. The result can be seen in Figure 13.13.

Program 128: Fix the Underwater Movie

```
import os

def changeRedAndGreen(pict,redFactor,greenFactor):
    for p in getPixels(pict):
        setRed(p,int(getRed(p) * redFactor))
        setGreen(p,int(getGreen(p) * greenFactor))
```

FIGURE 13.12
Frames from the too blue underwater movie.

FIGURE 13.13
Frames from the less blue movie.

```
def fixUnderwater(directory):
  num = 0
  dir="C://ip-book//mediasources//fish"
  for frameFile in os.listdir(dir):
    num = num + 1
    printNow("Frame: "+str(num))
    if frameFile.endswith(".jpg"):
      frame=makePicture(dir+"//"+frameFile)
      changeRedAndGreen(frame,2.0,1.5)
      writeFrame(num,directory,frame)
```

13.3 BUILDING A VIDEO EFFECT BOTTOM-UP

You may have seen the television commercials where actors "draw" in the air with a glow stick or flashlight, and the lines hang in the air as if drawn on a whiteboard. How do they do that? Given what we know about video and image processing, we can probably figure this out. Let's write a program to replicate the process, and we will do it in bottom-up, to exemplify that way of building programs.

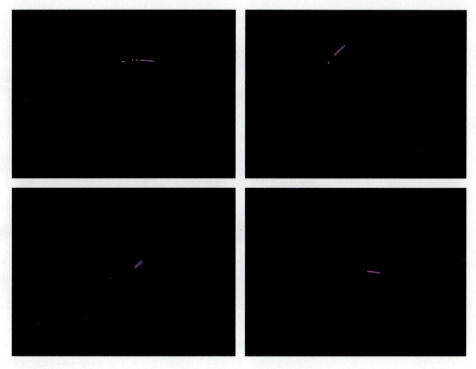

FIGURE 13.14
Frames of the source movie, with the glow stick being drawn in the air.

Figure 13.14 shows four frames of a movie of someone drawing with a glowstick in the air. We made this movie when it was dark out so that the glow stick would be a sharp contrast with the rest. How would we get the bright pixels from the glowstick to appear in all successive frames? We want the last frame of the created movie to look like Figure 13.15. We know that brightness is what we are measuring with luminance. What we could do is to copy from one frame to the next all those pixels above a certain luminance level. If we just repeat this for all frames, all those pixels that are brighter will get collected.

In bottom-up process, we start gathering the pieces that we need from standard libraries, or writing the pieces that we think that we will need. It's obvious that we will have to implement luminance at some point.

Program 129: `luminance` **for Combining Bright Pixels**

```
def luminance(apixel):
  return (getRed(apixel)+getGreen(apixel)+getBlue(apixel))/3.0
```

We should also test our pieces, as we develop them. Does our `luminance` function do what we expect? Let's make a pixel, and set its color to some extreme values to see if it is responding as we might expect.

FIGURE 13.15
Final frame of target movie, with the trace of the glow stick visible.

```
>>> pict = makeEmptyPicture(1,1)
>>> pixel=getPixelAt(pict,0,0)
>>> white
Color(255, 255, 255)
>>> setColor(pixel,white)
>>> luminance(pixel)
255.0
>>> black
Color(0, 0, 0)
>>> setColor(pixel,black)
>>> luminance(pixel)
0.0
```

Next, we'll need something that will tell us whether a pixel is bright *enough*. We need a *threshold* value as a comparison point. One might want the method `brightPixel` in a couple of different ways: where you provide a threshold value or where a default threshold value is used. Python gives us a way of doing both, by providing *keyword arguments* or sometimes called *optional arguments*. We specify an argument for a function with a default value.

Program 130: brightPixel for Combining Bright Pixels

```
def brightPixel(apixel, threshold=100):
  if luminance(apixel) > threshold:
    return true
  return false
```

How It Works

brightPixel takes a pixel as input, and optionally, a threshold value whose default value is 100. If the luminance of the pixel is greater than the threshold value, it returns true. If not, execution reaches the last line and it returns false. We can build brightPixel to take advantage of the fact that we've already written luminance.

We can use brightPixel by specifying the threshold value, or by leaving it out, or even by specifying it with an assignment.

```
>>> red
Color(255, 0, 0)
>>> setColor(pixel,red)
>>> luminance(pixel)
85.0
>>> brightPixel(pixel)
0
>>> brightPixel(pixel,80)
1
>>> brightPixel(pixel,threshold=80)
1
>>> setColor(pixel,white)
>>> brightPixel(pixel,threshold=80)
1
>>> brightPixel(pixel)
1
>>> setColor(pixel,black)
>>> brightPixel(pixel,threshold=80)
0
>>> brightPixel(pixel)
0
```

What other functions do we need? We can look over our description of the statement. We need to be able to get a list of all files from a directory, to get all the frames. Given a list of files, we will need to be able to get the firstFile as distinct from the rest of the files, restFiles, so that we take the first file, copy the pixels to the first of the rest of the files, and then continue the process. Let's write those pieces.

Program 131: Functions to Manipulate File Lists for Combining Bright Pixels

```
import os

def allFiles(fromDir):
  listFiles = os.listdir(fromDir)
  listFiles.sort()
  return listFiles

def firstFile(filelist):
  return filelist[0]
```

```
def restFiles(filelist):
  return filelist[1:]
```

How It Works

We have seen all three of these kinds of code before, so we are building on other elements. Here, we are just giving them good names and turning them into parameterized functions. allFiles just gets our list of files, then sorts it (to make sure it's in increasing order), and returns it. The [0]th item of a list is the first one, and [1:] is from the second item to the end of the list. Thus firstFile and restFiles give us the elements of the file we want. We should test these, to make sure that they work as we want.

```
>>> files = allFiles("/")
>>> files
['Recycled', '_314109_', 'bin', 'boot', 'cdrom',
'dev', 'etc', 'home', 'initrd', 'initrd.img',
'initrd.img.old', 'lib', 'lost+found', 'media',
'mnt', 'opt', 'proc', 'root', 'sbin', 'srv', 'sys',
'tmp', 'usr', 'var', 'vmlinuz', 'vmlinuz.old']
>>> firstFile(files)
'Recycled'
>>> restFiles(files)
['_314109_', 'bin', 'boot', 'cdrom', 'dev', 'etc',
'home', 'initrd', 'initrd.img', 'initrd.img.old',
'lib', 'lost+found', 'media', 'mnt', 'opt', 'proc',
'root', 'sbin', 'srv', 'sys', 'tmp', 'usr', 'var',
'vmlinuz', 'vmlinuz.old']
```

Now that we have built and tested all the individual pieces, we can write the top-level function, in terms of these smaller functions.

Program 132: Combining Bright Pixels into a New Movie

```
def brightCombine(fromDir,target):
  fileList = allFiles(fromDir)
  fromPictFile = firstFile(fileList)
  fromPict = makePicture(fromDir+fromPictFile)
  for toPictFile in restFiles(fileList):
    printNow(toPictFile)
    # Copy all the high luminance colors from fromPict to
      toPict
    toPict = makePicture(fromDir+toPictFile)
    for p in getPixels(fromPict):
      if brightPixel(p):
        c = getColor(p)
        setColor(getPixel(toPict,getX(p),getY(p)),c)
    writePictureTo(toPict,target+toPictFile)
    fromPict = toPict
```

How It Works

`brightCombine` takes two directories as input: where to get the frames of moving bright pixels and where to write the frames where the bright pixels are copied over. We get the list of frames, and make a picture (`fromPict`) from the first frame in the list. Now, `toPictFile` will be each of the other frame filenames, one at a time, and we will make a picture from it in variable `toPict`. We check all the pixels in the `fromPict` and those that are bright enough, get written to the `toPict`. We then make the *to* picture be the *from* picture, `fromPict = toPict`, and move on to the next frame. In this way, we copy all the bright pixels forward.

Of course, we should test `brightCombine` but we leave it to the reader to try it out. What you see in this process is building up individual elements, testing them, and building on top of those elements. The end result, the top-level function, might end up pretty much the same as in the top-down process. In the bottom-up process, we might not have a clear idea of where we're going (in this case, we did have a pretty good idea), and we focus on building from smaller to larger elements.

PROBLEMS

13.1   How many frames would you need for a two hour movie with a picture size of 1024 width by 728 height and 60 frames per second? How much disk space would this movie need if you stored every pixel's color? Remember that each pixel would require 24 bits to store the color.

13.2   What is AVI? What is QuickTime? What is MPEG? What does persistence of vision mean? What is frame-based animation?

13.3   Create a movie that has the frames slowly becoming sepia-toned.

13.4   Create a function that takes a picture and creates a movie with the picture slowing turning into the negative.

13.5   Create a new movie that has two rectangles moving a random amount (from −5 to 5) in each direction in each frame.

13.6   Create a new version of the `lineDetect` function (Program 43 (page 117)) that takes in a threshold and create a movie using `lineDetect` where the threshold changes depending on the frame number.

13.7   Create a new movie that has the kids crawling on the beach.

13.8   Create a new movie with Mark's face watching Katie dance.

13.9   Write a function to create a movie where one item is moving from the top to the bottom and another item is moving from the bottom to the top.

13.10 Write a function to create a movie where one item is moving from the left to the right and another item is moving from the right to the left.

13.11 Write a function to create a movie where one item is moving in a diagonal line from top left to bottom right and another item is moving from the right to the left

13.12 Write a function to create a movie where filled circles show up at random places on the background and then grow and shrink.

13.13 Write a function that draws a sun on the picture of a beach at different places on the picture so that it looks like the sun moving through the day.

13.14 Write a function to make a movie with text that starts out large near the bottom of the movie and then moves up towards the top and gets smaller each time it moves up. You can create a font style using `makeStyle(family,type,size)`.

13.15 Take a movie of some of your friends dancing in front of a green screen and use chromakey to make it look like they are dancing on the beach.

13.16 Take a movie of a location and a movie shot in front of a green screen and use chromakey to blend the two movies together.

13.17 Build an animation of at least three seconds in duration (30 frames at 10 fps, or 75 frames at 25 fps). You must have at least three things in motion during this sequence. You must use at least one composited image (a JPEG image that you scale (if necessary) and copy into the image) and one drawn image (a rectangle or line or text or oval or arc—anything that you draw). For at least one of the things in motion, change its *velocity* part-way through the animation—change the direction or the speed.

13.18 `http://abcnews.go.com` is a popular news site. Let's make a movie of it. Write a function that will input a directory as a string. Then:

- Visit `http://abcnews.go.com` and pick out the top three news story headlines. (*Hint*: the anchors for the news story headlines all have `<a href="/wire/` before them. Find that tag, then search for the beginning of the anchor `<a href="/wire/`, then you can find the anchor text, which is the headline.)

- Create a ticker tape movie on the 640×480 canvas of all three news stories. Have one come across at $y = 100$, another at $y = 200$, and the third at $y = 300$. Generate 100 frames, and don't have the ticker tapes move more than 5 pixels per frame. (In 100 frames, you won't make it all the way across the screen—that's fine.) Store the frames to files in the input directory.

13.19 Create a movie where a person seems to be fading out of the scene. You can base this on the `slowFadeout` function (Program 125 (page 307)).

13.20 Remember the blending of pictures in Program 44 (pages 118–120)? Try blending one picture into another as a movie, slowly increasing the percentage of the second (incoming) image while decreasing the percentage of the original (outgoing) image.

13.21 The example of tracing bright pixels in this chapter used the PAINT1 folder in the media sources. There is another example in PAINT2. Try running that one.

13.22 The end-result pixels are pretty dull in the bright pixel tracing example. Use the `makeLighter` function to brighten up the pixels that you copy across.

13.23 Will the bright pixel tracing function *only* work in darkness? Make your own movie with someone writing with a glowstick or flashlight, in normal brightness. Does the function still work? Do you need to use a different threshold value? Do you have to try a different approach to identify "bright" pixels (e.g., perhaps by comparing luminance a particular pixel to the pixels around it)?

PART 5

TOPICS IN COMPUTER SCIENCE

CHAPTER
14 Speed

Chapter Learning Objectives

- To choose between compiled and interpreted programming languages, based on an understanding of machine language and how computers work.
- To know the categories of algorithms based on their complexity and to avoid intractable algorithms.
- To consider processor choice based on an understanding of clock rates.
- To make decisions about computer storage options when aiming for optimizing speed.

14.1   FOCUSING ON COMPUTER SCIENCE

At this point, you probably have a lot of questions about what you've been doing in this book. You may be asking, for instance:

- Why is Photoshop so much faster than anything we do in JES?
- How fast can we get our programs to go?
- Does it always take this long to write programs? Can you write smaller programs to do the same things? Can you write programs more easily than this?
- What does programming look like in other programming languages?

The answers to most of these questions are known or are studied in *computer science*. This part of the book is an introduction to some of those topics, as a signpost to get you started in exploring computer science further.

14.2   WHAT MAKES PROGRAMS FAST?

Where does the speed go? You buy a really fast computer and Photoshop seems really fast on it. Colors change as quickly as you change the slider. But then you run programs in JES and they just take *forever* (or 30 seconds, whichever comes first). Why?

14.2.1   What Computers Really Understand

In reality, computers do not understand Python, or Java, or any other language. The basic computer understands only one kind of language—**machine language**. Machine-language instructions are just values in the bytes in memory and they tell the computer to do very low-level activities. In a real sense, the computer doesn't even "understand" machine language. The computer is just a machine with lots of switches that make data flow this way or that. Machine language is just a bunch of switch settings that make other switches in the computer change. We *interpret* these data switchings as addition, subtraction, loading data, and storing data.

Each kind of computer can have its own machine language. Windows computers can't run programs for older Apple computers, not because of any philosophical or marketing differences, but because each kind of computer has its own **processor** (the core of the computer that actually executes the machine language). They *literally* don't understand one another. That's why an .EXE program from Windows won't run on an older Macintosh and a Macintosh application won't run on a Windows computer. Executable files are (almost always) machine-language programs.

Machine language looks like a bunch of numbers—it's not particularly user-friendly. **Assembley language** is a set of human-readable words (or near-words) that corresponds one-to-one with machine language. Machine language instructions tell the computer to do things like store numbers into particular memory locations or into special locations (variables or registers) in the computer, test numbers for equality or comparison, or add numbers together or subtract them.

An assembley program to add two numbers together and store them somewhere (and the corresponding machine language generated by an **assembler**) might look like this:

```
LOAD #10,R0      ; Load special variable R0 with 10
LOAD #12,R1      ; Load special variable R1 with 12
SUM R0,R1        ; Add special variables R0 and R1
STOR R1,#45      ; Store the result into memory
                   location #45


01 00 10
01 01 12
02 00 01
03 01 45
```

An assembley program that can make a decision could look like this:

```
LOAD R1,#65536   ; Get a character from keyboard
TEST R1,#13      ; Is it an ASCII 13 (Enter)?
JUMPTRUE #32768  ; If true, go to another part of
                   the program
CALL #16384      ; If false, call func. to process
                   the new line


Machine Language:
05 01 255 255
10 01 13
```

```
20 127 255
122 63 255
```

Input and output devices are often just memory locations to the computer. Maybe, when you store a 255 to location 65,542, the red component of the pixel at (101, 345) is suddenly set to maximum intensity. Maybe each time the computer reads from memory location 897,784, it's a new sample just read from the microphone. In this way, these simple loads and stores can also handle multimedia.

Machine language is executed very quickly. Mark typed the first version of this chapter on a computer with a 900-megahertz (MHz) processor. What that means *exactly* is hard to define but roughly it means that this computer processes 900 *million* machine-language instructions *per second*. A 2-gigahertz (GHz) processor handles 2 *billion* instructions per second. A 12-byte machine-language program that corresponds to something like a = b + c executes on Mark's mid-range computer in something like 12/900,000,000 of a second.

14.2.2   Compilers and Interpreters

Applications like Adobe Photoshop and Microsoft Word are typically **compiled**. This means that they were written in a computer language like C or C++ and then *translated* into machine language using a program called a **compiler**. The programs then execute at the speed of the base processor.

However, programming languages like Python, Java, Scheme, Squeak, Director, and Flash are actually (in most cases) *interpreted*. They execute at a slower speed. It's the difference between *translating* and then doing instructions versus simply doing the instructions.

A detailed example might help. Consider this exercise:

Write a function doGraphics that will take a list as input. The function doGraphics will start by creating a canvas from the 640 × 480.JPG file in the mediasources folder. You will draw on the canvas according to the commands in the input list.

Each element of the list will be a string. There will be two kinds of strings in the list:

- "b 200 120" means to draw a black dot at *x* position 200 *y* position 120. The numbers, of course, will change, but the command will always be a "b." You can assume that the input numbers will always have three digits.
- "l 000 010 100 200" means to draw a line from position (0, 10) to position (100, 200).

So an input list might look like ["b 100 200","b 101 200","b 102 200","l 102 200 102 300"] (but have any number of elements).

Here's a solution to the exercise. We look at each string in the list, compare the first character as a "black pixel" command or a "list" command, then chop out the

```
>>> canvas=doGraphics(["b 100
    200","b 101 200","b 102
    200","1 102 200 102 300","1
    102 300 200 300"])
Drawing pixel at 100 : 200
Drawing pixel at 101 : 200
Drawing pixel at 102 : 200
Drawing line at 102 200 102 300
Drawing line at 102 300 200 300
>>> show(canvas)
```

FIGURE 14.1
Running the doGraphics interpreter.

right coordinates (converting them to numbers with int()), and doing the appropriate graphics command. This solution works—see Figure 14.1.

Program 133: Interpret Graphics Commands in a List

```
def doGraphics(mylist):
  canvas = makePicture(getMediaPath("640 x 480.jpg"))
  for command in mylist:
    if command[0] == "b":
      x = int(command[2:5])
      y = int(command[6:9])
      print "Drawing pixel at ",x,":",y
      setColor(getPixel(canvas, x,y),black)
    if command[0] =="l":
      x1 = int(command[2:5])
      y1 = int(command[6:9])
      x2 = int(command[10:13])
      y2 = int(command[14:17])
      print "Drawing line at",x1,y1,x2,y2
      addLine(canvas, x1, y1, x2, y2)
  return canvas
```

How It Works

We accept the list of graphics commands as input in mylist. We open a blank 640 × 480.jpg canvas for drawing on. For each string command in the input list, we check the first character (command[0]) to figure out what type of command it is. If it's a "b" (black pixel), we chop out the *x* and *y* coordinates from the string (since they're always the numbers of the same length, we know exactly where they'll be), then draw the pixel on the canvas. If it's an "l" (line), we get the four coordinates and draw the line. At the end, we return the canvas.

What we've just done is implement a new language for graphics. We have even created an *interpreter* that reads the instructions for our new language and creates the picture that goes along with it. In principle, this is just what Postscript, PDF, Flash, and AutoCAD are doing. Their file formats specify pictures in just the way that our graphics language does. When they draw (*render*) the image to the screen, they are *interpreting* the commands in that file.

While we probably can't tell from such a small example, this is a relatively slow language. Consider the program shown below—would it run faster than reading the list of commands and interpreting them? Both this program and the list in Figure 14.1 generate the exact same picture.

```
def doGraphics():
    canvas = makePicture(getMediaPath("640 x 480.jpg"))
    setColor(getPixel(canvas, 100,200),black)
    setColor(getPixel(canvas, 101,200),black)
    setColor(getPixel(canvas, 102,200),black)
    addLine(canvas, 102,200,102,300)
    addLine(canvas, 102,300,200,300)
    show(canvas)
    return canvas
```

In general, we'd probably guess (correctly) that the direct instructions given above will run faster than reading the list and interpreting it. Here's an analogy that might help. Mark took French in college but he says he is really bad at it. Let's say that someone gave him a list of instructions in French. He could meticulously look up each word, figure out the instructions, and do them. What if he was asked to do the instructions again? Go look up each word again. Ten times? Ten lookups. Now let's imagine that he wrote down the English (his native language) translation of the French instructions. He can very quickly repeat doing the list of instructions as often as you like. It takes him hardly any time to look up any word. In general, figuring out the language takes up some time that is just overhead—simply *doing* the instructions (or drawing the graphics) will always be faster.

Here's an idea: Could we *generate* the above program? Could we write a program that takes as input the list graphics language we invented, then writes a Python program that draws the same pictures? Turns out not to be that hard. This is a **compiler** for the graphics language.

Program 134: Compiler for New Graphics Language

```
def makeGraphics(mylist):
    file = open("graphics.py","wt")
    file.write('def doGraphics():\n')
    file.write('  canvas = makePicture(getMediaPath ("640 x 480.jpg"))\n');
    for i in mylist:
        if i[0] == "b":
            x = int(i[2:5])
            y = int(i[6:9])
            print "Drawing pixel at ",x,":",y
            file.write('  setColor(getPixel(canvas, '+str(x)+', '+str(y)+'),¬
            black)\n')
        if i[0] =="l":
```

¬These lines of the program should continue with the next lines. A single command in Python may not break across multiple lines.

```
        x1 = int(i[2:5])
        y1 = int(i[6:9])
        x2 = int(i[10:13])
        y2 = int(i[14:17])
        print "Drawing line at",x1,y1,x2,y2
        file.write('  addLine(canvas, '+str(x1)+','+str(y1)+','+ str(x2)+',¬
        '+str(y2)+')\n')
    file.write('  show(canvas)\n')
    file.write('  return canvas\n')
    file.close()
```

¬These lines of the program should continue with the next lines. A single command in Python may not break across multiple lines. ■

How It Works

The compiler accepts the *same* input as the interpreter, but instead of opening a `canvas` to write to, we open a `file`. We write to the file the start of a `doGraphics` function–the `def` and the code to create a `canvas` (indented two spaces so that it's inside the block of the `doGraphics` function). Note that we're not really *making* the `canvas` here—we're simply writing out the command to make the canvas, which will be executed *later* when `doGraphics` is executed. Then, just like the interpreter, we figure out which graphics command it is ("b" or "l") and we figure out the coordinates from the input string. Then we write out to the file the commands to do the drawing. At the end, we write out commands to `show` and `return` the `canvas`, and finally we `close` the file.

Now the compiler has a lot of overhead. We still have to look up what the commands mean. If we only have a small graphics program to run, and we only need it once, we might as well just run the interpreter. But what if we needed to run the picture 10 times, or 100 times? Then we pay the overhead of compiling the program *once*, and the next 9 or 99 times, we run it as fast as we possibly can. That will almost certainly be faster than doing the interpretation overhead 100 times.

This is what compilers are all about. Applications like Photoshop and Word are written in languages like C or C++ and are then *compiled* to *equivalent* machine-language programs. The machine-language program does the same thing that the C language says to do, just as the graphics programs created from our compiler do the same things as our graphics language says to do. But the machine-language program runs *much* faster than we could interpret the C or C++.

Jython programs are actually *interpreted* and not once but *twice*. Jython is written in Java and Java programs don't typically compile to machine language. (Java *can* be compiled to machine language—it's just not the normal thing that people do with Java.) Java programs compile to a machine language for a *make-believe processor*—a **virtual machine**. The *Java Virtual Machine* doesn't really exist as a physical processor. It's a definition of a processor. What good is that? It turns out that since machine language is *very* simple, building a machine-language *interpreter* is pretty easy to write.

The result is that a Java Virtual Machine interpreter can be very easily made to run on just about any processor. This means that a program in Java is compiled *once* and then runs *everywhere*. Devices as small as wristwatches can run the same Java programs that run on large computers.

When you run a program in JES, it's actually compiled to Java—an equivalent Java program is written for you. Then the Java is compiled for the Java Virtual Machine. Finally, the Java Virtual Machine interpreter runs the Java machine language of your program. All of which will always be slower than running a compiled form of the same thing.

That's the first part of the answer to the question "Why is Photoshop always faster than JES?" JES is interpreted *twice*, which will always be slower than Photoshop running in machine language.

Then why have an interpreter at all? There are many good reasons. Here are three:

- Do you like the Command Area? Did you even once ever type in some example code just to *try* it? That kind of interactive, exploratory, trying-things-out programming is only available with interpreters. Compilers don't let you try things out line by line and print the results. Interpreters are good for learners.

- Once a program is compiled to Java machine language, it can be used *anywhere*, as-is, from huge computers to programmable toaster ovens. That's a big savings for software developers. They only ship one program and it runs on anything.

- Virtual machines are safer than machine language. A program running in machine language might do all kinds of nonsecure things. A virtual machine can carefully keep track of the programs it is interpreting to make sure that they only do safe things.

14.2.3 What Limits Computer Speed?

The raw power of compiled as compared to interpreted programs is only part of the answer of why Photoshop is faster. The deeper part, and one that can actually lead to interpreted programs being *faster* than compiled programs, is in the design of the *algorithms*. There's a temptation to think, "Oh, it's okay if it's slow now. Wait 18 months, we'll get double the processor speed, and then it will be fine." There are some algorithms that are *so* slow they will never end in your lifetime and others that can't be written at all. Rewriting the algorithm to be *smarter* about what we ask the computer to do can have a dramatic impact on performance.

An **algorithm** is a description of the way a computer must behave to solve a problem. A program (functions in Python) consists of executable interpretations of algorithms. The same algorithm can be implemented in many different languages. There is always more than one algorithm to solve the same problem—some computer scientists study algorithms and come up with ways to compare them and state which are better than others.

We've seen several algorithms that appear in different ways but are really doing the same things:

- Sampling to scale a picture up or down or to lower or raise the frequency of a sound.

- Blending to merge two pictures or two sounds.

- Mirroring of sounds and pictures.

We can compare algorithms based on several criteria. One is how much *space* the algorithm needs to run. How much memory does the algorithm require? This can become a significant issue for media computation because so much memory is required to hold all that data. Think about how bad an algorithm would be that needed to hold *all* the frames of a movie in a list in memory at the same time.

The most common criterion used to compare algorithms is *time*. How much time does the algorithm take? We don't mean clock time, but how many steps the algorithm requires. Computer scientists use **Big-Oh notation**, or $O()$ to refer to the magnitude of the running time of an algorithm. The idea of Big-Oh is to express how much slower the program gets as the input data get larger. It tries to ignore differences between languages, even between compiled versus interpreted, and focus on the number of *steps* to be executed.

Think about our basic picture- and sound-processing functions like `increaseRed()` or `increaseVolume()`. Some of the complexity of these functions is hidden in functions like `getPixels()` and `getSamples()`. In general, though, we refer to these as being $O(n)$. The amount of time the program takes to run is proportional linearly to the input data. If the picture or sound doubled in size, we'd expect the program to take twice as long to run.

When we figure out Big-Oh, we typically clump the body of the loop into one step. We think about these functions as processing each sample or pixel once, so the real-time sink in these functions is the loop, and it doesn't really matter how many statements are in the loop.

Unless there is another loop in the loop body, that is. Loops are multiplicative in terms of time. Nested loops multiply the amount of time needed to run the body. Think about this toy program:

```
def loops():
  count = 0
  for x in range(1,5):
    for y in range(1,3):
      count = count + 1
      print x,y,"--Ran it ",count,"times"
```

When we run it, we see that it actually executes eight times—four for the x's, two for the y's, and $4 * 2 = 8$.

```
>>> loops()
1 1 --Ran it  1 times
1 2 --Ran it  2 times
2 1 --Ran it  3 times
2 2 --Ran it  4 times
3 1 --Ran it  5 times
3 2 --Ran it  6 times
4 1 --Ran it  7 times
4 2 --Ran it  8 times
```

How about movie code? Since it takes so long to process, is it actually a more complex algorithm? No, not really. Movie code is just processing each pixel once, so it's still $O(n)$. It's just that the n is really, *really* big!

Not all algorithms are $O(n)$. There is a group of algorithms called **sorting algorithms** that are used to sort data into alphabetical or numerical order. One simple algorithm called the **bubble sort** has a complexity of $O(n^2)$. In a bubble sort, you loop through elements in a list comparing two adjacent elements and swapping their values if they are out of order. You keep doing this until one pass through the list doesn't result in any swaps, which means the data is sorted.

For example, if we started with a list of (3, 2, 1) the following shows the changes in the list.

```
(3,2,1) # compare the 3 and 2 and swap order
(2,3,1) # compare the 3 and 1 and swap order
(2,1,3) # compare the 2 and 1 and swap order
(1,2,3) # no swaps, so the list is sorted
```

If a list has 100 elements, it'll take on the order of 10,000 steps to sort the 100 elements with this kind of sort. However, there are smarter algorithms (like the **quicksort**) that have complexity $O(n \log n)$. In quicksort, one of the values in the list to be sorted is picked as a pivot. Then the values in the original list are broken into two lists with all the values that are less than the pivot moved into one list and all the values greater or equal to the pivot moved to the other list. Then the two new lists are also sorted using quicksort. A list of one element is sorted, so if any of the lists ever reach that size quicksort just returns that list.

```
(5 1 3 2 7) # pick 3 as pivot
(1 2) 3 (5 7) # pick 2 and 7 as pivots
(1) 2 3 (5) 7 # all lists are of size 1 so
  just return them
(1 2 3 5 7) # combine all returned lists
```

The same list of 100 elements would only take 460 steps to process using quicksort. These kinds of differences start to have huge clock-time differences when you're talking about processing 10,000 customers.

14.2.4   Making Searching Faster

Consider how you might look up a word in the dictionary. One way is to check the first page, then the next page, then the next page, and so on. That's called a *linear search* and it's $O(n)$. It's not very efficient. The *best case* (the fastest the algorithm could possibly be) is that the problem is solved in one step—the word is on the first page. The *worst case* is n steps where n is the number of pages—the word could be on the last page. The *average case* is $n/2$ steps—the word is halfway through.

We can implement this as searching in a list.

Program 135: Linear Search of a List

```
def findInSortedList(something, alist):
  for item in alist:
    if item == something:
      return "Found it!"
  return "Not found"
```

```
>>> findInSortedList ("bear",["apple","bear","cat","dog",
"elephant"])
'Found it!'
>>> findInSortedList ("giraffe",["apple","bear","cat",
"dog", "elephant"])
'Not found'
```

But let's use the fact that dictionaries are already in sorted order. We can be smarter about how we search for a word and do it in $O(log(n))$ time ($log(n) = x$ where $2^x = n$). Split the dictionary in the middle. Is the word before or after the page you're looking at? If after, look from the middle to the end (e.g., again split the book, but from the middle to end). If before, look from the start to the middle (split halfway between start and middle). Keep repeating until you find the word or it couldn't possibly be there. This is a more efficient algorithm. In the best case, the word is in the first place you look. In the average and worst case, it's $log(n)$ steps—keep dividing the n pages in half, and you'll have at most $log(n)$ splits.

Here's a simple (i.e., not the best possible, but illustrative) implementation of this kind of a search, called a **binary search**.

Program 136: Simple Binary Search

```
def findInSortedList(something, alist):
  start = 0
  end = len(alist) - 1
  while start <= end: #While there are more to search
    checkpoint = int((start+end)/2.0)
    if alist[checkpoint]==something:
      return "Found it!"
    if alist[checkpoint]<something:
      start=checkpoint+1
    if alist[checkpoint]>something:
      end=checkpoint-1
  return "Not found"
```

How It Works

We start with the low-end marker `start` at the beginning of the list (0) and `end` at the end of the list (length of the list minus 1). As long as `start` is less than or equal to `end`, we continue to search. We compute the `checkpoint` as halfway between the start and end. We then check to see if we found it. If so, we're done and we `return`. If not, we figure out whether we have to move `start` up to one past the `checkpoint` or `end` down to one less than the `checkpoint`. And we continue searching. If we ever get through the whole loop, we didn't take the "Found it!" return, so we `return` that we didn't find what we were searching for.

To see what this is doing, stick in a line after the calculation of the `checkpoint` that prints the values of `checkpoint`, `start`, and `end`:

```
printNow("Checking at: "+str(checkpoint)+"
  Start:"+str(start)+" End:"+str(end))
>>> findInSortedList("giraffe",["apple","bear","cat",
  "dog"])
Checking at: 1 Start:0 End:3
Checking at: 2 Start:2 End:3
Checking at: 3 Start:3 End:3
'Not found'
>>> findInSortedList("apple",["apple","bear","cat",
  "dog"])
Checking at: 1 Start:0 End:3
Checking at: 0 Start:0 End:0
'Found it!'
>>> findInSortedList("dog",["apple","bear","cat",
  "dog"])
Checking at: 1 Start:0 End:3
Checking at: 2 Start:2 End:3
Checking at: 3 Start:3 End:3
'Found it!'
>>> findInSortedList("bear",["apple","bear","cat",
  "dog"])
Checking at: 1 Start:0 End:3
'Found it!'
```

14.2.5   Algorithms That Never Finish or Can't Be Written

Here's a thought experiment: imagine that you want to write a program that will generate hit songs for you. Your program will recombine bits of sounds that are some of the best riffs you've ever heard on various instruments—some 60 of them. You want to generate every combination of these 60 bits (some in, some out; some earlier in the song, some later). You want to find the combination that is less than 2 minutes 30 seconds (for optimal radio play time) and has the right amount of high and low volume combinations (and you've got a `checkSound()` function to do that).

How many combinations are there? Let's ignore order for right now. Let's say that you've got three sounds: a, b, and c. Your possible songs are a, b, c, bc, ac, ab, and abc. Try it with two sounds or four sounds and you'll see that the pattern is the same as what we saw earlier with bits: for n things, every combination of include-or-exclude is 2^n. (If we ignore the fact that there is an empty song, it's $2^n - 1$.)

Therefore, our 60 sounds will result in 2^{60} combinations to run through our length and sound checks. That's $1, 152, 921, 504, 606, 846, 976$ combinations. Let's imagine that we can do the checks in only a single instruction (unbelievable, of course, but we're pretending). On a 1.5-GHz computer, we can handle that many combinations in $768, 614, 336$ seconds. Spell that out: that's $12, 810, 238$ minutes, which is $213, 504$ hours, which is $8, 896$ days. That's 24 *years* to run the program. Now, since Moore's Law doubles process rates every 18 months, we will soon be able to run the program in much less time. Only *12 years!* If we cared about order, too (e.g., *abc* vs. *cba* vs. *bac*), the number of combinations has 63 zeroes in it.

Finding the absolutely optimal combination of just about anything is always time expensive. $O(2^n)$ like this is not an uncommon running time for these kinds of algorithms. But there are other problems that seem as if they should be do-able in a reasonable time but aren't.

One of these is the famous *Traveling Salesman Problem*. Imagine that you're a salesperson and you're responsible for many different clients—let's say 30, half the size of the optimization problem. To be efficient, you want to find the shortest path on the map that will let you visit each client exactly once, and not more than once.

The best-known algorithm that gives an optimal solution for the Traveling Salesman Problem is $O(n!)$. That's *n* factorial. There are algorithms that take less time to run that give close but not guaranteed shortest paths. For 30 cities, the number of steps to execute with one of these $O(n!)$ algorithms is 30!, or $265, 252, 859, 812, 191, 058, 636, 308, 480, 000, 000$. Go ahead and run that on a 1.5-GHz processor—it won't get done in your lifetime.

The really aggravating part is that the Traveling Salesman Problem isn't a made-up, toy problem. There really are people who have to plan the shortest routes in the world. There are similar problems that are basically the same algorithmically, like planning the route of a robot on a factory floor. This is a big, hard problem.

Computer scientists classify problems into three piles:

- Many problems, like sorting, can be solved with an algorithm whose running time has a complexity that's a polynomial, like $O(n^2)$. We call these *class P* (P for polynomial) problems.

- Other problems, like optimization, have known algorithms, but the solutions are so hard and big that we know we can't solve them in a reasonable time even for reasonable amounts of data. We call these problems *intractable*.

- Still other problems, like the Traveling Salesman, *seem* intractable, but maybe there's a solution in class P that we just haven't found yet. We call these *class NP*.

One of the biggest unsolved problems in theoretical computer science is proving either that class NP and class P are completely distinct (i.e., we'll never solve the Traveling Salesman optimally in polynomial time) or that class NP is within class P.

You may be wondering whether *anything* can be proved about algorithms. There are so many different languages and different ways of writing the same algorithm. How can we positively *prove* that something is doable or not doable? We can, it turns out. In fact, Alan Turing proved that there are even algorithms that *can't be written*.

The most famous algorithm that can't be written is the solution to the *Halting Problem*. We've already written programs that can read other programs and write out other programs. We can imagine a program that can read one program and tell us things about it (e.g., how many `print` statements are in it). Can we write a program that will input another program (e.g., from a file), then tell us whether the program will ever *stop*? Think about the input program having some complex `while` loops where it's hard to tell whether the expression in the `while` loop is ever `false`. Now imagine a bunch of these, all nested within one another.

Alan Turing proved that such a program could never be written. He used proof by absurdity. He showed that if such a program (call it H) could be written, you could try feeding that program to itself as input. Now H takes input, a program, right? What if you modified H (call it H2) so that if H said, "This one halts!" H2 would loop forever (e.g., `while 1:`). Turing showed that such a setup would announce that the program would halt only if it loops forever, and would halt only if it announces that it would loop forever.

The really amazing thing is that Turing came up with this proof in 1936—almost 10 years before the first computers were built. He defined a mathematical concept of a computer called a *Turing machine* and was able to make such proofs before physical computers even came into existence.

Here's another thought experiment: Is human intelligence computable? Our brains are executing a process that enables us to think, right? Can we write down that process as an algorithm? And if a computer executes that algorithm, is it thinking? Is a human reducible to a computer? This is one of the big questions in the field of **artificial intelligence**.

14.2.6   Why Is Photoshop Faster Than JES?

We can now answer the question of why Photoshop is faster than JES. First, Photoshop is compiled, so it runs at raw machine-language speeds.

But, secondly, Photoshop has algorithms that are smarter than what we're doing. For example, think about the programs where we searched for colors, like in Chromakey or in making Katie's hair red. We know that the background color and the hair color were clumped next to one another. What if, instead of linearly searching all the pixels, you just searched from where the color was what you were looking for until you didn't find that color anymore? Finding the boundary this way would be a smarter search. That's the kind of thing that Photoshop does.

14.3   WHAT MAKES A COMPUTER FAST?

Computers are getting faster all the time—Moore's Law promises us that. But knowing this doesn't help us to compare computers that all belong to the same Moore's Law generation. How do you compare ads in the paper and figure out which of the listed computers is *really* the fastest?

Simply being fast is only one criterion for picking a computer, of course. There are issues of cost, how much disk space you need, what kind of expansion features you

- AMD Athlon™ XP Processor 3000+ with QuantiSpeed™ Architecture
- 400MHz Front Side Bus
- 512KB L2 Cache
- DVD-ROM Drive
- CD-RW Drive
- 512MB DDR SDRAM
- 120.0GB Hard Drive

- Intel® Celeron® Processor 2.7GHz
- CD-RW Drive
- 400MHz Front Side Bus
- 128KB L2 Cache
- 256MB DDR SDRAM
- 40.0GB Hard Drive

FIGURE 14.2
A couple of sample computer advertisements.

need, and so on. But in this section we'll explicitly deal with what the various factors in computer ads mean in terms of computer speed (see Figure 14.2 for some examples).

14.3.1 Clock Rates and Actual Computation

When computer ads state that they have a "Some-brand Processor 2.8 GHz" or "Other-brand Processor 3.0 GHz," what they're talking about is the *clock rate*. The processor is the smarts of your computer—it's the part that makes decisions and does computation. It does all this computing work at a certain *pace*. Imagine a drill sergeant shouting, "Go! Go! Go! Go!" That's what the clock rate is—it tells you how fast the drill sergeant shouts "Go!" A clock rate of 2.8 GHz means that the clock *pulses* (the drill sergeant shouts "Go!") 2.8 *billion* times per second.

This doesn't mean that the processor actually does something useful with every "Go!" Some computations have several steps, so it may take several pulses of the clock to complete a single useful computation. But *in general* a faster clock rate implies faster computation. Certainly, for the same *kind* of processor, a faster clock rate implies faster computation.

Is there really any difference between 2.8 GHz and 3.0 GHz? Or is 1.0 GHz with processor X about the same as 2.0 GHz with processor Y? These are much tougher questions. It's not really that much different from arguing over Dodge versus Ford trucks. Most processors have their advocates and their critics. Some will argue that Processor X can do a certain search in very few clock pulses because of how well it's designed, so it's clearly faster even at a slower clock rate. Others will say that Processor Y is still faster overall because its average number of clock pulses per computation is so low—and how common is the type of search that X does so fast, anyway? It's almost like arguing about whose religion is better.

Many computers that you will purchase today have multiple *cores*. Each core is literally a whole other processor. A *dual core* computer then actually has *two* processors on its main chip. *Quad core* computers have *four* processors. Does this mean that these computers are two or four times faster? Unfortunately, it doesn't work that cleanly. Not all programs are written to take advantage of the multiple cores. It's hard to write a program that essentially says, "Okay, now the next piece of the computation can be done in *parallel*, so here's this piece and there's that piece, and here's how we'll put it together in the end." If none of your software is written to take advantage of multiple cores, then having them will not make things much faster at all. One of computer science's great challenges today is how to take advantage of all these multiple cores to make computers work faster for people.

The real answer is to try some realistic work on the computer that you're considering. Does it feel fast enough? Check reviews in computer magazines—they often use realistic tasks (like sorting in Excel and scrolling in Word) to test the speed of computers.

14.3.2   Storage: What Makes a Computer Slow?

The speed of your processor is only one factor in what makes a computer fast or slow. Probably a bigger factor is where the processor goes to get the data it works with. Where are your pictures when your computer goes to work on them? That's a much more complex question.

You can think about your storage as being in a hierarchy, from the fastest to the slowest.

- Your fastest storage is your **cache memory**. Cache is memory that is physically located on the same silicon chip as your processor (or very, very close to it). Your processor takes care of putting as much as possible in the cache and leaving it there as long as it's needed. Cache is accessed far faster than anything else on your computer. The more cache memory you have, the more things the computer can access very quickly. But cache (of course) is also your most expensive storage.

- Your *RAM* storage (whether it's called **SDRAM** or any other kind of **RAM**) is your computer's main *memory*. RAM (an acronym for **random access memory**) of 256 Mb (megabytes) means 256 *million* bytes of information. Memory of 1 Gb (gigabyte) means 1 billion bytes of information. RAM storage is where your programs reside when they're executing and it's where the data that your computer is directly acting upon is located. Things are in your RAM storage before they're loaded into the cache. RAM is less expensive than cache memory and is probably your best investment in terms of making your computer faster.

- Your **hard disk** is where you store all your **files**. Your program that you're executing now in RAM started out as an .exe (executable) file on your hard disk. All your digital pictures, digital music, word-processing files, spreadsheet files, and so on, are stored on your hard disk. Your hard disk is your *slowest* storage but it's also your largest. A hard disk of 40 Gb means that you can store 40 *billion* bytes on it. That's a *lot* of space—and it's pretty small these days.

Movement between levels in the hierarchy means a huge speed difference. It has been said that if the speed of access of cache memory is like reaching for a paper clip on your desk, then getting something off the hard disk means traveling to Alpha Centauri—four light years away from Earth. Obviously, we *do* get things off our disk at reasonable speeds (which really implies that cache memory is phenomenally fast!) but the analogy does emphasize how very different the levels of the hierarchy are in respect to speed. The bottom line is that the more you have of the faster memory, the faster your processor can get the information you want and the faster your overall processing will be.

You'll see advertisements occasionally mentioning the **system bus**. The system bus is how signals are sent around your computer—from video or network to hard disk, from RAM to the printer. A faster system bus clearly implies a faster overall system but a faster system bus may not influence (for example) the speed of your experience with JES or Photoshop. First, even the fastest bus is much slower than the processor—400 million pulses per second versus 4 billion pulses per second. Second, the system bus doesn't usually influence the access to cache or memory, and that's where most of the speed is won or lost anyway.

There are things that you can do to make your hard disk as fast as possible for your computation. The speed of the disk isn't that significant for processing time—even the fastest disks are still far slower than the slowest RAM. Leaving enough free space on your disk for **swapping** is important. When your computer doesn't have enough RAM for what you're asking it to do, it stores some of the data that it isn't currently using from RAM on your hard disk. Moving data to and from your hard disk is a slow process (relatively speaking, compared to access to RAM). Having a fast disk with enough free space that the computer doesn't have to search around for **swap space** helps with processing speed.

How about the network? In terms of speed, the network doesn't really help you. The network is magnitudes slower than your hard disk. There are differences in network speeds that do influence your overall experience but not necessarily the speed of processing of your computer. Wired Ethernet connections tend to be faster than wireless Ethernet connections. Modem connections are slower.

14.3.3   Display

How about the display? Does the speed of your display really affect the speed of your computer? No, not really. Computers are really, *really* fast. The computer can repaint everything even on really large displays faster than you can perceive.

The only application where the display speed may matter is really high-end computer gaming. Some computer gamers claim that they can perceive a difference between 50 frames per second and 60 frames per second updates of the screen. If your display was really large and everything had to be repainted with every update, then *maybe* a faster processor would make a difference you could perceive. But most modern computers update so quickly that you just wouldn't notice a difference.

PROBLEMS

14.1   What are each of the following:

- Interpreter
- Compiler
- Machine language
- RAM
- Cache

- Class P problems
- Class NP problems

14.2 Find animations of different sorting algorithms on the Web. Which is the fastest? Which is the slowest?

14.3 Write a function to do an insertion sort on a list.

14.4 Write a function to do a selection sort on a list.

14.5 Write a function to do a bubble sort on a list.

14.6 Write a function to do a quicksort on a list.

14.7 How many times will the following code print out the message?

```
for x in range(0,5):
  for y in range(0,10):
    print "I will be good"
```

14.8 How many times will the following code print out the message?

```
for x in range(1,5):
  for y in range(0,10,2):
    print "I will be good"
```

14.9 How many times will the following code print out the message?

```
for x in range(0,3):
  for y in range(1,5):
    print "I will be good"
```

14.10 What is the Big Oh of the method `clearBlue`?

14.11 What is the Big Oh of the method `lineDetect`?

14.12 Trace through the binary search algorithm in `findInSortedList` given the following input.

```
findInSortedList("8",["3","5","7","9","10"])
```

14.13 Trace through the binary search algorithm in `findInSortedList` given the following input.

```
findInSortedList("3",["3","5","7","9","10"])
```

14.14 Trace through the binary search algorithm in `findInSortedList` given the following input.

```
findInSortedList("1",["3","5","7","9","10"])
```

14.15 Trace through the binary search algorithm in `findInSortedList` given the following input.

```
findInSortedList("7",["3","5","7","9","10"])
```

14.16   You've now seen some examples of Class P problems (e.g., sorting and searching), intractable problems (optimization of the song elements), and Class NP problems (e.g., the Traveling Salesman Problem). Search the Web and find at least one more example of each class of problem.

14.17   Try something that takes a while in JES (e.g., chromakey on a large image) so that you can time it on a stopwatch. Now time the same JES task on several different computers with different amounts of memory and different clock rates (and different amounts of cache, if you can). See what difference the different factors make in terms of the time it takes to complete the task in JES.

14.18   Alan Turing is known for another important finding in computer science, besides the proof that the Halting Problem is unsolvable. He gave us our test for whether a computer has actually achieved intelligence. What is the name of this test and how does it work? Do you agree that it is a test of intelligence?

14.19   How do people get answers to problems that have algorithms that would take way to long to find the optimal result? Sometimes they use *heuristics*: rules that don't lead to a perfect solution but find a solution. Look up some heuristics used to compute the next move in a chess playing program.

14.20   Another way to deal with intractable problems is to use `satisficing` algorithms. These are algorithms that find a pretty good solution but not necessarily the best one. Find an algorithm that solves the Traveling Salesman problem in reasonable run time but isn't optimal.

TO DIG DEEPER

To learn more about what makes a program work *well*, we recommend reading *Structure and Interpretation of Computer Programs* [2]. It's not about gigahertz and cache memories but it tells a lot about how you should think about your programs to make them work well.

CHAPTER 15

Functional Programming

15.1 USING FUNCTIONS TO MAKE PROGRAMMING EASIER

15.2 FUNCTIONAL PROGRAMMING WITH MAP AND REDUCE

15.3 FUNCTIONAL PROGRAMMING FOR MEDIA

15.4 RECURSION: A POWERFUL IDEA

Chapter Learning Objectives

- To write programs more easily with more functions.
- To use functional programming to make powerful programs quickly.
- To understand what makes functional programming different from procedural or imperative programming.
- To be able to use else in Python.
- To be able to use global in Python.

15.1 USING FUNCTIONS TO MAKE PROGRAMMING EASIER

Why do we use functions? How can we use them to make programming easier? We have been talking about multiple functions at various points in this book. Let's summarize some of the benefits here, before we start talking about programming with functions in a more powerful way.

Functions are for managing complexity. Can we write all our programs as one large function? Sure, but it gets *hard*. As programs grow in size, they grow in complexity. We use functions—

- To hide away details so that we only focus on what we care about.
- To find the right place to make changes as you need to in a program—finding the right function is easier than finding a single line in few thousand lines of code.
- To make it easier to test and debug our programs.

If we break a program into smaller pieces, we can test each piece separately. Think about our HTML programs. We can test functions like doctype(), title(), and body() separately from the Command Area, rather than always having to test the whole thing. This way, you can deal with the smaller functions and smaller problems until they are solved—then you can ignore them and focus on the bigger problems.

```
>>> print doctype()
<!DOCTYPE HTML PUBLIC "-//W3C//DTD HTML 4.01
Transition//EN" "http://wwww.w3.org/TR/html4/
  loose.dtd">
>>> print title("My title string")
<html><head><title>My title string</title></head>
>>> print body("<h1>My heading</h1><p>My
  paragraph</p>")
<body><h1>My heading</h1><p>My paragraph</p></body>
  </html>
```

Being able to test small functions as shown above is useful when you are looking for problems (bugs). It also enables you to *trust* your functions. Try them in different ways. Convince yourself that the function always performs the task you're asking it to do. Once you have this trust, you can ask the function to do its task without thinking about it—then you can do some amazingly powerful things (see the next section).

Adding additional functions makes the whole program easier, if the functions are chosen well. If we have subfunctions that do smaller pieces of the overall task, we talk about changing the **granularity** of the functions. If the granularity gets too small, it swaps one kind of complexity for another. But at the right level, it makes the overall program easier to understand and to change.

Think about the home page program like this, with much smaller granularity than what we were doing before:

Program 137: Smaller Granularity Home Page Generator

```
def makeHomePage(name, interest):
  file=open("homepage.html","wt")
  file.write(doctype())
  file.write(startHTML())
  file.write(startHead())
  file.write(title(name+"'s Home Page"))
  file.write(endHead())
  file.write(startBody())
  file.write(heading(1,"Welcome to "+ name +"'s Home Page"))
  myParagraph = paragraph( "Hi!  I am " + name + ".  This is my home¬
  page! I am interested in " + interest + "</p>" )
  file.write(myParagraph)
  file.write(endBody())
  file.write(endHTML())
  file.close()

def doctype():
  return '<!DOCTYPE HTML PUBLIC "-//W3C//DTD HTML 4.01
    Transition//EN" "http://wwww.w3.org/TR/html4/loose.dtd">'

def startHTML():
  return '<html>'
```

¬These lines of the program should continue with the next lines. A single command in Python may not break across multiple lines.

```
def startHead():
  return '<head>'

def endHead():
  return '</head>'

def heading(level,string):
  return "<h"+str(level)+">"+string+"</h"+str(level)+">"

def startBody():
  return "<body>"

def paragraph(string):
  return "<p>"+string+"</p>"

def title(titlestring):
  return "<title>"+titlestring+"</title>"

def endBody():
  return "</body>"

def endHTML():
  return "</html>"
```

■

This version is even easier to test but now there's the new complexity of remembering all those function names you just made up!

Making It Work Tip: Use Subfunctions for the Hard Parts
Whenever you have a hard part in a program, break it into subfunctions so that you can debug and fix each of them separately.   ■

Think about the HTML program to generate a samples page. The loop was the hard part of the program, so let's break it into a separate subfunction. This makes it easier to change how links are formatted—it's all down in the subfunction.

Program 138: Samples Page Creator with a Subfunction
```
def makeSamplePage(directory):
  samplesFile=open(directory+"//samples.html","wt")
  samplesFile.write(doctype())
  samplesFile.write(title("Samples from "+directory))
  # Now, let's make up the string that will be the body.
  samples="<h1>Samples from "+directory+" </h1>"
  for file in os.listdir(directory):
    if file.endswith(".jpg"):
      samples = samples + fileEntry(file)
  samplesFile.write(body(samples))
  samplesFile.close()
```

```
def fileEntry(file):
  samples="<p>Filename: "+file+"<br />"
  samples=samples+'<img src="'+file+'" height="100" width="100"/></p>'
  return samples
```

Breaking out the pieces like this is part of **procedural abstraction**. Procedural abstraction is:

- State the problem. Figure out what you want to do.
- Break the problem into subproblems.
- Keep breaking the subproblems into smaller problems until you know how to write the program that solves the smaller problem.
- Your goal is for the main function to basically tell all the subfunctions what to do. Each subfunction should do *one and only one* logical task.

We can think about procedural abstraction as filling in a *tree* of functions (see Figure 15.1). Making modifications is a matter of changing *one* node (function) on this tree and making additions is a matter of adding a node. For example, adding in the functionality to handle WAV files in our samples page only requires changing the function `fileEntry`, when it's broken down like this (Figure 15.2).

15.2 FUNCTIONAL PROGRAMMING WITH MAP AND REDUCE

If you're willing to trust your functions, you can write fewer lines of code and get the same programs written. When you really understand functions, and trust that your

FIGURE 15.1
A hierarchy of functions for creating a samples page.

FIGURE 15.2
Changing the program is only a slight change to the hierarchy.

functions do what you meant them to do, you can do amazing things in a very few lines of code. We can write functions that apply functions to data and even have functions call themselves in a process called **recursion**.

Functions are just names that are associated with values that are pieces of code, rather than lists or sequences or numbers or strings. We invoke or call a function by stating its name followed by inputs in parentheses. Without parentheses, the name of the function still has a value—it's the function's code. Functions can also be *data*—they can be passed as inputs to *other* functions!

```
>>> print makeSamplePage
<function makeSamplePage at 4222078>
>>> print fileEntry
<function fileEntry at 10206598>
```

apply() is a function that takes as input another function and the inputs (as a sequence or list) to that function. Literally, apply() applies the function to the input.

```
def hello(someone):
  print "Hello,",someone
>>> hello("Mark")
Hello, Mark
>>> apply(hello,["Mark"])
Hello, Mark
>>> apply(hello,["Betty"])
Hello, Betty
```

A more useful function that takes functions as input is map(). It's a function that takes a function and a sequence as input. But map applies the function to *each* input in the sequence and returns whatever the function returns for each input.

```
>>> map(hello, ["Mark","Betty","Matthew","Jenny"])
Hello, Mark
Hello, Betty
Hello, Matthew
Hello, Jenny
[None, None, None, None]
```

filter() also takes a function and a sequence as input. It applies the function to each element of the sequence. If the *return value* of the function on that element is true (1), then the filter returns that element. If the return is false (0), then the filter skips that element. We can use filter() to quickly pull out data of interest to us.

```
def rInName(someName):
  # find returns -1 when not found
  if someName.find("r") == -1:
    return 0
  # if not -1 then found
  if someName.find("r") != -1:
    return 1
```

```
>>> rInName("January")
1
>>> rInName("July")
0
>>> filter(rInName, ["Mark","Betty","Matthew","Jenny"])
['Mark']
```

We can rewrite rInName() above (a function that returns true if the input word contains an 'r') in a much shorter form. Expressions actually do evaluate to 1 or 0 (true or false). We can perform operations on these *logical values*. One of these **logical operators** is not—it returns the opposite of its input value. So here's rInName() written using logical operators.

```
def rInName2(someName):
    return not(someName.find("r") == -1)

>>> filter(rInName2, ["Mark","Betty","Matthew","Jenny"])
['Mark']
```

reduce() also takes a function and a sequence but reduce *combines* the results. Below is an example where we total all the numbers: $1 + 2$, then $(1 + 2) + 3$, then $(1 + 2 + 3) + 4$, and finally $(1 + 2 + 3 + 4) + 5$. The total so far is passed in as the a input.

```
def add(a,b):
    return a+b

>>> reduce(add,[1,2,3,4,5])
15
```

Let's look at the example again: Doesn't it seem like a waste to have to create that add function when it's so small and does so little? It turns out that we don't have to give a function a name in order be able to use it. A nameless function is called a lambda. This is a very old term in computer science, one that dates back to one of the original programming languages, Lisp. Wherever you would otherwise use a function name, you can just stick in a lambda. The syntax of a lamda is the word lambda followed by input variables separated by commas, then a colon, then the body of the function. Here are some examples, including the above reduce example recreated with lambda. As you can see, we can define functions that are virtually identical to the ones typed in the Program Area by assigning a name to a lambda.

```
>>> reduce(lambda a,b:a+b, [1,2,3,4,5])
15
>>> (lambda a:"Hello,"+a)("Mark")
'Hello,Mark'
>>> f=lambda a:"Hello, "+a
>>> f
<function <lambda> 6>
>>> f("Mark")
'Hello, Mark'
```

Using `reduce` and `lambda`, we can do real computation. Here's a function that computes the **factorial** of the passed number. The factorial of some number *n* is the product of all the positive integers less or equal to n. For example, the factorial of 4 is $(4 * 3 * 2 * 1)$.

Program 139: Calculating Factorial Using `lambda` and `reduce`

```
def factorial(a):
    return reduce(lambda a,b:a*b, range(1,a+1))
```

How It Works

It's easier to read this program right to left. The first thing we do is to create a list of all the numbers from 1 to a with `range(1,a+1)`. We then use `reduce` to apply a function (the `lambda`) that multiplies all the numbers in the input list one by the next, by the next, and on until finished.

```
>>> factorial(2)
2
>>> factorial(3)
6
>>> factorial(4)
24
>>> factorial(10)
3628800
```

You might be thinking at this point, "Okay, `map`, `filter`, and `reduce` look like they might be useful. *Might*. Sometimes. But why in the world would anyone want to use `apply`? That's the same as just typing the function call ourselves, isn't it?" That's true but we can actually *make* `map`, `filter`, and `reduce` using `apply`. We can literally make any version of these that we might want ourselves using `apply`.

```
def myMap(function,list):
    for i in list:
        apply(function,[i])

>>> myMap(hello, ["Fred","Barney","Wilma","Betty"])
Hello, Fred
Hello, Barney
Hello, Wilma
Hello, Betty
```

This style of programming is called **functional programming**. What we've been doing in Python up to now might be called *procedural programming*, because our focus is on defining procedures, or *imperative programming*, because we are mostly telling the computer to do things and change variable values (also called *state*). Focusing on functions as data and on functions that use functions as input are key ideas in functional programming.

Functional programming is amazingly powerful. You apply layers upon layers of functions to other functions and you end up doing a lot in a few lines of program code. Functional programming is used in building artificial intelligence systems and in building prototypes. These are areas where the problems are hard and ill-defined, so you want to be able to do a lot with only a few lines of program code—even if those few lines are pretty hard to read for most people.

15.3   FUNCTIONAL PROGRAMMING FOR MEDIA

Remember the function to turn Katie's hair red—Program 36 (page 106)? Here it is again:

```
def turnRed():
  brown = makeColor(42,25,15)
  file="C:/ip-book/mediasources/katieFancy.jpg"
  picture=makePicture(file)
  for px in getPixels(picture):
    color = getColor(px)
    if distance(color,brown)<50.0:
      redness=int(getRed(px)*2)
      blueness=getBlue(px)
      greenness=getGreen(px)
      setColor(px,makeColor(redness,blueness,greenness))
  show(picture)
  return(picture)
```

We can write it as only a *single line* of program code. We need two utility functions—one that will check a single pixel for whether we want to turn the pixel red and another that will actually do it. Our single line of program code filters out the pixels that match our criteria for changing, then maps the change function to those pixels. In functional programming, you don't write functions with big loops. Instead, you write small functions and apply them to the data. It's like we're bringing the function to the data, rather than making the function go get all the data.

Program 140: Turn Hair Red, Functionally

```
def turnHairRed(pic):
  map(turnRed,filter(checkPixel,getPixels(pic)))

def checkPixel(aPixel):
  brown = makeColor(42,25,15)
  return distance (getColor(aPixel),brown)<50.0

def turnRed(aPixel):
  setRed(aPixel,getRed(aPixel)*2)
```

How It Works

The function turnRed takes a single pixel and doubles its redness percentage. The function checkPixel returns true or false if an input pixel is close enough to brown.

The function `turnHairRed` takes a picture as input, then applies `checkPixel` using `filter` to all the pixels in the input picture (using `getPixels`). If the pixel is brown enough, `filter` returns it. We then use `map` to apply `turnRed` to all the pixels that `filter` returns.

Here's how we use it:

```
>>> pic=makePicture(getMediaPath("KatieFancy.jpg"))
>>> map(turnRed, filter(checkPixel, getPixels(pic)))
```

15.3.1   Media Manipulation Without Changing State

Another important aspect of functional programming is programming *without state*. Our color manipulation functions (for example) change the object that is provided to the function as an input. Good functional programs do not do that. If an object is to be changed, a good functional program makes a copy of the object then modifies and returns the copied object. The advantage is that one can nest functions, passing the output of one to the input of the other, just as one can nest mathematical functions. No one expects that $sine(cosine(x))$ should change x any more than just $sine(x)$ changes x. Functions in the functional programming style should work the same. We say that these functions have no "*side effects.*" The functions only do what they are supposed to do and *return* a result. They don't change the inputs in any way.

Let's see what it would look like to create media manipulation functions that do not change state.

Program 141: Changing Colors Without Changing the Picture

```
def decreaseRed(aPicture):
  returnPic = makeEmptyPicture(getWidth(aPicture),getHeight(aPicture))
  for x in range(getWidth(aPicture)):
    for y in range(getHeight(aPicture)):
      srcPixel = getPixelAt(aPicture,x,y)
      returnPixel = getPixelAt(returnPic,x,y)
      setColor(returnPixel,getColor(srcPixel))
      setRed(returnPixel, 0.8*getRed(srcPixel))
  return returnPic

def increaseBlue(aPicture):
  returnPic = makeEmptyPicture(getWidth(aPicture),getHeight(aPicture))
  for x in range(getWidth(aPicture)):
    for y in range(getHeight(aPicture)):
      srcPixel = getPixelAt(aPicture,x,y)
      returnPixel = getPixelAt(returnPic,x,y)
      setColor(returnPixel,getColor(srcPixel))
      setBlue(returnPixel, 1.2*getBlue(srcPixel))
  return returnPic
```

How It Works

Both of these functions have the same basic structure. An object to be returned, `returnPic`, is created of the same size as the input picture. For each pixel in the input picture, we copy the color to the corresponding pixel in the `returnPic` picture. We then decrease red or increase blue. Finally, we return the `returnPic`.

With these functions, we can apply these to a picture without changing the original picture. We can nest the functions in any way we want. Now the functions are much more like mathematical functions.

```
>>> newp = increaseBlue(decreaseRed(p))
>>> show(newp)
>>> show(decreaseRed(p))
>>> show(decreaseRed(increaseBlue(p)))
>>> show(increaseBlue(p))
```

15.4 RECURSION: A POWERFUL IDEA

Recursion is writing functions that call *themselves*. Instead of writing loops, you write a function that loops by calling itself again and again and again. When you write a recursive function, you always have at least two pieces:

- What to do when you're done (e.g., when you're processing the very last item in the data); and
- What to do when the data are larger, which usually involves processing one element of the data, then recalling the function to deal with the rest.

Let's explore recursion with some simple textual functions, before we tackle media with recursion. Let's think about how we could write a function to do the following:

```
>>> downUp("Hello")
Hello
ello
llo
lo
o
lo
llo
ello
Hello
```

Recursion can be hard to get your head around. It really relies on you *trusting* your functions. Does the function do what it's supposed to do? Then just call it, and it'll do the right thing.

We're going to talk about recursion in three ways to help you understand it. The first way is **procedural abstraction**—breaking the problem down into the smallest pieces that we can write down easily as functions, and reusing as much as possible.

Let's think about `downUp` for one-character words. That's easy:

```
def downUp1(word):
  print word


>>> downUp1("I")
I
```

Now let's do `downUp` for two-character words. We'll reuse `downUp1` because we have it already.

```
def downUp2(word):
  print word
  downUp1(word[1:])
  print word
>>> downUp2("it")
it
t
it
>>> downUp2("me")
me
e
me
```

Now for three-character words:

```
def downUp3 (word):
  print word
  downUp2 (word[1:])
  print word

>>> downUp3("pop")
pop
op
p
op
pop
>>> downUp3("top")
top
op
p
op
top
```

Are we seeing a pattern yet? Let's try it:

```
def downUpTest(word):
  print word
  downUpTest(word[1:])
  print word
```

```
>>> downUpTest("hello")
hello
ello
llo
lo
o
The error was:java.lang.StackOverflowError
I wasn't able to do what you wanted.
The error java.lang.StackOverflowError has occured
Please check line 101 of C:\ip-book\programs\
    functional
```

The error is slightly different in regular Python, but means essentially the same thing.

```
>>> downUpTest("hello")
...
    File "<stdin>", line 3, in downUpTest
    File "<stdin>", line 3, in downUpTest
RuntimeError: maximum recursion depth exceeded
```

What happened? When we got down to one character, we just kept recalling downUpTest until we ran out of memory in an area called the *Stack*. We need to be able to tell our function "If we're down to only a single character, just print it and do *not* call yourself again!" The function shown below works.

Program 142: downUp Recursively

```
def downUp(word):
  print word
  if len(word)==1:
    return
  downUp(word[1:])
  print word
```

Here's our second way of thinking about recursion: good old tracing! We'll insert comments indented.

```
>>> downUp("Hello")
```

	The len(word) is not 1, so we print the word
Hello	
	Now we call downUp("ello") Still not one character, so print it
ello	
	Now we call downUp("llo") Still not one character, so print it

llo

> Now we call downUp("lo")
> Still not one character, so print it

lo

> Now call downUp(o")
> *Thats one character!* Print it, and return

o

> downUp("lo") now continues from its call
> to downUp("o")
> It prints again and ends.

lo

> downUp("llo") now continues (back from
> downUp("lo"))
> It prints and ends.

llo

> downUp("ello") now continues.
> It prints and ends.

ello

> Finally, the last line of the original
> downUp("Hello") can run.

Hello

A third way of thinking about this is to imagine a *function invocation* as an *elf*—a little person inside the computer who's going to do what you say.

Here are the downUp instructions to the elves:

1. Accept a word as input.

2. If your word has only one character, write it on the screen and you're done. Stop and sit down.

3. Write your word down on the screen.

4. Hire another elf to do the same instructions and give the new elf your word minus the first character.

5. Wait until the elf you hired is done.

6. Write your word down on the screen again. You're done.

I suggest trying this in your own class—it's fun and helps recursion make sense. It works something like this:

- We start out hiring our first elf with the input "Hello."

(Think of this as an abstraction of an elf.)

- The elf carrying "Hello" follows the instructions. He accepts the word as input, sees that it has more than character, and writes it on the screen: Hello. It then hires a new elf and gives it the input "ello."

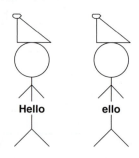

- The "ello"-carrying elf accepts the input, sees that it has more than one character, and writes it on the screen (ello, right under Hello). She then hires a new elf and hands it the input "llo."

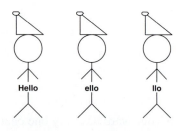

- At this point, we can make a few observations. Each elf is only aware of the elf to his left—the one he hired. He has to wait for that elf to finish before he can finish. When the elves start finishing, the first ones to finish will be the ones to the right, who were the last ones to be hired. We call this a **stack**—the elves "stack up" left to right, and the *last* one up is the *first* one out.

    If the original input was a really big word (e.g., "antidisestablishmentarianism"), you could imagine not having enough room for all the elves to stack up. We'd call that **stack overflow**—that's literally the error that Python gives you if the recursion gets too deep (i.e., too many elves).

- Imagine that we continue the simulation. We hire elves for "lo" and "o." The "o" elf writes down her o, then sits down.

- The "lo" elf now finishes up. She writes `lo` on the screen—which is below the `o` which is below the `lo`. And the "lo" elf sits down. That leaves us with three more elves awaiting their turns.

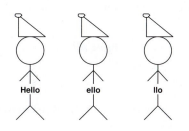

- The "llo" elf writes `llo` and sits down.

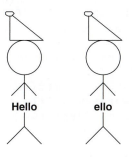

- The "ello" elf has been waiting for the "llo" elf to finish. He writes `ello` on the screen and sits down.

- Finally, the "Hello" elf writes down `Hello` for the second time and sits down. The stack is now empty.

Why use functional programming and recursion? Because it lets you do a lot in very few lines of code. It's a very useful technique for dealing with hard problems. Any kind of loop can be implemented with recursion. So many people feel that it's the most flexible, elegant, and powerful form of looping.

15.4.1   Recursive Directory Traversals

The earliest recursive structure that we met in this book was a directory tree. A folder can contain other folders, and so on, to any depth of folders. The easiest way to *traverse* (touch every file) in a directory structure is with a recursive method.

We know how to get all the files in a directory, using `os.listdir`. The challenge is to identify which of these files are directories. Fortunately, Java knows how to do this with its `File` object, which we can easily use from Jython. When we do find a directory, we can process just as we did the very first directory requested.

Program 143: Print All Filenames in a Directory Tree

```
import os
import java.io.File as File

def printAllFiles(directory):
  files = os.listdir(directory)
  for file in files:
    fullname = directory+"/"+file
    if isDirectory(fullname):
      printAllFiles(fullname)
    else:
      print fullname

def isDirectory(filename):
  filestatus = File(filename)
  return filestatus.isDirectory()
```

How It Works

We will need both Python's `os` module and Java's `java.io.File` class. To `printAllFiles` in a given `directory`, we get a list of all the files in the directory using `os.listdir`. For each of those files, we add the directory and the filename to get a full path. We then ask if that's a directory using `isDirectory`. Using the Java `File` object, we can ask it if it is a directory, then return that response.

Normally in this book, when we have to things to test, we use two `if` statements. Thus, we would write the first function above as:

```
def printAllFiles(directory):
  files = os.listdir(directory)
  for file in files:
    fullname = directory+"/"+file
    if isDirectory(fullname):
      printAllFiles(fullname)
    if not isDirectory(fullname):
      print fullname
```

However, every test of `isDirectory` requires a fairly complex file operation. That's expensive in terms of processing time. Rather than doing it repeatedly, we say, "If it's *not* a directory, i.e., `else`, do this." Thus, we use the `else` construct. An `else` is not as readable as the double `if` statements, but it does prevent us from repeating a test, and is thus, more efficient.

We will test this function on the folder shown in Figure 15.3.

FIGURE 15.3
What's in the sampleFolder.

```
>>> printAllFiles("/home/guzdial/Documents/sampleFolder")
/home/guzdial/Documents/sampleFolder/
  blueMotorcycle.jpg
/home/guzdial/Documents/sampleFolder/sounds/
  bassoon-c4.wav
/home/guzdial/Documents/sampleFolder/sounds/
  bassoon-g4.wav
/home/guzdial/Documents/sampleFolder/sounds/
  bassoon-e4.wav
/home/guzdial/Documents/sampleFolder/birds/bird3.jpg
/home/guzdial/Documents/sampleFolder/birds/bird2.jpg
/home/guzdial/Documents/sampleFolder/birds/bird1.jpg
/home/guzdial/Documents/sampleFolder/birds/bird5.jpg
/home/guzdial/Documents/sampleFolder/birds/bird4.jpg
/home/guzdial/Documents/sampleFolder/birds/bird6.jpg
/home/guzdial/Documents/sampleFolder/blue-mark.jpg
/home/guzdial/Documents/sampleFolder/butterfly.jpg
```

15.4.2   Recursive Media Functions

We can think about writing media functions like decreaseRed() recursively, like this.

Program 144: Decrease Red, Recursively

```python
def decreaseRedR(aList):
  if aList == []: # empty
    return
  setRed(aList[0],getRed(aList[0])*0.8)
  decreaseRedR(aList[1:])
```

How It Works

If the input list of pixels is empty, then we stop (`return`). Otherwise, we take the first pixel in the list (`alist[0]`) and decrease its red by 20% (multiply by 0.8). Then we call `decreaseRedR` on the *rest* of the list (`alist[1:]`).

We'd call this version like this: `decreaseRedR(getPixels(pic))`. *Warning:* it actually won't work even for reasonable-size pictures. Python (and the Java underlying Jython) don't expect recursion of this level of depth, so they run out of memory. It does work with *really* small pictures. This version of `decreaseRed` actually has two problems:

- First, it recurses once for every pixel. That's hundreds of thousands of times.
- Second, it passes the whole list of pixels for each call. That means, for every pixel processed, a copy of all the pixels is also stored in memory. That's a huge amount of memory.

We can write this function differently, so that we correct that second problem. We can avoid passing the whole list of pixels by declaring the variable containing the list of pixels as `global`. Then the variable is shared among the functions.

Program 145: Recursive decreaseRed with a Global Variable

```python
aPicturePixels=[]

def decreaseRedR(aPicture):
  global aPicturePixels
  aPicturePixels=getPixels(aPicture)
  decreaseRedByIndex(len(aPicturePixels)-1)

def decreaseRedByIndex(index):
  global aPicturePixels
  pixel = aPicturePixels[index]
  setRed(pixel, 0.8 * getRed(pixel))
  if index == 0: # empty
    return
  decreaseRedByIndex(index - 1)
```

How It Works

We first create the variable `aPicturePixels` outside of any function. The `global` statements tells Python that `aPicturePixels` should be one defined at the level of the file (module), not just local to this function. decreaseRedR puts all the pixels into aPicturePixels, then calls the helper function decreaseRedByIndex with the last index in the list of picture pixels, the length (len) of the list minus one. The function decreaseRedByIndex gets the pixel at the specified index and decreases the red in it by 80%. If the index is zero, the very first pixel, we simply return and stop. If it is not zero, we continue decreasing red by one less than the current index.

The problem is that this version still recurses once for every pixel. For even relatively small pictures (640 × 480), the stack overflows before we complete the picture processing. In general, processing pixel-by-pixel recursively is hard, maybe impossible, to do in Jython.

PROGRAMMING SUMMARY

Some of the functions and programming pieces that we met in this chapter.

FUNCTIONAL PROGRAMMING

apply	Inputs a function and a list as input to the function, where the list has as many elements as the function takes as input. Calls the function on the input.
map	Inputs a function and a list of several inputs to the function. Calls the function on each of the inputs and returns a list of the outputs (return values).
filter	Inputs a function and a list of several inputs to the function. Calls the function on each of the list elements and returns the *input element* if the function returns true (non-zero) for that element.
reduce	Inputs a function that takes two inputs and a list of several inputs to the function. The function is applied to the first two list elements, then the result of that is used as input with the next list element, then the result of that is used as input with the *next* list element, and so on. The overall result is returned at the end.
else:	After an if, executes the following block of code only if the test in the if statement is *false*.
global	Variables listed after the statement global are meant to reference a variable created *before* this function, at the level of the file (or module). This allows us to share a reference to an object, rather than duplicate it.

PROBLEMS

15.1   Here's a puzzle. You have six blocks. One of them weighs more than the other. You have a scale but you can only use it twice. Find the heaviest one. (a) Write down your process as an algorithm. (b) What search is this like?

15.2   Write a function to calculate the fibonacci of a number. Fibonacci of 0 is 0 and of 1 is 1. Fibonacci of n is $Fib(n) = Fib(n-2) + Fib(n-1)$.

15.3   Write a function to convert Celsius to Fahrenheit.

15.4   Write a function to calculate a person's body mass index given his/her weight and height.

15.5   Write a function to calculate a tip of 20 percent.

15.6   Look up Sierpinski's triangle. Write a recursive function to create Sierpinski's triangle.

15.7   Look up Koch's snowflake. Write a recursive function to create Koch's snowflake.

15.8   Change the functional `turnHairRed()` in Program 140 (page 346) into *only* a single line by recoding the utility functions as `lambda` functions.

15.9   Describe what this function does. Try different numbers as input.

```
def test(num):
    if num > 0:
        return test(num-1)
    else:
        return 0
```

15.10   Describe what this function does. Try different numbers as input.

```
def test(num):
    if num > 0:
        return test(num-1) + num
    else:
        return 0
```

15.11   Describe what this function does. Try different numbers as input.

```
def test(num):
    if num > 0:
        return test(num-1) * num
    else:
        return 0
```

15.12   Describe what this function does. Try different numbers as input.

```
def test(num):
    if num > 0:
        return num - test(num-1)
    else:
        return 0
```

15.13   Describe what this function does. Try different numbers as input.

```
def test(num):
    if num > 0:
        return test(num-2) * test(num-1)
    else:
        return 0
```

15.14   Write a recursive method to list all the files in a directory and in all subdirectories.

15.15   Try writing upDown():

```
>>> upDown("Hello")
Hello
Hell
Hel
He
H
He
Hel
Hell
Hello
```

Try to write it *both* recursively and without recursion. Which is easier? Why?

15.16   Try writing some of our sound and picture examples from the earlier chapters *functionally*, using structures like `filter` and `map`.

16 Object-Oriented Programming

Chapter Learning Objectives

- To use object-oriented programming to make programs easier to develop in teams, more robust, and easier to debug.
- To understand such features of object-oriented programs as polymorphism, encapsulation, inheritance, and aggregation.
- To be able to choose between different styles of programming for different purposes.

16.1 HISTORY OF OBJECTS

The most common style of programming today is **object-oriented programming**. We're going to define it in contrast with the procedural programming that we've been doing up until now.

Back in the 1960s and 1970s, procedural programming was the dominant form of programming. People used *procedural abstraction* and defined lots of functions at high and low levels, and reused their functions wherever possible. This worked reasonably well—up to a point. As programs got really large and complex, with many programmers working on them at the same time, procedural programming started to break down.

Programmers ran into problems with procedure conflicts. People would write programs that modified data in ways that other people didn't expect. They would use the same names for functions and find that their code couldn't be integrated into one large program.

There were also problems in *thinking* about programs and the tasks the programs were supposed to perform. Procedures are about *verbs*—tell the computer to do this, tell the computer to do that. But it's not clear whether that's the way people think best about problems.

Object-oriented programming is *noun-oriented programming*. Someone building an object-oriented program starts by thinking about what the nouns are in the *domain* of the problem—what are the people and things that are part of this problem and its solution? The process of identifying the objects, what each of them knows about (with respect to the problem), and what each of them has to do is called **object-oriented analysis**.

Programming in an object-oriented way means that you define variables (called **instance variables**) *for the objects* and you define functions (called **methods**) *for the objects*. You have very few or even *no* global functions or variables—things that are accessible everywhere. Instead, objects talk to one another by asking each other to do things via their methods. Adele Goldberg, one of the pioneers of object-oriented programming, calls this "Ask, don't touch." You can't just "touch" data and do whatever you want with it—instead, you "ask" objects to manipulate their data through their methods.

The term "object-oriented programming" was invented by Alan Kay. Kay is a brilliant multidisciplinary character—he holds undergraduate degrees in mathematics and biology, a Ph.D. in computer science, and has been a professional jazz guitarist. In 2004, he was awarded the ACM Turing Award, which is sort of the Nobel Prize of computing. Kay saw object-oriented programming as a way of developing software that could truly scale to large systems. He described objects as being like biological *cells* that work together in well-defined ways to make the whole organism work. Like cells, objects would—

- Help manage *complexity* by distributing responsibility for tasks across many objects rather than one big program.
- Support *robustness* by making the objects work relatively independently.
- Support *reuse* because each object would provide *services* to other objects (tasks that the object would do for other objects, accessible through its methods), just as real-world objects do.

The notion of starting from nouns is part of Kay's vision. **Software**, he said, is actually a *simulation* of the world. By making software *model* the world, it becomes clearer how to make software. You look at the world and how it works, then copy that into software. Things in the world *know* things—these become **instance variables**. Things in the world can *do* things—these become **methods**.

16.2   WORKING WITH TURTLES

Dr. Seymour Papert, at MIT, used robot turtles to help children think about how to specify procedures in the late 1960s. The turtle had a pen in the middle of it that could be raised and lowered to leave a trail of its movements. As graphical displays became available, he used a virtual turtle on a computer screen instead of a robotic turtle.

We are going to work with some turtle objects that move around a world. The turtles know how to move forward, turn left, turn right, and turn by some specified angle. The turtles have a pen in the middle of them that leaves a trail to show their movements. The world keeps track of the turtles that are in it.

16.2.1 Classes and Objects

How does the computer know what we mean by a turtle and a world? We have to define what a turtle is, what it knows about, and what it can do. We have to define what a world is, what it knows about, and what it can do. In Python we do this by defining classes. A class defines what things, objects (instances) of that class know and can do. We have created classes that define what we mean by a turtle and a world.

16.2.2 Creating Objects

Object-oriented programs consist of objects. But, how do we create those objects? The class knows what each object of that class needs to keep track of and what it should be able to do, so the class creates the objects of that class. You can think of a class as an object factory. The factory can create many objects. A class is also like a cookie cutter. You can make many cookies from one cookie cutter and they will all have the same shape. Or you can think of the class as a blueprint and the objects as the houses that you can create from the blueprint.

To create and initialize a world or turtle object you can use `makeClass (parameterList)` where the parameter list contains a list of items used to initialize the new object. Let's create a new world object.

```
>>> makeWorld()
```

This will create a world object and display a window that shows the world (Figure 16.1). It will just start as an all white picture in a frame titled, "World."

FIGURE 16.1
The display for a world object.

FIGURE 16.2
Creating a turtle in the world.

We didn't name the world so we don't have any way to refer to it. Let's try again and this time name the world object that gets created earth, and then create a turtle object in the world named earth. We will name the turtle object tina.

```
>>> earth = makeWorld()
>>> tina = makeTurtle(earth)
>>> print tina
No name turtle at 320, 240 heading 0.0.
```

① make World
② make Turtle (earth)

The turtle object appears in the center of the world (320, 240) and facing north (*a heading of 0*) (Figure 16.2). The turtle hasn't been assigned a name yet.

We can create many turtle objects. Each new turtle will appear in the center of the world.

```
>>> sue = makeTurtle(earth)
```

16.2.3   Sending Messages to Objects

We can ask the turtle to do things by sending a message to the turtle object. We do this using *dot notation.* In dot notation we ask an object to do something by specifying the name of the object and then a '.' and then the function to execute (name.function(parameterList)). We saw dot notation with strings in Section 10.3.1.

```
>>> tina.forward()
>>> tina.turnRight()
```

FIGURE 16.3
Asking one turtle to move and turn, while the other one remains.

```
>>> tina.forward()
```

Notice that only the turtle that we asked to do the actions moves (Figure 16.3). We can make the other one move by asking it to do things as well.

```
>>> sue.turnLeft()
>>> sue.forward(50)
```

Notice that different turtles have different colors (Figure 16.4). As you can see turtles know how to turn left, turnLeft() and right turnRight(). They also can go forward in the direction they are currently heading using forward(). By default they go forward 100 pixels. But, you can also specify how many pixels to go forward, forward(50). Turtles know how to turn a given number of degrees as well. Positive amounts turn the turtle to the right and negative amounts to the left (Figure 16.5).

Default = 100 pixels

specify # pixels

```
>>> tina.turn(-45)
.>> tina.forward()
```

— Degrees = left   ⊕ Degrees = Right

16.2.4   Objects Control Their State

In object-oriented programming we send messages to ask objects to do things. The objects can refuse to do what you ask. Why would an object refuse? An object *should* refuse if you ask it to do something that would cause its data to be wrong. The world that the turtles are in is 640 pixels wide by 480 high. What happens if you try to tell the turtle to go past the end of the world?

FIGURE 16.4
After the second turtle moves.

FIGURE 16.5
Turning a specified amount (−45).

```
>>> world1 = makeWorld()
>>> turtle1 = makeTurtle(world1)
>>> turtle1.forward(400)
>>> print turtle1
No name turtle at 320, 0 heading 0.0.
```

Recall that turtles are first positioned at (320, 240) heading north (up). In the world the top left position is (0, 0) and x increases to the right and y increases going down. By asking the turtle to go forward 400, we are asking it to go to (320, 240 − 400) which would result in a position of (320, −160) But, the turtle refuses to leave the world and instead stops when the center of the turtle is at (320, 0) (Figure 16.6). This means we won't lose sight of any of our turtles.

16.2.5 Other Turtle Functions

Turtles can do lots of other things as well as go forward and turn. As you have probably noticed when the turtles move they draw a line that is the same color as the turtle. You can ask the turtle to pick up the pen using penUp(). You can ask the turtle to put down the pen using penDown(). You can ask the turtle to move to a particular position using moveTo(x,y). If the pen is down when you ask the turtle to move to a new position the turtle will draw a line from the old position to the new position (Figure 16.7).

```
>>> worldX = makeWorld()
>>> turtleX = makeTurtle(worldX)
```

FIGURE 16.6
A turtle stuck at the edge of the world.

FIGURE 16.7
Using the turtle to draw a diagonal line.

```
>>> turtleX.penUp()
>>> turtleX.moveTo(0,0)
>>> turtleX.penDown()
>>> turtleX.moveTo(639,479)
```

You can change the color of a turtle using setColor(color). You can stop drawing the turtle using setVisible(false). You can change the width of the pen using setPenWidth(width) (Figure 16.8).

```
>>> worldX = makeWorld()
>>> turtleX = makeTurtle(worldX)
>>> turtleX.setVisible(false) #don't draw the turtle
>>> turtleX.penUp() # don't draw the path
>>> turtleX.moveTo(0,240)
>>> turtleX.penDown() # draw the path
>>> turtleX.setPenWidth(100) # width of pen
>>> turtleX.setColor(blue)
>>> turtleX.turnRight()
>>> turtleX.forward(300)
>>> turtleX.penUp() # don't draw the path
>>> turtleX.setColor(red)
>>> turtleX.moveTo(400,0)
>>> turtleX.turnRight()
```

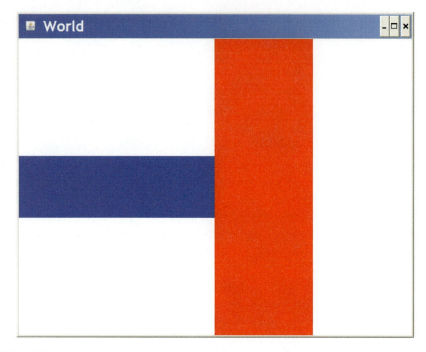

FIGURE 16.8
Drawing rectangles with the turtle.

```
>>> turtleX.setPenWidth(160)
>>> turtleX.penDown() # draw the path
>>> turtleX.forward(400)
```

16.3 TEACHING TURTLES NEW TRICKS

We have already defined a `Turtle` class for you. But, what if you want to create your own type of turtle and teach it to do new things? We can create a new type of turtle that will understand how to do all the things that turtle knows how to do, and we can also add some new functionality. This is called creating a *subclass*. Just like children inherit eye color from their parents our subclass will *inherit* all the things that turtles know and can do. A subclass is also called a *child* class and the class that it inherits from is called the `parent` class or `superclass`.

We will call our subclass `SmartTurtle`. And we will add a *method* that allows our turtle to draw a square. Methods are like the functions we have been using but they are defined inside a class. Methods also take a reference to the object of the class that the method is called on (usually called `self`). To draw a square our turtle will turn right and go forward 4 times. Notice that we inherit the ability to turn right and go forward from the `Turtle` class.

Program 146: Defining a Subclass

```
class SmartTurtle(Turtle):

  def drawSquare(self):
    for i in range(0,4):
      self.turnRight()
      self.forward()
```

Since the SmartTurtle is a kind of Turtle, we can use it in much the same way. But, we will need to create the SmartTurtle in a new way. We have been using makePicture, makeSound, makeWorld and makeTurtle to make our objects. These are functions we have created to make it easier to make these objects. But, the actual way in Python to create a new object is to use ClassName(parameterList). So to create a world you can use worldObj = World() and to create a SmartTurtle you can use turtleObj = SmartTurtle(worldObj).

```
>>> earth = World()
>>> smarty = SmartTurtle(earth)
smarty.drawSquare()
```

Our smart turtle now knows how to draw a square (Figure 16.9). But, it can only draw squares of size 100. It would be nice to be able to draw different size squares. We can add another function that takes a parameter that specifies the width of the square.

FIGURE 16.9
Drawing a square with our SmartTurtle.

Program 147: Defining a Subclass

```
class SmartTurtle(Turtle):

    def drawSquare(self):
        for i in range(0,4):
            self.turnRight()
            self.forward()

    def drawSquare(self, width):
        for i in range(0,4):
            self.turnRight()
            self.forward(width)
```

You can use this to draw different size squares Figure 16.10.

```
>>> mars = World()
>>> tina = SmartTurtle(mars)
>>> tina.drawSquare(30)
>>> tina.drawSquare(150)
>>> tina.drawSquare(100)
```

FIGURE 16.10
Drawing different size squares.

16.4   AN OBJECT-ORIENTED SLIDE SHOW

Let's use object-oriented techniques to build a slide show. Let's say that we want to show a picture, then play a corresponding sound and wait until the sound is done before going on to the next picture. We'll use the function (mentioned many chapters ago) *blockingPlay()* which plays a sound and waits for it to finish before executing the next statement.

Program 148: Slide Show As One Big Function

```
def playSlideShow():
    pic = makePicture(getMediaPath("barbara.jpg"))
    sound = makeSound(getMediaPath("bassoon-c4.wav"))
    show(pic)
    blockingPlay(sound)
    pic = makePicture(getMediaPath("beach.jpg"))
    sound = makeSound(getMediaPath("bassoon-e4.wav"))
    show(pic)
    blockingPlay(sound)
    pic = makePicture(getMediaPath("church.jpg"))
    sound = makeSound(getMediaPath("bassoon-g4.wav"))
    show(pic)
    blockingPlay(sound)
    pic = makePicture(getMediaPath("jungle2.jpg"))
    sound = makeSound(getMediaPath("bassoon-c4.wav"))
    show(pic)
    blockingPlay(sound)
```

This isn't a very good program from any perspective. From a procedural programming perspective, there's an awful lot of duplicated code here. It would be nice to get rid of it. From an object-oriented programming perspective, we should have slide objects.

As we mentioned, objects have two parts. Objects *know* things—these become *instance variables*. Objects can *do* things—these become *methods*. We're going to access both of these using dot notation.

So what does a slide know? It knows its *picture* and its *sound*. What can a slide do? It can *show* itself, by showing its picture and playing its sound.

To define a slide object in Python (and many other object-oriented programming languages, including Java and C++), we must define a slide **class**. A class defines the instance variables and methods for a set of objects—that is, what each object of that class knows and can do. Each object of the class is called an *instance* of the class. We'll make multiple slides by making multiple instances of the slide class—just as our bodies might make multiple kidney cells or multiple heart cells, each of which knows how to do certain kinds of tasks.

To create a class in Python, we start with:

```
class slide:
```

What comes after this, indented, are the methods for creating new slides and playing slides. Let's add a *show()* method to our slide class.

```
class slide:
   def show(self):
      show(self.picture)
      blockingPlay(self.sound)
```

To create new instances, we call the class name like a function. We can define new instance variables by simply assigning them. So here is how to create a slide and give it a picture and sound.

```
>>> slide1=slide()
>>> slide1.picture = makePicture(getMediaPath("barbara.jpg"))
>>> slide1.sound = makeSound(getMediaPath("bassoon-c4.wav"))
>>> slide1.show()
```

The `slide1.show()` function shows the picture and plays the sound. What is this `self` stuff? When we execute `object.method()`, Python finds the method in the object's class, then calls it, using the instance object as an *input*. It's Python style to name this input variable `self` (because it is the object itself). Since we have the object in the variable `self`, we can then access its picture and sound by saying `self.picture` and `self.sound`.

But this is still pretty hard to use if we have to set up all the variables from the Command Area. How could we make it easier? What if we could pass in the sound and picture for the slides as *inputs* to the `slide` class, as if the class were a real function? We can do this by defining something called a **constructor**.

To create new instances with some inputs, we must define a function named `__init__`. That's "underscore-underscore-i-n-i-t-underscore-underscore." It's the pre-defined name in Python for a method that *initializes* new objects. Our `__init__` method needs three inputs: the instance itself (because all methods get that), a picture, and a sound.

Program 149: A Slide Class

```
class slide:
   def __init__(self, pictureFile, soundFile):
      self.picture = makePicture(pictureFile)
      self.sound = makeSound(soundFile)

   def show(self):
      show(self.picture)
      blockingPlay(self.sound)
```

We can use our slide class to define a slide show like this.

Program 150: Playing a Slide Show, Using Our `slide` Class

```
def playSlideShow2():
   pictF = getMediaPath("barbara.jpg")
```

```
soundF = getMediaPath("bassoon-c4.wav")
slide1 = slide(pictF,soundF)
pictF = getMediaPath("beach.jpg")
soundF = getMediaPath("bassoon-e4.wav")
slide2 = slide(pictF,soundF)
pictF = getMediaPath("church.jpg")
soundF = getMediaPath("bassoon-g4.wav")
slide3 = slide(pictF,soundF)
pictF = getMediaPath("jungle2.jpg")
soundF = getMediaPath("bassoon-c4.wav")
slide4 = slide(pictF,soundF)
slide1.show()
slide2.show()
slide3.show()
slide4.show()
```

One of the features of Python that make it so powerful is that we can mix object-oriented and functional programming styles. Slides are now objects that can easily be stored in lists, like any other kind of Python object. Here's an example of the same slide show where we use map to show the slide show.

Program 151: Slide Show, In Objects and Functions

```
def showSlide(aSlide):
  aSlide.show()

def playSlideShow3():
    pictF = getMediaPath("barbara.jpg")
    soundF = getMediaPath("bassoon-c4.wav")
    slide1 = slide(pictF,soundF )
    pictF = getMediaPath("beach.jpg")
    soundF = getMediaPath("bassoon-e4.wav")
    slide2 = slide(pictF,soundF)
    pictF = getMediaPath("church.jpg")
    soundF = getMediaPath("bassoon-g4.wav")
    slide3 = slide(pictF,soundF)
    pictF = getMediaPath("jungle2.jpg")
    soundF = getMediaPath("bassoon-c4.wav")
    slide4 = slide(pictF,soundF)

    map(showSlide,[slide1,slide2,slide3,slide4])
```

Is the object-oriented version of the slide show easier to write? It certainly has less replication of code. It features **encapsulation** in that the data and behavior of the object are defined in one and only one place, so that any change to one is easily changed in the other. Being able to use lots of objects (like lists of objects) is called **aggregation**. This is a very powerful idea. We don't always have to define new classes—we can often use the powerful structures we know, like lists with existing objects, to great impact.

16.4.1 Joe the Box

The earliest example used to teach object-oriented programming was developed by Adele Goldberg and Alan Kay—it's called *Joe the Box*. Imagine that you have a class Box like the one below:

```
class Box:
  def __init__(self):
    self.setDefaultColor()
    self.size=10
    self.position=(10,10)
  def setDefaultColor(self):
    self.color = red
  def draw(self,canvas):
    addRectFilled(canvas, self.position[0],
self.position[1], self.size, self.size, self.color)
```

What will you see if you execute the following code?

```
>>> canvas = makeEmptyPicture(400,200)
>>> joe = Box()
>>> joe.draw(canvas)
>>> show(canvas)
```

Let's trace it out.

- Obviously, the first line just creates a white canvas that is 400 pixels wide and 200 pixels high.

- When we create joe, the __init__ method is called. The method setDefault Color is called on joe, so he gets a default color of red. When self.color=red is executed, the *instance variable* color is created for joe and gets a value of red. We return to __init__, where joe is given a size of 10 and a position of (10,10) (size and position both become new instance variables).

- When joe is asked to draw himself on the canvas, he's drawn as a red, filled rectangle (addRectFilled), at *x* position 10 and *y* position 10, with a size of 10 pixels on each side.

We could add a method to Box that allows us to make joe change his size.

```
class Box:
  def __init__(self):
    self.setDefaultColor()
    self.size=10
    self.position=(10,10)
  def setDefaultColor(self):
    self.color = red
  def draw(self,canvas):
    addRectFilled(canvas, self.position[0],self.
    position[1], self.size, self.size, self.color)
  def grow(self,size):
    self.size=self.size+size
```

Now we can tell joe to grow. A negative number like -2 will cause joe to shrink. A positive number will cause joe to grow—though we'd have to add a move method if we wanted him to grow much and still fit on the canvas.

Now consider the following code added to the same Program Area.

```
class SadBox(Box):
  def setDefaultColor(self):
    self.color=blue
```

Note that SadBox lists Box as a superclass (parent class). This means that SadBox *inherits* all the methods of Box. What will you see if you execute the code below?

```
>>> jane = SadBox()
>>> jane.draw(canvas)
>>> repaint(canvas)
```

Let's trace it out:

- When jane is created as a SadBox, the method __init__ is executed in class Box.
- The first thing that happens in __init__ is that we call setDefaultColor *on the input object* self. That object is now jane. So we call jane's setDefaultColor. We say that SadBox's setDefaultColor *overrides* Box's.
- The setDefaultColor for jane sets the color to blue.
- We then return to executing the rest of Box's __init__. We set jane's size to 10 and position to (10,10).
- When we tell jane to draw, she appears as a 10×10 blue square at position (10,10). If we haven't moved or grown joe, he will disappear as jane is drawn on top of him.

Note that joe and jane are each a different *kind* of Box. They have the same instance variables (but different *values* for the same variables) and mostly know the same things. Because both understand draw, for example, we say that draw is *polymorphic*. The word polymorphic just means many forms.

A SadBox (jane) is slightly different in how it behaves when it created, so it knows some things differently. Joe and Jane highlight some of the basic ideas of object-oriented programming: inheritance, specialization in subclasses, and shared instance variables while having different instance variable values.

16.4.2   Object-Oriented Media

Of course, we've been using objects already. Pictures, sounds, samples, and colors are all objects. Our lists of pixels and samples are certainly examples of aggregation. The functions we've been using are actually just covering up the underlying methods. We certainly can just call the objects' methods directly. We can also create a picture using the normal constructor.

```
>>> pic=Picture(getMediaPath("barbara.jpg"))
>>> pic.show()
```

Here's how the *function* show() is defined. You can ignore raise and __class__. The key point is that the function is simply executing the existing picture method show.

```
def show(picture):
    if not picture.__class__ == Picture:
        print "show(picture): Input is not a picture"
        raise ValueError
    picture.show()
```

Did you notice that we defined the method show() for slides, the same name that we have for showing pictures? First of all, we can clearly do that—objects can have their own methods with names that other objects also use. Much more powerful is that each of these methods with the same name can achieve the same *goal*, but in different ways. For both slides and pictures, the method show() says, "Show the object." But what's really happening is different in each case: pictures just show themselves, but slides show their pictures and play their sounds.

Computer Science Idea: Polymorphism

When the same name can be used to invoke different methods that achieve the same goal, we call that **polymorphism**. It's very powerful for the programmer. You simply tell an object show()—you don't have to care exactly what method is being executed and you don't even have to know exactly what object it is that you're telling the object to show. You the programmer simply specify your *goal*, to show the object. The object-oriented program handles the rest.

There are several examples of polymorphism built into the methods that we're using in JES.[1] For example, both pixels and colors understand the methods setRed, getRed, setBlue, getBlue, setGreen, and getGreen. This allows us to manipulate the colors of the pixels without pulling out the color objects separately. We could have defined the functions to take both kinds of inputs or to provide different functions for each kind of input, but both of those options get confusing. It's easy to do with methods.

```
>>> pic=Picture(getMediaPath("barbara.jpg"))
>>> pic.show()
>>> pixel = pic.getPixel(100,200)
>>> print pixel.getRed()
73
>>> color = pixel.getColor()
>>> print color.getRed()
73
```

Another example is the method writeTo(). The method writeTo(filename) is defined for both pictures and sounds. Did you ever confuse write-PictureTo() and writeSoundTo()? Isn't it easier to just always write writeTo(filename)? That's why that method is named the same in both classes,

---

[1]Recall that JES is an environment for programming in Jython, which is a specific kind of Python. The media supports are part of what JES provides—they're not part of the core of Python.

and why polymorphism is so powerful. (You may be wondering why we didn't introduce this in the first place. Were you ready in Chapter 2 to talk about dot notation and polymorphic methods?)

Overall, there are actually many more methods defined in JES than functions. More specifically, there are a bunch of methods for drawing on pictures that aren't available as functions.

- As you would expect, pictures understand `pic.addRect(color,x,y,width, height)`, `pic.addRectFilled(color,x,y,width,height)`, `pic.addOval-(color,x,y,width,height)`, and `pic.addOvalFilled(color,x,y,width, height)`.

  See Figure 16.11 for examples of rectangle methods drawn from the following example.

  ```
  >>> pic=Picture (getMediaPath("640x480.jpg"))
  >>> pic.addRectFilled (orange,10,10,100,100)
  >>> pic.addRect (blue,200,200,50,50)
  >>> pic.show()
  >>> pic.writeTo("newrects.jpg")
  ```

  See Figure 16.12 for examples of ovals drawn from the following example.

  ```
  >>> pic=Picture (getMediaPath("640x480.jpg"))
  >>> pic.addOval (green,200,200,50,50)
  >>> pic.addOvalFilled (magenta,10,10,100,100)
  >>> pic.show()
  >>> pic.writeTo("ovals.jpg")
  ```

- Pictures also understand *arcs*. Arcs are literally parts of a circle. The two methods are `pic.addArc(color,x,y,width,height,startAngle,arcAngle)`

FIGURE 16.11
Examples of rectangle methods.

FIGURE 16.12
Examples of oval methods.

FIGURE 16.13
Examples of arc methods.

and `pic.addArcFilled(color,x,y,width,height,startAngle,arcAngle)`. They draw arcs for `arcAngle` degrees, where `startAngle` is the starting point. 0 degrees is at 3 o'clock on the clock face. A positive arc is counter-clockwise and negative is clockwise. The center of the circle is the middle of the rectangle defined by (x, y) with the given `width` and `height`.

- We can also now draw colored lines, using `pic.addLine(color,x1,y1, x2,y2)`.

See Figure 16.13 for examples of arcs and lines drawn from the following example.

```
>>> pic=Picture (getMediaPath("640x480.jpg"))
>>> pic.addArc(red,10,10,100,100,5,45)
>>> pic.show()
>>> pic.addArcFilled (green,200,100,200,100,1,90)
>>> pic.repaint()
>>> pic.addLine(blue,400,400,600,400)
>>> pic.repaint()
>>> pic.writeTo("arcs-lines.jpg")
```

- Text in Java can have styles, but these are limited to make sure that all platforms can replicate them. `pic.addText(color,x,y,string)` is the one we would expect to see. There is also `pic.addTextWithStyle(color,x,y, string,style)`, which takes a style created from `makeStyle(font,emphasis, size)`. The font is `sansSerif`, `serif` or `mono`. The emphasis is `italic`, `bold`, or `plain`, or sum them to get combinations (e.g., `italic+bold`. `size` is a point size).

    See Figure 16.14 for examples of text drawn from the following example.

```
>>> pic=Picture (getMediaPath("640x480.jpg"))
>>> pic.addText(red,10,100,"This is a red
      string!")
>>> pic.addTextWithStyle (green,10,200,"This is a
      bold, italic, green, large string",
      makeStyle(sansSerif, bold+italic,18))
>>> pic.addTextWithStyle (blue,10,300,"This is a
      blue, larger, italic-only, serif string",
      makeStyle(serif, italic,24))
>>> pic.writeTo("text.jpg")
```

FIGURE 16.14
Examples of text methods.

The older media functions that we wrote can be rewritten in method form. We will need to create a subclass of the `Picture` class and add the method to that class.

Program 152: Making a Sunset Using a Method

```
class MyPicture(Picture):
  def makeSunset(self):
    for p in getPixels(self):
      p.setBlue(int(p.getBlue()*0.7))
      p.setGreen(int (p.getGreen()*0.7))
```

■

This can be used like this.

```
>>> pict = MyPicture(getMediaPath("beach.jpg"))
>>> pict.explore()
>>> pict.makeSunset()
>>> pict.explore()
```

We can also create new subclasses of the Sound class and new methods to work on sound objects. The methods for accessing sound sample values are `getSampleValue()` and `getSampleValueAt(index)`.

Program 153: Reverse a Sound with a Method

```
class MySound(Sound):
  def reverse(self):
    target = Sound(self.getLength())
    sourceIndex = self.getLength() - 1
    for targetIndex in range(0,target.getLength()):
      sourceValue = self.getSampleValueAt(sourceIndex)
      target.setSampleValueAt(targetIndex,sourceValue)
      sourceIndex = sourceIndex - 1
    return target
```

■

This can be used like this.

```
>>> sound = MySound(getMediaPath("always.wav"))
>>> sound.explore()
>>> target = sound.reverse()
>>> target.explore()
```

16.4.3 Why Objects?

One role for objects is to reduce the number of names that you have to remember. Through polymorphism, you only have to remember the name and the goal, not all the various global functions.

More importantly, though, objects encapsulate data and behavior. Imagine that you wanted to change the name of an instance variable and then all the methods that use the variable. That's a lot to change. What if you miss one? Changing them all in one place, together, is useful.

Aggregation is also a significant benefit of object systems. You can have lots of objects doing useful things. Want more? Just create them!

Python's objects are similar to the objects of many languages. One significant difference is in access to instance variables, though. In Python, any object can access and manipulate any other object's instance variables. That's not true in languages like Java, C++, or Smalltalk. In these other languages, access to instance variables from other objects is limited and can even be eliminated entirely—then you can only access objects' instance variables through methods called **getters** and **setters** (to get and set the instance variable).

Another big part of object systems is **inheritance**. As we saw with our turtle and box examples, we can declare one class (*parent class*) to be *inherited* by another class (*child class*). Inheritance provides for instant polymorphism—the instances of the child automatically have all the data and behavior of the parent class. The child can then add more behavior and data to what the parent class had. This is called making the child a *specialization* of the parent class. For example, a 3-D rectangle instance might know and do everything that a rectangle instance does by saying `class rectangle3D(rectangle)`.

Inheritance gets a lot of press in the object-oriented world but it's a trade-off. It reduces even further the duplication of code, which is a good thing. In actual practice, inheritance isn't used as much as other advantages of object-oriented programming (like aggregation and encapsulation), and it can be confusing. Whose method is being executed when you type the below? It's invisible from here, and if it's *wrong*, it can be hard to figure out where it's wrong.

```
myBox = rectangle3D()
myBox.draw()
```

So when should you use objects? You should define your own object classes when you have data in groups (e.g., pictures and sounds) and behavior that you want to define for all instances of the group. You should use existing objects *all the time*. They're very powerful. If you're not comfortable with dot notation and the ideas of objects, you can stick with functions—they work just fine. Objects just give you a leg up on more complex systems.

PROGRAMMING SUMMARY

Some of the programming pieces that we met in this chapter.

OBJECT-ORIENTED PROGRAMMING

`class`	Lets you define a class. The keyword `class` takes a class name and an optional superclass in parentheses, ending with a colon. Methods for the class follow, indented within the class block.
`__init__`	The name of the method called on an object when it's first created. It's not required to have one.

GRAPHICS METHODS

addRect, addRectFilled	The *methods* in the Picture class for drawing rectangles and filled rectangles.
addOval, addOvalFilled	The methods in the Picture class for drawing ovals and filled ovals.
addArc, addArcFilled	The methods in the Picture class for drawing arcs and filled arcs.
addText, addText-WithStyle	The methods in the Picture class for drawing text and text with style elements (like boldface or sans serif).

addLine	The method in the Picture class for drawing a line.
getRed, getGreen, getBlue	The methods for both Pixel and Color objects for getting the red, green, and blue color components.
setRed, setGreen, setBlue	The methods for both Pixel and Color objects for setting the red, green, and blue color components.

PROBLEMS

16.1 Answer the following questions.

- What is the difference between an instance and a class?
- How are functions and methods different?
- How is object-oriented programming different from procedural programming?
- What is polymorphism?
- What is encapsulation?
- What is aggregation?
- What is a constructor?
- How did biological cells influence the development of the idea of objects?

16.2 Answer the following questions.

- What is inheritance?
- What is a superclass?
- What is a subclass?
- What methods does a child class inherit?
- What instance variables (fields) does a child class inherit?

16.3 Add a method to the Turtle class to draw an equilateral triangle.

16.4   Add a method to the `Turtle` class to draw a rectangle given a width and height.

16.5   Add a method to the `Turtle` class to draw a simple house. It can have a rectangle for the house and an equilateral triangle as the roof.

16.6   Add a method to the `Turtle` class to draw a street of houses.

16.7   Add a method to the `Turtle` class to draw a letter.

16.8   Add a method to the `Turtle` class to draw your initials.

16.9   Create a movie with several turtles moving in each frame.

16.10 Add another constructor to the `Slide` class that takes just a picture filename.

16.11 Create a `SlideShow` class that holds a list of slides and shows each slide one at a time.

16.12 Create a `CartoonPanel` class that takes an array of `Pictures` and displays the pictures from left to right. It should also have a title and author and display the title at the top left edge and the author at the top right edge.

16.13 Create a `Student` class. Each student should have a name and a picture. Add a method, `show`, that shows the picture for the student.

16.14 Add a field to the `SlideShow` class to hold the title and modify the show method to first show a blank picture with the title on it.

16.15 Create a `PlayList` class that takes a list of sounds and play them one at a time.

16.16 Use the methods in the `Picture` class to draw a smiling face.

16.17 Use the methods in the `Picture` class to draw a rainbow.

16.18 Rewrite the mirror functions as methods in the `MyPicture` class.

16.19 Make some modifications to Joe the Box.

- Add a method to `Box` named `setColor` that takes a color as input, then makes the input color the new color for the box. (Maybe `setDefaultColor` should call `setColor`?)
- Add a method to `Box` named `setSize` that takes a number as input, then makes the input number the new size for the box.
- Add a method to `Box` named `setPosition` that takes a list or tuple as a parameter, then makes that input the new position for the box.
- Change `__init__` so that it uses `setSize` and `setPosition` rather than simply setting the instance variables.

*16.20 Finish the Joe the Box example.

(a) Implement `grow` and `move`. The method `move` takes as input a relative distance like (-10,15) to move 10 pixels up (*x* position) and 15 pixels to the right (*y* position).

(b) Draw patterns by creating `joe` and `jane`, then move a little and draw, grow a little and draw, then repaint the new canvas.

16.21 Create a movie with boxes growing and shrinking in it.

TO DIG DEEPER

There is lots more to do with Python in exploring procedural, functional, and object-oriented programming styles. Mark recommends the books by Mark Lutz (especially [30]) and Richard Hightower [24] as nice introductions to the deeper realms of Python. You might also explore some of the tutorials at the Python Web site (`http://www.python.org`).

APPENDIX A

Quick Reference to Python

A.1   VARIABLES

Variables start with a letter and can be any word *except* one of the *reserved words*. These are: and, assert, break, class, continue, def, del, elif, else, except, exec, finally, for, from, global, if, import, in, is, lambda, not, or, pass, print, raise, return, try, while, yield.

We can use `print` to display the value of an expression (e.g., a variable). If we simply type the variable without `print`, we get the internal representation—functions and objects tell us about where they are in memory, and strings appear with their quotes.

```
>>> x = 10
>>> print x
10
>>> x
```

```
10
>>> y='string'
>>> print y
string
>>> y
'string'
>>> p=makePicture(pickAFile())
>>> print p
Picture, filename C:\ip-book\mediasources\
    7inX95in.jpg height 684 width 504
>>> p
<media.Picture instance at 6436242>
>>> print sin(12)
-0.5365729180004349
>>> sin
<java function sin at 26510058>
```

[handwritten: string ← Without ' ']

[handwritten in left margin: print picture = Picture, filename, MediaPath Height, Width]

A.2   FUNCTION CREATION

We define functions with `def`. `def x(a,b):` defines a function named "x" that takes two input values which will be bound to variables "a" and "b." The body of the function comes after the `def` and is indented.

The function can return values using the `return` statement.

A.3   LOOPS AND CONDITIONALS

We create most of our loops using `for`, which takes an index variable and a list. The body of the loop is executed once for each element of the list.

```
>>> for p in [1,2,3]:
...         print p
...
1
2
3
```

The list in a `for` is often generated using a `range` function. `range` can take one, two, or three inputs. With one input, the `range` is from zero to the input. With two, the `range` starts at the first input and stops *before* the second. With three, the `range` starts at the first, takes steps of the third, and ends *before* the second.

```
>>> range(4)
[0, 1, 2, 3]
>>> range(1,4)
[1, 2, 3]
```

[handwritten: from 0 → n−1]

[handwritten in left margin: 1 input]

[handwritten in left margin: 2 inputs   from n, m−1]

```
>>> range(1,4,2)
[1,  3]
```

3 inputs [handwritten annotation]

The `while` loop takes a logical expression and executes its block as long as the logical expression is true.

```
>>> x = 1
>>> while x < 5:
...            print x
...            x = x + 1
...
1
2
3
4
```

this function up till [handwritten annotation]
x < 5 [handwritten annotation]

A `break` immediately ends the current loop.

An `if` statement takes a logical expression and evaluates it. If it is true, the `if`'s block is executed. If it is false, the `else:` clause is executed, if one exists.

```
>>> if a < b:
...            print "a is smaller"
... else:
...            print "b is smaller"
```

A.4   OPERATORS AND REPRESENTATION FUNCTIONS

+, -, *, /, **	Addition, subtraction, multiplication, division, and exponentiation. Order of precedence is algebraic.
<,>, ==, <=, >=	Logical operators less-than, greater-than, equal-to, less-than-or-equal, greater-than-or-equal.
< >, !=	Logical operators not-equal (both of them are equivalent).
and, or, not	Logical conjunctives and, or, and not.
int()	Returns the integer part of the input (floating-point number or string).
float()	Returns a floating point version of the input.
str()	Returns a string representation of the input.
ord()	Given an input character, returns the ASCII numeric representation.

A.5   NUMERIC FUNCTIONS

abs()	Absolute value.
sin()	Sine.
cos()	Cosine.
max()	Maximum value of the inputs (including a list).
min()	Minimum value of the inputs (including a list).
len()	Returns the length of the input sequence.

A.6   SEQUENCE OPERATIONS

Sequences (strings, lists, tuples) can be added together for concatenation (e.g., s1 + s2).

Elements of a sequence can be accessed using slices:

- seq[n] accesses the *n*-th element of the list (the first element is zero).
- seq[n:m] accesses the elements starting at the *n*-th up to *but not including* the *m*-th.
- seq[:m] accesses elements from the start up to but not including the *m*-th.
- seq[n:] accesses elements from the *n*-th to the end of the sequence.

A.7   STRING ESCAPES

\t	Tab character
\b	Backspace
\n	Newline
\r	Return
\uXXXX	Unicode character, hexadecimal XXXX

Precede a string with "r" as in r"C:\mediasources" to treat a string in raw mode, ignoring escapes.

A.8   USEFUL STRING METHODS

- count(sub): returns the number of times sub appears in the string.
- find(sub): returns the index where sub appears in the string, or returns −1 if not found. find can take an optional starting point and an optional ending point. rfind takes the same inputs but works right to left.
- upper(), lower(): convert the string to all upper or all lowercase.

- `isalpha()`, `isdigit()`: return true if all the characters in the string are alphabetic or all numeric, respectively.
- `replace(s,r)`: replaces all instances of "s" with "r" in the string.
- `split(d)`: returns a list of sublists where the character d is the split point.

A.9 FILES

[handwritten margin note: Files opened with open (filename, file mode) file mode = r w a + t (for text) b (binary)]

Files are opened with open with two inputs: the filename and a file mode. The file mode is "r" for reading, "w" for writing, and "a" for appending, concatenated with a "t" for text or a "b" for binary. File methods include:

- `read()`: returns the whole file as a string.
- `readlines()`: returns the whole file as a list of strings delimited by lines.
- `write(s)`: writes the string s to the file.

A.10 LISTS

Lists are indexed like sequences using "[]". They are concatenated using +. List methods include:

[handwritten note: [ ] = Indexed   + = Concatenated]

- `append(a)`: appends the item a to the list.
- `remove(b)`: removes the item b from the list.
- `sort()`: sorts the list.
- `reverse()`: reverses the list.
- `count(s)`: returns the number of times that the element s appears in the list.

A.11 DICTIONARIES, HASH TABLES, OR ASSOCIATIVE ARRAYS

Dictionaries are created with {}. They can be accessed by a key.

```
>>> d = {'cat':'Diana', 'dog':'Fido'}
>>> print d
{'cat': 'Diana', 'dog': 'Fido'}
>>> print d.keys()
['cat', 'dog']
>>> print d['cat']
Diana
```

A.12 EXTERNAL MODULES

Modules are accessed using `import`. They can also be input as an alias, e.g., `import javax. swing as swing`. Specific pieces can be imported, without any need for dot notation to access them, using `from module import n1, n2`. All pieces of a module can be imported and accessed without dot notation using `from module import *`.

A.13   CLASSES

Classes are created using the `class` keyword followed by the name of the class and, in parentheses, an optional superclass (one or more). Methods follow and are indented. *Constructors* (which are called when a new instance of the class is created) must be named `__init__`. You can have more than one constructor in a Python class as long as they take different parameters.

A.14   FUNCTIONAL METHODS

`apply`	Inputs a function and a list as input to the function, where the list has as many elements as the function takes as input. Calls the function on the input.
`map`	Inputs a function and a list of several inputs to the function. Calls the function on each of the inputs and returns a list of the outputs (`return` values).
`filter`	Inputs a function and a list of several inputs to the function. Calls the function on each of the list elements and returns *the input element* if the function returns true (non-zero) for that element.
`reduce`	Inputs a function that takes two inputs and a list of several inputs to the function. The function is applied to the first two list elements, the result of this is used as input with the next list element, then the result of this is used as input with the *next* list element, and so on. The overall result is returned at the end.

Bibliography

1. AAUW, *Tech-Savvy: Educating Girls in the New Computer Age*, American Association of University Women Education Foundation, New York, 2000.

2. HAROLD ABELSON, GERALD JAY SUSSMAN, AND JULIE SUSSMAN, *Structure and Interpretation of Computer Programs*, 2d ed., MIT Press, Cambridge, MA, 1996.

3. KEN ABERNETHY AND TOM ALLEN, *Exploring the Digital Domain: An Introduction to Computing with Multimedia and Networking*, PWS Publishing, Boston, 1998.

4. ACM/IEEE, *Computing Curriculum 2001*, http://www.acm.org/sigcse/cc2001 (2001).

5. BETH ADELSON AND ELLIOT SOLOWAY, "The Role of Domain Experience in Software Design," *IEEE Transactions on Software Engineering* **SE-11** (1985), no. 11, 1351–1360.

6. JENS BENNEDSEN AND MICHAEL E. CASPERSEN, "Failure Rates in Introductory Programming," *SIGCSE Bulletin* **39** (2007), no. 2.

7. RICHARD BOULANGER (ed.), *The Csound Book: Perspectives in Synthesis, Sound Design, Signal Processing, and Programming*, MIT Press, Cambridge, MA, 2000.

8. AMY BRUCKMAN, "Situated Support for Learning: Storm's Weekend with Rachael," *Journal of the Learning Sciences* **9** (2000), no. 3, 329–372.

9. JOHN T. BRUER, *Schools for Thought: A Science of Learning in the Classroom*, MIT Press, Cambridge, MA, 1993.

10. ALAN J. DIX, JANET E. FINLAY, GREGORY D. ABOWD, AND RUSSELL BEALE, *Human–Computer Interaction*, 2d ed., Prentice Hall, Upper Saddle River, NJ, 1998.

11. CHARLES DODGE AND THOMAS A. JERSE, *Computer Music: Synthesis, Composition, and Performance*, Schirmer-Thomson Learning, New York, 1997.

12. MATTHIAS FELLEISEN, ROBERT BRUCE FINDLER, MATTHEW FLATT, AND SHRIRAM KRISHNAMURTHI, *How to Design Programs: An Introduction to Programming and Computing*, MIT Press, Cambridge, MA, 2001.

13. ANN E. FLEURY, "Encapsulation and Reuse as Viewed by Java Students," *Proceedings of the 32nd SIGCSE Technical Symposium on Computer Science Education* (2001), 189–193.

14. JAMES D. FOLEY, ANDRIES VAN DAM, AND STEVEN K. FEINER, *Introduction to Computer Graphics*, Addison Wesley, Reading, MA, 1993.

15. ANDREA FORTE AND MARK GUZDIAL, *Computers for Communication, Not Calculation: Media as a Motivation and Context for Learning*, HICSS 2004, Big Island, HI, IEEE Computer Society 2004.

16. DANNY GOODMAN, *JavaScript & DHTML Cookbook*, O'Reilly & Associates, Sebastapol, CA, 2003.

17. MARTIN GREENBERGER, "Computers and the World of the Future," transcribed recordings of lectures at the Sloan School of Business Administration, April 1961, MIT Press, Cambridge, MA, 1962.

18. RASHI GUPTA, *Making Use of Python*, Wiley, New York, 2002.

19. MARK GUZDIAL, *Squeak: Object-Oriented Design with Multimedia Applications*, Prentice Hall, Englewood, NJ, 2001.

20. MARK GUZDIAL AND KIM ROSE (eds.), *Squeak, Open Personal Computing for Multimedia*, Prentice Hall, Englewood, NJ, 2001.

21. MARK GUZDIAL AND ALLISON ELLIOT TEW, "Imagineering Inauthentic Legitimate Peripheral Participation: An Instructional Design Approach for Motivating Computing Education," paper presented at the International Computing Education Research Workshop, Canterbury, UK, ACM, New York, NY, 2006.

22. IDIT HAREL AND SEYMOUR PAPERT, "Software Design as a Learning Environment," *Interactive Learning Environments* **1** (1990), no. 1, 1–32.

23. BRIAN HARVEY, *Computer Science Logo Style*, 2d ed., Vol. 1: *Symbolic Computing*, MIT Press, Cambridge, MA, 1997.

24. RICHARD HIGHTOWER, *Python Programming with the Java Class Libraries*, Addison-Wesley, Reading, MA, 2003.

25. DAN INGALLS, TED KAEHLER, JOHN MALONEY, SCOTT WALLACE, AND ALAN KAY, "Back to the Future: The Story of Squeak, a Practical Smalltalk Written in Itself," *OOPSLA'97 Conference Proceedings*, ACM, Atlanta, 1997, pp. 318–326.

26. JANET KOLODNER, *Case-Based Reasoning*, Morgan Kaufmann, San Mateo, CA, 1993.

27. HEATHER PERRY, LAUREN RICH, AND MARK GUZDIAL, *A CS1 Course Designed to Address Interests of Women*, ACM: New York ACM SIGCSE Conference 2004, Norfolk, VA, 2004, pp. 190–194.

28. MARGARET LIVINGSTONE, *Vision and Art: The Biology of Seeing*, Harry N. Abrams, New York, 2002.

29. FREDERIK LUNDH, *Python Standard Library*, O'Reilly and Associates, Sebastapol, CA, 2001.

30. MARK LUTZ AND DAVID ASCHER, *Learning Python*, O'Reilly & Associates, Sebastopol, CA, 2003.

31. JANE MARGOLIS AND ALLAN FISHER, *Unlocking the Clubhouse: Women in Computing*, MIT Press, Cambridge, MA, 2002.

32. DAN OLSEN, *Developing User Interfaces*, Morgan Kaufmann Publishers, San Mateo, CA, 1998.

33. M. RESNICK, *Turtles, Termites, and Traffic Jams: Explorations in Massively Parallel Microworlds*, MIT Press, Cambridge, MA, 1997.

34. JEANNETTE WING, "Computational Thinking," *Communications of the ACM* **Vol-49** (2006), no. 3, 33–35.

35. CURTIS ROADS, *The Computer Music Tutorial*, MIT Press, Cambridge, MA, 1996.

36. ROBERT SLOAN AND PATRICK TROY "CS 0.5: A Better Approach to Introductory Computer Science for Majors," *Proceedings of the 39th SIGCSE Technical Symposium on Computer Science Education*, ACM Press: New York, 2008, 271–275.

37. ALLISON ELLIOT TEW, CHARLES FOWLER, AND MARK GUZDIAL, "Tracking an Innovation in Introductory CS Education from a Research University to a Two-Year College," *Proceedings of the 36th SIGCSE Technical Symposium on Computer Science Education*, ACM press: New York, 2005, 416–420.

Index